THE AMA HANDBOOK OF E-LEARNING

THE AMA HANDBOOK OF E-LEARNING

EFFECTIVE DESIGN, IMPLEMENTATION, AND TECHNOLOGY SOLUTIONS

➤EDITED BY GEORGE M. PISKURICH

AMACOM AMERICAN MANAGEMENT ASSOCIATION

New York | Atlanta | Brussels | Buenos Aires | Chicago | London | Mexico City
San Francisco | Shanghai | Tokyo | Toronto | Washington, D. C.

Special discounts on bulk quantities of AMACOM books are available
to corporations, professional associations, and other organizations.
For details, contact Special Sales Department, AMACOM, a division
of American Management Association, 1601 Broadway, New York, NY 10019.
Tel.: 212-903-8316. Fax: 212-903-8083.
Web site: www. amacombooks.org

This publication is designed to provide accurate and authoritative information
in regard to the subject matter covered. It is sold with the understanding
that the publisher is not engaged in rendering legal, accounting, or other
professional service. If legal advice or other expert assistance is required,
the services of a competent professional person should be sought.

Library of Congress Cataloging-in-Publication Data

The AMA handbook of e-learning : effective design, implemenation, and
technology solutions / edited by George M. Piskurich.

    p.   cm.
   Includes bibliographical references and index.
   ISBN 0-8144-0721-8
   1. Employees—Training of—computer assisted instruction—Handbooks,
manual, etc. 2. Employees—Training of—Data processing—Handbooks,
manuals, etc. 3. Internet in education—Handbooks, manuals, etc. I.
Piskurich, George M. II. American Management Association.

HF5549.5.T7A496 2003
658.3′124′0285—dc21

                        2003000649

Printing number

10 9 8 7 6 5 4 3 2 1

CONTENTS

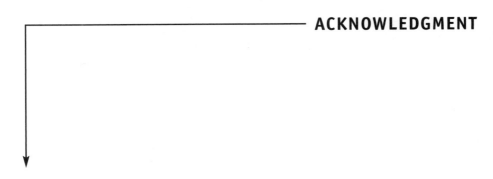

ACKNOWLEDGMENT

The editor would like to acknowledge the large contribution that Janice Meagher made to the conceptualization and completion of this book. Without her guidance during its origination this book would not have been.

THE AMA HANDBOOK OF E-LEARNING

CHAPTER 1

EDITOR'S INTRODUCTION: WHAT IS E-LEARNING?

➤GEORGE M PISKURICH

WHAT IS E-LEARNING?

What a great question! I wish I had a great answer for you. Everyone more or less agrees that e-learning has something to do with technology, and most (though not all) feel it also has something to do with computers. But that's about where the agreement ends. Does e-learning include the creation of nonstructured learning communities through bulletin boards and chat rooms? Are administrative processes such as on-line registration and electronic learning resource catalogues really e-learning? Are unstructured and even structured technology-enabled knowledge-sharing interventions e-learning? Is a CD-ROM based program e-learning? More great questions!

One of the problems with e-learning is that it has evolved from earlier concepts such as TBT (technology-based training), CBT (computer-based training), and a good number of other half-forgotten acronyms that have been created over the years. As many of these concepts had no agreed upon definition, the chance that e-learning would or will is pretty remote.

Another problem is that e-learning is a still-evolving discipline, and what might be considered a good definition today may not even be in the ballpark tomorrow. If you have a problem agreeing with this, check out Clark Aldrich's chapter on the future of e-learning. It will astound you!

As with any book, however, "ya gotta start (or in this case stop) somewhere." So for the sake of some clarity (not to mention the editor's sanity) we decided that for this handbook the defining characteristic of e-learning would be the use of a computer network or the web for delivery of the learning.

There was another of those old (and ill-defined) acronyms floating around once upon a time, computer mediated instruction or CMI. I figured that CMI meant using a computer to assist in or enhance learning, covering a range of concepts from complete delivery through a computer to simple administration of records by a computer. Many of the blended learning processes that we use today would have been termed CMI years ago. This concept doesn't exactly describe the scope of this book, but the basic idea is the same. If it's concerned with computer networks and learning, we've tried to cover it here.

Of course that leaves a number of aspects of learning technology uncovered. For example, while you may find references to satellite or telephone mediated distance learning in this book, there are no chapters on these concepts, and while stand-up classroom technologies can be very electronic, they are not covered here, either. Knowledge management falls into this category, and the same is true of learning strictly via CD-ROM.

That's not to say that chapters such as Larry Israelite and Nanette Dunn's on "Designing for Asynchronous e-Learning," or Wayne Turmel's "Evaluating Your e-Learning Implementation" are not highly applicable to these other delivery systems, but only that this book does not cover these concepts as specific topics. There are a number of fine books available on these topics, so we chose to stay with what is newer and has received much less coverage, e-learning.

So, all that being said, why would you want to own this book? Well, I could quote statistics to you about how e-learning availability has doubled in the last two years and is expected to triple in the next two, how it saved one company 25 percent on its training costs and reduced another's by 40 percent, or go the other way and state that while most companies are adopting e-learning, only 12 percent of their learners prefer it over classroom instruction. We'll cover the pros and cons of all these bits of information and many more throughout the book.

I could overwhelm you by cataloging the many e-learning approaches you should be familiar with, such as sandwiches, club sandwiches, on-line universities, electronic performance management systems, virtual seminars, and electronic surround. We'll discuss all of these and more in the chapters to come.

But perhaps the best answer to that question—*What is e-learning?*—is to consider the book's purpose as I tried to explain it to our expert authors when I enlisted them for this undertaking:

Our purpose is to create a book that you keep on your shelf and refer to when you need questions answered concerning any aspect of e-learning. It is not a series of academic essays, though it contains enough theory to give it the proper credentials, nor is it a best practices relating of "how I did it" by an individual who might have had one e-learning experience. Rather, it is a discussion of "what it is" and "how to do it," whether the "it" is designing effective web-based training or how to choose the proper learning portal host provider for your organization's needs. The chapters are written by authors who have been there, done it, and understand how it can work or not work for others.

This book is a complete reference that can provide you with the ability to make decisions concerning the applicability of the various aspects of e-learning to your situation, the knowledge to use the concepts as appropriate, and guidance on where to go to obtain more information if it is needed.

Because e-learning is a wide-ranging and still-evolving process, the chapters are not homogenous in design; however, most include a discussion of the topic, an explanation of how to do/use it effectively, a list of tips or helpful hints, and either a case study, decision making guide, or performance aid as appropriate. Each chapter also contains a resource area comprised of at least three to five recommended readings and resources. Some have more extensive lists of books, articles, and websites that can further illuminate the topic if you find you have a need for more information.

Our hope is that you will find this handbook easy to read and straight to the point in covering its various topics. We've tried to include every aspect of e-learning that we thought might appear on your radar screen, including all the basics such as Bray Brockbank's definitive chapter on learning management systems, Harvey Singh's discussion of e-learning software, and Loretta Donovan's look at implementing e-learning.

We've also dealt with more advanced topics, such as John Hartnett's discussion of bandwidth and other technical issues, and Saundra Wall William's consideration of building on-line communities.

And to whet your appetite for what's next, we have Tom Labonte discussing the relationship of e-learning to performance, and both Clark Aldrich and Elliott Masie gazing into their crystal balls for a look at the near and far future of e-learning.

As you begin to read the chapters you'll find that to help you use this book more effectively, we have compiled a list of twenty-five "burning" e-learning questions and tried to answer one or more of them in each chapter. At the start of almost every chapter, therefore, you'll find the title, "Your e-learning questions answered by this chapter," followed by the questions that the authors felt their chapter answered from our list of twenty-five.

There are considerably more than twenty-five questions floating around concerning e-learning. A process where a request for a quote on a small project can range from $57,000 to $112,000 has any number of important questions unanswered. A discipline (and I use that term somewhat loosely) that easily can have six or eight different pricing options ranging from "price per seat" to "pay for use" likely has a lot of very focused questions yet to ask. Is anyone really confident (or competent) enough to describe the difference between a website and a learning portal, or how either is used by an application service provider? And what about those standards for an LMS, or a CLMS, or learning objects, or. . . .

So how did we decide on only twenty-five questions, and where did they come from?

They basically came from you, or, if not you directly, your colleagues who are in the same state of confusion as you might be concerning e-learning.

When we began to organize this book, we conducted a few surveys of practitioners to find out where they were having problems understanding e-learning. These surveys were not particularly scientific, but they served their purpose. We wanted the real scoop on what the problems were out there, not simply answers to a series of formal questions that might be interpreted in many different ways.

We also didn't want to ask the experts—as everybody always asks them and they often don't remember—what it was like when they were just starting out on the e-learning road. Their concerns now go well beyond "What do you do with a learning object?" or "How can I make my PowerPoint slides into e-learning?" We wanted the questions of people who might not even be sure of how to spell e-learning, but somehow knew that it was important to them and their companies to learn.

So we went to a number of professional conferences and gatherings where people were talking about e-learning, listened to the talk, and then talked to the attendees ourselves. We held individual discussions, group discussions, arranged for later telephone discussions, and in some cases even passed out carefully designed forms such as the one shown in Figure 1-1.

To add an uncertain measure of validity to our surveys, we asked our question a number of different ways at different gatherings:

What are your burning e-learning questions?

What about e-learning keeps you up at night?

What do you wish you knew about e-learning?

In response, we received more than 400 different questions, running the gamut from the very specific:

➤ How do you monitor the use of company time for employees engaged in e-learning?

➤ What price should we expect to pay for one hour of good, customized, asynchronous e-learning?

➤ How do you implement e-learning in a highly diverse work force?

➤ What tools can I use to assess my learners' readiness to be e-learners?

➤ How do I get my instructor-led classroom culture to give e-learning a chance?

```
AMA  American Management Association


We'd Like to Know:     What e-learning questions keep you up at night?


1.


2.


3.
```

FIGURE 1-1. **EXAMPLE OF A CAREFULLY DESIGNED FORM.**

➤ How do we take our customized in-house classes and put them on line?

➤ Is e-learning an effective tool for training our customers?

To the very general:

➤ How do I spot a good e-learning package?

➤ How do we get started?

➤ How do I find all the on-line resources available?

➤ How do I determine which e-learning product best suits my business need?

➤ Is e-learning really effective for soft skills training?

To some that didn't fit any category, and were at times a bit surprising:

➤ What about job security for trainers?

➤ What's a better name for e-learning?

➤ How can we roll e-learning out effectively to 20,000 people at once?

➤ How do I get them to use the e-learning and stop calling me?

➤ How many e-learning projects can one person be working on at any one time?

➤ Why spend money on e-learning if your learners don't need to travel?

This didn't make them any less valid concerns though.

An analysis (also none too scientific) of our questions found that the majority of them dealt with these five basic issues:

➤ Getting support from the company to start e-learning and from managers to allow time to do it.

➤ Motivating learners to attempt e-learning and to complete the courses.

➤ Making decisions on which vendors and off-the-shelf programs best meet learning needs.

➤ Measuring the success of e-learning.

➤ Designing effective e-learning efficiently.

It was a difficult task, but we combined some questions, reworded others, and came up with what we believe are your twenty-five most pressing e-learning questions:

25 QUESTIONS CONCERNING E-LEARNING

1. How do I motivate my employees to be responsive to e-learning?

2. Can small organizations afford e-learning?

3. Is e-learning effective for all levels and types of learners, particularly those with low literacy levels?

4. How do I create time for e-learning?

5. What are the minimum technology requirements for effective e-learning?

6. How do I retool my stand-up trainers to become e-proficient? What is available to help me?

7. How do I work with corporate IT to communicate my e-learning needs?

8. How do we create e-learning that can migrate easily to other platforms and customer networks?

9. Can e-learning be designed so there is no need for downloads?

10. What criteria do I use to pick the best e-learning programs?

11. Is it more efficient to deal with e-learning internally or to use outside agents? Do I build it or buy it?

12. What strategies do I use to get executives involved in not only supporting e-learning but in helping to implement it and make time for it?

13. What technical or other problems can be anticipated and avoided when getting started with e-learning?

14. How do I determine the ROI of e-learning?

15. What is the right blend of e-learning and classroom instruction?

16. Is e-learning effective for soft skills?

17. How do we measure e-learning success rates?

18. Are there ways to reduce e-learning development time?

19. Can e-learning be effective cross-culturally?

20. How do I pick the best e-learning tools, software, platforms, and so on?

21. How much should e-learning cost?

22. Whom should I target with my e-learning first—top executives, middle managers, or individual contributors?

23. What do I need to do to support and maintain my e-learning process?

24. How do we make e-learning interesting?

25. How do I transition my learners to e-learning?

As already noted, each chapter answers one or more of these questions to a greater or lesser extent. Sometimes the answers may be a bit obscure, and not readily obvious from the chapter's general theme; but if the authors say the answers are there, then they are there, and we hope in a way that you can understand. Most of the authors have given you contact information in case you didn't find the answer in their chapter.

There is also a lot of overlap, so one question may have half a dozen chapters that discuss it at various levels.

You can use the questions as a guide in choosing the right chapter to read if you have a specific e-learning question, or simply as an organizer to help you determine what the chapter has to offer.

We hope that we've covered the majority of your questions with ours, but if you can't find an answer, or if you have a question that we didn't address, give me a call or drop me an e-mail. I probably won't know the answer, but chances are I'll know someone who does.

To further assist you as you navigate around this new and sometimes confusing world of e-learning, the authors contributed to and then agreed upon a list of basic definitions for common terms related to e-learning. To help get you started, here they are:

COMMON E-LEARNING TERMS AND DEFINITIONS

E-learning: Learning that uses computer networks or webs as the delivery or mediation mechanism. By this definition neither CD-ROM-based nor satellite-based delivery would be considered as e-learning.

Distance learning: Situation in which the instructor and students are separated by time, location, or both. Distance learning courses can be synchronous or asynchronous in nature.

Synchronous e-learning: Real-time, instructor-led, online learning in which all participants are logged on at the same time and communicate directly with each other and the instructor through the computer and possibly other means as well.

Asynchronous e-learning: A more or less self-paced learning event in which learners are accessing programs online at different times, and cannot communicate without a time delay.

Bandwidth: The information (text, audio, and/or video) carrying capacity of a communications channel.

Streaming audio/video: Audio or video files that are played as they are being downloaded over the Internet instead of having the user wait for the entire file to download first.

URL (uniform resource locator): The address of a homepage on the World Wide Web. For example, http://www.elearnhere.com.

Learning portal: A website that offers learners or organizations access to learning and training resources. Operators of learning portals are often called content providers, aggregators, or hosts.

Learning content management system: Software that allows for both the administrative and content-related functions of e-learning. It combines a learning management system (LMS) and a content management system (CMS) in one package.

Authoring tools: Software that is used to produce e-learning materials. These programs bring together components of a course, such as text presentation, graphics, tracking, and links.

HTML (hypertext markup language): The code used to create and to access documents over the Web.

Content provider: A vendor that provides complete off-the shelf e-learning courses that have been developed by the vendor to organizations through a private or public learning portal. Most content providers will also create custom programs that reside on their website for clients.

Aggregator: A vendor that offers complete off-the shelf e-learning courses that have been developed by numerous providers through a public or private learning portal. The aggregator controls the program specifics to make sure that they will run through the website. Some aggregators provide development of custom programs while some do not.

Web host: A vendor that provides learning portals to clients. Strict web hosts offer no content, but simply the mechanisms to create and administer a learning portal. It is the customers responsibility to develop or otherwise obtain the programs that will reside there.

Plug-in: An accessory program that adds more capabilities to a program. Plug-ins can help deliver animations, video, and graphics.

Firewall: A process by which organizations limit access to and from the Internet in order to retain the security of their network.

Application service provider (ASP): Vendor that supplies software applications and/or software-related services over the Internet. ASP is a general term that covers web hosts, aggregators, and content providers.

User interface: The method by which an e-learner navigates through a program, finds information, and basically achieves his or her learning goals.

Hot spots: Areas on e-learning screens that provide dynamic links to other media, such as audio, video, or graphics files, or that are linked electronically to other websites or pages on the Internet.

Blended learning: Usually the combining of e-learning with face-to-face instruction, job aids, or other common instructional techniques, it can also include readings, special projects, practicum, writing, and so on.

Learning object: A reusable, program-independent chunk of information used as a building block for e-learning content.

Chat room: An on-line facility that allows communication between e-learners using text. The messages are sent between learners in real-time as in a conversation but by typing on the computer rather than by talking.

Discussion board: An on-line facility where e-learners involved in a learning program can post text messages for other users to read.

Browser: Software that allows users to find and view information on websites.

EPSS (electronic performance support system): A computer program or piece of software that enables workers to access information or resources to help them achieve a task or performance.

FAQ (frequently asked questions): A file containing questions and answers new users often ask concerning an e-learning program or system.

Learning needs: The skills and knowledge required for individuals to achieve the performance expectations associated with their position.

Business needs: The measurable goals of a business unit or of an organization.

This is by no means given to you as a comprehensive, list of e-learning terms. Like our book itself, the list is more a primer, something to get you started down the road to understanding e-learning. There are many more terms and definitions in the chapters to come, and extensive content to enhance your understanding of them.

In its entirety, this is it. The authoritative resource on e-learning. I hope it is as useful for you to use as it was fun for me to edit.

➤ABOUT THE AUTHOR

George Piskurich is an organizational learning and performance consultant specializing in e-learning design, performance improvement analysis and interventions, and telecommuting initiatives.

With more than twenty years of experience, he has been a classroom instructor, instructional designer, and corporate training director. He has developed classroom seminars, multimedia productions, and distance learning programs.

Piskurich has been a presenter at more than thirty conferences and symposia, including the International Self-directed Learning Symposium and the ISPI and ASTD international conferences.

He has authored books on learning technology, self-directed learning, instructional design, and telecommuting, edited two books on Instructional Technology, and written many journal articles and book chapters on various topics. He can be reached at *GPiskurich@cs.com* or through his Web site, *GPiskurich.com*.

YOUR E-LEARNING QUESTIONS
ANSWERED BY THIS CHAPTER

➤ Is e-learning effective for all levels and types of learners, particularly those with low literacy levels?

➤ What strategies do I use to get executives involved in not only supporting e-learning but in helping to implement it and make time for it?

➤ What is the right blend of e-learning and classroom instruction?

CHAPTER 2

INTRODUCTION: IS E-LEARNING BETTER THAN . . . ?

➤**BILL ELLET**

➤**ALARIC NAIMAN**

Who are you, and why are you reading this book?

You might be a seasoned practitioner of e-learning, looking for tips and new ideas or checking on what other people consider to be the state of the art. Or a recent entrant, who is not quite sure where to begin and who wants a boost up the e-learning curve. Perhaps, instead, you are a manager of e-learning resources or of a department that will be a customer for them. Maybe you are another type of stakeholder: a nonelectronic trainer or someone else whose position may be challenged by the emergence of e-learning. Or an IT professional who may be responsible for implementing e-learning on your current systems.

Whoever you are, welcome to the party! We hope that you will find, throughout this chapter and book, ideas that will help you to get what you want from e-learning—and, in whatever way best suits you, to contribute your own knowledge, skill, and creativity to this important discipline.

THREE WAVES, FOUR VIEWS, SIX THESES

A movement as potentially transformative as e-learning may generate as much comment as content. Even though universally accepted definitions must await universal applications, we offer this historical snapshot of the state of the art:

➤ The first wave in e-learning included both basic research in AI (artificial intelligence) and related disciplines, the development of critical technology components such as user interfaces, and quasi-interactive instructional programs for both elementary and professional education. Groundbreaking programs like MIT's ELIZA virtual therapist tested the public's willingness to project human characteristics onto computers. This early work gave rise to computer-based curricula ranging from how to fill out government forms to PC hardware and software self-tutorials.

➤ The second wave, which may be cresting now, can best be described as the initial commercial foray. Improvements in computing capacity and cost, telecommunications infrastructure, coding, and interfaces have supported an evolving comfort with thinking machines, and corporations are now sometimes willing to treat complex education systems as a safe commodity.

➤ The emerging third wave embodies several improvements. Delivery may exceed expectations, systems will work out-of-the-box and still be readily customized, and there will be an expansion in the range of subject matter available. Statistical rather than anecdotal evidence will support marketing. Hence the buying field will be level. It will be incumbent on non-e-learning training vendors to demonstrate that their offerings can compete with the offerings from e-learning vendors on capability and value.

The question "Is e-learning better than traditional training?" implies something against which to compare e-learning—some other practices that serve a similar function more or less well. It thus implies the existence of criteria by which such a judgment may be made. Let's compare two extreme and two moderate responses to the question:

➤ "E-learning is in such a nascent state of development that only hucksters and the gullible will get involved any time soon." Or, even more cynically, "second mouse gets the cheese"—let someone else make all the mistakes.

➤ "E-learning is the only intelligent way to deliver modern training."

➤ "E-learning is rapidly emerging as an effective and efficient way to deliver certain classes of training in specific environments."

➤ "I don't know if we need e-learning just now, but we could gain a lot by inquiring further."

The first view, that e-learning is a failure, is selfish and self-limiting. Late entries sometimes do capitalize on others' learning, but so narrow a calculation neglects the historical necessity for community involvement in any new venture. If it takes a village to raise a child, then it takes a fair cross-section of the global village to bring to maturity a new vehicle for humans to share and propagate their capabilities.

The second view, that e-learning is the only way to deliver training, is too bold. It may become true in a decade or three, but it is certainly not so now. For example, e-learning may never be as effective in delivering "soft" skills as human trainers. That extreme view also compresses the range of criteria for evaluating a training vehicle, ignoring such factors as availability of capital infrastructure, challenges in applying "generic" content to a company's unique requirements, and so on. A fine line separates enthusiasm and zealotry. And yet, every major advance requires the commitment of early adopters, whose passion yields both failures and breakthroughs.

The third view—that e-learning is rapidly emerging as an effective and efficient way to deliver training—is closer to reality. It is probably already true in some cases and may soon apply to many more. Further, it is a legitimate affirmation rather than a slogan. It gives an incomplete process a sense of direction rather than boldly asserting an exaggeration that never can (and probably never should) be true.

Perhaps even more important is the fourth view: that you may be unsure if you even need e-learning or are interested in exploring it further. Assume nothing, and ask if there is anything useful to be learned. Even successful early adopters might be wise in returning sometimes to this stance and reviewing the field with a beginner's mind. As the great sociologist Yogi Berra noted, sometimes we can observe a lot just by watching.

Here, then, are six broad suggestions for maintaining perspective on this exciting, important and rapidly evolving field.

Adventures in Time and (Parameter) Space

The question "Is e-learning better than . . . ?" invites a binary answer—yes or no. Framing your thinking about e-learning with this question incurs at least three risks: making the wrong choice now, limiting future choices, and curtailing learning. Einstein warned: Everything should be made as simple as possible but not any simpler.

By inviting a range of possibilities, you can expand the discussion of e-learning to such generative questions as:

➤ Under what circumstances is e-learning best applied?

➤ With what subject matter and delivery mechanisms is e-learning most effective?

➤ What classes of benefits may result, and how do these compare with those now available?

➤ How do costs and risks differ from those of other training modalities?

➤ If you do wish to proceed with e-learning , what resources are available, both internally and externally?

➤ Where in our training program could e-learning offer best results, fastest return, lowest risk? What might be a good forward plan?

And finally,

➤ Is e-learning our best choice for now or for later? and for what goals or outcomes?

Very few important questions about training are simple. Even with concrete skills—for example, state wiring codes, a new version of Microsoft Office, hazardous materials handling—there are uncertainties about who will take the training, who will deliver it, and the like. E-learning provides an extensible platform, one that can serve many uses and add new capabilities in the future. The price of access to these generous benefits is a complex trade-off requiring a choice among diverse and sometimes bewildering choices.

The formidable-sounding "parametric optimization" offers a way out of bewilderment. The term means that costs and benefits of different types of e-learning are simultaneously balanced. Time is also a critical factor because different types of benefits are sown and reaped on different time schedules. A simple parametric optimization timeline (or "development trajectory") might look like the one shown in Figure 2-1. The basic principle is an ordered set of steps with specific criteria for each. The figure is tailored to an e-learning implementation.

A well-managed parametric flight path serves business and organizational needs in a way that maximizes buy-in and benefits while minimizing risks and costs at each stage. Such a tightly managed trajectory makes possible a "rolling wave" analysis, one that is very detailed for the next step, less precise into the future. Implementation plans can then be made with full awareness of:

➤ A systemic view of intended benefits to be derived from e-learning;

➤ A systemic view of necessary changes required to implement e-learning;

➤ A careful appraisal of possible contingencies and responses, for example, a change in corporate training strategy or IT infrastructure or downsizing that makes a particular program impractical;

➤ Reasonable knowledge of implementation options

E-learning requires a compelling economic case, but an excessive focus on dollars and cents can cheat the corporation of benefits whose value may greatly exceed that of the training itself; for example, needed changes to the company culture or upgrades to IT systems. These "secondary" benefits can be so compelling that persuading stakeholders to take a systemic view may be easy. But where do you begin?

Action	Criteria
Identify an isolated and concrete training need; develop and deliver to a select target group	Minimize risk and need for extended buy-in

Solve a specific problem

Give a promising vendor a chance to display capability

Make an easy introduction to e-learning for our IT department |
| Conduct a small learning review with all involved parties; feed this into a choice of larger, riskier, more visible trainings | Build from success so reluctant stakeholders will give some support or at least not interfere

Better define needs and system requirements for increased learning

Develop cadre of satisfied initial trainees who will spread the word |
| Repeat several times as effectiveness increases | Build more support

Reduce costs

Enhance efficiency

Develop cadre of internal training agents

Reduce unfamiliarity and resistance |
| Target more ambitious trainings: larger scale, less cooperative trainees or other stakeholders, more abstract or relational content | Test limits for strategic planning in HRD and other areas |

FIGURE 2-1. **A PARAMETRIC FLIGHT PATH**

First Step of the Journey

Even though the longest trek begins with a single stride, a journey can be a lot easier if the first step is in the right direction—and if someone has prepared a good map in advance. An optimal e-learning development plan lies between two common errors:

➤ Narrowly focused action with no thought beyond alleviating an immediate problem, leading to no generalizable learning or capabilities;

➤ Attempting a universally capable system from the start but instead getting something unwieldy, hard to teach or learn, expensive, and irretrievably flawed.

The first outcome typically arises when ad-hocracy prevails, when resources are limited below the breaking point, or when corporate strategy is unknown to those charged with implementing it. There is usually no evil intent. Solving problems and capturing opportunities is what we are all paid to do, but solutions that create more problems ultimately hurt everyone.

The second error, that of trying to do too much too fast, may occur when an enthusiast without delivery responsibility controls design or when too many stakeholders are competing. The resulting e-learning initiative may be a monster that collapses under its own weight. In the case of a new approach like e-learning, this failure may delay progress much longer than if the initial attempt had never been made. Painful examples surround us in software, major infrastructure—highways, bridges, subways—and even legal codes and social systems. Instead, it is prudent to build flexible, modular, evolvable platforms. Here are some proven guidelines for where to start your e-learning journey:

➤ What training objectives and enabling systems will produce early, convincing, practical outcomes?

➤ What choices are likeliest to produce at least a "good enough" result? For example, how can we please a few key stakeholders with a program that has little risk?

➤ What training program designs will produce useful learning and a compelling demonstration of principles, that in turn will elicit continued support even if not all business goals are met the first time?

And for choice of systems and vendors, there are two alternative criteria:

➤ What programs are in the best state of development and offered by the most stable vendors, thus minimizing risk?

➤ What programs are stable and well-supported but still early enough in development that we can influence their design to suit our purposes?

A pair of complementary metaphors may be useful here. One is that the most efficient path between any two points is often not visible from either. Many "best routes" head out in the opposite direction from the objective, but in that way miss unseen perils mapped by prior travelers. And deep-space probes may begin their journeys into the universe by dropping toward the sun, then using gravitational slingshot effects from inner planets to gain free boost before flying outward again. A careful planner will begin by mapping both obstacles and supportive forces that can guide the choice of development paths.

The second metaphor is a classic of linear programming, the "Traveling Salesman Problem." Given several cities to be visited, what is the most efficient routing? For more than a dozen or so destinations, a precise solution is almost non-computable. And yet, humans—even (especially?) children—can quickly and intuitively select a route very close to ideal. The moral may be that in our planning, we should strive for excellence rather than unattainable perfection.

In practical terms, this means doing some kind of collective analysis on a wide range of cost, risk, and benefit factors, all as a function of time. The Pareto approach lies between rigorous optimization and gut feel: order factors by importance, and choose to include only the most important. This can follow a sequence of planning steps as shown in Figure 2-2.

This rational, inclusive approach should yield a sound business case for using e-learning or not. But does a business case guarantee that all stakeholders will agree with and lend full support to the proposed program?

Barriers Beyond the Business Case

Not all of the many defunct dot-com businesses were half-baked. Some had a reasonable business case for investors, customers, and other stakeholders. A business case, however, is not a guarantee of success. In proposing e-learning, advocates may not recognize that they are embarking on a major change effort that can challenge or violate entrenched practices and comfort zones in an organization. E-learning is not a new delivery system that leaves the training function unchanged. The effects of e-learning range well beyond the training function, from cultural

Stage	Action
Pilot	Identify opportunity for early returns that are cheap, fast, safe, visible, etc.
Initial learning cycle	In parallel to the pilot, plan for and capture organizational learning related to people, systems, technology, ancillary issues and opportunities
Cultural integration	Consolidate both business and learning gains. With initial results in, Pareto ordering may de-emphasize risk and (possibly) payback time
Full-scale rollout	Integrate long-term learning and process development with specific projects throughout the company

FIGURE 2-2. **A PARETO PATH**

stresses and turf wars to the need for new competencies and revised business processes.

Once past the business case, those responsible for e-learning must negotiate a variety of barriers related to the change process, company and culture, trainees, trainers, and business processes.

The Change Process

Most of us learned to learn in classrooms. That includes even the youngest members of the workforce. For that reason alone, e-learning is a major change. Suddenly, many trainees must learn how to learn in a different way. But even before learners feel the effects, trainers confront their own set of challenges. They need to learn how to train in a new way; they must master new types of information, new processes and procedures, and new working relationships. Other stakeholders such as line managers also must adapt to the needs and vulnerabilities of e-learning.

Although e-learning has been touted as revolutionary, stakeholders responsible for implementation may want to handle it as a transaction or a training program enhancement in order to lower barriers to acceptance. Unwittingly, they may raise them. A recent joint study from ASTD and the Masie Center [1] notes that the companies included in its study believe they are marketing e-learning effectively; their e-learning users don't agree. The study recommends "intentional, dynamic, and continuous marketing activities, as well as traditional marketing methods."[2] The narrow focus on marketing suggests a business-as-usual approach. Marketing is important as a part of managing change, but it is just one tool in a much larger process. A narrow incremental approach can founder on rocks it simply doesn't see. The biggest rock is the sobering statistical reality that more change efforts fail than succeed. But the numbers don't mean change is futile; they remind us of the Boy Scout motto, "Be prepared."

Organizations should be asking themselves, How good are we at introducing substantive change? If we're good at it, what are the success factors? If we don't have a good track record, how can we improve? How is e-learning different from or similar to changes we've made in the past? If the company has resident change experts, they should be sought out and asked to help. An outside consultant—one attuned to change as much as e-learning— might not hurt either.

Company and Culture

Fit to company and culture is a critical factor in determining the success or failure of change. A change antithetical to either faces long odds, while a highly compatible one should be much easier to establish. We can speculate about both companies and cultures favorable and unfavorable to e-learning using a simple two-by-two matrix (see Figure 2-3). The matrix has two scales, the values an organization places on technology and on learning.

The core businesses of organizations influence both values. The four classes of organizations the matrix defines are:

> ➤ Cutting Edge: values both learning and technology highly because both are crucial to the organization's competitive strength. Example: the U.S. military.

We're committed to doing better.

	Low	Value of Technology	High
High	**Added Value** High learning Low technology Example: Law firm, consulting firm	**Cutting Edge** High learning High technology Example: High tech companies, military	
Value of Learning	**Steady State** Low learning Low technology Example: Cement company, government	**Efficiency Machine** Low learning High technology Example: Call center, mail order company	
Low			

It ain't broke, so don't fix it.

Low   Value of Technology   High

FIGURE 2-3. **THE E-LEARNING CULTURAL MATRIX**

➤ Added Value: values learning highly because the organization competes on knowledge but technology is not an important factor in its core business. Example: consulting firm.

➤ Efficiency Machine: places a low value on learning because the core business doesn't require deep knowledge but is dependent on technology for efficiency. Example: a brokerage firm.

➤ Steady State: values neither learning nor technology highly because core business provides little incentive for either. Example: construction company.

Here are brief studies that illustrate how core businesses influence the adoption of e-learning.

Steady-State to Added Value

A city government is a Steady-State organization. Residents expect it to deliver the same basic services year in and year out. They put a premium on reliability. Efficiency is less important. Technology generally doesn't have a large role in the delivery of city services.

In Green Hills, however, the new city manager is aiming for "a total learning organization." (The city's name has been changed.) He has found that learning opportunities improve employee retention. At the same time, he seems intent on moving the organization from a Steady-State model to an Added Value one. If his interesting strategy works, it seems likely the city will pursue e-learning technologies.

Currently, though, more than 90 percent of the city's training is delivered in the classroom. The training manager sees a very limited role for e-learning in an important area: "I don't think you can teach a lot of soft skills using e-learning." For desktop training, she's purchased online courses and is thinking about buying more. A closed-circuit TV system may be used soon for mandatory safety training. Otherwise, there isn't a push or a pull for e-learning initiatives.

Efficiency Machine

A big brokerage is a highly regulated sales organizations in which small cadres of high-salaried professionals make the investment decisions, while large numbers of young people work the phones and counters. Transaction efficiency is what makes the big machine hum.

The industry has a steep initial learning requirement: a six-week course leading to a brokerage license. After the license exam, the requirement is much lower, consisting primarily of keeping current with regulatory changes.

Although the industry has huge investments in technology and could not do business without it, it is "pretty married to the classroom model of instruction," in part because of the heavy use of subject matter experts. Trainers feel no pressure to adopt e-learning. A move to a blended approach is slowly taking shape, including virtual classrooms run by experts on government regulations.

Cutting Edge

The U.S. military is one of the largest training organizations in the world. To say that it embraces technology is an understatement. It is more like a bear hug. The combination drives large-scale e-learning.

A continuing challenge is the training of reservists. They are dispersed and have limited training time, yet must be kept at an adequate state of readiness. One reserve course, the Army's Armor Captain's Career Course (ACCC), had a correspondence course portion that trained only 15 percent of the tasks trained in the 10-month resident course offered to active duty officers. The paper format was not hospitable to group exercises that could accelerate learning.

Over four years, civilian employees, contractors, and uniformed personnel painstakingly developed, tested, and refined an online version of the course. Along the way, the team built its own learning management system, not because they wanted to reinvent the wheel, but because at the time no commercial product met their requirements. The course was finally rolled out in 2000.

The adaptation from paper to web improved the course itself. Because content could be added fairly easily to the online version, the reservists' course now teaches content comparable to the active duty course. Students can easily communicate with their peers and instructors wherever they're studying. They can learn in new ways from dynamic interactive content. Their progress can be monitored continuously.

From the beginning, the self-study portion of the course was not seen as a stand-alone product but as a component of blended learning. Overall, the course uses a rich design of media delivery and face-to-face instruction.

Case Study Conclusions

The two most favorable classes of companies for e-learning are Cutting Edge and Added Value firms. Cutting Edge organizations readily use technology that gives them an advantage and may be more willing than other classes of organizations to experiment with untried systems. The marriage of technology and learning is a perfect match for them. Knowledge is crucial to Added Value firms. Although technology is not a key factor in their business, technology that gives them a knowledge advantage should have great interest for the nimble. The critical factor in Added Value firms is how well advocates make the case to decision makers and users that e-learning can enhance learning for the organization.

Steady State and Efficiency Machine organizations are not good candidates for e-learning because knowledge does not figure prominently in what they do and how they succeed. Ironically, these very companies may be strongly attracted to e-learning as a cost-cutting tool. But they are going to trip over a variety of obstacles if they introduce e-learning. Their employees have little incentive or motivation to adapt to the system and use it. Both employees and middle managers will be tempted to ignore or suppress e-learning-related requirements. Where learning is not tightly integrated with promotion ladders, is not an essential part of performance evaluations or personal development plans, and is not relentlessly promoted as a key human resource and strategic asset, a troubled e-learning rollout has more to do with culture than anything else.

In weak learning cultures, however, e-learning can provide a starting point for renovation. A possible e-learning investment can be a lever to pry the lid off neglect and indifference and to look at learning and training in a new way. The provision of new systems to facilitate training could provide a Hawthorne Effect[3] among employees that may convince them the new direction is not a "program du jour."

A related cultural barrier stems from the subtle hypocrisy of pushing e-learning for employees but not managers and executives. Where executives and senior managers receive training in consultant-led internal seminars or in outside programs, while the troops are required to pick from rented libraries of online courses, the employees take notice. When top people signal that something is not important to them, the message ripples through the entire company. The ASTD–Masie Center survey noted in passing that a large majority of users in the study said e-learning courses weren't considered prestigious in their companies.[4] Could this be evidence that the people at the top have sent the wrong message?

Learners

Let's consider what students may lose when they are asked to give up the classroom. Most of us have spent more time in a classroom than in any other setting outside the home until we reach the age of 38, not counting years spent in organized daycare or graduate studies. We have an intimate knowledge of and comfort with classroom workings—procedures, norms, and roles. In the classroom, learners are afforded a protected time and place to study. The learning is by definition social and collaborative; a student interacts with a teacher, peers, content, and others such as a guest presenter or subject matter expert.

In a classroom learners can influence the instruction through feedback, including nonverbal expression. Students profit from the best feedback system currently on the market: an instructor answering a student's question—or, sometimes more important, the question behind the question. Bored students can coax an instructor to move on or shift the approach, while social norms prevent them from leaving. Later in the class or afterwards, they may discover something of importance. Sometimes the realization can take years.

Poorly implemented e-learning can remove or reduce many educational benefits possible in a live classroom.

Second generation e-learning isolates the user. A student interacts with rote content that is text-based, has low interactivity, and evaluates learning (actually reading comprehension) with multiple choice quizzes. The user has no real influence on the instruction. Even with preassessments allowing users to opt out of content they already know, the second-generation course is comparable to a lecture with no questions allowed and a test at the end that most students are expert at gaming. No tangible learning community exists, or there are only traces of one. And the social function of corporate classroom training shouldn't be overlooked. The opportunity to see old friends and make new ones and the social activities that revolve around a class are now gone. The feedback, no matter how cleverly disguised, is canned. Bored students can click the mouse and leave, and they do in droves. Students exercising this freedom may miss learning that could benefit them.

In the ASTD–Masie Center study, start rates of e-learning courses were low.[5] Anecdotal evidence has suggested even lower completion rates. In the absence of research, poor completion rates are interpreted as a benefit of e-learning: users exit when they've learned what they need to know. But many of the courses in the field study were mandatory; the sponsoring organization thought the content of the entire course important. As proxies for learners, reviewers for *Training Media Review* have said again and again that much online content is not engaging or challenging.

They say that the combination of rote content and technical glitches can prompt a quick exit.

Both vendors and the training community have recognized the weaknesses of second-generation e-learning and are beginning to offer improvements. E-learning platforms are starting to integrate as standard features links to instructors, mentors, subject matter experts, and, most importantly, peers. Developers are trying hard to break the isolation of second-generation systems by fostering virtual learning communities; in other words, they are learning from the strengths of superior classroom instruction. The thinking about the blending of different teaching and training methods is also important. Although no consensus definition of "blended" has emerged and the push and pull of differing agendas adds to the confusion, the new direction will benefit everyone. So will the further development of "learning objects." The notion of e-learning "courses" was borrowed from the classroom. In some subjects, the chunking of content into the smallest meaningful units (learning objects) may allow students to assemble the learning they need as opposed to slogging through one-size-fits-all courses. Of course, identifying learning objects in actual content and assuring some kind of coherence in their use is no easy feat.

Two other learner-related barriers have turned up in recent studies. The popularity of open office designs has been an unanticipated problem for e-learning. A cubicle is by design a compromise between private and public. The tradeoffs don't necessarily work well for e-learning. Ringing phones, e-mail alerts and faxes, work emergencies, drop-ins, meetings, and hallway conversations intrude, and even the yellow police tape that people are said to string across the openings to their bays is a poor substitute for classroom walls. An ASTD–Masie Center study strongly confirms that this barrier is a significant impediment to effective e-learning.[6]

The research has also turned up a barrier of time. Early in the discussions of anywhere, anytime learning, the question Whose time? was raised. Americans are working more hours than they ever have. They work longer than the population of any other developed nation. Americans have faced a relentless lengthening of the workweek and increasing difficulty in balancing work and private life. Workers seem to regard the anytime mantra as an encroachment on personal time, above all, when the training is mandatory. According to the ASTD–Masie Center study, 87 percent of learners preferred to take compulsory training during working hours.[7]

Trainers

E-learning drives classroom learners into a major transition, but its effects on trainers are even greater. Their primary role has been—and remains, according to the data—in the classroom. In e-learning, the trainer is not there anymore. That simple change changes everything. Trainers have been educated to function in a classroom system. They have become used to working in certain ways, following certain procedures, using certain tools. Suddenly, everything is up in the air. Trainers' learned, intuitive, and unconscious classroom methods don't seem to be relevant any longer. They can have legitimate worries about the difficulty of mastering new systems that they don't yet understand. They can wonder whether their current skills will have any relevance to e-learning. In this type of situation, the change doctor can write out a prescription for resistance long before its onset.

In this condition of uncertainty, trainers need information. They need to know the features, functions, and possibilities of the technology relevant to training. They must educate themselves about technology at a level of detail for which many are unprepared. In the recent past, however, the e-learning industry hasn't been of much help. Industry participants tend to identify with the technology world, not training. Their strong sense of identification is played out in language, which is a powerful way of confirming and reinforcing membership in a community. That is understandable and is not a problem because technologists usually sell to other technologists. In the e-learning market, however, technologists have been selling to trainers, and there has been a pervasive failure to communicate. Trainers often ask questions that cannot be answered ("How much will e-learning cost in my company?"), and vendors often give opaque answers to simple questions ("All of our content is SCORM compliant").

Fortunately, this barrier is slowly coming down. More vendors are making an effort to think of themselves as learning companies and talk about their products in terms their customers can understand. The 2001 economic decline and the general distress of the technology sector added urgency to vendors' desire to connect with customers. More shows and seminars on e-learning are being offered, although both can be heavily laced with marketing. Professional associations have jumped into the gap and are trying to act as educators.

Trainers also need information on their new job as e-trainers. So far, they are having trouble finding it. The dearth of information is understandable because the job is new and the fund of experience to draw on for best practices is small. Still, the void can be a barrier, and the faster the industry and the profession can fill it, the better for e-learning acceptance.

E-learning is typically described as a team effort. Trainers are consummate team players; if they aren't, they don't usually last in the job. E-learning puts trainers on teams with different members, issues, outputs, and parameters of action than they are used to. In classroom training, trainers may work with IT as a service provider that helps them project laptop content on a screen. On an e-learning team, IT is a key player with influence on and responsibility for a host of technology-related matters. The commonly accepted lifecycle of a team—forming, storming, norming, performing—takes time. For virtual e-learning teams, the first three stages may be harder and longer. With new teams, and especially cross-functional ones, turf, authority, and budget issues have to be negotiated from scratch, and it is a near certainty that these issues will be central to the storming stage. All of this work takes time, effort, and patience. Trainers energized by and fully committed to e-learning will take a deep breath before starting the long march. Trainers less thrilled by e-learning may seek other routes.

One early-stage barrier is the workload of trainers. Like everyone, they are overworked and have their hands full keeping current activities running smoothly.

Training departments run lean under any circumstances. In bad economic times, trainers are too often among the first to be let go, leaving even more work for those left behind. A retail sales organization formed from several merged companies let go of "redundant" trainers, leaving one individual responsible for the IT training of nearly 1,000 field sales reps. The person also serves as the internal IT hotline. The company has always delivered training in the classroom, and employees strongly prefer it, but the trainer wants to convert much of it to online. The heavy teaching load has put the hoped-for move to e-learning on indefinite hold. A trainer newly hired by a city government department arrived with great plans to introduce CBT. After a year, she has made no progress. She captures the problem perfectly: "Other things always seem to take precedence."

The last trainer-related barrier has little to do with e-learning and much to do with human nature. Planning for change typically involves a close and critical look at practices and people. The scrutiny can be painful in any case and excruciating when it exposes inefficiency or incompetence. The prospect can provoke fear in those being scrutinized. So can the perception that the scrutiny may be predisposed to discovering fault. It is not unheard of for outside consultants to feel the need to justify their existence (and fees) by finding problems. New hires or transfers brought in to lead the charge may want to make their mark by criticizing current practices and contrasting them with the improvements they are going to make. That demoralizing scenario can lead to all kinds of well-disguised acts of resistance.

Business Processes

Long after everyone else is on board the e-learning ship, the people in accounting may impound the vessel until they can get some straight answers. They may have no information about which departments have the authority to sign off on requisitions and invoices for e-learning purchases. They may not be aware that a new budget category has been created, and three different departments can draw on it. When the time comes to make a large infrastructure purchase, none of the specification forms used by IT or Trainer can capture all the necessary information. Finance won't approve a purchase with incomplete specs. And how are the large costs of implementation going to be allocated? As the rollout approaches, IT, Training, and HR may each think the other is responsible for user orientation. As a result, the rollout has to be postponed while the parties straighten things out.

Mundane? Yes. Trivial? Hardly. The breakdowns are suggestive of an entire category of barriers that can impede an e-learning initiative by slowing progress, discouraging supporters, and emboldening naysayers. When process, responsibility, and coordination are unclear, a host of problems arise, including:

➤ Missing procedures and paper systems

➤ Inappropriate specification, approval, purchase, and implementation structures

➤ Underdefined responsibilities; for example, between Training and IT departments

> Unbalanced allocation of costs and rewards; for example, IT pays, Training gets most of the benefits

Clearing the Obstacles

How do you deal with obstacles beyond making the business case? First, recognize they exist, and carefully diagnose your situation. Second, understand that the inclusion of all stakeholders, including learners, early in the process is important. It is a basic recommendation of change management that if you build commitment early, you will experience less resistance later on. A process aimed at winning over stakeholders includes:

> Persuasive explanation of the business goals to be achieved and demonstration that e-learning is the best route for achieving them

> Clear definition of responsibilities and probable benefits

> Open negotiation or fair assignment of responsibilities

> Prior agreement to site and timing

> Specification of rewards and their magnitude

> Convincing demonstration that needed education and other support will be available as part of a coherent rollout plan

> Avoidance of overstatement or oversell to gain stakeholder buy-in

The change process's greatest enemy is the flight from clarity. Anyone who has ever worked in an organization has done it or experienced it. In clarity there is commitment—to the diagnosis of a problem, to the recognition of an opportunity or a need to change, to the definition of new roles, and so on. Clarity is usually the first victim of fear and strong resistance. Without it, any process bogs down and may collapse or yield bad decisions.

The process should also include a realistic assessment of organizational gains and losses. As a result of an e-learning initiative:

> Subject matter experts may gain more control over course development at the expense of the training department.

> Employees may lose classroom time they enjoy.

> IT may have to take on additional responsibilities it doesn't welcome and have to make technical compromises it doesn't like.

Every party may gain other benefits, but the losses need to be acknowledged and prepared for. Crucially, they need to be accepted. Public recognition matters, but private acceptance is probably the key. No certain way exists to assure the latter, but good leaders take notice and give personal attention as required to influence the individuals affected.

The Vice of Extremism

At one end of the e-learning market, two classes of buyers leap at new products: techno-geeks who believe in change for the sake of change and bleeding-edge early adopters. The bleeding-edgers perform a community service. They take on new systems, test them, suffer the slings and arrows of their audacity, and help push the systems to the next level. In the end, they may help the rest of us more than themselves. At the other extreme, the second-mouse-gets-the-cheese camp waits and waits until it judges the technology is safe, though by that point, they may have been left in the dust by competitors.

The two extremes are essentially impervious to marketing. The techno-geeks and early adopters will buy whatever is new. The second mice will wait until the technology either vanishes or becomes the gold standard. In between are potential customers that can be swayed by salesmanship.

Hype is a tested tactic for lowering resistance to purchase. With mature technology such as automobiles, hype does not pose a threat to its subject. Buyers are familiar with the product, and their view of it is not going to be altered by oversell. When the subject of the oversell is a new product unfamiliar to buyers, hype can have the benign effect of encouraging trial, giving the product a chance to prove its worth. Nevertheless, it is a double-edged sword. It can cut through resistance, and it can cut the other way, damaging the very thing it is trying to sell. E-learning is a new and vulnerable technology; its impact on business problems and results is not yet known with any precision. Mistakes are going to be made; in fact, they have to be made for the technology to develop and for training to prosper from it. Some disappointment is inevitable and healthy. But if reality begins to stand in stark contrast to the oversell, the situation becomes precarious. E-learning hype exacts a price in three ways:

➤ Disillusionment with e-learning, not just with a particular product

➤ Fear of being outmoded and obsolete

➤ Distortions in the necessary dialogue about e-learning

Categorical Disillusionment

The most common and toxic reactions to hype are suspicion, skepticism, and doubt. These reactions become particularly harmful when they are applied to an entire product category, not just a specific product. Throwing the baby out with the bathwater is far more likely when the category includes new and untested products. We will illustrate the point with a brief case study from the dot-com world.

E-retailers claimed many advantages over traditional bricks-and-mortar competitors. One was that they would transform gift giving. They touted anywhere, anytime shopping, fast transactions, ship-with-a-click service. No longer would you buy something in a store, take it home, wrap it, and stand in a slow-moving line at the post office. Neither would you have to find a gift in a mail order catalog, wait in an interminable phone queue, make the transaction (unless the item was out of stock), and provide shipping information.

These capabilities did sound transformative until the Christmas of 1999. At the most critical moment of the retail year, e-tailer shipments didn't ship, and many buyers didn't find out until after the holiday. E-tailers improved their service after the virtual Grinch stole Christmas, but the damage to customer confidence was done.

Among the trainers we've talked to and interviewed, we've seen signs of hype-induced skepticism about e-learning. The predictions of explosive geometrical growth have been way off the mark. A report from the American Society for Training & Development (ASTD) revealed that the use of e-learning in U.S. companies actually peaked in 1997.[8] ASTD's latest State of the Industry report says e-learning use increased in 2000. Another respected industry survey reports a continuing decline.[9] Whichever report is correct, the fact remains e-learning is struggling to gain a foothold. Economic problems and the disaster of 9/11 certainly are contributing factors. Yet, they are far from the only ones.

The drumbeat of analyst predictions of geometrical growth has set up a situation in which anything less looks like a failure. The shaky state of the e-learning industry and its performance to date suggest to many in the training community that the technology is not what it was cracked up to be. Trainers can feel justified in being less interested in e-learning and less urgent about testing it. Skepticism can lead to the shelving of trials and the delay or elimination of important learning that would flow from them. In reality, the e-learning industry may be exactly where it should be. In the short run, losing money may be a symptom of truly innovative products and learning a market in the school of hard knocks.

Rank-and-file trainers have difficulty evaluating the promised benefits of e-learning because they can't find clear explanations of the technologies that are supposed to bring the benefits. Time and again, we've heard trainers ask, What is a learning management system? What they mean is, What is relevant about a learning management system to my role and function? Direct answers are rare. Both sides are experiencing an application of Gresham's Law: bad information drives out good. Hyperbolic end results are touted and celebrated, but the means are not discussed. Then, when trainers receive explanations of the means laced with jargon and technical terms, these explanations can sound like another easily dismissed dose of hype.

Fear

The training community has heard the hype. They can't attend a professional meeting, read a journal or magazine, or subscribe to a list serve and miss it. At professional meetings lately, e-learning has crowded out other training topics. The same has been true in professional publications. Many in the training community accepted the first wave of hype as another amusing iteration in the cycle of Great Educational Claims that then must face reality; for example, educational television, programmed learning, the many "back to basics" movements. But this new generation of hype packed a punch. E-learning was positioned as a one-for-one substitute for classroom instruction, and the industry had a plausible case for large cost savings, especially for big corporations. Suddenly, trainers faced a long-term job threat that had nothing to do with the business cycle. This time, the hype might prevail. The net result was fear and uncertainty.

Since then, the leadership of our profession has advised the community to ride the wave. The advice itself is not hype, but it is hard to differentiate from oversell in a rhetorical greenhouse. The message has benign meaning: "E-learning offers new capabilities that trainers need to learn about and incorporate into practice. You shouldn't be distracted by current responsibilities or deterred by fear." It also has a hard-edged meaning: "If you want a job, you will jump on this train before it leaves the station—do or die." Both parts of the message are probably true. The overall message can inspire both hope and fear.

Even the ASTD–Masie Center report—remembering that the ASTD is the principal training professional association—can feed the fear. In the last year, "blended learning"—the combination of e-learning, face-to-face instruction, and other methods—has become a rallying point for the industry. According to an ASTD study, "Blended learning is likely to be the immediate-term successor to traditional instructor-led classroom training."[10] The statement is ambiguous. What is the destination of the implied transition? Could blended learning be just a point on a line leading to instructorless learning?

Distorted Dialogue

In a column in the *Boston Globe*, Josh Hyatt asked, "Who killed all those Internet retailers?"[11] Most observers would tick off the usual suspects: callow twenty-somethings, delusional venture capitalists, gullible media, costly Big Bang business strategies, unbridled greed. The comic strip character Pogo once said, "We have met the enemy and he is us." Echoing Pogo, Hyatt says the enemy of the e-tailers was us—the majority of us who "refused to understand that transacting business over the Internet was the best way to buy everything."

The dot-com bubble was inflated by volumes of hot air. More and more hype was pumped into the balloon until it burst. Underlying the hype and oversell was an assumption that customers would behave in the way the industry wanted them to. Customers would see the value offered to them, do without the palpability of physical goods and bricks-and-mortar stores, and regard shopping as a transaction, not a social event. Customers were pushed to sites by the hype and found that their experience didn't equal the expectations created by the sell. When the push weakened, there wasn't enough pull left to sustain the industry.

There's a parallel here to the e-learning industry.

Before the dot-com implosion, industry forecasters and analysts were predicting that e-learning would account for 90 percent or more of training. The shift would be astonishingly fast, no more than three or four years. After the collapse and the declaration of the official recession, analysts are still saying the same thing with the disclaimer that they can't pinpoint the year of the big percentage leap. The year of the e-volution has been pushed out steadily as the numbers always lag the projected curve. Although presentations about the industry currently have titles like "E-learning on Rations," the assumption of dominance is still alive and well.

It is not just the industry, with an economic stake in the outcome, that believes e-learning should and will dominate. So do people in training. At a conference in 2001, a session participant called traditional live classroom training "spoon feeding." The new breed of e-trainers talk about "rewiring" learners' brains. E-learning, they say, demands a new level of maturity and responsibility from learners, who must recognize that they alone are responsible for their own learning.

The full argument seems to read this way: Too many of us have been spoiled by the classroom. We show up where and when we're supposed to, do what we're told to do, and leave as soon as we're allowed. Throughout our lives, we're the same passive learners we have been trained to be. Hence, we need to be reformed from the ground up as independent learners.

The lecture method of education can stamp out a sense of responsibility for one's education. In business schools, case method teaching comes as a shock to many students. Students who have been lectured to for much of their schooling expect the instructor to take most of the air time and tell them what to think, something good case method teachers never do. Suddenly, they are responsible for the class discussion or the class literally disappears; in addition, they have to test out ideas and positions for themselves. In other words, they must take charge of their own learning in a way that few of them ever have.

However, to assume that a majority of adults takes little responsibility for their learning and that this problem is the underlying cause of resistance to e-learning is wrong. We hope we are not seeing the rehearsal of the futile argument that e-learning is being undermined by those of us who "refuse to understand that e-learning is the best way to learn everything." As the dot-comers discovered, nothing is gained by blaming the customer. In this case, blaming the learner creates a barrier to seeing them—their needs, their strengths and weaknesses—as they really are. At the same time, a one-sided view makes an objective evaluation of the technology and its strengths and weaknesses unlikely.

Distortions anywhere in a system tend to distort the whole system. A dialogue with your doctor is going to be compromised if you withhold crucial facts related to your health. Likewise, distorting the learner's responsibility will distort the general dialogue about e-learning. The same rule holds for all the other issues that make up the dialogue.

Learning About Learning about Learning

A balanced path has been charted, the business case made, stakeholders broadly recruited, and a realistic objective asserted. Success is assured. . . .

According to some definitions, teaching is about learning to know, and training is about learning to do. (While many use these terms interchangeably, some such distinction is useful in many learning situations.) E-learning certainly has the potential to encompass both. The concern of teaching, by that definition, is efficient information transfer. The methods of training, by contrast, focus on the activation of cognitive and behavioral strategies that allow trainees to reproduce not just ideas but operational competence. As such, teaching is fundamentally algorithmic: learn this information and demonstrate understanding in standard applications. Training, however, is fundamentally heuristic (discovery-based): find or build your own best internal strategies and demonstrate behavioral competence in situations that extend beyond the learning environment.

Some of e-learning's greatest early successes have been in the field of IT training. There are several possible reasons for this. Those who produce IT training will in many cases already be capable in IT but less familiar with other subject matter. More subtly, both curriculum designers and prospective participants in e-learning programs may preselect themselves according to comfort with the delivery mechanism. This self-sorting will naturally deliver the most receptive and, in some ways, capable trainees to e-learning courses with major IT content.

A key challenge to e-learning, then, is whether it can have the potential to deal effectively with "soft" subjects like relational and sales skills, the practice of coaching, or even relatively formless sensitivity training.

Some assert that effective skills transfer requires some kind of modeling process. Modeling, in this context, refers to the student's development of enabling beliefs, cognitive processes, decision strategies, and behaviors. Exceptionally effective teachers often use such strategies unconsciously, matching what is offered to students' capabilities and value systems. Increasingly, however, trainers are being taught these skills and attitudes very consciously, for example, in accelerated learning and NLP.

The methods of training apply to almost any kind of content. While highly technical or algorithmic subjects do require mastery of a fundamental knowledge base, the point of training is to do something more than mere rote memorization or application to formal problems. And the most contentious subjects—like influence skills, counseling, interviewing, and facilitation skills themselves—are almost purely heuristic. By this we mean that there exist only fuzzy guidelines requiring much awareness and choice. True learning of such topics is largely a matter of guided self-discovery.

Some current e-learning assumes that the methods of informational training can be used for soft skills. This is manifestly not the case. Maslow's observation that when one has just a hammer, the world appears to contain only nails seems to apply here. Part of the job of the third wave of e-learning theorists and practitioners will be to exercise greater discrimination in the matching of e-learning methods to subject matter.

When Pull Meets Push

Historically, most innovations fail not in the physical world but in the imaginations of their intended customer base. "I know what it can do for you" can rarely overcome "I don't see what it can do for me."

We use a term in training to decide when a subject has received attention enough. GEIGER—Good Enough Is Good Enough, Right?—reminds us to focus on what counts and on the point of diminishing returns. For most people most of the time, desires accommodate to circumstances, as advised in Niebuhr's famous Serenity Prayer. It is mainly Shaw's "unreasonable men,"[12] who insist on changing the world to meet their own vision, who are readiest to consider or demand new ideas. And somewhere between the poles of complacency and change for its own sake lies the proper place for such new methods as e-learning.

Technology push is the domain of enthusiasts, boffins, techno-geeks. "It's really cool so let's (get someone else to) use it" can be modeled as a process of What It Is → What It Does → What It Does For Me. What the customer actually wants comes last! Needs-based marketing begins with Who, asks What benefits are wanted, and only then moves to How can we best achieve this.

Buddhists, with one of the most venerable of training traditions, speak of "skillful means" (Sanskrit, *upaya*). Effective buy-in may be gained in many ways. For early adopters, it is often just a matter of making information on new opportunities available, and getting out of the way (see→buy). But to gain the committed attention of a large organization without use of positional authority, either careful "market" segmentation or satisfaction of universal needs is necessary.

Responsibility for the success of e-learning therefore vests, to some degree, in every one of us.

E-Learning and Wisdom

This chapter is intended to be both descriptive, with perspective on how far our field of e-learning has come; and prescriptive, to help it continue to evolve in the most valuable directions. We can summarize in a few lines:

➤ Use discrimination or don't use e-learning—have a real, committed purpose for which e-learning is demonstrably the best solution.

➤ Be honest, broad, and dispassionate when evaluating costs, risks, and benefits.

➤ View e-learning as it is—a tool, not an objective—and be creative in seeking multiple organizational benefits from its use.

➤ Then implement a balanced plan that manages costs and risks, captures visible benefits early, and best satisfies the most stakeholders.

Adaptation of e-learning to training in "soft" skills will be challenging, and it will happen. Similarly, our community must and will find new ways to share knowledge and experience. Wisdom will emerge from practice. It is this collective wisdom that will guide e-learning to deliver its full potential: value to the business community, to the recipients of training, to the theorists and technologists whose work will enable the next level of development, and to the smooth running and positive evolution of society as a whole.

CASE STUDIES

Here are brief studies that illustrate how core businesses influence the adoption of e-learning. You may want to refer to Figure 2-3 as you read these studies.

Steady-State to Added Value

A city government is a Steady-State organization. Residents expect it to deliver the same basic services year in and year out. They put a premium on reliability. Efficiency is less important. Technology generally doesn't have a large role in the delivery of city services.

In Green Hills, however, the new city manager is aiming for "a total learning organization." (The city's name has been changed.) He has found that learning opportunities improve employee retention. At the same time, he seems intent on moving the organization from a Steady-State model to an Added Value one. If his interesting strategy works, it seems likely the city will pursue e-learning technologies.

Currently, though, more than 90 percent of the city's training is delivered in the classroom. The training manager sees a very limited role for e-learning in an important area: "I don't think you can teach a lot of soft skills using e-learning." For desktop training, she's purchased online courses and is thinking about buying more. A closed-circuit TV system may be used soon for mandatory safety training. Otherwise, there isn't a push or a pull for e-learning initiatives.

Efficiency Machine

A big brokerage is a highly regulated sales organization in which small cadres of high-salaried professionals make the investment decisions, while large numbers of young people work the phones and counters. Transaction efficiency is what makes the big machine hum.

The industry has a steep initial learning requirement: a six-week course leading to a brokerage license. After the license exam, the requirement is much lower, consisting primarily of keeping current with regulatory changes.

Although the industry has huge investments in technology and could not do business without them, it is "pretty married to the classroom model of instruction," in part because of the heavy use of subject matter experts. Trainers feel no pressure to adopt e-learning. A move to a blended approach is slowly taking shape, including virtual classrooms run by experts on government regulations.

Cutting Edge

The U.S. military conducts operations regularly but trains every day. In fact, it is one of the largest training organizations in the world. And to say that the modern military embraces technology is an understatement. It is more like a bear hug.

The reserves are an essential component of our military forces, and they require a voluminous distance learning system. One reserve officer course of 240 hours has always been conducted as a correspondence course. Among other things, the medium was cumbersome and hard to update; it did not allow dynamic and interactive exercises helpful for military training; and it did not allow easy or timely progress reports.

Over four years, civilian employees, contractors, and uniformed personnel painstakingly developed, tested, and refined an online version of the course. Along the way, the team built its own learning management system, not because they wanted to reinvent the wheel but because at the time no commercial product met their requirements. The course was finally rolled out in 2001.

E-learning advocates tout the fast course development enabled by development tools and reusable content. Commercial vendors have pumped out large libraries of online courses in a short time. This government team believes that quality takes time. In their view, the turtle always wins the long race.

TIPS AND HINTS

Begin with a well-formed outcome. Some key factors: what benefits will be delivered, when, and to whom? What costs and risks will be incurred, when, and by whom? Who will do what, when, and with what resources? Who will track all this, and by what metrics?

Learning for a change. Introduction of e-learning is a change process. Like any other, it requires careful planning and management from both business and cultural perspectives.

Easy does it. Major benefits and new opportunities often emerge over time, while costs and risks can be handled in small steps. Anticipate and mitigate acceptance barriers, and keep expectations reasonable.

Have it (approximately) your way. This field is evolving so quickly that many aspects are still developmental. So be bold in specifying program designs according to your needs. You might get exactly what you want and will help the field and the market evolve to meet each other.

Don't try to do it alone. Many roles and responsibilities are involved. Sharing the load early can also help to gain buy-in of key stakeholders; it can also involve people with skills whose value might not have been obvious at first and resources that turn out to be important.

Think big and think broad. These steps should be part of a strong vision, integrated with strategy and embodied in a credible and balanced plan. Much of the benefit may accrue beyond the primary targets.

Take responsibility for the field. E-learning is still so new that every major initiative can be defining for the entire endeavor. Be careful, be honest, be bold, be optimistic. *Accept pleasant surprises!*

NOTES

1. *E-Learning: If We Build It, Will They Come?*, American Society for Training & Development–The Masie Center, 2001.
2. *E-Learning*, p. 29.
3. The principle that any group that is singled out for special study or consideration will have its performance positively affected by the knowledge that it has been so selected.
4. *E-Learning*, p. 21.
5. *E-Learning*, p. 15.
6. *E-Learning*, pp. 22–23.
7. *E-Learning*, p. 23.
8. 2002 State of the Industry Report, American Society for Training & Development, 2002, p. 44.
9. Tammy Galvin, Industry Report 2001, *Training Magazine*, October 2001, p. 10.
10. *E-Learning*, p. 11.
11. *Boston Globe*, Oct. 18, 2001, p. C4.
12. The reasonable man adapts himself to the world: the unreasonable one persists in trying to adapt the world to himself. Therefore all progress depends on the unreasonable man. From *Man and Superman*.

RESOURCES

Readings

Brown, John Seely, and Duguid, Paul (2000). *The Social Life of Information.* Cambridge, MA: Harvard Buisness School Press.

Van Buren, Mark E. (2001). *State of the Industry Report 2001.* ASTD.

Websites

American Society for Training & Development, *www.astd.org*
www.education-world.com
http://elearners.com
www.e-learningcentre.co.uk
www.elearningforum.com
ELIZA, *http://i5.nyu.edu/~mm64/x52.9265/january1966.html*
http://mse.byu.edu/projects/elc/
NLP and accelerated learning: *http://nlp.org*
Training Media Review, www.tmreview.com

►ABOUT THE AUTHORS

Bill Ellet is editor and co-owner of *Training Media Review*, an online service and print publication. TMR (*www.tmreview.com*) uses a reviewer network of training and human resource professionals to evaluate media-delivered business training (online, CBT, video, and print). The company offers consulting services in training media-related areas. Mr. Ellet is a member of the Editorial Board of T+D magazine, a publication of the American Society for Training & Development. He writes and edits media reviews for *Training Media Review* and is overseeing a series of evaluative reports on e-learning products and vendors. He is also a writing consultant to the MBA Program at Harvard Business School. He has degrees from the University of Chicago and University of California at Berkeley. He can be reached at 617-489-9120 and *wellet@tmreview.com*.

Alaric Naiman, Ph.D., is a technical and organizational consultant specializing in innovation processes and culture change. His focus for some years has been the study of cognitive strategies, values, and other factors that enable cultural transformation and enhanced personal and corporate effectiveness. He began as a chemist, with thirteen years' industrial R&D following studies at Harvard, Berkeley and Oxford. During eight years at a European management consultancy, he codeveloped a branded practice in structured innovation and coaching. He has delivered training and advanced facilitation in 16 countries on subjects ranging from energy production and intellectual property rights strategy to project planning, sales, and negotiation skills. He is now principal of Transition States, part of a network of specialist consulting groups in training and OD, branding and product design, and selected technical fields. He can be reached at 781-929-5693 and *naiman@tstates.com*.

YOUR E-LEARNING QUESTIONS ANSWERED BY THIS CHAPTER

➤ Is e-learning effective for all levels and types of learners, particularly those with low literacy levels?

➤ How do I determine the ROI of e-learning?

➤ Are there ways to reduce e-learning development time?

➤ How do I transition my learners to e-learning?

CHAPTER 3

ANALYZING THE ORGANIZATION'S NEED FOR E-LEARNING

➤TOM FLOYD

INTRODUCTION—HAS THIS EVER HAPPENED TO YOU?

Every training department within your company is in a total state of chaos. Senior executives have just returned from a national conference, and have declared e-learning is the wave of the future in training. Senior managers throughout the company begin to state in meetings with fellow employees that e-learning is going to save your company X amount of dollars each year, which will help the overall organization immensely in the tough economy looming ahead.

The Director of the company's largest training group, Global Training Organization (GTO), has stated all existing training curricula must be evaluated immediately, and converted to a Web-based, e-learning format as quickly as possible. Audiences are affected everywhere: external and internal, U.S.-based audiences as well and international audiences residing in regions where your company has a presence.

The curricula affected by this declaration currently exist in a variety of formats, including instructor-led training, self-paced documentation, job-aids, and CD-based computer-based training (CBT). A variety of topics are covered within each curriculum, which range all over the board from soft skills subjects such as communication to application training on how to use various software programs.

As the Program Manager responsible for your curricula, you have been tasked with converting your current training to e-learning. You have never developed e-learning before, and are not sure if it even makes sense for your audience. You are feeling a little overwhelmed—and do not know where to begin.

CHAPTER OVERVIEW

If you have ever found yourself in a situation similar to the scenario described on the previous page, then this chapter is for you. In this chapter, you are going to learn how to scope, plan, and determine if your organization is ready for e-learning by conducting a needs analysis. At a high level, this chapter will:

> ➤ Define the needs analysis process

> ➤ Discuss how to conduct an audience analysis

> ➤ Provide an overview of the primary deliverables created during an e-learning needs analysis

The goal of this chapter is to provide you with the information and tools you will need to conduct a needs analysis within your group that maximizes the time, effectiveness, and budget associated with your curriculum.

WHAT IS A NEEDS ANALYSIS?

The term **needs analysis** is often used to describe the process of identifying performance or skills gaps, analyzing data, and determining the most effective strategy to roll out a training curriculum.

There are several primary needs analysis models used in the training and human resource development profession. These models include:

> ➤ Robert Mager's Model of Analyzing Performance Problems,

> ➤ Allison Rossett's Training Needs Assessment Model, and

> ➤ Many, many others.

These models are excellent examples for those with an instructional design and human resource development background in training, but may not be as practical for an overwhelmed training manager who just wants to learn a "down and dirty" approach for conducting a needs analysis specific to their particular curriculum.

The approach identified in this chapter provides a fundamental process that can be used by newcomers to the world of needs analysis and e-learning.

E-Learning Needs Analysis

An e-learning needs analysis is very similar to the assessment process you would use for any other form of training delivery. The basic model includes:

➤ Determining training objectives

➤ Analyzing the needs and skills of the audience receiving the training by collecting data

➤ Reviewing the data for trends and consistencies

➤ Designing a high-level course outline for the e-learning curriculum

➤ Developing training recommendations based on the data collected

➤ Compiling a project plan and budget for the e-learning curriculum moving forward

➤ Summarizing the needs analysis results and presenting them to management

However, it is also important to note there are several factors to consider that make conducting an e-learning needs analysis very different from one for a traditional training medium like instructor-led training.

E-Learning is a Newer Delivery Medium

E-learning as a training medium has been around since the late 1990s, and is still a relatively new delivery method most training professionals are fairly unfamiliar with. Because fewer people have "been there, done that," there are few definitive guides to follow when delivering training in a Web-based format.

Technology

Technology also plays a huge role in the e-learning world—and even affects how e-learning is defined. While many training professionals use the term loosely to apply to one specific medium, the term actually refers to multiple delivery methods including:

➤ Virtual Synchronous Classroom Delivery

➤ Virtual Asynchronous Classroom Delivery

➤ Electronic Performance Support Systems

➤ Web-CBT

➤ On-line Assessment

Additionally, there are several technologies such as learning portals, Web-based assessment applications, Web-content development engines, and other tools to consider when scoping these projects that add a layer of additional complexities that make defining these projects a little more challenging.

Fear of Technology

The technologies associated with e-learning can be complicated and daunting to newcomers to the e-learning world. A certain level of training and "upskilling" is usually required to get both training managers and executives involved in the e-learning buying process familiar with the tools and approach that is going to be used. It is important to factor in the time associated with increasing the comfort level of those who will be driving, supporting, and contributing to e-learning projects.

Geography

The location and distribution of the learners who will be receiving the training becomes a critical component when determining how to deliver an e-learning curriculum. In many cases, the geography and location of the audience is the sole factor driving the decision to implement e-learning and thus control the costs associated with training. The complexities associated with geography open up a new can of training issues that have not played as important a role on projects involving other media. These issues include, but are not limited to:

➤ Bandwidth

➤ The hardware and software used at each audience location

➤ Course location and accessibility

➤ Learner registration

➤ Global issues such as localization of course content and translation

Curriculum Design Becomes Even More Important

Due to some of the factors associated with the geography and distribution of the audience who will be receiving the training, curriculum design becomes even more important. When developing the initial course outline for the e-learning curriculum, new emphasis will need to be placed on factors such as:

➤ Number and length of learning modules

➤ "Chunking" of content

➤ Learner course engagement and interactivity

➤ Primary speaking language of each audience

➤ Cultural factors and behaviors to be considering when developing content

➤ Navigation, layout, and ease-of-use of curriculum

Different Players

Unlike many projects in the past that could be limited to a few key players including a training program manager, one instructional designer/trainer, and a primary subject matter expert, the number of resources required to effectively implement an e-learning curriculum is considerably larger. These resources can include:

➤ Corporate executives or sponsors

➤ Multiple project leads or project managers

➤ Teams of subject matter experts from around the world

➤ Multiple instructional designers and/or trainers

➤ Technical experts such as Web programmers, database programmers, and other e-learning development technical resources who are responsible for developing and supporting the training to be delivered

Time

The amount of time required to consider, research, plan, and develop the project plan for the project is longer than some of the traditional "day or two" scoping that can be done on smaller projects involving less complex training media. This time can often come as a huge surprise to executives who are hoping for a quick roll out of the e-learning program.

Cost

Cost is probably one of the biggest differences between conducting an e-learning needs analysis and a more traditional needs analysis. Because many managers and executives are used to this cost being minimal, if *anything*, managers develop "sticker shock" when they learn that, for example, it could cost anywhere between $20,000 and $40,000 to determine how to implement and deliver their e-learning strategy—which is completely separate from the cost of actually developing the training and rolling it out.

Deliverables

The final element that makes an e-learning needs analysis different from conducting a traditional training needs analysis is the type of deliverables that need to be created. These deliverables can include:

➤ Surveys

➤ Audience analysis matrices

➤ Audience analysis summaries

➤ Course outlines

➤ Recommendations documents

➤ Delivery project plans

➤ Budgets

➤ Proposals

Even though all of these deliverables may not be relevant for every e-learning project, it has been this author's experience that the majority of these are required to achieve executive buy-in, determine an effective strategy, and roll out the curriculum.

HOW TO CONDUCT AN E-LEARNING NEEDS ANALYSIS

The remainder of this chapter is going to focus on the process you can follow to conduct an e-learning needs analysis. This process can be broken down into the following steps:

➤ Determine the objectives of the training program

➤ Conduct an audience analysis

➤ Analyze the data gathered during the audience analysis

➤ Develop a high-level course outline

➤ Develop a recommendations document

➤ Present the needs analysis findings and recommendations to management

Determine Objectives of Training Program

A common problem that can develop on many e-learning projects has to do with gaining support of the executives who are funding the project. Many training managers proceed with developing elaborate e-learning solutions for their audiences that fail to meet the expectations of corporate sponsors due to:

➤ Lack of buy-in from the executive or team funding the project

➤ Misinterpretation of the goals and objectives for delivering the project

➤ Miscommunication and noncommunication with corporate sponsors about key decisions and issues

Before any thought is given to what the appropriate strategy is for a specific e-learning curriculum, it is critical the training manager or program manager meet with the executive sponsor(s) funding the project to set expectations and ensure team alignment.

Executives have a wealth of knowledge and perspective that helps provide the e-learning team with objectives for the program, the project budget, possible vendors to contact, and what content the sponsor would like to see conveyed to the audience.

It is during this phase of the project that you as the primary resource on the needs analysis should work with your corporate sponsor and other executives to:

➤ Determine key internal players on the project,

➤ Create an initial contact log capturing the necessary e-mail, phone, and other information you will need to arrange meetings with other players identified,

➤ Set and agree on program objectives, and

➤ Talk openly with your sponsor about what their vision is for the curriculum.

One way to open the conversation up with your sponsor is to ask them what their "magic wand" solution is for the curriculum. In other words, if they could wave a magic wand, what would they like the curriculum to look like—and how would they deliver it?

Your sponsor's answer to this question can provide you with an initial vision and plan to work from moving forward. For example, your sponsor might say "I was at a training conference a few weeks ago, and saw some excellent examples of e-learning from a vendor called ACME Company. I would really like to see us either work with that vendor or develop something similar we could deploy to our audience." From conversations like this you can create an action plan that contains items like:

➤ Names of vendors or consulting firms to follow up with,

➤ Ideal start and end dates for the project,

➤ A range of budgets, to work within, or

➤ Ideas of what the sponsor would like to see and would like NOT to see happen on the project.

By ensuring alignment and open communication with your corporate sponsor and executive team, you can greatly improve your chances of developing an appropriate strategy, delivering an effective e-learning curriculum that meets corporate goals, and "hitting a home run" with your e-learning program in the executive team's eyes.

Return on Investment

Another very important conversation to have with your corporate sponsor or executive team should focus on the return on investment (ROI) of the e-learning curriculum. In other words, you need to make sure the objectives you agree on with the sponsor are measurable items that can be used to indicate the success or failure of the curriculum.

Oftentimes, creating measurable objectives and determining how the ROI will be measured will involve you educating your sponsor on the difference between direct ROI measurements and indirect ROI measurements.

Many executives will want to see the ROI measured in terms of dollars saved or other factors they can use to demonstrate the e-learning curriculum had a direct impact on the "bottom line" within your corporation. In a good majority of circumstances, however, increases or decreases in the "bottom line" cannot be directly correlated with the success or failure of the e-learning itself.

Direct ROI

It is very important for the executive team to understand the difference between direct ROI measurements and indirect ROI measurements. Direct ROI can be correlated back to the e-learning curriculum itself. Direct ROI can involve establishing metrics and ensuring specific baselines are in place before development of the curriculum begins. For example, learners' baseline knowledge of the content of the e-learning curriculum could be surveyed and measured before training and then after. So if the learners rank their knowledge of the course content in pre- and post-assessments or surveys, this would provide a direct measurement that could be used to demonstrate the impact of the curriculum on the learner's overall knowledge.

Another way to directly examine the impact or effectiveness of e-learning is by examining statistics related to user participation or completion of training. There are several ways to measure this, including:

➤ Number of people registered to take the training

➤ Number of people who completed the curriculum

➤ Number of people who were able to pass assessment tests and receive certificates as a result of the training

These numbers can be used to initiate questions about the effectiveness of the curriculum. For example, if you noticed that 1,000 people registered for the course but only 100 individuals completed it, additional research could be done by interviewing learners or by examining course evaluations. You may learn a course was too long, or that the content was not relevant or interesting to the learners. Regardless of what the case may be, you can then come up with a plan to modify the e-learning as appropriate based on the feedback you gathered to ensure it is more effective moving forward.

Indirect ROI

Items such as increased revenue that are based on "bottom line" factors are *indirect* measurements of ROI. Although these items can be linked to training indirectly, there is not a direct correlation that says these factors changed as a direct result of learners completing the e-learning curriculum.

For example, learners could complete a product-based e-learning curriculum that had a goal of increasing revenue of a product in a specific region. Learners may be able to demonstrate an increased knowledge of the content through assessment tests, knowledge on the job, and other factors as a result of completing the course. However, the e-learning itself cannot be held solely accountable if revenues of the product do or do not increase in the region. Various factors beyond the training such as cost, marketing, location, cultural perceptions, and quality of the product could also have significant influences on the revenue of the product in the region. A thorough investigation of each of those factors would need to occur as well.

To summarize, a reliable method to use to demonstrate the ROI of an e-learning curriculum is to focus on evaluating factors that can be directly linked to the e-learning itself—such as the ability to demonstrate and apply knowledge gained from the curriculum.

Audience Analysis

Once you have ensured alignment with your executive sponsors and have definitive information related to the objectives and return on investment of the proposed e-learning curriculum, your next step is to gather information about your audience you will need to develop the strategy and recommendations for your curriculum moving forward.

The process of gathering information, creating profiles, and analyzing data specific to the needs of your learners is referred to as an audience analysis. The audience analysis is the most critical phase of any needs analysis. The data you gather during this phase is used to create the foundation upon which your recommendations for the curriculum will be built. To ensure your audience analysis is successful, you are going to need to know:

➤ What to ask,

➤ Whom to ask, and

➤ How to ask it.

What To Ask

There is a variety of data you will need to gather to determine the best strategy for delivering an e-learning solution to your audience. This information can be grouped into several categories including:

➤ Background information,

➤ Technology,

➤ Existing training delivery, and

➤ Current knowledge of content.

Background information includes basic data about your audience such as location, primary speaking language, job title, education level, gender, and age. Although some of this information can be very sensitive for some groups, it is essential to gather this data to form an accurate profile of your learners. For example, if you discover the majority of your audience is nonnative English speaking males between the ages of 41 and 55 with post-graduate educations, the solution you develop would be significantly different than a curriculum designed for a population of 21- to 28-year-old males and females with a highschool education.

Developing a clear understanding of the technological environment in which your audience is operating is essential in determining what type of solution their location can support. For example, if connectivity and bandwidth are identified as major constraints for your learners, you will need to ensure the e-learning solution you choose addresses those constraints and is as streamlined as possible.

Existing training delivery is a subject that can sometimes fall through the cracks during an e-learning needs analysis. It is very important to address both how training is currently delivered to your learners in addition to what their comfort level is with various training media. The results of these questions may surprise you—an audience you felt might be resistant to e-learning delivery may indicate their comfort level or willingness to accept it is higher than you expected; however, you should also be willing to address possible scenarios where the audience is not comfortable with e-learning. Although it could lead to a difficult conversation with the sponsors of the program, you must be willing to acknowledge the data you gather could indicate e-learning is not the best solution for your group.

As was mentioned earlier in this chapter, determining your audience's current knowledge of the content that training will be developed for is necessary to form a baseline that can be used as a means to demonstrate the effectiveness of the curriculum. Not only can this data be used to demonstrate ROI, but it can also become a critical source of information for your instructional designers as they design and develop each module or lesson.

For examples of the types of questions to ask related to each of these categories, please review Appendix 3-A, Survey Sample, at the end of this chapter.

Who To Ask?

You will need to gather information from a well-rounded blend of individuals with different perspectives and needs related to your e-learning curriculum. These individuals should include:

➤ Managers,

➤ Subject matter experts, and

➤ Learners.

Managers within each audience will tend to be experts on their audience's overall expectations of the curriculum. They also will be able to provide you with facts specific to how training is currently delivered for their group, in addition to information specific to the types of training that have been well received. Managers will also know whom to contact within their groups to find out additional details related to subjects like technology, infrastructure, and budget. You may even find managers within some groups are willing to contribute funds to the overall curriculum if it meets specific needs they are hoping to achieve.

Subject matter experts (SMEs) provide a wealth of information specific to the content for the e-learning curriculum. The expertise these individuals offer is used during the needs analysis process to gather data on their expectations for the content for your training. SMEs also become invaluable as reviewers to approve course outlines, storyboards, and other deliverables created during future phases of your project.

It is important to note you will need to carefully weigh the information these individuals contribute. While they will provide you with an assessment of what the curriculum should cover, they also may go into "content overload"—and burden you with extraneous details that are not essential to the learners or the curriculum.

The most critical group for you to gather data from is the learners themselves. These are the people who need the content you are delivering, and who will provide you with excellent information related to their individual needs, comfort levels, and expectations. You will use the data gathered from this group to identify the characteristics of the "average" learner within your audience. Although the curriculum you deliver should cater to multiple adult learning styles and preferences, the majority of your training should be designed with this average learner in mind.

Your audience analysis should contain a sprinkling of managers and SMEs, but should focus the majority of its energy on the learners. You must ensure you sample as many of these individuals as possible, given the time, budget, or other considerations for your project.

Because the information gathered during your audience analysis will depend on a combination of tools including in-person interviews, teleconferences, and surveys, it will be essential for you to determine an appropriate sample size within your audience upon which to focus. The science of identifying and determining the appropriate population and sample size is complex, and warrants volumes of publications and books on its own.

Although this chapter will not go into a complete explanation of statistics, sampling, and surveying methodologies, here are some basic guidelines to keep in mind.

- ➤ Decide how much sampling error can be tolerated (in terms of a percentage),
- ➤ Determine how large your population (audience) is, and
- ➤ Remember the size of your sample has a significant impact on the accuracy of your data (the larger your sample, the more accurate your data will be).

How To Ask It?
The information you gather during your audience analysis will be done using a combination of in-person interviews, teleconferences, and surveys. Due to the limited amount of time available to conduct a full-blown audience and needs analysis on most training projects, the fastest way to gather this information is to use surveys as your primary data collection tool, and to follow up with in-person conversations and teleconferences as necessary. This approach allows you to maximize both your time and your respondents' time, and generally provides a high rate of return on information if you manage the process proactively.

Your surveys can be distributed using a variety of formats, including:

➤ Word documents sent via e-mail,

➤ HTML-based Web surveys accessed via a URL, and

➤ Web-based survey-assessment software.

These formats tend to produce the quickest and most effective results. Regardless of how you choose to distribute your surveys, make sure you choose a solution that allows you to compile, review, and analyze the data as quickly as possible. The bibliography at the end of this chapter provides a list of Web-based surveying tools that can be used as an excellent means to quickly distribute and compile your data.

Finally, before sending the surveys out to your audience, you must make sure you have definitive parameters in place related to your surveying process that affect your overall timeline. These parameters should include:

➤ The sample size (what is the minimum number of surveys you must receive back),

➤ Due date (what is your cut-off date for accepting surveys), and

➤ Follow-up and communication (do you have a plan in place to communicate with your audience, answer questions as needed, and provide them with gentle reminders of when surveys are due?)

Having these parameters in place will allow you to make effective use of your surveying time, and will provide you with the closure on the process you will need to move onto to the next phase of the process—data analysis.

Data Analysis

Once you have received the minimum number of surveys back that meets the requirements identified for your audience sample, your next step is to compile and analyze the data. Like surveying, the science of data analysis is complex, and there are volumes of information in existence that describe various models and methods used for data analysis related to items such as probability, distribution, and frequency. Although having a background or experience in formal data analysis is certainly ideal, it is not required for the everyday Training Manager or Program Manager who needs to make some basic inferences about the data collected.

Some general guidelines to follow when analyzing the data gathered from your audience analysis revolve around:

➤ Organization,

➤ Summation, and

➤ Presentation.

The data you collect should be organized and grouped logically into basic categories related to your curriculum. At a minimum, the data should at least be grouped into the categories upon which your survey questions were built in the earlier part of the audience analysis. These categories are:

➤ Background information,

➤ Technology,

➤ Existing training delivery, and

➤ Current knowledge of content.

Depending on the medium you used to distribute your surveys, these categories, in addition to the others you specify, should be used to group your data into subsets within a deliverable or report called an audience analysis matrix.

An audience analysis matrix can either be a report run and customized from a Web-based survey assessment software program or "manually" created on your own using a spreadsheet application like Excel. The audience analysis matrix is the tool you will use to summarize and make inferences about your data. At a high-level your matrix should be able to:

➤ Group your results by the categories you specify,

➤ Provide a breakdown of results by individual,

➤ Compare each individual's results against the larger audience sample, and

➤ Provide you with percentages, averages, means, and other statistics related to individuals answers to each question identified in your survey.

Hands down, one of the easiest ways to create an audience analysis matrix is to use a Web-based surveying package, and to just select a report within that package to serve as the basis for your matrix. This data could then be exported to a spreadsheet program like Excel, and modified for your needs.

In their book, *Statistical Methods and Data Analysis*, R. Lyman Ott and Michael Longnecker remind those using any type of surveying software that designers of these programs tend to include everything in the output a user could conceivably want. It is important to realize some of the output will be irrelevant to you. The authors are absolutely correct. For an e-learning needs analysis, you should focus on the information you need to determine:

➤ If an e-learning curriculum is appropriate for your audience,

➤ How you should deploy it,

➤ What content you should develop your curriculum around,

➤ How the content should be designed, and

➤ What the profile is of the average learner within your audience.

Within each category you group your data into, there are going to be specific statistics or results that will influence the items in the list above. For example, the

TABLE 3-1. **BACKGROUND DATA ANALYSIS FACTORS**

Topic	Question to Ask	What to Identify
Age	Do a large number of respondents fall within a specific age group?	The age group(s) that contain the largest number of respondents
Job Title	Do a large number of respondents perform a similar line of work?	The most common job titles identified by respondents.
Primary Speaking Language	What languages do respondents within my audience most commonly speak?	The primary speaking languages in order from most spoken to least spoken identified by respondents.

results of the background information gathered about your audience are used to create the profile of the average learner within that group. Table 3-1 below provides an example of some of the factors you could look for in your data analysis to help build this profile.

Once you have analyzed and reviewed the data you have collected, your next step is to summarize this information in an easy-to-read document called an audience analysis summary. An audience analysis summary provides a factual, high-level overview of the results of your data analysis and summarizes key findings within each category. This deliverable is the document you should share with managers, program sponsors, and others within your organization who will only want to know the big picture results from your analysis.

The audience analysis summary should not contain your recommendations for how to proceed. It should be written in a factual and unbiased format, and used as a basis for your recommendations. Appendix 3-B, ACME Audience Analysis Summary, provides a template you can use to create this deliverable.

Develop a High Level Course Outline

Once you have finalized your audience analysis summary, your next step is to create a high-level, preliminary course outline. Based on the information gathered from SMEs and learners during the audience analysis, you should be able to develop a basic outline that contains:

➤ A list of lessons for the curriculum

➤ A list of primary topics and subtopics within each lesson

➤ Ideas related to instructional activities within each lesson

> An assessment approach for each lesson

> Ideas related to interactivity and activities within each lesson

> An estimate of how many pages each lesson will contain

This preliminary course outline should not be confused with the detailed course outline that will later need to be created that contains a step-by-step breakdown of each lesson. The purpose of this initial high-level outline is to provide the sponsors of the program and others within your group of an idea of the type of information the curriculum will contain.

This outline is also critical from a scoping and planning perspective. As you create the project plan and budget for the development phase of your project, you will need to identify the total number of hours that will be necessary for development. As you begin to work with vendors, instructional designers, programmers, and others who may be involved in the next phase, it will be easier for them to tell you how long it will take to complete a development task if they know the number of topics and pages within each module or lesson of your curriculum. For example, an instructional designer may be able to determine from looking at this outline that it will take around 120 hours to develop storyboard content for a curriculum containing five lessons and approximately 100 pages. This estimate could then be used in the project plan to determine the due date for storyboards in the next phase.

Appendix 3-C, *Course Outline*, provides you with a one-page template that can be used for developing a preliminary course outline of this nature.

Develop a Recommendations Document

With the completion of the course outline, you should now have a solid base of information you can use to build your recommendations for the curriculum for your e-learning project. The recommendations you identify are summarized in a deliverable called a recommendations document.

The recommendations document is the primary deliverable you should present to the managers and corporate sponsors of your program. It should contain easy-to-read, high-level information about your findings during the needs analysis, and should include your recommendations, and strategy for moving forward.

The recommendations document contains the following sections:

> Executive Summary

> Background

> Audience Analysis

> Recommendation Overview

> Instructional Strategy

> Assessment strategy

- ➤ Delivery strategy
- ➤ Communication strategy
- ➤ Maintenance strategy
- ➤ Project Plan
- ➤ Budget

Executive Summary

The Executive Summary should provide a one-page description of the objectives of the program, and should outline why this program is critical to your organization. The main purpose of this section is to ensure that all of the stakeholders for your project are on the same page. It should reinforce the commitment and objectives expressed by each sponsor during your initial meetings with them at the beginning of the needs analysis.

Background

The Background section should provide information specific to the methodology or approach that was used to conduct the analysis, in addition to:

- ➤ An overview of the players on the project,
- ➤ An explanation of roles and responsibilities,
- ➤ A summary of the existing training program,
- ➤ Any issues or concerns that have been identified within the existing curriculum that have indicated an e-learning solution may be appropriate to moving forward.

Audience Analysis

The Audience Analysis should draw heavily upon the information and summaries identified in the audience analysis summary document. This section should not be a verbatim summary of both the audience analysis summary and audience analysis matrix, but should reference them as appropriate as it provides the reader with an overview of:

- ➤ The average learner profile,
- ➤ What the technological environment looks like,
- ➤ What learners' comfort level is with e-learning and other media, and
- ➤ How the audience feels about the content for the curriculum.

The summary of information you present in this section should be used to help build your case for the recommendations you present in the Recommendation section.

Recommendations

The Recommendations section is the most critical section with your document. This section should provide a clear, concise explanation of your recommendations in one to two pages. The recommendation(s) identified within this section should be explained further in the remaining sections outlined within the document. The Recommendations section should be the one page the sponsor of your program can turn to for a quick, two-minute explanation of what you are proposing.

Instructional Strategy

The Instructional Strategy section should contain an explanation of the overall e-learning curriculum and the approach that will be taken for each lesson. The preliminary course outline you have created should be referenced within this section. This section should paint a very accurate picture of what your vision for the curriculum is, and should discuss such features as:

- ➤ Learning objectives
- ➤ Number of lessons
- ➤ Topics within each lesson
- ➤ Length of lessons
- ➤ Interactivity within lessons
- ➤ Instructional activities and case studies that will be used within lessons
- ➤ Media such as graphics, Flash, audio, and video
- ➤ Technology or programs that will be used to enhance each lesson

Assessment Strategy

The Assessment Strategy section should identify how learners will be measured or evaluated throughout the curriculum. It is within this section you should discuss the types of assessments that will be used, tracking and scoring of questions answers, pass/fail indicators, and other factors used to measure the impact of the curriculum on the overall knowledge of each learner.

Delivery Strategy

The Delivery Strategy section should contain the overall plan and technological considerations that must be taken into account when rolling the e-learning curriculum out to your audience. This section can include such items as architecture diagrams, explanation of installation procedures, the navigation strategy for the course, and other items affecting how the curriculum will be installed and delivered. The Delivery Section should also contain a list of any requirements necessary to view and access the training related to:

- ➤ Bandwidth and connectivity
- ➤ Web browsers

- ➤ Operating platform
- ➤ Plug-ins required
- ➤ Page dimensions

Communication Strategy

An important component many individuals forget to address when recommending an e-learning curriculum is communication. Many training managers can adopt an "If I build it, they will come" approach to their strategy similar to the baseball field created in the movie, *Field of Dreams.*

Unfortunately, many e-learning curricula are underutilized because learners do not know these tools are available to them. The Communication Strategy of your document should clearly state:

- ➤ What media or channels will be used to communicate the existence of your curriculum to your audience
- ➤ Who will be responsible for this communication
- ➤ How often this communication will occur

Maintenance Strategy

Although it often falls through the cracks, your recommendations should address the issue of maintenance. You must have a strategy that lists:

- ➤ How updates will be incorporated to the curriculum
- ➤ How often these updates will occur
- ➤ Who will responsible for implementing these updates

The Maintenance Strategy section of your recommendations document should identify all of these items, in addition to any other issues specific to your e-learning solution.

Project Plan

The recommendations document you present to your corporate sponsor or executive committee should contain a big picture project plan that lists:

- ➤ A proposed start date and end date
- ➤ The length of the project in weeks
- ➤ The resources involved on the project
- ➤ Key deliverable due dates and milestones
- ➤ The total hours by resource for the project

The project plan you present in your recommendations document should not provide a week-by-week, activity-by-activity breakdown of the entire project.

Because such factors as the start date, resources involved, and budget available for the project may change between the time your recommendations are made and the project begins, a best practice is to create the detailed week-by-week project plan after these factors have been approved and finalized.

Budget

The last few pages of your recommendations document will contain the information many of your corporate sponsors will be the most anxious to see—the budget. The Budget section of your recommendations document should contain a breakdown of all internal and external costs associated with the project. It should include such factors as:

➤ Cost of development hours required by external vendors or consultants

➤ Cost of internal resources in terms of hours and time required

➤ Hardware and software costs

➤ Hosting costs

➤ Maintenance costs

As a rule of thumb, when preparing the budget for your e-learning project, you should prepare for your worst-case scenario. Preparing for the possible worst case allows you to secure the budget you very well may need for your project—without going over-budget. In projects in the past where bare-bones budgets were identified, the projected costs associated with the project have tended to skyrocket when unexpected factors or dependencies that were not taken into consideration ended up affecting the overall project and increasing the number of hours or dollars required. By preparing for your worst-case scenario, your chances of coming in under budget are much higher than your chances of working with a budget based on optimal project conditions.

Present Needs Analysis Findings

Once you have finalized your recommendations document, your last step in the needs analysis project is present your recommendations along with all of the deliverables you have created for the project to your executive sponsors. While many of the executives and managers sponsoring your program will review every deliverable you have created in detail, many of them will appreciate a one to two hour presentation from you that explains your recommendations and walks them through your recommendations document.

This presentation is your opportunity to:

➤ Make the case for your recommendations internally

➤ Answer questions your sponsors may have

➤ Outline proposed next steps for moving forward with your management team

At the end of this presentation, you should feel confident you have provided your sponsors with the information they need to make a decision about your e-learning curriculum moving forward.

SUMMARY

This chapter provided you with a high-level overview of the information and deliverables needed to complete an e-learning needs analysis. Specifically this chapter:

- ➤ Provided you with an overview of the needs analysis process
- ➤ Listed the deliverables created during an e-learning needs analysis
- ➤ Discussed how to establish program objectives with your executive sponsors and obtain buy-in
- ➤ Compared and contrasted the difference between direct return on investment and indirect return on investment
- ➤ Identified a step-by-step approach for conducting an audience analysis
- ➤ Reviewed the key components to list within an e-learning recommendations document
- ➤ Discussed how to present your findings to the executive sponsors of your e-learning curriculum

RESOURCES

Readings

Gupta, Kavita (1999). *A Practical Guide to Needs Assessment.* San Francisco, CA: Jossey-Bass Pfeiffer.

Ott, R., and Longnecker, M. (2001). *Statistical Methods and Data Analysis.* Pacific Grove, CA: Duxbury.

Rea, L., and Parker, R. (1997). *Designing and Conducting Survey Research.* San Francisco, CA: Jossey-Bass Pfeiffer.

Rosenberg, Marc (2001). *e-Learning: Strategies for Delivering Knowledge in the Digital Age.* New York: McGraw-Hill.

Salant, P., and Dillman, D. (1994). *How To Conduct Your Own Survey.* New York: John Wiley & Sons, Inc.

Needs Analysis References

Bartham, S., and Gibson, B. (2000). *The Training Needs Analysis Toolkit.* Human Resource Development Inc.

Rosset, Allison (1987). Training Needs Assessment (Techniques in Training and Performance Development Series). Educational Technology Publications.

ACME Program

Survey

We are in the process of evaluating the existing curriculum for the ACME Program. Both our U.S. and global audiences are currently using the ACME curriculum. The existing curriculum is going to be modified and updated for delivery within your group during the next few months.

In order for us to ensure that the existing curriculum will be effective in meeting the requirements within your group, we are asking that you complete the following survey.

If you could please complete the survey below and e-mail this document back to Jane Doe at jdoe@ecompanyx , we'd really appreciate it. All surveys are due by 8:00 am EST on Monday September 10th, 2001.

Thank you in advance for your feedback and participation!

Background Information

Please provide us with the following information:

Name:	Male	Female
Location:	Age	
Telephone number:		
E-mail:		

1. What is your job title?

2. How long have you been in this position?

3. What is the highest level of education that you have completed? (Please select all that apply.)
   ☐ High school
   ☐ College or university undergraduate degree
   ☐ Postgraduate master's degree
   ☐ Postgraduate doctorate or Ph.D.
   ☐ Other

4. What is your primary speaking language? (Please select one language from the list below.)
   ☐ Cantonese
   ☐ English
   ☐ French
   ☐ German
   ☐ Hindi
   ☐ Italian
   ☐ Japanese
   ☐ Korean
   ☐ Mandarin
   ☐ Portuguese
   ☐ Spanish
   ☐ Other

5. What secondary languages do you speak? (Please select <u>all</u> that apply.)
   ☐ Cantonese
   ☐ English
   ☐ French
   ☐ German
   ☐ Hindi
   ☐ Italian
   ☐ Japanese
   ☐ Korean
   ☐ Mandarin
   ☐ Portuguese
   ☐ Spanish
   ☐ Other

6. What is your primary reading language? (Please select <u>one</u> language from the list below.)
   ☐ Cantonese
   ☐ English
   ☐ French
   ☐ German
   ☐ Hindi
   ☐ Italian
   ☐ Japanese
   ☐ Korean
   ☐ Mandarin
   ☐ Portuguese
   ☐ Spanish
   ☐ Other

7. What other languages can you read? (Please select <u>all</u> that apply.)
   ☐ Cantonese
   ☐ English
   ☐ French
   ☐ German
   ☐ Hindi
   ☐ Italian
   ☐ Japanese
   ☐ Korean
   ☐ Mandarin
   ☐ Portuguese
   ☐ Spanish
   ☐ Other

Technology
8. How would you rate yourself as a computer user?
   ☐ Beginner
   ☐ Intermediate
   ☐ Expert

9. What operating system do you use?
   ☐ Windows 95
   ☐ Windows 98

☐ Windows 2000
☐ Macintosh
☐ UNIX
☐ Other

10. Do you feel comfortable using the Internet and World Wide Web?
☐ Yes   ☐ No

11. Which Web browsers does your location support? (If other, please list the Web browsers your theater supports.)
☐ Microsoft Internet Explorer
☐ Netscape
☐ Other

12. Which versions of the following browsers does your location support?
Microsoft Internet Explorer
☐ Version 5.5
☐ Version 5.01
☐ Version 5.0
☐ Version 4.0
☐ Version 3.02
☐ Other
☐ Not applicable

Netscape
☐ Version 6.0
☐ Version 4.7
☐ Version 4.6
☐ Version 4.5
☐ Version 4.0
☐ Version 3.0
☐ Other
☐ Not applicable

13. What hardware systems are used to access the Internet and World Wide Web in your location? (Please select all that apply.)
☐ Desktop PCs
☐ Laptops
☐ Dedicated workstations
☐ Personal Digital Assistant (PDA)
☐ Mobile/cell phone
☐ Other

14. How do the majority of users within your location access the Internet and World Wide Web? (Please select all that apply. If other, please explain.)
☐ Corporate LAN or WAN
☐ Dial-up 56K
☐ Dial-up 33.6K
☐ Dial-up 28K
☐ DSL 1.5M
☐ DSL 384K
☐ ISDN
☐ Cable

APPENDIX 3-A. *Continued*

☐ All of the above
☐ Not known
☐ Other

15. Which media does your computer support? (Please select all that apply.)
    ☐ Audio
    ☐ Video
    ☐ Neither of the above
    ☐ Not applicable

16. Do you feel there have been bandwidth/technology constraints associated with e-learning courses that have been delivered in your location in the past? (If yes, please list some of the constraints your location has experienced.)
    ☐Yes   ☐No

17. How are technical/IT issues currently resolved in your location? (If other, please explain.)
    ☐ Regional IT help desk or response center
    ☐ Local IT help desk or response center
    ☐ Other

18. Can you provide us with the name of a primary IT contact in your location that we can speak with?

Existing Training Delivery

19. How many hours each month do you currently dedicate to training?
    ☐ 1 – 5 hours
    ☐ 6 – 10 hours
    ☐ 11 – 20 hours
    ☐ Over 20 hours each month

20. Please list the training courses that you are currently required to complete for your job role.

21. Please list any optional training courses that are available to you.

22. How is training currently delivered within your location? (Please select all that apply.)

    ☐ Instructor-led
    ☐ Coaching/individual mentoring
    ☐ Web-based training or e-learning
    ☐ Computer-based training via CD
    ☐ Virtual synchronous classroom (Placeware, WebEx, Centra, etc.)
    ☐ Linear video (VHS, PAL, SECAM)
    ☐ Video on Demand (VOD)
    ☐ Self-paced documentation (user guides, student guides)

☐ On-line help or reference documentation
☐ Other

23. On a scale from 1 to 5, with 1 = uncomfortable and 5 = comfortable, how comfortable are you receiving training via each of the following mediums?

Instructor-led training	1	2	3	4	5
Coaching/individual mentoring	1	2	3	4	5
Web-based training or e-learning	1	2	3	4	5
Computer-based training via CD	1	2	3	4	5
Virtual synchronous classroom	1	2	3	4	5
Linear video (VHS, PAL, SECAM)	1	2	3	4	5
Video on Demand (VOD)	1	2	3	4	5
Self-paced documentation (user guides, student guides)	1	2	3	4	5
On-line help or reference documentation	1	2	3	4	5
Other	1	2	3	4	5

24. What primary language is used in your location to deliver training via each of the mediums listed below?

Instructor-led training
Coaching/individual mentoring
Web-based training or e-learning
Computer-based training via CD
Virtual synchronous classroom (Placeware, WebEx, Centra, etc.)
Linear video (VHS, PAL, SECAM)
Video on Demand (VOD)
Self-paced documentation (user guides, student guides)
On-line help or reference documentation
Other

25. On a scale from 1 to 5, with 1 = uncomfortable and 5 = comfortable, how comfortable are you receiving training via each of the mediums below in *English*?

Instructor-led training	1	2	3	4	5
Coaching/individual mentoring	1	2	3	4	5
Web-based training or e-learning	1	2	3	4	5

APPENDIX 3-A. *Continued*

Computer-based training via CD	1	2	3	4	5
Virtual synchronous classroom (Placeware, WebEx, Centra, etc.)	1	2	3	4	5
Linear video (VHS, PAL, SECAM)	1	2	3	4	5
Video on Demand (VOD)	1	2	3	4	5
Self-paced documentation (user guides, student guides)	1	2	3	4	5
On-line help or reference documentation	1	2	3	4	5
Other	1	2	3	4	5

26. When do you normally attend or participate in training? (Please select all that apply.)
   ☐ During the course of a normal working day (8:00 am to 5:00 pm)
   ☐ In the evening after 5:00 pm
   ☐ On weekends

27. Do you view training as critical to your job? (If no, please explain your response.)

   ☐ Yes   ☐ No

28. Have e-learning courses been well received in your location in the past?   (If no, please explain your response.)

   ☐ Yes   ☐ No

29. What are some of the things that you have liked about e-learning courses that you have taken in the past?

30. What are some of the things that you have not liked about e-learning courses that you have taken in the past?

Existing Curriculum

<Insert Next Question>

Thank you for taking the time to complete this survey!

This document provides several sample pages that you might find within an audience analysis summary document. The purpose of an audience analysis summary is to provide a big-picture overview of the data compiled within the audience analysis matrices developed for your project.

This document provides an analysis of data gathered from respondents within the following ACME organizations:

- Organization X
- Organization Y
- Organization Z

This information was gathered using a combination of in-person interviews, teleconferences, and Web-based surveys gathered using www.xyzsurveycompany.com. Please review the following attachments, *Attachment A – Organization X Audience Analysis Matrix, Attachment B – Organization Y Audience Analysis Matrix,* and *Attachment C – Organization Z Audience Analysis Matrix* for specific information gathered from each respondent.

Each audience identified within this document contains a brief overview and high-level summary of findings. Each summary of findings is broken down into the following sections:

- Background information
- Technology
- Additional topic 1
- Additional topic 2
- Additional topic 3

Recommendations specific to how training should be delivered within each theater based on this data will be identified within our Recommendations Document. These recommendations will be presented to the *<insert names of corporate sponsors>* the week of *Month, xxth.*

Organization X

Introduction

Organization X contains a diverse audience of 500 Account Managers and other ACME sales personnel distributed among ACME offices in countries around the world. These countries included:

- The United Kingdom
- France
- Germany
- Italy
- Israel
- India
- China
- Japan
- Mexico

Data was gathered from a sample of 200 respondents within each of these countries to form a profile of the average learner within each location.

The distribution of respondents from each country was as follows.

Sample Population

Country of Residence	UK	France	Germany	Italy	Israel	India	China	Japan	Mexico	Total
Account Managers	10	15	12	6	4	20	20	18	15	120
Sales Title 1	5	5	6	2	2	10	10	2	8	50
Sales Title 2	2	3	4	1	2	5	5	2	6	30
Grand Total Respondents										200

Background

Overview:
Within each survey, individuals were asked to provide information related to gender, age, education level, and primary speaking language. This information was used to create a profile of the average learner within each area, and can be used as a factor in determining the approach, instructional strategy, and tone of a training curriculum deployed for that audience.

For example, if data gathered had indicated that the majority of respondents were college-educated males between the ages of 18 and 25, training materials would need to be designed quite differently than those appropriate for a large audience of postgraduate females between the ages of 35 and 49.

Another critical factor that should be taken into consideration when deploying a global training curriculum for this audience is language. A general rule of thumb is to develop materials in the language or languages spoken by the majority of learners within any given group.

Due to the variety of cultures within Organization X, there were generally a variety of languages spoken among respondents, including English, French, German, Spanish, Japanese, and Mandarin.

Summary of Findings:
- *The sample was composed of 120 males, and 80 females.*

- *Data gathered from respondents related to gender and age indicated that the majority of males within the sample were between the ages of 31 and 40 (40%), and the majority of females were between the ages of 31 and 40 (35%) as well:*

Age	Male	Female
21 – 30	25%	20%
31 – 40	40%	35%
41 – 50	25%	30%
51 – 60	5%	10%
61 +	5%	5%

APPENDIX 3-B. *Continued*

- *The majority of respondents surveyed had received a college or undergraduate degree:*

Education	Respondents
High School	200
College or university undergraduate degree	175
Postgraduate master's degree	40
Postgraduate doctorate or Ph.D.	10
Other	24

- *The information gathered in this analysis indicated that a good majority of respondents within this organization do not speak English as a primary speaking language. Primary speaking languages used by respondents were broken out as follows:*

Technology

Overview:

Basic information was gathered from all respondents to form an understanding of the technological environment in which they are working. Individuals were asked to provide data specific to:

- *Current hardware used at their locations*
- *Operating platform*
- *Browser type and version*
- *Internet connectivity and speed*

When developing e-learning or Web-based training, it is very important to gather this information to determine how much bandwidth and other constraints will affect the design of on-line courses delivered in a given region.

Summary of Findings:

- *Although Netscape Navigator is the common platform used by the majority of respondents within Organization X, a large number of respondents use Internet Explorer as well.*

Browsers Used to Access the Internet and World Wide Web

Browser	Respondents
Netscape Navigator	60%
Internet Explorer	40%

- *The majority of respondents within Organization X indicated that traditional desktops and laptops are used as the primary hardware to access the Internet and World Wide Web.*

- *Respondents use a variety of operating platforms to access the Internet as well. While platforms range from Windows 95 to UNIX, Windows 2000 was clearly the platform used by the majority of respondents.*

- *As far as media used by respondents to gain access to the Internet and World Wide Web, corporate LAN is the clear majority for all respondents. However, it is also important to note that for the majority of respondents, multiple media are used to access the Internet in addition to corporate LANs.*

Media Used to Access the Internet and World Wide Web

Media	Respondents
Corporate LAN	100%
Dial-up 56K	58%
Dial-up 33K	42%
Dial-up 28K	42%
DSL 1.5 M	30%
DSL 384K	20%
ISDN	5%
Cable	33%
No access to Internet and WWW	0%

- Although surveyed individuals within Organization X seem to have the technological capacity to support e-learning courses, a significant portion of respondents (30%) indicated that bandwidth has been an issue with e-learning courses they have taken in the past.

APPENDIX 3-B. *Continued*

Preliminary Course Outline
ACME Program
Last Updated: January 1, 20xx

Module 1: <Insert Title>

Description

<Insert description of module 1>

Objectives

At the end of this module, you will be able to:

- *<Insert Objective 1>*
- *<Insert Objective 2>*
- *<Insert Objective 3>*
- *<Insert Objective 4>*
- *<Insert Objective 5>*

Assessment Questions

This lesson will contain multiple choice review questions that will provide users with correct/incorrect feedback as each question is completed.

9 Multiple Choice Questions

- 1 Question About Objective 1
- 2 Questions on Objective 2
- 2 Questions on Objective 3
- 3 Questions on Objective 4
- 1 Question on Objective 5

Instructional Activities

- 2 Simulations
- 2 Drag and Drop Exercises
- 2 Interactive Case Studies with Video

APPENDIX 3-C. **PRELIMINARY COURSE OUTLINE**

Media

- 15 - 20 Screen Shots
- 10 – 15 Custom Graphics or Photos
- 2 3-4 Minute Video Clips for Case Studies

Web Pages

- This module will contain between 30 – 40 Web pages.

High-Level Course Outline

1.1. **Topic 1**
    1.1.2. Sub-topic
    1.1.3. Sub-topic

1.2. **Topic 2**
    1.2.2.1.Sub-topic
    1.2.2.2.Sub-topic
    1.2.2.3.Sub-topic
    1.2.2.4.Sub-topic

1.3. **Topic 3**
    1.3.2. Sub-topic
    1.3.3. Sub-topic

1.4. **Topic 4**
    1.4.2. Sub-topic
    1.4.3. Sub-topic

1.5. **Topic 5**
    1.5.2. Sub-topic
    1.5.3. Sub-topic

1.6. **Topic 6**
    1.6.2. Sub-topic
    1.6.3. Sub-topic

Module 2: <Insert Title>

Description

<Insert description of module 2>

Objectives

At the end of this module, you will be able to:

- *<Insert Objective 1>*
- *<Insert Objective 2>*
- *<Insert Objective 3>*
- *<Insert Objective 4>*
- *<Insert Objective 5>*

Assessment Questions

This lesson will contain…...

- *<Insert type and approximate number of questions>*

Instructional Activities

- *<Insert instructional activity 1>*

Media

- *<Insert media type 1>*

Web Pages

- *<Insert approximate number of Web pages>:*

High-Level Course Outline

2.1. *<Insert high-level course outline for module 2>*

➤ABOUT THE AUTHOR

Tom Floyd is a Senior Educational Consultant with Crawford & Associates International, a training consulting firm located in Palo Alto, California. Tom has conducted both domestic and global e-learning needs analyses for Fortune 500 companies located in the San Francisco Bay Area. He has played a pivotal role in developing the design, implementation, and assessment strategies for a variety of audiences using both synchronous and asynchronous e-learning media.

Tom is currently driving the global implementation of an e-learning curriculum designed for Sales and Marketing audiences located within the United States, Europe, and Latin America.

CHAPTER 4

SELLING E-LEARNING TO YOUR ORGANIZATION

➤**DARIN HARTLEY**

INTRODUCTION

One of the attractions at Walt Disney World is the "It's a Small World" boat ride. How prophetic were the folks at Disney with the premise of this ride. The world is actually getting smaller every minute (or is that every microsecond) with the explosion of the Internet and its related industries and technologies. People are hyperconnected now to each other with a myriad of technological systems and devices. If the folks at Disney were to revamp the ride, it might be called "It's an e-World." We have e-commerce, e-banking, e-loans, e-mail, e-zines, and so on, ad infinitum. Now, of course, we have e-learning.

How does one define e-learning? ASTD defines it as: "Anything delivered, enabled, or mediated by electronic technology for the

71

explicit purpose of learning. It also refers to the technology and services that help create, deliver, and manage those activities." This definition helps give you an idea of the scope of e-learning and what it entails, and doesn't entail. If you know the definition you can start to talk about this to others in your organization. Note that this is not the only definition of e-learning that exists. In fact, if you got any group of ten people together and asked for their definition of e-learning, the responses would be widely divergent.

E-learning is being used by thousands of organizations now across the world. There are even companies and organizations that have entire e-learning departments. Many financial institutions and brokerages now have full-time e-learning analysts on their staffs. These people create reports that focus on the e-learning sector. This would have been unheard of even ten years ago. Many of these financial institutions are predicting the e-learning business to be valued in the multiple billions of U.S. dollars in the coming five years.

In this chapter we will deal with the following three questions:

➤ If e-learning is the greatest thing to happen in the learning field in recent history, why do I have to sell it to my organization?

➤ What information/tools do I need to be able to make the case for e-learning?

➤ What kinds of resistance can I expect from the organization when I am selling e-learning?

Having said all of the preceding concerning the importance of e-learning, why would anyone have to try to "sell" e-learning in their organization? If it is such a hot commodity, shouldn't senior management be pushing their training organizations for enterprisewide e-learning implementations . . . now? On the surface, this may seem to be the case. However, there is much noise that has to be filtered out to enable e-learning in an organization. How much does this stuff cost? Who can implement it? What do I do with the existing training staff? How will this affect our operating systems? What is the learning curve for our end-users and also for the new e-learning personnel in the organization?

ASSESSING E-LEARNING READINESS

These are just a few of the questions that can help muddy the decision to use e-learning in an organization. And then there are other issues associated with e-learning readiness: organizational culture, instructor readiness, technology infrastructure, support/maintenance, and business/fiscal readiness. Let's take a look at each of these in a little more detail.

Organizational Culture

A major potential issue in any enterprise, commercial, nonprofit, or public, is the organizational culture of the organization. What is the primary mode of communication in the organization? Do most people meet face-to-face on a regular basis or are e-communications the modus operandi? How do people like to learn in the organization? Do they prefer self-paced instruction or classroom-based instruction? What is the organization's change tolerance? How easy is it to catalyze change in the organization?

All of these questions (and other similar questions) help address the organizational culture of the organization that is considering adopting e-learning. If the culture is extremely contrary to the notion of e-learning, then it will be hard to sell e-learning to the organization. So you will need to assess the organizational culture to help determine e-learning readiness.

Instructor Readiness

Next look at instructor readiness. This is a key issue when organizations are contemplating the use of e-learning. If no one in the organization can support the e-learning from a training/facilitator standpoint, then it can be difficult to sustain and enrich the e-learning program.

Contrary to popular belief, e-learning entails much more than posting a static website and walking away. For e-learning to be effective, it has to be kept fresh and updated. This, generally, means that someone will have to be manually making changes to some types of e-learning media or making changes to the databases that support nonstatic media.

So, who will do that in an organization that is considering the use of e-learning? There are courses that internal people can take to help get them up to speed, however, during an initial implementation of e-learning it might require some consulting services. You can work with e-learning consultants who can help you with your e-learning implementation and also improve the internal staff's abilities with e-learning.

Technology Infrastructure

Another important factor as you explore the use of e-learning in your organization is the technology infrastructure of your organization. For e-learning to be successful, you need a technology infrastructure that will support it at some level.

That's not to say that everyone in an organization has to have the latest rocket computer with all the latest upgrades. It does mean that everyone in an organization that will be using e-learning will need to have some baseline level of hardware, software, and network access to help ensure a viable e-learning undertaking.

For instance, if you want your customer support department to take online courses from an Internet-based supplier, one of the most basic technology requirements is that these people have access to computers that have access to the Internet.

Support and Maintenance Structure

Another important aspect of readiness for your organization is the support/maintenance structure of the organization. As mentioned earlier, a solid e-learning program required regular updates to help ensure that the content is viable and that it continues to draw people to the e-learning intervention and also to ensure that once folks are there, they are getting what they need. It is important that organizations build in this kind of support/maintenance resources and funding into their e-learning business cases or in the end, they will shortchange themselves and/or their clients.

Business Readiness

Finally, for an organization to be ready for e-learning its business must be ready for it. This means that there must be management, philosophical, and financial support from business leadership for the undertaking, meaning that leadership must be a proponent for this new type of learning and must take actions to demonstrate and communicate this to its employees.

For example, Microsoft CEO Bill Gates wanted a "paperless office" and challenged his department leadership to reduce the number of forms from the greater than 1,000 that were in house in 1996. By 1999, this was reduced to a company-wide total of 60 forms (50 of which are required in paper by law and/or organizations that are still paper-based. [*Business @ the Speed of Thought*, Bill Gates, Warner Books, NY, 1999, p. 49]). This type of leadership enables change and parallels the implementation of e-learning in organizations.

It is also important to ensure that an organization has the fiscal infrastructure to be ready for e-learning. There will be costs associated with implementing e-learning and if there is no way to manage this aspect of the implementation easily, e-learning implementations can be stopped in their tracks, by bureaucracy, lack of funding, and so on.

GATHERING INFORMATION AND TOOLS TO MAKE THE CASE

Now that you are familiar with the e-learning readiness, you will want to go back and assess where your organization is. If you are pretty confident that you are ready to start with e-learning, then you can proceed with the next part of the "selling e-learning" process, which is gathering evidence for support.

Evidence Gathering

In a sense, you are making a persuasive argument when you are pitching e-learning to a new group. In order to persuade people about something, it is often very helpful to have supportive evidence. So it is when you are trying to sell the concept of e-learning. You will need evidence to help make your case, and that evidence can include industry trends, success stories, and news.

Industry Trends

Let's break the types of evidence into more detail. The first group is industry trends. Every industry has trends associated with it. Learning, training, and performance consulting are no different. One of the latest and most powerful trends in the learning industry is the movement towards e-learning. We have mentioned that brokerage houses have analysts that cover the e-learning industry.

There are also some research and financial analysis firms that are focused solely on the e-learning industry. Check out www.thinkequity.com as an example. If there were no promise of a bright future in this sector, we wouldn't see organizations like these in place.

We know that technology is becoming more prevalent. We know that computer prices, Internet access, and even broadband access is decreasing in cost. More countries outside the United States are "getting wired" and this all points to the need for additional sources of learning, including technology-enabled learning.

Finally, there is a trend to hire as few people as possible. In fact, during 2001 the U.S. economy experienced an economic slowdown that led to waves of layoffs and other economic uncertainty. This means, in general, that most organizations are going to have fewer people to do more work. It can be a career-limiting move as a trainer in an organization to recommend more classroom-based training as the solution for the next business initiative.

The last thing management wants to have in situations like this is more classroom-based training. It means that their already horizontally loaded workforce has additional time requirements placed on it for training.

Success Stories

Another source of evidence for your e-learning business case is success stories. There are many companies and organizations in the world today that are having success implementing e-learning. Their success might result in greater employee efficiency, reduced costs, greater impact, and so on, which are some of the benefits that will be discussed in more detail in this chapter. When you can find e-learning success stories from comparable businesses (and even sometimes competitors) you can help make the case in your organization.

Where can you find these success stories? They are available in lots of places. One of the easiest and quickest ways to find sources is to go to a search engine and type in the phrase "e-learning success story." You will be amazed at the number of responses that get returned after such a query. Review the findings that you get from the Web and then start to dig down.

When you discover stories that seem really appropriate, it might be a good idea to contact the marketing or public relations department of the organization to see if there is additional information you can get from the story. Always ask for permission prior to printing or distributing success stories inside your organization. This is a professional courtesy and legal responsibility when dealing with copyrighted materials, though, normally, you will get an affirmative response to the request.

News and Current Events

One other area of interest for evidence gathering to support e-learning is in the news and current events happening all around us. One thing that is quite possible for some folks in the training industry to do is to get so focused on creating learning solutions that they have no time to look outside their cubicles to see what is happening around them. This doesn't help the person trying to implement e-learning. There is industry news and technology news that can be used as evidence for most people.

Where can you find these sources of news? They are in multiple places. They might be in the technology (or business) section of your newspaper. There are sources of relevant news all over the Internet, not to mention desktop delivery of lots of news. You can also find it on television and the radio.

We are nearly continuously bombarded with news and related information that often contains sources of evidence to support your case for e-learning. For instance, it is a known fact that microprocessors are getting smaller in size, bigger in computer power, and lower in cost.

What might this say about the future of learning? How could you use this news to support an argument for e-learning? Well . . . One hypothesis might be: If there are fewer people in organizations doing more work, then it is going to be harder to get them out of the work space to go to traditional classroom training. Because microprocessors are shrinking so fast in cost and size, couldn't they be used in products in people's workspaces to promote learning? The answer is "yes."

We are already seeing work and learning being shrunk down into small components and brought to the job. The personal digital assistant (PDA) that is so pervasive in our world today, is a relatively powerful tool that enables folks to get lots of information they need, wherever they may be, when they need it. If you aren't paying attention to the news, then you lose the potential opportunity to exploit it.

You can see that evidence gathering is important in the process of selling e-learning in your organization. One thing you might consider doing in this process is to keep file folders (some paper based and others electronic) that contain the evidence and other supporting information you need to make your case. In this way, each time you create a case, you don't have to start completely from scratch. You can use the information you have gathered from previous business cases to support the new case.

Identify the Benefits

One of the next steps you will need to take is to identify the benefits of e-learning for your organization. No organization is going to undertake new endeavors unless the benefits outweigh the potential risks. So, as the e-learning evangelist in your organization, you will want to clearly identify the benefits. Each organization has business initiatives that might be more pressing for them than for other organizations, so ideally, you should identify benefits that most closely parallel the direction the organization is heading.

Benefits can include:

➤ cost savings

➤ increased efficiency

➤ greater learner control

➤ greater impact—quicker

➤ reduced time in training

Your task is to identify the benefit(s) for your organization that will facilitate making your business case. There are other benefits not listed here that you might identify as well. Let's look at each of these in more detail now.

Cost Savings
The first benefit identified is cost savings. Depending on your existing technology infrastructure and technology, the cost to implement some of the e-learning solutions can be relatively low. Many e-learning solution companies are offering application service provider (ASP) solutions that don't require hardware or software investments in-house.

Instructional Costs
Where you can really start to save money is in the cost of instructors, classroom space, print-based materials, travel, and in other areas. If you are conducting a Web-based course for 100 people, you don't have to try to herd them into a classroom over three or four sessions to get the same content. They can learn the content from their desktops, which minimizes travel costs associated with training (even forty-five minute round trips from one campus to another start to add up).

Instructor costs can be huge. Changes for contract instructors can range from $50 per hour to whatever. Again, using e-learning these costs could be minimized or eliminated completely.

Opportunity Costs
Another example of cost savings is minimized opportunity costs. If a field-based salesperson has to be brought into the home office, 1,000 miles away for two days to get two hours worth of product updates, he or she cannot provide support to his or her accounts during that time. This is an example of opportunity costs that occur every day as people are taken from where they need to be to best support their managers, employees, clients, and/or customers.

Increased Efficiency
Increased efficiency is another example of a benefit that can be obtained from e-learning. Employees can use e-learning to get knowledge, just-in-time, which helps them perform on the job better. If you need to learn about project management for an upcoming project and can't get into a traditional classroom on the subject for three months because of limited classroom size or long wait lists, you can't be as efficient as you could be if you could get the information on demand.

Learner Control

Another tremendous benefit of e-learning is increased learner control. For years, the training world has been giving lip service to the notion of learner-centered instruction—that is, instruction where the student or participant drives the learning. The fact is that this still is not happening in most classrooms. The instructor tells the participants when to do everything from which handout to read to the time to take a break or lunch. The learner is not getting to make the decision about anything in the session.

The other issue here is that invariably people in a classroom will have different levels of knowledge about the topic at hand, so that those with advanced levels of knowledge are bored and those with little knowledge are continually trying to get to the level of the rest of the group. If a student is forced to learn what he or she already knows, this is not learner-centered instruction.

Impact

The impact e-learning has versus traditional training can be astronomical. When organizations have business and organizational initiatives that require training, traditional classroom-based learning can take so long that by the time everyone in the organization gets trained, the original need is passed or is obsolete.

Here's an example.

Let's say that two equal-sized companies have to train their employees on a new component that will be used in their products. Companies A and B have their training ready for implementation on the same day. However, Company A is using an Internet-based solution that can be implemented to its 1,000 employees 24/7 in a short amount of time. Company B is herding groups of 25 people into classrooms to get their training. With makeups, no shows, and other scheduling issues, Company B's implementation of the four-hour classroom course will take many months to get everyone through it. This is how e-learning can have a greater impact . . . quicker. This is truly a benefit of the solution.

Reduced Time

It has already been stated that the more time spent in training increases the opportunity cost associated with training due to lost time on the job and away from where the employee normally should be. So, it makes sense that anything that can reduce time spent in training would be a plus. E-learning can decrease the time spent in training in several ways.

First, many kinds of e-learning are built with preassessments that allow participants to challenge a course and to bypass information they already know. These types of courses then lay out a recommended learning path that focuses on just what the participants need to know. In a traditional classroom, people are at various levels of competency; yet get the same lesson delivery.

Second, many e-learning courses are structure nonhierarchically, like the Web. Ten learners could get the same course, navigate through it completely differently, and still meet the end goal of the course. Since people get just the learning they need and not all of the excess fluff, there is less time spent in training. Less time spent in training means more time spent where the employees need to be. This is a benefit to the entire organization.

As you've read, there are lots of potential benefits for e-learning. Some are more appropriate to focus on for your organization than others. Your task is to identify those benefits that will parallel or mesh well with the strategic direction of your organization.

Making the Case

Now that you have identified the benefits of implementing e-learning for your solution, you will need to actually start putting the case together. One of the best ways to do this is with a template. There is a good possibility that once you start implementing e-learning solutions that you will have to do it more than once. So, a reusable e-learning business case template is a must. What are some things that should be included in the template?

➤ business case title

➤ purpose

➤ submission date

➤ project team

➤ major tasks

➤ milestones

➤ deliverables

➤ costs

➤ benefits

➤ forecasted ROI

➤ risks

➤ list of potential suppliers (if appropriate)

➤ success metrics

➤ interactions needed with other departments

➤ interactions needed with legacy systems

➤ change management plan

There might be other categories required for your template based on specific requirements that your organization has, but these form the basis of the business case. The template can be created in a word processor and saved for later use. They can also be done as websites and shared through your Intranet or possibly the Internet.

Alternatively, you could put the business case on a CD-ROM and couple it with presentations and other supporting information. Use appropriate graphics to enhance the appearance of your business case too.

Let's look at some of the items you should cover in the business case and how you might want to approach them.

Title—When you create a title for the business case make it provocative. Make it action-based so people will be compelled to pick it up and read it. Which of the following business case titles are you more likely to pick up and read? *E-Learning Business Case for the ABC Corporation* or *Web-Based Collaboration: The Next Communications Revolution?* Most people would probably pick up the latter.

Purpose—Let the readers know very quickly why they are reading the business case and what implementation of the e-learning solution will accomplish.

Project Team—Identify the team and departments they represent. Generally, you should have representation from more departments than just Human Resources and/or Training. Include contact information for each team member.

Major Tasks—List the major tasks that will be involved in getting the e-learning solution implemented. This helps the people reviewing the business case to get a sense of what the project actually entails.

Milestones—Identify the major milestones of the project. These let the reader understand where key parts of the project are and probably where project reviews will be occurring.

Deliverables—List the deliverables and specifications for them.

Costs—It will be nearly impossible for a management team to approve an e-learning project without understanding the costs associated with the project. Don't hide costs! Identify all costs associated with the project. If you underestimate the costs, then you might not be able to complete a project without seriously overspending on it. This is a surefire way to have management disapprove your future requests.

Forecasted ROI—ROI stands for return on investment. Every good business person wants to have an estimate of what the forecasted return on their investment is before they will make an investment in any new project. Work with your finance department and operations personnel to help create this. In the bibliography for this chapter you will find a URL for a free ROI Calculator.

Risks—If you are trying to make a business case for e-learning, you might think you shouldn't list any of the risks involved. This is bound to come back to bite you if you don't. Risks themselves don't stop a new initiative from occurring. Risks that are identified with no contingency planning can be showstoppers. Identifying risks also shows organizational leadership in that you are being objective about the case you are making.

List of Potential Suppliers—If you know, for example, that you are trying to bring a Learning Management System (LMS) into your organization, there are lots of suppliers out there in this space. It is okay to list some of these in the business case and shows evidence that you've started thinking about different ways to implement the solution.

Success Metrics—How will the organization recognize that the initiative was a success? You will want to identify these so that you can report on the results after the end of the initiative or during the initiative's maintenance phase.

Interactions Needed with Other Departments—Usually implementation of a new e-learning system or solution touches multiple departments in organizations. The only time this might not be true is if an end-user is loading a CD-ROM onto his or her desktop. Enterprise or Web-based learning has the potential to touch many departments. If your e-learning solution will require another department's resources, the decision makers need to know this so that they can be assured that there is proper preparation taking place. If you need someone from the Information Technology (IT) organization to write code for you or to help install an application on a server, then the IT department needs to know about it in advance.

Interactions Needed with Legacy Systems—Most organizations have operational hardware and software that drives its business. For instance, companies that have manufacturing plants need inventory control software, payroll needs, payroll software, and so on. If implementation of your e-learning solution can potentially affect a legacy or operational system, this needs to be denoted clearly in the business case. You don't want to be the training manager who has just shut down the Sales Account System by implementing a new enterprisewide e-learning solution on coaching.

Change Management Plan—How will changes to the business case be managed? Who will capture them? Who will communicate them? How often can changes be made, and so on? These are the types of questions you will need to answer in this section.

Now you've seen some of the information to be included in your business case document. There are other sections that you might add that reflect specific needs that you might have. That's fine. This is a guide to help get you started. Remember to save your template and any completed business cases so they can be used for reference in the future.

When you are preparing your business case, continue to look at trends that are occurring in the industry and in the world. These trends could add weight to your argument. For example, at the time of this writing, unemployment was high. This means that there are fewer people doing more work, which means less time for people to be in the classroom. This trend helps support the need for e-learning, since it can minimize the time spent in the classroom.

Practice the Presentation

You've gathered evidence, identified the benefits, created a report and are ready to make the case to management. One thing that is important for you to do is to practice your presentation multiple times. You want your delivery to be as smooth as possible. There are times when you will want to demonstrate a sample of the technology you are considering. For these types of sessions you will want to ensure that you are comfortable using and demonstrating the technology. If you are not, you can ask vendors to demonstrate the products for you. They will normally do this at no cost to you, and it will allow you to focus on making the case.

One additional thing you can do to prepare for the presentation is to make it in front of people who know little or nothing about e-learning. They will ask some of the same questions that management will when you make the presentation to them. This will prepare you with responses to those questions.

DEALING WITH RESISTANCE

You're making the presentation and you're getting some objections from management. Is this typical? Sure, you need to worry if you aren't getting some tough questions asked. How do you respond to the objections that they may have? Most objections can be addressed in two ways.

The first is to educate the management team about e-learning. If they understand what e-learning is and maybe even get to practice using e-learning prior to or during the business case presentation, it is easier to make the case.

The second way to combat objections is to relay to management how the e-learning solution will provide equivalent or better learning opportunities than the traditional classroom environment when used properly. As adults, most of us have spent literally thousands of hours in the classroom from kindergarten through graduate school and beyond. We are very comfortable sitting passively in neat rows and being talked to. This is what we know. So, as a change catalyst in your organization you will have to help people learn some new skills and new ways of learning to really take ownership of the e-learning process.

Rejection

You've made the presentation of the business case to the management team. They rejected the idea. It hurts. Does this means that you give up on e-learning completely? No. It means that you at least have gotten the seed in management's head and making the case will be easier the next time. Answer the questions they had and be prepared for related questions in the future. A tiger only makes a kill once for every ten attempts. Does the tiger give up after the first missed kill? No. Be persistent and you will be rewarded.

Making a case for e-learning is a complicated business as you have seen. It takes tremendous preparation, work, and resilience. The key in all of this is to make your audience as savvy as they can possibly be in the e-learning space, within the time constraints that you have. Make a solid business case, deliver a polished presentation, respond gracefully to objections, and demonstrate perseverance in your pursuit of e-learning, and you will make the case for e-learning in your organization.

TIPS AND HINTS

- ➤ Define e-learning for your target audience.

- ➤ Discover whether or not your organization is ready for e-learning.

- ➤ Gather various types of evidence to support your case: industry trends, success stories, and news.

- ➤ Identify the benefits of e-learning to your organization. These might include:

  - ➤ cost savings

  - ➤ increased efficiency

  - ➤ greater learner control

  - ➤ greater impact—quicker

  - ➤ reduced time in training

- ➤ Use a template to create your business case. Save the template and any created business cases for future reference.

- ➤ Review industry trends prior to making the actual business case presentation.

- ➤ Practice, practice, practice the presentation (remember to practice with people who don't know what e-learning is, too.)

- ➤ Address objections by letting management know how you can help up-level employee skill and knowledge of e-learning and related technologies.

- ➤ Be prepared for rejection.

- ➤ Be persistent!

- ➤ Use the business case checklist in Appendix 4-A to help make your case.

Use this checklist to verify that you are ready to make your business case.

Business need identified for e-learning

Baseline solution identified

Best provider for the e-learning solution identified

Non-disclosure agreement in place with vendor (if necessary)

Business case written

Cost benefit study conducted

Risks of proceeding and not proceeding identified

Timeline and task list created

Presentations have been made to team(s) that will approve projects

End users of proposed solution have had opportunity to try the new solution

Contract in place with vendor if appropriate

Marketing plan developed for e-learning solution

Work authorized to start

Solution piloted

Solution implemented

APPENDIX 4-A. **BUSINESS CASE CHECKLIST[1]**

NOTES

1. Gates, Bill (1999). *Business @ the Speed of Thought*, New York: Warner Books. Hartley, Darin (2001). *Selling E-Learning*, ASTD Press.

RESOURCES

Readings

Abbey, Beverly (2000). *Instructional and Cognitive Impacts of Web-Based Education*. Hershey, PA: Idea Group Publishing, Hershey.

Davis, Stan, and Meyer, Christopher (1998). *Blur*. Reading Massachusetts: Addison-Wesley.

Driscoll, Marcy P. (1994). *Psychology of Learning for Instruction*, Boston: Allyn and Bacon.

Hartley, Darin E (2000). "All Aboard the E-Learning Train." *Training & Development Magazine*. 56.

Hartley, Darin (2000). *On-Demand Learning: Training in the New Millennium.* Amherst, MD: HRD Press.

Hartman, Amir, and Sifonis, John (with John Kador) (2000). *Net Ready.* New York: McGraw-Hill.

Levine, Rick, Locke, Christopher; Searls, Doc; and Weinberger, David (2000). *The Cluetrain Manifesto.* Cambridge, MA: Perseus Publishing.

Rosenberg, Marc. J. (2000). *e-Learning.* New York: McGraw-Hill.

Schank, Roger. (1997). *Virtual Learning.* New York: McGraw Hill.

Schank, Roger (2000). *Coloring Outside the Lines.* New York: Harper Collins Publishers.

Van Adelsberg, David, and Trolley, Edward A. (1999). *Running Training Like a Business.* San Francisco: Berrett-Koehler Publishers, Inc.

Websites

www.astd.org
www.brandon-hall.com
www.click2learn.com
www.corpu.com
www.ddiworld.com
www.eduventures.com
elearningguild.com

www.learningcircuits.com
www.learn2now.com
www.masie.com
www.macromedia.com
www.smartforce.com
www.thinkequity.com

Magazines

T+D
American Society for Training & Development (ASTD)
1640 King Street, Box 1443
Alexandria, VA 22313-2043, USA
Phone: 703-683-8100

TRAINING
Training magazine, 50 S. Ninth St., Minneapolis, MN 55402
Phone: 800-707-7749   Fax: 612-333-6526

e-learning
Publishing Office
201 Sandpointe Ave., Suite 600
Santa Ana, CA 92707
Phone: 714-513-8400
Fax: 714-513-8632

►ABOUT THE AUTHOR

Darin Hartley has been working in the training industry for the past twelve years and has undergraduate and graduate degrees in Corporate Training and Training Management. He is the Developer of New Business Ventures for ASTD. Prior to ASTD he was the Program Manager of the Customer-Focused E-Learning Solutions Department of Dell Computer Corporation's training organization, Dell Learning. Darin has presented previously at ISPI International, ASTD International, and the ASTD Technical Skills Training Conference on a variety of topics. He has authored articles for *T+D*, *Technical & Skills Training* and *WorkForce* Magazines, and books, entitled *Job Analysis at the Speed of Reality*, *On-Demand Learning: Training in the New Millennium*, and *Selling E-Learning*.

CHAPTER 5

ARE YOUR LEARNERS READY FOR E-LEARNING?

➤ PAUL J. GUGLIELMINO
AND LUCY M. GUGLIELMINO

HOW IMPORTANT IS THIS QUESTION?

Crucial. If your learners are truly ready for e-learning, it is an efficient, effective, and economical approach. If they are not, the attempt to use e-learning may lead to frustration, battered egos, wasted
time, incomplete learning, and program failures. Even though some
learners may be able to breeze through well-designed e-learning
frameworks, others, especially the novices, are likely to need transition structures. Both need learner support systems that they can turn
to for additional resources or assistance with problems.

WHAT FACTORS AFFECT LEARNER SUCCESS IN E-LEARNING?

What factors affect the successful use of electronic distance learning? There appear to be two categories of variables, those elements

that are controllable from the perspective of the learner and those that are uncontrollable. Uncontrollable variables include environmental factors, such as the content and design of the material to be learned, and personal issues, such as job transfers, accidents, sickness, and other acts of chance. Although the learner can react to these factors in a variety of ways, he or she cannot control them or prevent their occurrence.

Controllable factors are those factors that are believed to be in the control or relative control of an individual learner: such things as one's knowledge, attitudes, skills, and habits. This chapter will focus on the controllable factors that affect success in electronic distance learning.

WHAT ARE THE COMPONENTS OF LEARNER READINESS FOR E-LEARNING?

Technical skills are the first component of learner readiness for e-learning that occurs to many people. Whereas technical skills are certainly important, research and opinion reported in the literature indicates that readiness for self-direction in learning, or the ability to manage one's own learning, is even more important. There are two major components necessary for successful e-learning to occur that are within the control of the learner: *Technical Readiness* and *Readiness for Self-Directed Learning*. These two components can be examined by using the KASH mode (Guglielmino and Klatt 1996), which breaks each component into Knowledge, Attitudes, Skills, and Habits. In addition to having the knowledge needed to do something, learners must have the right attitudes, required skills, and positive habits.

Technical Readiness for E-learning: KASH

Logically, an individual who has the requisite KASH basis in technology will have an advantage over the novice in terms of readiness for e-learning. What knowledge, attitudes, skills and habits form the basis for technical readiness for e-learning?

Technical Knowledge
The technical knowledge needed for e-learning includes a basic knowledge of the components and operations of the technical system being used to deliver the e-learning as well as a knowledge of resources for technical assistance that can be used if technical problems are encountered. Learners using the Blackboard system, for example, would need to have basic knowledge of word processing and e-mail functions, including how to attach and download files; and possibly how to create PowerPoint presentations (depending on the course requirements). They would also need to learn the components of the Blackboard system, especially the discussion board and group chat features, as well as becoming familiar with the online help function.

Technical Attitudes
The central attitude involved in technical readiness for e-learning is a positive feeling toward the use of technology as a delivery system for learning; in other words,

a lack of technophobia. Confidence in one's ability to manage the basic technology contributes to technical readiness as well, and with the rapid changes in technology, a positive expectation in terms of being able to master new technical challenges is important.

For example, an e-learner working in a web-based system might be asked to make the transition from using e-mail to chat rooms or from posting a project to a discussion board to actually presenting it online using Real Player. A positive attitude keeps these technical challenges from becoming roadblocks.

Technical Skills

An obvious part of technical readiness is the ability to competently apply the basic skills needed in order to use the technical system selected for e-learning. For example, a learner using a web-based delivery system would need to have the skills necessary to access the internet, perform basic e-mail functions, perform basic word processing functions, and other skills as required. In using the Blackboard system, for example, they will need to learn to navigate the site to access documents, web links, and assignments; learn how to post their comments or reports to the discussion board and respond to others' comments (asynchronous discussion); and participate in real-time discussion using the group chat feature.

Technical Habits

Habits contributing to technical readiness would, of course, vary with the technology used for the e-learning. Developing habits to ensure appropriate participation, submission of work, and saving of work completed is vital. As an example, if a web-based platform were being used, habits such as maintaining an organized desktop and backing up regularly would be important.

Readiness for Self-Directed Learning: KASH

The most predominant characteristic associated with success in e-learning in the literature is variously referred to as independence, self-direction, or autonomy in learning. The construct of readiness for self-directed learning is a logical link for readiness for e-learning, with learner *autonomy, initiative, and independence* being central aspects of that construct. After a Delphi study on the characteristics of highly self-directed learners, L. Guglielmino (1977) proposed the following description of a highly self-directed learner:

> A highly self-directed learner, based on the survey results, is one who exhibits initiative, independence, and persistence in learning; one who accepts responsibility for his or her own learning and views problems as challenges, not obstacles; one who is capable of self-discipline and has a high degree of curiosity; one who has a strong desire to learn or change and is self-confident; one who is able to use basic study skills, organize his or her time and set an appropriate pace for learning, and to develop a plan for

completing work; one who enjoys learning and has a tendency to be goal-oriented.

The definition suggests a variety of knowledge, attitudes, skills, and habits which comprise readiness for self-directed learning (SDL).

SDL Knowledge

Readiness for self-directed learning requires, first, self-knowledge: an understanding of oneself as a learner based on an honest appraisal. This can be accomplished through reflection, by using self-assessment instruments and exercises, or some combination of these methods. SDL readiness is enhanced by a knowledge of one's preferred learning style, the best ways to take in new information. Readiness for self-directed learning also involves an understanding of self-direction in learning, ways of managing one's own learning, and an understanding that it is a skill that can be learned and further developed.

SDL Attitudes

Attitudes forming the basis for success in self-directed or self-managed learning are based in a strong desire to learn or change. The individual who has a strong curiosity, enjoys learning new things, is focused on continuous self-improvement and views learning as a path to problem solving is likely to be a successful e-learner. A second fundamental attitude is confidence in oneself as a competent, effective learner: seeing oneself as a "can-do" learner and taking the initiative in learning.

Closely related to this attitude are the *acceptance of responsibility for one's own learning* and the viewing of problems as challenges, rather than obstacles. The successful self-directed learner believes that the primary onus for learning is on the learner. He or she is the one who needs to recognize needs for learning and take the responsibility for making it happen. This learner will find a way to make the learning occur regardless of the course design, other inviting activities, unforeseen occurrences—all the distractions that are used by some as an excuse for truncated learning.

Creativity and independence in learning are also crucial in many (well-designed) e-learning settings. Many individuals see themselves as competent learners because they are able to do exactly what is asked of them and present the products in exactly the format requested, but flounder when asked to think creatively or develop their own thoughts and processes for identifying and solving problems. They are good "memorizers" and are good at following directions, but become anxious when asked to apply or create.

A *willingness to seek help* also facilitates self-directed learning. The idea of the self-directed learner as a lone wolf struggling to find answers in isolation is a myth. The effective self-directed learner uses all the tools available, then invents those that are not. Those individuals who are reluctant to "show their ignorance" by asking questions, seeking clarification, and seeking out expert advice handicap themselves in terms of learning progress. Those who are willing to ask for help reduce the time involved in responding to problems and challenges and avoid frustration that can lead to poor completion rates.

Another helpful attitude is the *valuing of one's own learning*—a belief in the importance of learning achieved on one's own. Our educational system has, in the past, consistently devalued the learning achieved outside of formal classroom situations, promoting the idea that unless an instructor tells you what to learn, delivers the information to you, and then tests you on it, that learning doesn't count. The expansion of knowledge in the information age makes this concept not only foolish, but potentially damaging: in some arenas, where new challenges and obstacles are being presented daily, if individuals wait for someone else to tell them what to learn, they and their organizations will lag behind instead of leading.

SDL Skills

Logically, basic academic skills are an important part of readiness for e-learning, especially reading skills. Depending on the instructional design, writing skills can also be critical. Self-directed learners are also usually skilled at identifying and analyzing their learning needs. Key skills related to meeting these learning needs include the ability to set learning goals, develop a learning plan, identify resources for learning (both human and material), implement the learning, and evaluate the learning. Time management skills and document or report preparation skills support this process as well.

SDL Habits

One of the most important habits of the successful self-directed learner is the habit of persistence: the refusal to be deterred from reaching a goal because of problems, boredom, or other factors or events that might derail a less determined learner. Habits such as systematic planning, productive organization of learning media and materials, and completing tasks within the time scheduled can streamline and anchor the effective e-learning.

Two other habits are worth emphasizing: the habits of reflection and environmental scanning. The reflective individual is regularly thinking about events and actions, his or her own performance, possible results of actions or events, how his or her own actions are being interpreted, possible motivations for others' actions, analyzing his or her own learning, learning processes, and learning outcomes (meta-learning)—in other words, looking at things from both a macro and a micro view in a search for new insights and meaning. A part of this reflection is environmental scanning, an ongoing, active awareness of changes in the environment and their possible implications, including possible needs for new learning. Even though it is not easy to assess whether a learner has these skills, their presence or absence have a major impact on ability to foresee needs for change within the organization and act on them. Good e-learning design promotes their development.

HOW DO WE FIND OUT IF LEARNERS ARE READY FOR E-LEARNING?

The simplest way to determine learner readiness for e-learning is to use some form of assessment. Many are available. How do you choose one? The vast majority of the "free," noncopyrighted assessments that are available on the web focus on assessing technical skills; some extend to five pages of questions related to the use of databases and spreadsheets, downloading skills, e-mail proficiency, and the like. However, it is pointless to assess readiness on the basis of a wide range of technical skills that may not be needed for a particular course. It is generally agreed that those who are committed to e-learning and are self-directed can learn the specific tech skills needed for a particular learning activity if they already possess basic technical knowledge. As previously mentioned, technical skills are not the central element of readiness for e-learning. Independence, autonomy, and self-direction in learning are even more important.

Many business organizations and educational institutions have used the *Self-Directed Learning Readiness Scale (SDLRS)* (L. Guglielmino, 1977) to assess readiness for e-learning. This instrument has consistently demonstrated strong reliability and validity in identifying those who are ready for self-directed learning in its 26-year history.

In an attempt to more closely target the two major components of readiness for e-learning (technical and self-directed learning readiness), we surveyed professors and HRD professionals involved in delivering distance learning as well as learners participating in e-learning (Guglielmino and Guglielmino 2001). On the basis of the national survey results, we developed the Distance Learning Readiness Assessment (DLRA), which incorporates items from the SDLRS with new items related to technical readiness. This new assessment tool offers another promising option for assessing readiness for e-learning. Appendix 5-A provides a quicklist for learner readiness.

HOW CAN WE MAXIMIZE THE POSSIBILITY OF SUCCESS FOR E-LEARNERS?

Organizational Commitment

An important and often overlooked support for the e-learning process is clear evidence of the organization's acceptance of e-learning as a legitimate, effective process. Are upper-level managers voicing support for e-learning? Is e-learning being highlighted in internal publications such as newsletters and company websites? Is it being promoted via bulletin boards, memos, catalogs of training and development options? Do e-learners receive the same level and type of recognition as those involved in face-to face learning? And, finally, the all-important money question: Is adequate funding provided for the necessary research and development and provision of human and material support?

If all or most of these questions can be answered in the affirmative, the organization has created a positive climate for e-learning success.

Support for the Individual

Within the context of an organizational environment supportive of continued learning, including e-learning, specific services and resources for the individual learner must also be developed. Among the most important are opportunities for self-assessment, transition structures for new e-learners, and continuing e-learning support systems.

Assessment

As mentioned earlier, e-learners can perform better if they understand their learning styles and preferences. At a minimum, they should have an opportunity to assess their readiness for e-learning, including self-directed learning readiness and technical competence, and their preferred learning styles (how they best perceive and process new information). They can then make informed decisions about:

1. the types of learning opportunities to enroll in: class-based, partly class-based and partly e-based, or totally e-based;

2. the learning strategies to use within the selected course or program. If they are visual learners, for example, they may choose to avoid programs that are exclusively text-based.

Transition Structures

New e-learners or those with lower levels of readiness for online learning may need additional support in their first learning experiences.

GRADUAL INTRODUCTION OF TECHNICAL FUNCTIONS WITHIN A LEARNING ACTIVITY

As good instructional design moves from simple to complex in terms of content, good instructional design for new e-learners moves from simple to complex technical skills. A learner unfamiliar to an online classroom platform such as Blackboard, for example, might be overwhelmed if required to use the virtual classroom, group chat, and discussion board functions, all in the first learning activity. The first learning activities should make use of the simpler technical functions, then gradually add the more complex ones, with reference to the available user's manual.

DELIVERY OPTIONS PROVIDING VARYING LEVELS OF SUPPORT FOR E-LEARNERS

Learners benefit from having a variety of delivery options to choose from, including traditional, class-based learning; partially class-based, partially e-based; and totally e-based. Many of the problems involved in the introduction of e-learning can be traced to the "sink or swim" or "all or nothing" mentality. Excited by the promise of e-learning, some organizations have invested large amounts of money into designing e-learning, then simply announced that a particular learning experience will only be available in that format. Often completion rates are low or learners' complaints are strident, because they were inadequately prepared for the change.

Many organizations have found that learners become accustomed to e-learning with much less stress and far fewer problems if they first have an opportunity to participate in learning experiences which alternate between class-based and e-learning environments. The psychological comfort of knowing there will be a "real person" to answer their questions at the next session is almost as important as the face-to-face access. In addition, some topics lend themselves better to either class-based or e-based learning formats. For example, learning the principles of conflict resolution or negotiation via e-learning would be very effective, and good e-based simulations might help to build skills, but transfer to practice would be more likely if some face-to-face practice was included.

Technical and Content Support

Ideally, e-learners should have access to an online help desk. The opportunity to obtain both technical and content support on an as-needed basis would be invaluable in ensuring productive learning time. Obviously, this type of support is beyond the reach of some organizations. Less ambitious but still very useful support systems include reference documents of frequently asked questions or ways to resolve typical problems that can be accessed as needed. A search capability for these aids would be a valuable plus.

Even the simplest of support systems can enhance learner success in distance learning. A simple pairing of the less technically skilled with the more technically skilled can greatly reduce frustration.

Learner assessment and learner support can greatly enhance success rates in e-learning; however, they are not sufficient to ensure success. Good instructional design, reliable technology, appropriate and timely feedback, and many other factors also have a strong impact on success rates in electronic distance learning. Since e-learning holds so much promise in terms of efficiency and cost-effectiveness, it is worth the effort to carefully examine our approaches and outcomes to maximize success. Appendix 5-B provides an organizational support assessment.

RESOURCES

Readings

Bernt, F.L., and Bugbee, A.C. (1993). "Study Practices and Attitudes Related to Academic Success in a Distance Learning Programme." *Distance Education 14*(1), 97–112.

Coggins, C.C. (1988). "Preferred Learning Styles and Their Impact on Completion of External Degree Programs." *The American Journal of Distance Education 2*(1), 25–37.

Cole, R.A. (Ed.) (2000). *Issues in Web-Based Pedagogy: A Critical Primer.* London: Greenwood Press.

Guglielmino, L. (1977). *Development of the Self-directed Learning Readiness Scale.* Doctoral disseration, The University of Georgia.

Guglielmino, L. M., and Guglielmino, P. J (1991). *Enhancing Your Readiness for Self-Directed Learning: A Workbook for the Learning Preference Assessment.* King of Prussia, PA: HRDQ.

Guglielmino, P. J., and Guglielmino, L. M. (2001). "Learner characteristics affecting success in electronic distance learning." In H. B. Long & Associates, *21st Century Advances in Self-Directed Learning.* Schaumberg, IL: Motorola University Press.

Guglielmino, P., and Klatt, L. (1996). "Toward a Theory of Entrepreneurship Education." *The Art and Science of Entrepreneurship Education,* v.4.

Hiltz, S. R. (1994). "Predictors of Success in the Virtual Classroom." Chapter 12 in *The Virtual Classroom: Learning Without Limits via Computer Networks.* Norwood, NJ: Ablex Publishing Corporation.

Kouki, R., and Wright, D. (1999). *Telelearning via the Internet.* Hershey, PA. Idea Group Publishing.

Piskurich, G., Beckschi, P., and Hall, B. (Eds.). *The ASTD Handbook of Training Design and Delivery.* New York: McGraw-Hill. (Section on electronic and self-directed learning.)

Websites

Internet Literacy Classes Online:
http://www.pbs.org/als/alliance/participation/checklist_visitor.htm
http://www.udel.edu/ce/internet_literacy_ncr.html

Assessment Of Readiness For Self-Directed Learning:
Organizational profile or research study:http://www.guglielmino734.com
Self-scoring format for use in workshops (Learning Preference Assessment):
http://www.hrdq.com/products/load-lpa.htm

International Symposium On Self-Directed Learning:
http://www.sdlglobal.com

Workbook For Expanding Readiness For Self-Directed Learning:
http://www.hrdq.com/products/load-lpa.htm

General Information:
http://www.ecollege.com
http://www.elearningforum.com/
http://www.elearningmag.com/issues/nov01/winning.asp
http://www.hungrymindsuniversity.com/
http://ocl.nps.navy.mil/instruction/default.htm

➤ Although there are some uncontrollable factors that affect e-learning success, there are many factors that can be addressed by the learner and the organization.

➤ The major components of readiness for e-learning are:

  ➤ Technical readiness

  ➤ Readiness for self-direction in learning

➤ Both technical readiness and readiness for SDL are comprised of

  ➤ Knowledge

  ➤ Attitudes

  ➤ Skills

  ➤ Habits (KASH)

➤ A variety of assessment tools for technical readiness or SDL readiness are available.

➤ Other factors that can help the learners in your organization to become ready for e-learning and maximize their chances for success include:

  ➤ Evidence of organizational commitment to learning and to electronic delivery of learning

  ➤ Available support for the individual, including

    ➤ Assessment/diagnosis of learning needs

    ➤ Transition structures built into learning designs

    ➤ A variety of delivery options for learners with different levels of readiness for e-learning

    ➤ Technical and content support

APPENDIX 5-A: **QUICKLIST FOR LEARNER READINESS FOR ONLINE LEARNING**

1. Is our commitment to e-learning reflected in our organizational communications?

   ➤ Managers' and supervisors' comments   __Yes __No

   ➤ Newsletters   __Yes __No

   ➤ Signage/Bulletin boards   __Yes __No

   ➤ Website   __Yes __No

   ➤ Training notices   __Yes __No

2. Do e-learners receive the same level and type of recognition as those involved in face-to-face learning? (Certificates, training hours, credit, promotions)   __Yes __No

   3. Have funds been allocated for research, development, and implementation of e-learning?   __Yes __No

4. Do prospective e-learners have an opportunity for self-assessment?

   ➤ Of their readiness for e-learning?   __Yes __No

   ➤ Of their learning styles?   __Yes __No

   ➤ Of prerequisite content knowledge or skills (if required)   __Yes __No

5. Are a variety of e-learning formats available to ease the transition for new e-learners?

   ➤ An introductory workshop or learning activity   __Yes __No

   ➤ Learning activities which alternate between e-learning and onsite   __Yes __No

6. Are learner support systems available?

   ➤ For technical help   __Yes __No

   ➤ For content help   __Yes __No

   7. Has follow-up been done to determine learner satisfaction and to obtain suggestions for improvement?   __Yes __No

APPENDIX 5-B: **ORGANIZATIONAL ASSESSMENT:**
HOW WELL ARE WE SUPPORTING OUR E-LEARNERS?

►ABOUT THE AUTHORS

Dr. **Paul Guglielmino** is an Associate Professor of Management at Florida Atlantic University. He teaches undergraduate and graduate level courses in the area of general management, entrepreneurship, and new business formation. In 1998, Dr. Guglielmino was selected University Distinguished Teacher of the Year at Florida Atlantic University. He has served as an advisory board member at Walt Disney World in Orlando and has consulted with companies such as Disney, Motorola, AT&T, Johnson & Johnson, and Medtronic. Dr. Guglielmino is a member of the Academy of Management and a past member of the Academy of International Business. He has published more than 30 academic articles and book chapters.

Dr. **Lucy Guglielmino** is currently Professor of Adult and Community Education and Director of the E.O. Melby Community Education Center at Florida Atlantic University in Boca Raton, Florida. Her doctorate is in Adult Education from the University of Georgia (1977). Dr. Guglielmino is best known for her development of the Self-Directed Learning Readiness Scale (with a self-scoring form known as the Learning Preference Assessment). The SDLRS has been translated into twelve languages and used in more than three dozen countries. In addition, Dr. Guglielmino has authored or co-authored more than 90 books, chapters, articles, monographs, and other written materials on various aspects of adult learning, training, and development. She is listed in many honoraries, including Notable American Women, Who's Who in America, and Who's Who in the World.

Phone/FAX: (561) 392-0379
Web site: *http://www.guglielmino734.com*

> YOUR E-LEARNING QUESTIONS
> ANSWERED BY THIS CHAPTER
>
> ➤ How do I motivate my
> employees to be responsive
> to e-learning?
>
> ➤ What strategies do I use to
> get executives involved in not
> only supporting e-learning but
> in helping to implement it and
> make time for it?

CHAPTER 6

INCREASING LEARNER INVOLVEMENT AND PARTICIPATION

➤RUSS BROCK

Imagine for a moment that you are a new employee in an organization and you have been asked by your manager to participate in a new e-learning program designed to train you in a new job skill. So you position yourself at your desk—which they're now calling your *learning station*, even though you call it your *desk*—and you log-on to the website they've given you and you begin the registration process by entering the requested data. Then you click on the button that says "Tour" and you observe the screen change to new webpages with video and lots of flashy graphics and animation. And then the tour ends with a webpage that has your name in big bold letters, thanks you for being a part of the tour, and invites you to join everyone else in the first session. Are you *involved* in e-learning? Are you *interacting* with the e-learning program? Are you *participating?* Can we surmise how *motivated* you are to learn at this point?

Involvement, interaction, participation, motivation. Different aspects of a process for actively engaging a person—mentally, emotionally, and physically—in a learning experience. This is an important distinction because involvement is not just entering data or clicking on a button; it is not involvement unless and until the learner's mind is cognitively engaged, and there is present an emotional readiness/receptivity to the learning activity.

Given this, it is possible for a person in your organization to register and "attend" an e-learning program, yet not be actively engaged. In this sense, e-learning is challenged with the same questions faced by traditional classroom training: Why do people sign up for a program and then just sit there, waiting for something to happen? Why do other people not sign up for the program at all? Why do some not complete the learning activity? In what ways are the people who flourish in the activity different from those who don't? How can the learning experience be changed in order to serve the needs of more people? In short, how do we increase the level of involvement and participation?

INERTIA AND LEVEL OF COMPETENCE AS OBSTACLES TO INVOLVEMENT

The tradition of a classroom as the center of learning and training is still deeply rooted in our culture—even among the younger workforce. And within this tradition has formed a set of persistent norms and expectations about learning—who it's intended for, who is involved, how it's achieved, what roles each person has, when is it completed, and so on. The archetype of this tradition, of course, is the classroom teacher who possesses knowledge and dispenses it to students sitting at his or her feet (yes, pedagogy), passively absorbing the new information for later recall. After a dozen or so years of this, the students' learning period is deemed over. This model is still ingrained in our notions about learning, even among training professionals. As a result, while we are entranced by the rapid growth of e-learning, we still face a workforce that has anxiety about the new methodology and a majority of people who are neither adequately prepared for, nor desirous of, self-directed and lifelong learning models.

A barrier of this magnitude obviously requires a change effort on multiple fronts, including efforts by employers and workforce development professionals. But there are other individual factors that directly affect an e-learner's level of involvement in a learning activity. Before an e-learning program can hope to achieve high levels of involvement and participation, designers must, from the outset, consider three *core competence* dimensions:

➤ Basic literacy—an individual's competence in basic reading, writing, and math skills

➤ Computer literacy—an individual's competence in using computers and related technology for processing information

➤ Motivation for learning—an individual's drive to acquire and apply knowledge; the receptivity to self-directed learning and self-management skills

Trainers have always encountered learners who possess weak basic skills and/or low motivation for learning. With the advent of e-learning, however, we must overcome not only these two "classic" learning barriers but also deal with the added difficulties associated with learning a new technology and methodology. By definition, e-learning adds a dimension of complexity to an already challenging assignment faced by training staff and e-learners alike.

As depicted in Table 6-1, we can roughly categorize learners by their level of competence in each of the three dimensions.

The Core Competence Matrix provides a simple framework for understanding a person's readiness for e-learning and, at the same time, offers insight into what you can do to increase learner involvement and participation. As a case in point, an individual with weak basic literacy skills, weak computer skills, and weak motivation for learning (cells I/IV/VII) will likely struggle in an e-learning program designed for a learner presumed to have strong basic literacy skills, strong computer literacy skills, and a strong motivation for learning (cells III/VI/IX). Without a stretch of your imagination, you might readily predict the first individual would soon become less involved in such an activity.

Certain components of e-learning present challenges to people, especially if they prefer traditional classroom methodology. In some regards, e-learners have to work harder to stay involved with the content because they must contend with difficulties imposed by distance, technology, and new learning environments. Even with synchronous, instructor-led e-learning events, learners may struggle to stay motivated because of variables such as:

➤ Less social interaction among students

➤ Difficulty in detecting discreet nuances in interactions with other learners

➤ Lag time in responses between student–instructor–other student interactions

➤ Extraneous distractions at the remote learning station (the microwave just beeped in the kitchen, drop-in visitors in the office)

TABLE 6-1. **Core Competence Matrix**

Dimension	Level of Readiness		
	Weak	Moderate	Strong
Basic literacy	I	II	III
Computer literacy	IV	V	VI
Motivation for learning	VII	VIII	IX

➤ Fatigue in the form of eye strain, soreness in hands or neck

➤ Problems in using the equipment, especially for new e-learners

The implications should be clear: If you ignore the inherent differences in learners' core competence and learning preferences, and, instead, design a "one size fits all" e-learning activity, then you essentially replicate the traditional classroom model and confine your e-learning program to lower levels of involvement and participation.

Considerations for Your E-Learning Strategic Plan:

➤ Collaborate with local workforce development agencies and educational institutions to ensure a continual and reliable source of employees possessing core competence. This may take the form of helping schools in designing a curriculum, outsourcing your basic skills training to partnering agencies, developing creative arrangements for student–employer learning experiences, arranging for educational specialists (instructional media, instructional staff, etc.) to assist your organization in the design and development of the e-learning program, providing your own employees with an opportunity to work in schools and instruct students in core competencies.

➤ Expect the instructional design of e-learning activities to be diverse enough to accommodate people with different learning needs and interests; or, consider a separate instructional design for identified target groups of individuals who share common levels of core competence. Both approaches may raise the front-end costs of design and development, but it tends to produce a higher dividend on the back-end level of involvement and performance results.

➤ Explore a blended learning approach, in which a mix of delivery methods, content and timing are linked to the learning needs of the individual.

BUT DO THEY WANNA?

Even if your organization is fortunate enough to recruit, hire, and retain people who have the basic literacy and computer literacy competence to be successful e-learners (not always an easy task in the current workforce), the job of developing an engaging e-learning program for them remains. And just as the basic literacy level may vary widely in your organization, so too will the level of motivation among e-learners.

The motivation to participate for some e-learners may be little more than fear of job security—as one participant remarked, "My boss made me sign up for this . . . now there are *two* things I don't like about this job." Granted, it is a very fragile drive, but at least you have something to work with.

Luckily for us, most e-learners have a more positive—or, at least a benign "show me"—approach to participating in a learning activity. The nature of their motivation will differ: some will be eager to develop a new skill; some will strive for a personal learning goal; some will desire a certification so they can advance their careers; some will want merely to join their friends in a common event.

The reason people choose not to complete a learning activity will similarly vary. Reasons often cited include: not enough time, overwhelmed with other work assignments, completion was not needed (learner got what was essential and then left the activity), problems with technology and navigation, lack variety in lessons, needs were not met by the program, instructor was slow to respond to e-mails, preference for traditional classroom training methods, not prone to self-directed learning. Note how most reasons given are organizational factors and not a matter of the learner's intrinsic motivation.

We can describe the learning topography, then, as including some who won't/can't get involved on one end and some who flourish and excel on the other end. In between, we have varying degrees of those who participate but don't want to, some who are involved but will not complete, some who are getting by satisfactorily. Or, as one currently popular aphorism states: If you build it, they won't necessarily come; and if they do, they won't necessarily stay.

What's an instructional designer to do?

FROM THE LEARNER'S POINT OF VIEW

Before we can design e-learning that raises the level of involvement and participation, we first ought to understand the learning situation and perceive the experience from the learner's frame of reference. There is almost a Zen quality to this task: To better understand a learner, be a learner. The Exercise in Figure 6-1 might help.

Take a moment to recall the very first time you used a computer and all the emotions that were attached to using the equipment. Was there an initial enthusiasm about the chance to get started? Did your enthusiasm and confidence quickly fade once you encountered terms and procedures that were totally unfamiliar to you? How hesitant were you to ask a friend, or an instructor, or a manager for help simply because you didn't want them to know how much you didn't know? When you pressed a key and the computer froze, did you feel stupid or worried that you had broken the equipment? If you checked with the user manuals, did you have the impression they were written in the Klingon language or designed only for people who have degrees in engineering or programming? How long did it take you to make another attempt after your first failure? When you finally got the computer to do what you wanted it to do, did you suddenly have a feeling of elation? That you were, indeed, the master? You *ruled*!

FIGURE 6-1. **AN EXERCISE IN EMPATHY**

For most people, each swing in mood—from excitement, to bewilderment, to shame, to paralysis, to trepidation, to anticipation, to triumph—becomes a decision point of whether or not to remain involved. Beginning e-learners, especially, may experience a similar roller coaster ride of feelings towards their e-learning assignment. How many are sitting there paralyzed by fear? How many feel embarrassed? How many are just gaining the courage to make a first attempt? How many are already gaining confidence and moving into fast forward mode? Are we selling the idea of e-learning to those who are technologically aversive or who have low-core competence, and then not giving the support they really need? How much of our content is written in jargon? Are the navigation job aids written in the Klingon language?

It's easy for instructional designers and other training professionals to forget, or dismiss, the anxieties felt by many learners, whether they're in a classroom or on a remote computer. Within the e-learning realm of professionals, we seem to work effortlessly, pressing the correct function keys, cutting and pasting, writing HTML, surfing from one website to another, talking to colleagues in a chat room. Then we pick up our professional journals and latest book—just like this one—and we read what other people are doing in our field. Over time, we unwittingly form the assumption that *everyone* must know what we ourselves know. Surely they must all be as excited about this as we are!

We serve individuals, however, who, like the person in the preceding exercise, may sit there—wondering if they should make the next move . . . or quit. They're not concerned whether you know the latest—coolest—way to use frames in a web page. They don't want to know how you've used XML, JavaScript, or cascading style sheets to manipulate knowledge objects on a web page.

But if you observe closely, you'll learn what they *are* concerned with. And if you're really sensitive to their situation, you'll hear the clues that tell you they're ready to click out of your e-learning program:

➤ Why won't this computer let me log-on to the Internet?

➤ Plug-ins, streaming video, HTML, Java, cookies. I don't understand any of this gibberish.

➤ Look, all I want to do is turn on the computer and have it show me the things I need to know.

➤ Is it always this slow? I could have read the book and gone back to work by now.

➤ I'm not going to call that help desk. Whenever I do, they make me feel like a fool.

➤ I can't read this web page. Tiny letters, light purple type on a black background. This hurts my eyes!

➤ I had to click on twelve different web pages just to get the course description!

➤ I've been told by my friends never to give this information over the Internet.

➤ The boss is making me do this, so I'm not going to do any more than I absolutely have to.

➤ I have so many things I have to do, I'll get around to this e-learning stuff later.

➤ I already know this stuff; I've been doing it for twenty years.

The assertion offered here is: If you fully understand the learner's frame of reference, if you empathize with the range of emotions experienced by the learner, if you know their expectations and work climate, then you can have better insight into why and how learners *want* to be involved, as well as why they may or may *not* want to participate in e-learning. Thus, by "walking a mile in the learner's shoes" we expand our options for finding creative ways to attract, motivate, and retain learners.

GET LEARNER INVOLVEMENT RIGHT FROM THE START

As we have observed in other organizational change efforts (such as goal-setting, employee participation, teambuilding, process improvement, etc.) the more involved a person is throughout the e-learning dialogue (ideation, exploration, planning, design, development, implementation, evaluation, feedback), the greater the level of interaction and participation.

There is sound reason, therefore, to get e-learners involved early and throughout. But the benefit extends beyond that of the individual involved, because a neural path is built as others interact with the involved person. In relatively short time, the involved employee can serve as a center of influence—a person who helps other prospective e-learners know the why's, how's, purpose, scope, benefits, and limits of the program.

A proven way to get early involvement of people in the e-learning process is to invite people to participate in a *steering team* of key stakeholders. Besides individuals from the training staff, the team can also include representatives of all levels of management, employees from different geographic locations or divisions, people who serve as e-learning facilitators and mentors, a sample of targeted learners, IT and financial staff, and work unit leaders. It's also suggested the team have input from noncomputer users and from those who are not prone to self-directed learning. The advantage of having a steering team is that the e-learning effort will be more user-driven, rather than a design imposed solely by the training staff.

Teams that consist of ten to twenty-five members can typically provide you with sufficient input from key areas of the organization, without being too small to get a critical mass for change, or too large to manage effectively. Some projects, however, may require input from a greater number of people—for example, when content is particularly complex or when your organization faces unusually strong resistance to change. In these cases, the steering team can invite others to get involved with subgroups, such as ad hoc study teams, global interface teams, survey teams, "search the web" teams, and so on. Expanding e-learner involvement in this way can broaden support for the program as well as ensure that key design elements are not omitted.

Team members quickly lose energy and interest if they do not have the support of top management or do not have a clearly defined charter. Ideally, the team has direct input to a chief knowledge officer or top-level workplace learning and performance executive, giving the team the ability to influence e-learning strategy and policy and to serve the following purposes:

- ➤ Act as a communications link to the rest of the organization on matters concerning e-learning.

- ➤ Explore the efficacy of e-learning as a methodology to serve the organization's business needs compared to alternative methods.

- ➤ Clarify and communicate the organization's vision and values that will be conducive to effective e-learning.

- ➤ Create an organizational roadmap for the integration of organizational learning, knowledge management, and lifelong learning in the workplace.

- ➤ Articulate, in broad terms, the charter of e-learning, including what it is, its importance, purpose, constraints, boundaries, and indicators for expected outcomes of e-learning.

- ➤ Ensure the e-learning process remains focused on its intended purpose— in particular, the business needs, critical operating tasks, and core competencies needed by the organization.

- ➤ Serve as a firewall against counter-productive influences; that is, protect the integrity of the program from influences that would jeopardize the e-learners' trust and involvement in the program.

- ➤ Provide a forum for receiving input from throughout the organization in terms of the effectiveness and needs for program modification.

- ➤ Identify the range of potential users and the resources needed to service them.

- ➤ Champion a culture of risk-free, lifelong learning throughout the organization.

Within the scope of the steering team, there is a wide range of tasks members can work on while furthering the cause of e-learning.

- ➤ Involve top management in building commitment and ensuring adequate resources to achieve the goals of e-learning.

- ➤ Conduct an environmental scan of the organization's technological capacity to meet the expected demand for e-learning.

- ➤ Determine the needs and expectations of current and potential users.

- ➤ Benchmark programs in other organizations; visit other organization's facilities or get permission to visit their learning portals as guests.

- ➤ Identify current users and uses of e-learning within the organization; assess its value to the individuals and the organization; identify what aspects of your program work best.

- ➤ Forecast scenarios of worst/probable/best-case outcomes for e-learning in the organization.

- ➤ Gather ongoing feedback from employees using surveys, force-field analysis, focus group interviews, and so on.

- ➤ Identify levels of e-learner readiness and best opportunities for pilot testing or initial implementation.

- ➤ Build support within the organization by using centers of influence, supportive champions, key sponsors, and key events that lead to organizationwide change.

- ➤ Explore and recommend possible changes in the organization's structure, systems, and policies that encourage, support, and reward e-learning.

- ➤ Assist various work units as they work through issues of resistance, competing goals, territoriality, and so on.

- ➤ Serve as e-learner models or mentors to those just beginning.

REDUCING ORGANIZATIONAL BARRIERS TO LEARNER PARTICIPATION

Although the level of involvement depends substantially upon an individual's core competence, the importance of your organization's support system for e-learning cannot be overlooked. This issue is made clearer when we ask, "What does our organization do to prevent our learners from successfully participating in an e-learning program?" That's been the lesson from the field of organization behavior over the past quarter century. People *will* show surprising motivation to use computer technology for learning new material—*when* we remove organizational barriers and make the learning experience one of intrinsic value to the learner. The most common support system factors that interfere with learner participation include (1) technology, (2) organizational structures and social systems, and (3) inadequate user interface.

Technology as a Barrier to Involvement

Technology shapes, to a very large extent, the nature and growth of e-learning. At the core of effective e-learning programs is an information infrastructure (appropriate computer hardware and software, telephony/fax systems, bulletin boards, e-learner e-mail list, etc.) that ensures dependable access and reliable communication systems. The frustration that builds as a result of unreliable technology quickly dampens the level of participation. The steering team can be useful in remedying such problems as:

➤ Problems logging on (password nonacceptance, busy line, pressed wrong key, etc.)

➤ Connection frequently "dropped" by the network or ISP while online

➤ Inadequate hardware and/or software (slow modems, small bandwidth, inadequate RAM or hard disk memory, etc.)

➤ Difficulties encountered by geographically dispersed learners (such as, lack of local dial-up access, the effect on quality and context of communications due to time delays when interacting online, etc.)

➤ Lack of uniformity and standards in using e-learning programs from location to location (different browsers and operating systems may not handle various multimedia and web-based features, different software programs may not be able to translate and open downloaded files, etc.)

➤ No accessibility for e-learners with disabilities (Section 508 of the Rehabilitation Act is directed at people who have some form of impairment that effectively precludes or severely limits them from involvement in e-learning)

Organizational Structures and Social Systems as Obstacles to Involvement

Many organizations have found it especially difficult to adopt structures, work processes, and social systems—such as organizational learning, knowledge management, and autonomous work team models—that are conducive to the long-term success of e-learning. To be sure, there are organizations—GE being perhaps the most notable example—that take a new concept and successfully drive it deep into its culture and processes. There are far more organizations, however, unwilling or unable to change in fundamental ways, leaving new methodologies like e-learning hampered and falling far short of their potential.

Organizational factors interact directly with and influence your involvement in any e-learning experience. For example, you may be sufficiently prepared for an e-learning program, yet meet with unfavorable results because of some organizational factor (lack of time available, negative consequences for participating, obsolete equipment or software, etc.). It should go without saying that your motivation to continue an e-learning experience will weaken after repeated frustrations from an organizational system that isn't ready.

Sometimes the organization's culture—in particular, its norms and values—interfere with the level of involvement. Imagine trying to maintain your enthusiasm for your self-directed study when you hear your manager say, "If you're on the Internet, or taking a class at home, then you're not doing the work we hired you for." It's crucial, therefore, for top management and the steering team to foster a culture that values learning as a legitimate part of work.

The organization's balance of consequences plays an integral part in demonstrating your support for e-learning. We all witness or experience the balance of consequences every day in numerous work situations.

1. A person participates in an e-learning program (desired behavior) and earns a certification to perform a new job task (rewarded).

2. A person participates in an e-learning program (desired behavior) and is admonished by the manager to quit wasting time and do something productive (punished).

3. A person does not participate in an e-learning program mandated for all employees (undesired behavior) but is allowed to perform the new job task anyway (rewarded).

4. A person does not participate in an e-learning program mandated for all employees (our undesired behavior) and is denied the pay-for-knowledge adjustment given to those who participate (punished).

An effort needs to be made to assure that desired behaviors are rewarded, not punished. As obvious as that appears, however, it's not easy to do in practice. E-learning, for example, may eliminate travel to classroom training for some or all employees. If the travel had been perceived as a reward for their work, however, then e-learning may be viewed with resentment by the employees. In this case, the reward attached to participation in an e-learning program may not outweigh the perceived negative consequence of losing their travel. This is where you can use a steering team to tap into employees and find a balance of consequences that will work satisfactorily for your organization.

Other ways you can strengthen organizational structures and social systems include:

➤ Modify the job design to build relevancy for participation in e-learning activities. Job enrichment, for example, could be used to allow learners to perform new tasks or solve a work-related problem while participating in an e-learning program. Jobs can also incorporate flextime and shared-time concepts to permit one or more people to productively schedule time for e-learning activities.

➤ Help employees organize their time and work in ways that permit opportunities for e-learning.

➤ Let your e-learners know the rules of the game up front. Develop a formal policy regarding the use of computers and e-learning: when they can be used, under what circumstances they cannot be used, who owns rights to material created and/or stored on computers, what time is available for the purpose of e-learning programs and self-directed study, compensation for time devoted to self-directed study, tuition/fees costs, standards for enrolling and successful completion, and so on.

➤ Assign a learning mentor for first time users. Because of technology, mentors can be readily available, even when they're not located in the same building . . . or country. Best results seem to occur when experienced e-learners are matched with first-time users, and when people are matched with others learning the same content area.

➤ Position e-learning as a primary means for expanding a person's job opportunities (job enlargement, job enrichment, job advancement).

➤ Consider developing a pay-for-knowledge incentive (such as 15 cents per hour differential if a critical module is completed) or a certification process for job advancement.

User Interface as a Source of Obstacles for E-Learning:

The e-learning element that is most immediately apparent to a learner is the user interface. It's here that learners most generally see content, send messages to instructors and other students, enter data, engage in class discussions, and more.

For the most part, e-learning programs have been developed by individuals who possess sophisticated computer skills. They are often technology-savvy and intrigued by what a computer *can* do, versus what the e-learning program *needs* to do. Granted, Java Scripts that produce mouse over buttons, pop-up windows, and other bells and whistles, can add variety to a web page. But we need to make certain that such design elements do not, in and of themselves, become the blockages to learning. Just because a designer can make a site "really neat" from his/her perspective doesn't make it a better site for the user. In fact, it may be the very aspect of e-learning that causes the user to click the "exit program" button.

As is the case with most other learning methodologies, e-learning is a blend of technical skill and artistic talent. In order to be effective, the user interface must combine the right mix of technical and artistic elements in order to achieve the following attributes:

➤ Creatively flows from the learners' needs as determined from a needs analysis

➤ Helps overcome the learner's resistance or preoccupation with outside issues

➤ Pulls the learner into the lesson and engages the person cognitively

➤ Permits easy navigation within each web page and between different web pages

➤ Provides clear and easy paths for learners who want to "drill down" for greater depth in content or click to different levels of competence

➤ Requires some level of reflective thinking by the learner

➤ Minimizes learner waiting time

A major frustration expressed by e-learners is the amount of time waiting for content to appear on the screen. Complaints surface even in light of today's faster processors and growth of broad bandwidth systems. From the learner's point of view, a long period of waiting erodes the motivation to continue. If a web page takes more than thirty seconds to appear, the learner tends to click off the page. [In reality, that's still a rather generous amount of time. Conventional reading habits of people actually reveal much less tolerance. People scan a newspaper or magazine page, for instance, in a matter of seconds. If they don't see anything of interest, they turn the page. And advertisers have known for years that they have a one- to three-second time period with which to attract your attention and interest.]

What you can do with the user interface is limited only by your own imagination, but there is now a track record of design elements that improve the learner's ability to navigate within an e-learning environment successfully:

➤ Make it easy for any employee, even those who have just been hired, to sign up and get started.

➤ Design the initial page so that critical navigational and program knowledge is just one or two clicks away

➤ Avoid graphic-intensive web pages that slow down the learning activity. Many e-learners, particularly those conducting their learning sessions at home, typically have slower modems and computers.

➤ Test any and all interactivity devices before starting a session. If not compatible across platforms or with browsers other than Netscape or Internet Explorer, then you exclude a segment of your learners from participation.

➤ Make text simple and easy to read. Screen resolutions vary; eyesight varies more.

➤ Develop convenient job aids to help people use the system and solve interface and technical problems easily

➤ Construct safety nets, especially in the early stages, that quickly route learners back to areas where they feel a sense of control, success, and comfort.

➤ Shape the attitudes towards e-learning early by introducing new employees to short, easy-to-succeed modules as part of their initial orientation and job training.

➤ Design the program so that learners don't have to read excessively just to navigate. Provide easy-to-access tools (such as glossary, course map, icons, clear labels, hyperlinks, toll free help desk, etc.) so that learners can determine their own way through the program.

JOB AID: 20 WAYS TO INCREASE INTERACTIVITY AND PARTICIPATION WITH LEARNERS

1. Use the organization's website or learning portal to show online examples and video clips of instructors. Include a sample as a "teaser"—a job aid or some content that has immediate value to the prospective participant and that will encourage the learner to explore more and/or return.

2. Make certain that foundational, critical information is in manageable chunks, easy to download, and easy to navigate.

3. Provide short exercises for learners while online, for both group and individual assignments.

4. Instructors can use an electronic whiteboard that permits e-learners to contribute their own comments for all to see, for instance, by adding text to an instructor's agenda or presentation notes. During the first session, this technique could be used to indicate where each learner is located on a displayed map.

5. Encourage interaction with the instructor and other users beyond the class time. Show learners how to access and use chat rooms and threaded discussions.

6. Create an introductory module so people can take a quick, easy tour of the entire program, or visit a "play" area where they can learn to navigate, get familiar with the content, and so on.

7. Personalize the learner's involvement. One easy method of doing this is to employ cookies to track learners' usage patterns and responses and then customize content for them. Allow user preferences that enable a learner to turn off or discard components they don't need or desire (such as browser frames).

8. Explore ways to reinforce learners (recognition in company newsletter, emails, etc.) to enroll, continue, gain knowledge, complete, discover something new, offering suggestions for program improvement, contributing content/materials, and so on.

9. When appropriate, employ games (for example, trivia questions about the content or company), but be judicious in their use; when overused or inappropriately applied, games tend to trivialize the learning process and culture.

10. Use the program as part of your staff meetings (this also demonstrates the manager's support of the e-learning system).

11. Offer a short module (20 to 40 minutes) during new employee orientation that can serve many people, promote consistency in your message, require less direct training time by the training staff, and promote a culture of e-learning at the outset of employment.

12. Consider offering some e-learning courses for family members of employees, or customers. Examples include time management, managing stress, public speaking, overview of the company, interpersonal skills, and so on.

13. Develop some "training to go" for employees who travel frequently. Modules can be placed on laptops and accessed during "down" times.

14. Make the foundational knowledge modules accessible anytime (24/7/365).

15. Design a simulation that models an organizational task, procedure, or process. Millions of students have dissected a frog on the Internet; millions of people have flown an airplane on software.

16. Show learners the larger context of the material by providing advance organizers, such as a concept map, session outlines, summary paragraphs, key word lists, and so on.

17. Incorporate mnemonic techniques such as acronyms (the continuous improvement method of Plan-Do-Study-Act becomes *PDSA*), and word substitutes (the musical scale of G-clef is often learned by students who memorize the lines E-G-B-D-F with "every good boy does fine" and the spaces F-A-C-E with "face").

18. When possible, integrate collaborative learning, allowing learners to work together to solve problems, and so on.

19. Build-in capabilities for collaborative group work, group scheduling and planning, file storage (many web-based services such as Yahoo! Groups and Intranet.com provide these options for users).

20. Ensure that instructors are actively involved with chat rooms, threaded messages with students. Encourage quick acknowledgement and response to emails from learners. Provide in-service training for instructors so they know how to facilitate e-learning sessions, use equipment, work with asynchronous learners, work with agenda timing, and so on.

RESOURCES

Readings

Argyris, Chris (1993). *Knowledge for Action: A Guide to Overcoming Barriers to Organizational Change*. San Francisco: Jossey-Bass.

Beer, Valorie (2000). *The Web Learning Fieldbook: Using the World Wide Web to Build Workplace Learning Environments.* San Francisco: Jossey-Bass.

Galbraith, Jay R., Lawler, E. E., III, and others (1993). *Organizing for the Future: The New Logic for Managing Complex Organizations.* San Francisco: Jossey-Bass.

Rosenberg, Marc J. (2001). *e-Learning: Strategies for Delivering Knowledge in the Digital Age.* New York: McGraw-Hill.

Additional Readings

Alden, Jay (1998). *Trainer's Guide to Web-Based Instruction.* Alexandria, VA: American Society for Training and Development.

Cyrs, Thomas E. (ed.) (1997). *Teaching and Learning at a Distance: What It Takes to Design, Deliver, and Evaluate Programs.* San Francisco: Jossey-Bass.

Driscoll, Margaret, and Alexander, Larry (1998). *Web-Based Training : Using Technology to Design Adult Learning Experiences.* San Francisco: Jossey-Bass.

Eckes, George (2001). *Making Six Sigma Last : Managing the Balance Between Cultural and Technical* Change. New York: John Wiley & Sons.

Feyten, Carine M., and Nutta, Joyce W (1999). *Virtual Instruction: Issues and Insights from an International Perspective.* Englewood, CO: Libraries Unlimited, Inc.

Harvey, Don, and Brown, Donald R (1996). *An Experiential Approach to Organization Development, 5th ed.* Upper Saddle River, N.J.: Simon & Schuster Co.

Kruse, Kevin , and Keil, Jason (1999). *Technology-Based Training: The Art and Science of Design, Development, and Delivery.* San Francisco: Jossey-Bass.

Lawler, Edward E., III, Mohrman, Susan Albers, and Benson, George (2001). *Organizing for High Performance: Employee Involvement, TQM, Reengineering, and Knowledge Management in the Fortune 1000: The CEO Report.* San Francisco: Jossey-Bass.

Shapiro, Nancy S., and Levine, Jodi (1999). *Creating Learning Communities: A Practical Guide to Winning Support, Organizing for Change, and Implementing Programs.* San Francisco: Jossey-Bass.

Williams, Marcia L., Paprock, Kenneth, and Covington, Barbara (1999). *Distance Learning: The Essential Guide.* Thousand Oaks, CA: SAGE Publications.

➤ABOUT THE AUTHOR

Russ Brock is managing partner of the Center for Innovation and Inquiry, an organization development and change management agency. With more than twenty-five years experience in organization development, Russ has worked with a variety of organizational systems design and change management projects. Much of his work is directly involved with corporate IT departments and network consulting firms. Prior to forming the center, he held positions as director of a management consulting agency at Bowling Green State University, and as Dean for the Center for Applied and Professional Education at another university, where he managed satellite distance-learning programs. His current work includes helping organizations apply web-based services for collaborative work groups and online training.

Phone: 1-614-794-9062
e-mail: *ciigroup@earthlink.net*

CHAPTER 7

SYNCHRONOUS COLLABORATION, LIVE E-LEARNING, AND BEYOND

➤HARVEY SINGH

INTRODUCTION

Some of the very first Internet technologies to be used for learning or distance education were the World Wide Web and e-mail. The World Wide Web allowed multimedia or hypermedia (HTML) based instructional content to be loaded on a Web server and browsed using HTML based browsers and Internet-based e-mail systems allowed learners and facilitators to correspond asynchronously—anytime, anyplace.

However, one of the most significant contributions of Internet based technologies toward learning in the last few years has been the introduction of synchronous collaboration technologies (often described as live e-learning or virtual classrooms).

Synchronous collaboration technologies truly create a new medium that brings facilitators and participants together in a dynamic and live environment through which highly interactive communication can occur—closing down the barriers for communication and learning.

The introduction of the telephony allowed participants to connect and communicate via voice over great distances. Today, Internet-based synchronous collaborative technologies create a multidimensional and multisensory environment for communication through voice, multimedia and interactivity—the right medium for learning and knowledge transfer.

Furthermore, advances in Internet technologies and availability of sufficient bandwidth allow synchronous collaboration to occur among a very large number of participants.

Prior to the introduction of synchronous and live e-learning, one of the main objections toward online learning or e-learning was lack of human interaction. Synchronous e-learning attempts to address that objection in a very powerful way.

Thousands of organizations—business, academic, and government are exploiting synchronous collaboration and live e-learning technologies successfully to revolutionize enterprise learning and demonstrating tremendous and immediate return on investment.

DEFINING SYNCHRONOUS E-LEARNING

Internet-based Synchronous collaboration allows two or more people to communicate simultaneously using a computer and a Web browser-based client software module or add-on. Participants only need a PC and Web browser to begin a synchronous collaboration session.

Participants join at the same time (a designated time) from different locations (the greater the distances, higher the payoffs). Synchronous e-learning software modules include viewer function, which allows participants to share content (slides, visuals, graphics, web pages, or other software applications) while they converse via Internet-based audio protocol (also known as Voice over IP).

The facilitator's ability to use the capabilities and tools within the synchronous collaboration environment to choreograph the experience is central to success any live e-Learning program. This includes presenting the right content, but more importantly encouraging the use of tools like "hand-raising" (where a participant can click on the hand-raise icon on the application window) and shifting the control by "handing the microphone" (a microphone icon shows up against the name of the participant who is speaking) to a participant.

TYPES OF SYNCHRONOUS COLLABORATION

The Synchronous collaboration technology can be used in a variety of configurations including those described in the next few sections.

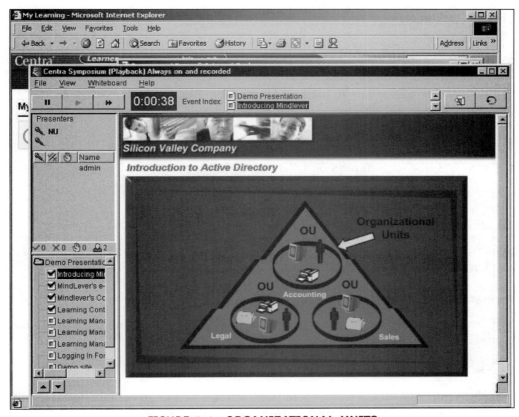

FIGURE 7-1. **ORGANIZATIONAL UNITS**

e-Meetings

Far more effective than teleconferencing or expensive video systems, Web-based e-Meeting augments face-to-face meetings, presentations, briefings, and other ad hoc business interactions in a secure, highly interactive, online work environment. An e-Meeting system enables organizations to easily coordinate all aspects of meeting scheduling, attendee participation, information, and content for Web-based meetings.

E-Meetings are highly effective for small group interactions and can be used for maintaining remote office hours, e-learning project management, or coaching sessions (see Figure 7-1).

e-Conferences

Web conferencing and online presentations allow you to assemble large audiences on the Web without sacrificing the important benefits of real-time, face-to-face interaction, communication, and learning. E-conferences can be used in various online learning initiatives such as product launches and demonstrations, large and remote lectures, and executive broadcasts.

Virtual Classrooms

With a virtual classroom, organizations can bring together large groups of people to interact and learn in a highly collaborative e-learning environment while dramatically reducing travel, facilities, and telecommunications costs.

Virtual classrooms can be used for focused and highly interactive training programs where the orchestration of participant feedback and retention of knowledge and application of that knowledge are essential desired outcomes.

THE BENEFITS OF SYNCHRONOUS OR LIVE E-LEARNING

There are numerous benefits to synchronous collaboration or live e-learning.

Extending Reach

Synchronous collaboration instantly extends the reach of events to participants far and wide by overcoming travel, distance, and time barriers.

Accelerating Time to Market

Synchronous events can be put together and rolled out faster with decreased time to market.

Higher Completion Rates

Collaboration, live interpersonal communication, and human contact increases the percentage of learning programs' completion rates when compared with completion rates of a self-paced online learning program by itself.

Higher Retention Rates

Presentation of content in smaller, digestible chunks or smaller virtual classroom or live e-learning events increases the likelihood that participants will retain and apply the information and knowledge in the workplace.

Target Multiple Learning Styles

Because synchronous collaboration deploys a variety of modes of communication—audio, video, graphics, interactivity, and text chat—it provides multichannel stimuli to address different learning styles.

ROI—Cost and Time Savings

Synchronous collaboration technologies provide an easier business case or return on investment (ROI) calculations than traditional classroom training or synchronous e-learning. The time- and cost-saving dimensions include: reduction in travel time and cost, reduction in need for training facilities, reduced time away from work for participants, reduced logistics and content distribution costs.

Leveraging Existing Talent and Infrastructure

Synchronous collaboration technologies leverage the existing computer and Internet infrastructure already deployed within most organizations. In addition, the existing staff resources—trainers and subject matter experts—can quickly learn new skills to manage live e-learning events.

Continuous Learning

Synchronous and live e-learning facilitates the creation of ongoing and continuous learning programs that are available in a just-in-time and just-enough basis.

SYNCHRONOUS E-LEARNING TOOLBOX

A suite of tools or features may be used within a synchronous e-learning environment. Some of these are based on the physical classroom metaphor, such as flipcharts in the form of whiteboard, while others are unique to the computer/web-based environment, such as application sharing. When used effectively, these tools help the learning and collaboration process to be choreographed to achieve the desired results. Different software products vary considerably in their implementation of these features or tools.

Content/Presentation View

One of the most significant aspects of a synchronous collaboration environment is the content/presentation area. The session leader can load a variety of different content items, such as PowerPoint slides, and share them with the participants.

The key to synchronous and live e-learning is that a session leader and the participants view the same content at the same time. The leader moves from one slide or frame to the next and provides commentary, and encourages questions and responses from the audience. The participants' screens refresh synchronously as the leader moves between different slides/frames.

Another very useful function from the learning standpoint is the ability to pull a piece of content (PowerPoint slide, document, or a Web page) dynamically into the viewing area during the session or conversation.

Participant List View

The participant list pane provides several useful pieces of information: names of the participants, number of participants, the name of a person speaking at any given time. In addition, the session leader can invite the participants to agree or disagree (yes/no response) to a question and the participant list provides visual indication about the participants' response.

Agenda

The agenda tool allows session leaders to assemble and sequence the content from various sources, including PowerPoint slides, documents, web pages, and graphic files, and preload it onto the server and associate the agenda with an event.

Setting the agenda is especially desirable in a structured classroom or lab session or large conference presentation or broadcast.

Voice (One-Way and Two-Way)

The ability to directly talk through the computer and the Internet through a revolutionary technology called Voice over IP or Internet Protocol (also referred to as VoIP) without needing the telephone has simplified the collaboration and event-management process. In addition, there are great cost savings achieved through Internet-based conferencing versus communication over standard phone lines, especially when participants are located farther apart, can be dramatic.

Voice, especially live human speech, can add a completely new dimension to the learning experience. It makes the participants more attentive and responsive to the issues, ideas, and questions being presented. The participants' ability to ask questions in real-time and correspond with a "real" human being on the other side gives them a sense of support and affirmation that is invaluable in the learning process.

Content Markup

The session leader can markup the presentation in the viewing area (à la football broadcaster John Madden) and draw attention to a specific part of the screen or text message. For example, the leader can use the painting and drawing tools and underline or bold certain areas of a slide by simply pointing and clicking with the computer mouse. Content markup adds a dynamic quality to the session beyond a static and potentially mind-numbing slide presentation.

Learner Participation

Beyond the content presentation and voice interaction, there a number of tools the participants can use to communicate during a synchronous event. The facilitator can use these devices to solicit interactions and responses from the audience including: "passing the microphone," "hand-raising," emotional expressions (laughter, clapping), agreeing/disagreeing, and so on.

If the content viewing area provides the visual stimulus and the voice provides the auditory input, the interactions provide the kinesthetic dimensions to the learning experience. These senses can be used in conjunction with one another to orchestrate an effective knowledge transfer program by addressing multiple learning styles and preferences.

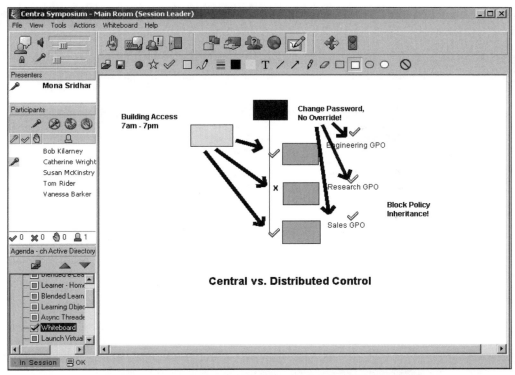

FIGURE 7-2. **CONTROL VERSUS DISTRIBUTED CONTROL**

White Boards

A white board (see Figure 7-2) is similar to the notion of a flipchart in a physical classroom; however, in a synchronous collaboration application, the white board can be used more easily by any of the participants (the permissions can be controlled) to share ideas, paste graphics, or write text messages.

From a learning standpoint, white boards can be an invaluable interlude to an online collaboration session, including: discussing key points, illicit participant input, illustrating or elaborating ideas, and brainstorming.

Application Sharing

In addition to sharing PowerPoint slides, documents, or Web pages, participants can also present and share desktop applications within the content view of synchronous collaboration application (see Figure 7-3).

The implications for computer application training and collaborative work are enormous through collaborative application sharing; some of key knowledge transfer opportunities include: new software product demonstration and training, enterprise application rollouts/training, and desktop application training and certification.

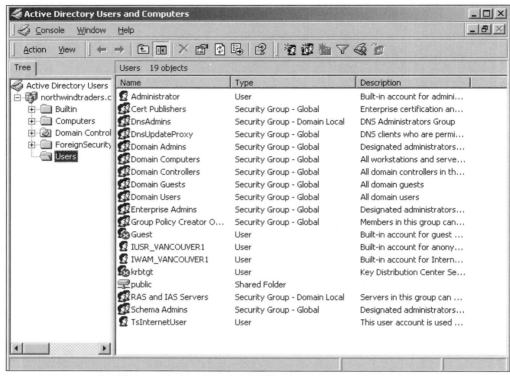

FIGURE 7-3. **ACTIVE DIRECTORY USERS AND COMPUTERS**

Text-based Chat

Text-based chat (see Figure 7-4) is a handy tool for communication between the facilitator and participants using text messages. A separate window is used to type the messages and direct them to the relevant individuals. Text-based chat is great way for participants to input questions to be discussed during or after the live event.

Video

A one-way or two-way video feature can be deployed to present the speaker (usually in a small viewing area) using a desktop video camera. Most synchronous collaboration tools allow the video to be shown to one participant at a time. More sophisticated synchronous collaboration applications allow the video streaming rate to be automatically adjusted based on available bandwidth.

The biggest advantage of a video window is to provide a visual picture of the speaker/participant that could be desirable if the participants have not met in person. The video window could also be used to conduct role-play or interpersonal learning scenarios. However, gratuitous use of brand-width hungry video tools should be avoided especially in circumstances where it distracts from the conversation and other more appropriate content that participants need to focus on in the content/presentation window.

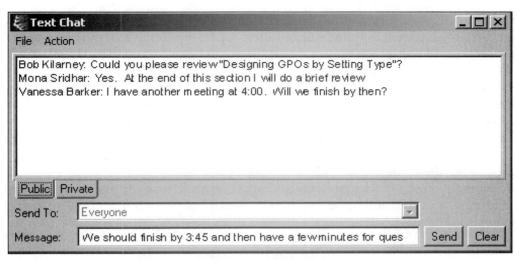

FIGURE 7-4. **TEXT CHAT**

Surveys/Polls

Computer/Web-based synchronous collaboration applications provide another unique tool which is harder or much more expensive to implement in a physical classroom setting—real time surveys and polls. Surveys and polls create interactivity, and when used appropriately they allow the facilitator and the participants to visualize the group's agreement, disagreement, or opinions.

Assessments and Evaluations

Online assessments and evaluations allow event facilitators to build feedback mechanisms and ensure the delivery of effective training programs. For example, they can create pre- or posttests and evaluate the participants comprehension and retention. Synchronous collaboration applications provide some basic assessment capabilities, but these can be combined with asynchronous learning tools, such as authoring and content management systems, to build more advanced content with higher degree of media and interactivity.

Breakout Rooms

A breakout room is a metaphor from the physical classroom that the virtual classroom tries to emulate by allowing the participants to be divided in groups. Each group can have a different set of conversations, presentations, or assignments.

Each breakout room can be facilitated by a different trainer or the same trainer can visit different breakout rooms during the virtual class.

Recording and Playback

Physical meetings and classrooms lack a fundamental characteristic—the knowledge generated and shared during the event is mostly lost and people who could not be at the meetings are usually out of luck. This is another area where computer/web-based synchronous collaboration application fulfill a large need—to be able to record the interactions, conversations, and presentation sequences, store the content as "knowledge objects," and play the content on demand.

Recordings ensure that the content can be revisited as a refresher by those who attended the event and by those who could not attend the original event. The recordings can be stored and managed on a Web server and can even be edited by a facilitator who can post it to be used as self-paced course.

One of the serendipitous uses of recordings and playback is that many organizations use the recording and playback option as a way to author content without intending to host a synchronous collaboration event. In fact, the intended purpose of using it as a rapid authoring tool is to build self-paced content and allow participants to view that content using a browser in an on-demand fashion.

Administrative Interface

The administration system serves as a front-end portal through which administrators, leaders, or participants connect to the synchronous collaboration server. The administrative system provides access to various key functions including: registration, enrollment, user management (adding, dropping users), notification, tracking, and reporting.

A built-in administrative interface makes the synchronous collaboration application self-contained without requiring a full enterprise learning management system (LMS) to administer the access and launching of collaboration events. However, if an organization already has an enterprise LMS deployed then the synchronous collaboration application can be integrated into that LMS using an application programming interface (API).

BRINGING LEARNING DIMENSION INTO SYNCHRONOUS COLLABORATION MEDIUM TIPS AND TECHNIQUES

Learning is a process and synchronous collaboration technology can facilitate that process. However, just as the presence of the physical classroom by itself does not create learning, synchronous collaboration software infrastructure and related tools by themselves don't, either.

Learning occurs by virtue of well thought out content, facilitator and learner preparation, and coordination to create engaging conversations, inquiry, active participation, and dialog between the facilitator and the participants during the learning process.

The following tips and techniques may be applied to make the computer/web-based synchronous collaboration learning process more effective:

➤ Keep the session length short and provide many breaks: since participants use the computer to connect with the content and they cannot see one another face-to-face, participants' attention spans are expected to be shorter than what they may be in a physical classroom.

- ➤ Provide basic or remedial learning content asynchronously via self-paced content prior to the synchronous event so that the discussion can focus on problem solving and higher level discussions and interactions.

- ➤ Make the synchronous event interactive; in other words, incorporate many activities into the event rather than just stare at the monitor for a long period of time. There are numerous ways in which inter-activity can be achieved, for example, surveys and polls, assignments during breakout rooms, clicking agree/disagree icons, white board sharing, asking participants to take control of the application during application sharing.

- ➤ Build your event agenda based on clearly defined learning objectives and then build appropriate presentation, media, and activities driven by those objectives.

- ➤ Set up follow-on activities and communication.

STRETCHING THE BOUNDARIES OF VIRTUAL CLASSROOMS

In a more traditional view, virtual classrooms can be mapped to the physical classroom training experience and viewed as a one-time event. However, with the advent of Internet, e-learning, and just-in-time learning methodologies, learning can be designed to be a continuous process.

Here are some examples how learning is being redefined.

Blended Learning

The future of learning is moving toward the notion of blended learning, where two or more delivery mechanisms may be involved in a given learning program. A blended learning program may include computer/web-based self-paced learning modules, live e-learning events, asynchronous discussion forums, and online tests and references.

Furthermore, the blended learning programs may be further personalized based on learners prior knowledge/skill and learning styles.

Content Management

One of the most significant ideas related to blended learning is the notion of content management, where an organization can build a content repository and provide a ubiquitous web browser access to a learning resource catalog. This catalog can contain learning resources in various delivery formats: documents, virtual classrooms, discussions forums, recorded synchronous and live events in the form of knowledge objects, online assessments, and self-paced modular content. Furthermore, the ability to combine and recombine these disparate types of resources in meaningful sequences will provide the means to the ultimate promise of personalized learning. For an example, see the screen in Figure 7-5.

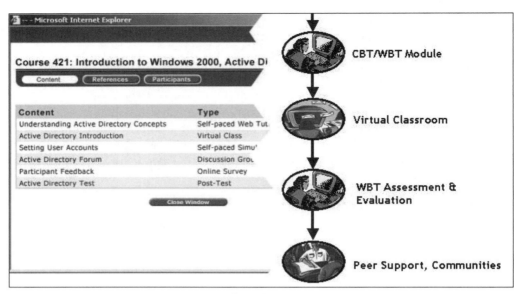

FIGURE 7-5.

Different Models for e-Learning

Synchronous collaboration technologies will be used more creatively in the future to go far beyond the replication of physical classroom metaphor in the form of a computer/web-based virtual classroom. New models of synchronous collaboration may include:

➤ Coaching—a knowledge-worker may invite an expert at the moment of need to provide more information on the process

➤ Help Desk—a customer support representative may help a customer resolve a problem using application sharing

➤ Virtual Office Hours—A trainer may maintain office hours

➤ Collaborative Work—Participants and co-workers may do collaborative work by sharing applications, notes, ideas, and tasks

SUMMARY

Synchronous collaboration application is a "killer app" in the field of Internet-based learning and knowledge management and is expected to become part of computer facilitated knowledge work. Live e-learning and collaboration applications are expected to become an integral part of day- to-day work and learning just as MS Office and e-mail have become a part of day-to-day office work.

Furthermore, the usefulness of synchronous collaboration technologies is certain to expand from an innovative technology being applied to selected learning

FIGURE 7-6. **LEARNER HOMEPAGE**

and training initiatives to a mainstream delivery platform for broad-based, ongoing and corporatewide initiatives, especially when it is blended with other forms of learning and knowledge delivery options and offerings.

Synchronous collaboration and live e-learning leverage a fundamental principle that each knowledge worker is a learner and a knowledge expert and it is the ability of an organization to tap into that expertise at the right place and right time that creates the ultimate competitive advantage. For an example, see the learner home page in Figure 7-6.

RESOURCES

Reading

Hofmann, Jennifer (2000). *The Synchronous Trainer's Survival Guide.*

Website

(http://www.insynctraining.com/pages/books.html)

►ABOUT THE AUTHOR

Harvey Singh is a pioneer in the field of e-learning, performance engineering, and knowledge management and is the founder of NavoWave, an e-learning and performance services company. Prior to NavoWave, Harvey served as the Chief Learning Technology Officer at Centra Software after the company he cofounded, MindLever, merged with Centra Software. Harvey also served as an advisor to e-learning standards organizations like ADL and IMS and was nominated as e-Learning Executive of the Year in 2001.

Contact Information: NavoWave, Inc.
                         920 Main Campus Dr.
                         Suite 400
                         Raleigh, NC 27606
                         hsingh@navowave.com

CHAPTER 8

OUTSOURCING VERSUS INSOURCING YOUR E-LEARNING PROJECTS

➤TRAVIS PIPER

Outsourcing the organization's requirements for generic training is extremely cost-effective. This is especially true for IT-related training where "how to print a document" using Word is the same for organization A as it is for organization B. Per-learner pricing for this type of training via e-learning is a fraction of the per-learner price to conduct traditional training. In today's increasingly global economy, however, it is the unique culture, processes, and skills of an organization's personnel that set it apart from the competition. E-learning solutions for these in-house advantages are not going to be available as part of a generic e-learning library. They must be custom developed. It has been said that "if you want generic people, use generic training." This chapter addresses the pros and cons of either developing the ability to conduct customized e-learning development internally or outsourcing it.

If you decide to hire an internal staff for custom e-learning development, then at least two of the remaining questions from the "Top Questions Concerning E-learning" survey must be answered. These are also addressed in this Chapter:

➤ How do I retool my stand-up trainers to become e-proficient? What is available to help me?

➤ What do I need to do to support and maintain my e-learning process?

WHAT IS OUTSOURCING?

Outsourcing means, quite simply, hiring an outside resource to do the job. It's much like hiring a contractor to remodel your kitchen. Examples of outsourcing in the e-learning arena can range from quite small tasks such as hiring an outside programmer to create a simple scoring routine, to hiring a vendor to develop and perhaps even host a custom e-learning course or entire curriculum of courses.

Can I Outsource?

The first question to be answered concerning outsourcing is "can I outsource?" If the answer is "Yes," then the next question has to be "What are the guidelines I must work within?"

Because e-learning involves computer equipment and, for the most part, internal computer networks, you must understand the impact that your outsourcing endeavor will have on those networks. If, for example, you decide to outsource some of your training requirements to an e-learning provider of video-intensive Intranet-based training, you need to get your IT organization involved in the discussions early on. We had an approved purchase order from one organization to develop an e-learning solution for them. When they finally involved IT (which we had advised them to do months earlier), the project *had to be cancelled* due to the requirements IT added to the development process. The issues to be discussed with IT are centered around hosting requirements and bandwidth.

PROS AND CONS

So you might ask, Why not hire my own e-learning staff instead of outsourcing to a custom e-learning development firm? Table 8-1 summarizes the pros and cons of the hire/internal versus outsource/external decision for custom development. Each point is discussed in the text.

The PROs and CONs of Creating an INTERNAL Organization (the "Hire")

PRO—Easier to Set Priorities

What could be better than hiring your own e-learning staff members? *You* can determine the priorities of what gets worked on first and how and when it's going to get done. *You* are in charge of your own destiny.

TABLE 8-1. Custom Development: Internal Staff versus Outsourcing

Pros	Cons
Internal	
➤ Easier to set priorities	➤ Can "overprioritize"
➤ Lower Rates	➤ Need to cover downtime
➤ Better Control	➤ Requires non-core job skills
➤ Can hire the "right" people	➤ Have to create "from scratch"
➤ Can mold into a team	➤ Hard to retain sought-after skills
➤ Can get started right away	➤ Have to learn as you go
External	
➤ Have own facilities/equipment	➤ Need to communicate effectively
➤ Team of seasoned veterans	➤ Higher rates
➤ Shorter timeframes possible	➤ Higher rates
➤ Quicker reaction to problems	➤ Higher rates

CON—Can "Overprioritize"

What can go wrong when you hire your own e-learning staff members? *You* have to determine the priorities of what gets worked on first and how and when it's going to get done *with the resources you have hired*. It's easy to overcommit those resources and, because they are a limited resource, there is just so much you can do. Typically you must hire in "whole person" increments. If you have a staff of ten people and you need two more for two months to finish a project, chances are you won't be able to hire two additional people for two months. If you are outsourcing, however, the vendor can assign additional resources as needed to meet your deadline at an additional cost.

PRO—Lower Rates

It is true that you will pay less per hour to hire someone than you will to outsource to them on an hourly basis. Outsourcing rates seem high because the vendor has factored in not only a profit margin and overhead, but has anticipated "downtime" (nonbillable hours).

CON—Need to Cover Downtime

You need to look closely at your *real* cost to hire an e-learning specialist, especially in terms of downtime. How many *productive* "e-learning development" hours will that person truly be able to put in every year as a member of your team? Assume you have one large project that will take a team of six people eighteen months to complete. What if you end up paying premium dollars to hire and equip a staff for that project only to have nothing for them to do after eighteen months? Your costs of acquisition, equipment, training, startup, management, and dismissal will far exceed the cost of paying the "big bucks" to a vendor with an equipped, coordinated team already in place that can "ebb and flow" with the project as it progresses. When you outsource, if there is no project, there is no cost.

PRO—Better Control
Much like setting priorities, you have total control over the project.

CON—Requires Noncore Job Skills
Controlling the job assignments of an e-learning team could be an entirely different experience for your organization's culture. You need to be sensitive to creating an environment where instructional designers, storyboard writers, graphic artists, and programmers will feel welcome and can be managed as the independent professionals they are. Consider too that these specialists are doing tasks that may be unique within your entire organization. They need to be made to feel that they are a part of the company culture. Consider too that they may or may not be interested in job advancement opportunities outside of the e-learning group.

PRO—Can Hire the *Right* People
A big plus in hiring a new team is that all members are *charter* members of the organization and share a sense of ownership and camaraderie.

CON—Have to Create the Team *From Scratch*
It is most likely that this has not been done before in your organization; you run the risk of making a mistake and having the entire project fail. Even if you don't make any mistakes, if the organization doesn't understand the new group and its role, you may find yourself under attack at the same time you're trying to get the job done.

PRO—Can Mold Into a Team
Because the team is hired as a cohesive unit, with good management, it can be "coached" into the proverbial "well-oiled machine."

CON—Hard to Retain Sought-After Skills
The stronger members of the team will be sought after by outside organizations with job offers. If you fall into template-based course development after the initial program launch, an outside position with a firm doing a wide variety of projects for multiple clients will be quite appealing to your creative employees.

PRO—Can Get Started Right Away
Once you have approval to hire, you can quickly get a team in place, assuming you have permission to hire from the outside or that there are qualified individuals within the organization with the requisite skills.

CON—Have to Learn As You Go
The employees needed for an effective e-learning team could be completely unlike individuals in the current organization. Managing an e-learning team has its own

unique challenges. Hiring an experienced manager from the outside is an advantage, but now the manager needs to learn the culture of the organization, while at the same time, try to get the job done.

The PROs and CONs of Outsourcing to an EXTERNAL Organization

PRO—Have Own Facilities/Equipment and Software

A reputable outside vendor is fully equipped to handle your project with state-of-the-art hardware and software. It is practically impossible to anticipate all of the equipment and software you will need if you decide to hire your own staff. The computers and authoring products are obvious. Less obvious are the required scripting, graphics (2D and 3D), animation, and audio and video software and hardware components, not to mention pricey annual software support licenses with key software vendors. You can't afford to have a project on hold at the last minute because you can't call the software vendor to obtain resolution of a "bug." You also need to anticipate upgrading all software and some hardware every year or two to keep up with the current releases and models. Another requirement is to have all necessary test platforms at your disposal. If your organization supports Windows 98, 2000, and NT on equipment ranging from Pentium 200 and higher, you need to have "one of each" at your disposal for testing. If some learners will be using dial-up and others using T-1 connections, you need to have the necessary equipment configurations to test all combinations of access on every supported piece of equipment. The permutations can be significant.

CON—Need to Communicate Effectively

Communication with an outside organization presents different challenges than if the individuals were just "down the hall." A good vendor is already experienced in dealing with clients "from a distance." It is a good idea to begin with an initial on-site meeting to put faces with names and to discuss the design and development process. Beyond that, you can send files back and forth to communicate what is desired and expected until the final set of files produce the desired product to everyone's satisfaction.

PRO—Team of Seasoned Veterans

An outside vendor already has a cohesive team in place. These are individuals that are already working together. They have developed their own "language" that quickly lets a graphic designer and a programmer reach a decision as to how best to make a graphic appear on the screen in the quickest time possible. They can relate your (new) project to similar projects they have done in the past, again speeding the communications between team members. Most importantly, they can bring experience and even coding routines to bear on your project that were developed for other projects, thereby allowing you to benefit from their already-acquired learning curve as opposed to having your own team needing to learn everything "new" for the first time.

Another key factor is that the vendor can retain the team of veterans because they are all kept busy working on e-learning projects, which is what they have chosen to do as a profession. To illustrate, one member of our team recently retired after eighteen years. Another has been with us for seventeen years, another eight years, and so on.

An internal team may, at times, need to be diverted to other organization tasks (teaching a class, writing a policy, building a nontraining related database, etc.). This can be disconcerting to the true e-learning professional who may decide to leave your organization and seek employment elsewhere. You then have to backfill that person and "start over" to build that expertise from within or hire from the outside. An outside vendor will have more *depth* and can backfill more rapidly because of having other similarly skilled personnel already on staff.

Also, many organizations are always trying to promote from within. A key member of your team may be promoted to a position outside the team, causing you to have to find a replacement (if there isn't a hiring freeze in effect). Vendors typically have team members in place who see e-learning as their career. As long as they can grow and learn at their job, they will stay.

The following is excerpted from an article titled "Yellow Light on Insourcing," which appeared in the January 25, 2000, issue (Vol. 2, No. 44) of *Online Learning News*, an information and idea service of VNU Business Media.

> "If you're considering bringing development of Web-based training in house after initially having it done by outside designers—think carefully," warns Dave Rogers . . . a science-course coordinator with Open Learning Agency in Victoria, British Columbia, which develops Web-based courses for senior high schools. . . . If development of your courses require programmers and programming, Rogers' warning goes double. "The market for programmers is extremely tight these days," he cautions, "and your in-house effort could become dependent on staff you cannot hire.
>
> . . . any training which has the learner interacting with a server computer," says Rogers, "will require a programmer or programmer/analyst to keep it running. . . . The cost will be steep, since programming is expensive—but the cost of not being able to hire rare staff will be steeper."

CON—They Don't Know Our Business

The question is often asked: "who should I hire to be an author"—a subject matter expert who already knows the material, or an instructional designer who already knows how to organize it and present it? The answer is to hire the instructional designer who is skilled at interfacing with the subject matter experts, "picking their brains" and structuring the gathered information in a concise, cohesive design to make it clearly understandable by the audience. A good vendor of external resources will first send in one or more instructional designers to gather information about the subject. Once that has been structured and organized, it is fed back to the organization for review, asking questions like "Did we understand you correctly?" and "Did we miss anything?" Often just the process of creating clear behavioral objectives makes the organization realize that there are elements of the subject that even they haven't been communicating clearly to their learners. Having "another pair of eyes" with an external orientation often brings fresh and unanticipated benefits to the design and creation process.

PRO—Shorter Timeframes Possible
Outsourcers can work on a project full time, all day, every day with multiple people. Internal people are often pulled off their *development* tasks to do other work.

CON—Higher Rates
When you consider higher rates versus a shorter time frame, think again of the kitchen remodeling example. You can "do it yourself," buying new tools, having dust and appliances scattered throughout the house for weeks, or you can hire a professional who is in and out with minimal disruption, though you'll probably still have the dust. Some e-learning projects may be tied to the launch of a new product or system. Every week that the e-learning is late can cost the organization significantly in terms of lost revenue or lost opportunity. When timeliness is paramount, you cannot afford to have development disrupted by other organizational pressures. You must constantly be looking out for the organization's bottom line. While the rates for outsourcing may seem high initially, when you take into account factors like facilities, equipment, software, depth of experience, and turnover, outsourcing is very cost-effective, as companies who already use *body shops* for contract labor can attest.

PRO—Quicker Reaction to Problems
The vendor's team will typically have "depth" that is not possible in an internal organization. Different technicians with varied experiences can pool their knowledge and ideas to help find the "best" solutions to technical problems. The result is a solution that is not only the most effective to implement, but the most effective for the client from a maintenance and performance standpoint. A program that is designed with ease of revision in mind can greatly reduce ongoing maintenance costs. Occasionally a solution will come up that even the authoring software vendor hasn't realized. An outsource vendor's "closeness" to the project and varied experience with other custom projects is often a better resource than the authoring software vendor who is more focused on insuring a stable product than creating new ways to use it. The savings possible as a result of identifying the "best" solution also help to counter the perception of the higher cost of outsourcing.

While the *pros* and *cons* of hiring versus outsourcing are many, the key question comes down to whether you are looking for a "long haul" solution or a single project solution. You must take into account the organization's commitment to custom-developed in-house e-learning. Later in this chapter you will find guidelines for hiring the in-house staff as well as a checklist for dealing with external vendors.

Lesson Learned

Internal Projects

1. *Employees with special training can leave.* One firm needed updates to an e-learning course they had developed internally. They purchased Authorware, hired a person, sent them to Authorware training and had them write the course. By the time the course needed maintenance, their "author" had left the firm.

2. *Internal resources can be waylaid.* Another firm already has significant internal resources for e-learning development. They have issued a contract to handle the translation of a project into Chinese. The project has been continually delayed because the client's resources are continually being diverted to other projects due to internal priorities.

3. *Internal resources can "lose touch."* A publishing vendor decided to get into the e-learning business. They sent one of their staff to Director classes, then hired a summer intern to develop their first project for a major client. They brought in a vendor for some initial consulting assistance to get the program started and recommend techniques. At the end of the summer, the intern returned to school. The in-house Director trainee had not worked enough on the program during the summer to be able to effectively complete the project. The firm had to call in the vendor again to complete the project and meet their client's deadline. They have now decided that e-learning is not their "thing", and they plan to outsource all future work.

Outsourced projects

1. *SME costs can be high.* A firm outsourced the initial writing and all authoring/programming. However, they also had to contract for all of the SME support for the project. Even though the e-learning development worked out to be cheaper than could have been done internally, the SME consulting fees were much higher than anticipated and after nearly half of the curriculum was completed, the client firm decided against continuing the project.

2. *Providing easily understandable materials to the vendor make the project go smoothly, which leads to more projects.* A firm provided a user's guide and the software to a vendor to develop e-learning for a new version of their in-house software being rolled out to more than 300 employees who work alone out of their homes. The vendor designed, storyboarded, and programmed the training, requiring only that the client provide a liaison and review personnel. The client anticipates additional needs in the future. In the meantime, they are incurring no additional costs.

Outsourced, then internal projects

1. *Work with a vendor on the initial project to learn how it's done.* A firm outsourced all design and development of their e-learning and asked that their people be allowed to work with the vendor. At the end of the project, ongoing maintenance was transitioned to the client, and they have been self-sufficient ever since.

SUPPOSE I DECIDE TO HIRE

The most important rule for setting up an internal capability is to hire the right type of people for the required positions. A successful e-learning team must include:

➤ Instructional designer: Effective design is the key to effective e-learning. Well-designed e-learning can be highly effective even if the graphics are clipart and the programming is simple. Conversely, a poorly designed "Hollywood" production costing ten times more to develop can impart absolutely nothing to the learners. A good instructional designer doesn't need to *be* highly technical, but does need to be able to grasp technical concepts and to be able to clearly communicate them to writers, graphic artists, programmers, and authors to insure the attainment of the behavioral objectives defined for the content being covered.

Possible sources:

1. Trained instructional designers,

2. Persons with experience in adult learning theory,

3. Creative individuals with good speaking, listening and design skills

Unlikely sources: Trainers or teachers who would rather present than write (don't confuse delivery with design). Design is all about being able to clearly write and illustrate ideas and concepts that communicate all facets of the project to the other team members.

➤ Storyboard writer: Needs to be able to translate the design document into succinct onscreen text, graphic descriptions, and audio and video scripts laid out in a storyboard format that clearly communicates all media elements to the client for review and to the "team" for total understanding before any media element development begins.

Possible sources: Individuals with excellent writing skills.

Unlikely sources: Trainers. While at Xerox, we tried to transition standup instructors into authoring roles. One out of eight made the transition; that one, as it turned out, preferred "desk work" to "teaching". She was probably in the wrong job to begin with. Trainers are trainers because they like the face-to-face contact. They are "people" people.

They don't like the solitude of being at a desk. Their preferred method of communication is oral versus written.

➤ Graphic designer: insist on individuals with experience in computer graphics for computer display. Don't assume that a person who has created artwork for print-based publication can create graphics that will display effectively and look good via a slow dialup connection.

Possible sources: Web Designers

Unlikely sources: artists or illustrators with limited experience with graphic software or who can only work on nonstandard hardware or software. Most artistic people are "right brained" (free, creative, self-expressive). Much of computer graphic development in a production e-learning environment is "left brained" (structured, methodical, standards-driven, based on palettes and compression formats, etc.). Be sure these factors are clearly understood by those you consider for this position.

➤ Author (the person who "programs" the storyboard): insist on individuals with a programming background. No matter how "friendly" your chosen authoring product(s) claim to be, you will need to have at least one authoring "techie" on your team who has a direct line to the vendor of your authoring product(s). We have "cleaned up" many projects over the years that ran poorly, took up excessive space, and were a nightmare to maintain due to haphazard coding structures created by "multimedia" personnel who were somewhere between a graphic designer and a programmer, but not necessarily good at either skill.

➤ Marketeer: To keep the team busy you must have someone constantly "selling" to obtain new projects. This person should know the organizational structure and be able to "follow the money" to the organization's priority projects. He or she should also clearly understand the benefits of e-learning and when it is and is not appropriate.

Possible Sources: persons with prior marketing experience and a "history" with the organization.

Unlikely Sources: persons with e-learning experience but no "sales" skills.

Although it is not considered correct to generalize, it is unlikely that the following phrases are unfamiliar: *temperamental artists, pride of authorship, argumentative programmers.* The point to understand is that each person on the team is a professional and (like the story of the six blind men) sees his or her part of the "elephant" differently. Artists are called temperamental because they can get quite defensive about their work. The reviewer will never understand the process and the dedication the artist put into the creation. Similarly, the writer's "pride of authorship" is attacked each time a suggestion is made to change a word. Only the writer understands how or why that particular word was chosen. Finally, the argumentative programmer could have spent considerable time developing an extremely efficient block of code that exactly matches the specifications, only to find that the specifications have changed. Dealing with the various people on an e-learning team can be rewarding and yet a constant challenge to get oils and waters to mix together into a homogeneous team.

WHAT DO I NEED TO DO TO SUPPORT AND MAINTAIN MY E-LEARNING PROCESS?

Having briefly addressed hiring the team, we can now address the question of supporting an ongoing process.

1. Have plenty of work for your team. It is probable that one project which may take the entire team three months to finish may only involve the storyboard writer for one month, or the graphic designer for only two or three weeks. You need to insure that you have sufficient work for all individuals to keep them challenged and productive at all times. At least three concurrent projects at all times is highly desirable.

2. You must implement and continue a constant marketing effort to managers and project leaders within the organization and, if permitted, outside the organization. This requires a marketing individual. Not only does this person need to keep work coming in, but also needs to assist clients with promoting the work already done. Too many organizations have canceled their e-learning initiative only because they built the courses but "nobody came". Because e-learning just passively sits "out there" waiting to be taken, it must be constantly marketed to derive the benefits that were anticipated when the "go with e-learning" decision was made. One organization garnered hundreds of registrations for e-learning by putting colorful three-sided printed cardstock "towers" on the lunch tables in the cafeteria. Another sent large posters with an interesting photograph of the development team out to branch locations. Each poster had small tear-off descriptions of individual courses available for free registration.

3. You must create e-learning that continues to sell its own benefits. For example, your program can have an automatic ROI tracking capability which compares traditional classroom training time against e-learning training time. The in-house client can update an online table with information such as typical learner wages, instructor wages, classroom, meals and travel costs, and traditional class duration. Each month, the ROI program can determine the actual average e-learning completion time and, using the other values from the table, can calculate and report to management the savings that month (and year-to-date) resulting from using e-learning versus traditional training.

You can also determine the ROI of e-learning by identifying startup costs from previous experiences that are reduced or eliminated. One e-learning project replaced a previous user guide that was used to train a remote audience. The "user guide" implementation required twelve persons providing telephone "training" to the readers of the "guide." The e-learning implementation had only two persons assigned to the phones and they rarely rang.

4. Plan to send your team members for training and to conferences. Your team must constantly be exposed to new and different ways of doing their jobs. Not only will these activities be a welcome change and perceived benefit for the individual, they can often result in timesaving and moneysaving lessons that can far outweigh the costs of sending the person to the event.

HOW DO I RETOOL MY STAND-UP TRAINERS TO BECOME E-PROFICIENT? WHAT IS AVAILABLE TO HELP ME?

My personal opinion is that the most effective use of e-learning is employing it in conjunction with instructor-led training. I have long felt that trying to get trainers excited about e-learning is like trying to get assembly line workers excited about robotics. Not only is the technology seen as a threat that will eliminate their jobs, but it also requires them to develop skills that are not compatible with their innate preferences. We all migrate toward a profession where it lets us do what we "like" to do. If I "like" the social interaction of being in front of a class and seeing the "aha!" in the learners' eyes, I will be very reluctant to give that up to sit at a desk and *write* or *author*. If you look closely, many trainers today are still using flipcharts and overhead projectors as their "technology of choice" despite the possibility of enhancing those same presentations using laptops, computer projection equipment, and infrared mouse controls.

Some trainers will make the transition to e-learning developers. As I mentioned earlier one of eight did so in my experience at Xerox; however, the optimal way to retool stand-up trainers to become e-proficient is not to make them developers, but to help them understand how and where e-learning can be developed to augment their current jobs. As one example, we developed a training simulator of a military field radio. The instructor initially felt threatened by the training. In reality, once the simulator was completed, the instructor would hand out laptops for the learners to use to learn how to operate the radio. "Before the simulator," he explained, "I would teach a process then turn everyone loose on their own radio to practice it. Invariably two or three individuals would get hopelessly lost. I could only work with one of them at a time. Eventually it would be time to stop for a break. After the break we had to move on to the next process so those lost individuals never did get trained on that process, plus they remained frustrated during the remaining training because they felt they had failed on the one process. Now, using the simulator, I introduce a process and all individuals use the simulator to practice what

I've just explained. If they have difficulty, they can review the demo. This saves me having to go over the material again. If they get off track in the simulator, it explains the incorrect action and helps them get right back on track. I can spend my time offering remedial assistance to the slower learners and providing additional background information to the quicker learners who finish early. I know that everyone sitting through my sessions now completes every exercise correctly because the simulator insures that for me. The training is now so much more rewarding for me than before the e-learning component was added."

As For "What is Available To Help Me?"

Before attempting to retrain your current stand-up trainers into e-learning team members, first describe the various team positions to them and ask them to honestly assess their own likes and dislikes in terms of changing to an entirely different set of job duties. Have them take an "aptitude" test. You may both be surprised to learn what a person might be suited for. Finally, have them review the current classes they are teaching and identify areas where an e-learning component would help them do their job better. By getting them involved in this way, you insure their buy-in as development of the component gets underway and as it eventually becomes available to them to incorporate into their class.

SUPPOSE I DECIDE TO OUTSOURCE

If you decide to outsource, your first step is to identify potential vendors. A good place to start is a search on the Internet for "custom CBT" Then you need to put together an effective Request for Proposal (RFP) to describe to those vendors what you are seeking.

A Checklist for Potential Vendors

1. Has an established track record

2. E-learning development is their main business (not a sideline).

3. Gathers all the information before recommending specific media recommendations for the project. Demonstrates state-of-the-art technology in current projects (even though it might not be appropriate for yours).

4. Work with a variety of authoring/development products.

5. Uses the current releases of the development products they recommend.

6. Provided demos illustrate sound principles of instructional design.

7. Their definitions of terms such as "interactive" and "engaging" agree with yours.

8. Their idea of what constitutes great material agrees with yours.

9. Recommends *nonproprietary* technology that is commercially available.

10. Development team possesses all of the skills required for the project.

11. The team members that will be assigned to the project have worked together before.

12. Provides good customer support (from your own preproject experience and from the experience of the vendor's references that you interview).

13. Can convince you that they know all of the proper steps to complete your project to your satisfaction.

14. Pricing is in line with other quotations (Be careful of the ultra-low bid to get the foot in the door or the ultra-high bid that accompanies claims of a superior deliverable).

15. Is in the custom e-learning development business where each project's design is unique to achieve specific objectives (as opposed to being a commercial developer where a "generic" design is applied to all projects).

16. The vendor is flexible. They are willing to do just some of the work (e.g., you do the storyboard design and content development and they do the programming).

17. The physical location of the development personnel is not an issue. Remember, you are developing written communication and graphics. All are easily transmitted as e-mail attachments or via overnight delivery of a CD, regardless of where the vendor is located.

18. The vendor is willing to come work at or near your facility, if necessary. If you insist on the vendor being on-site, consider the occasional on-site meeting. Even with travel costs factored in, a "right-priced" vendor can still be more cost-effective than a local provider.

19. Has or has access to video- or web-conferencing facilities if a "face to face" is required over a distance.

20. The vendor does not insist on retaining any rights to the program. If they do, look elsewhere. Future "rights" entanglements can be costly.

21. The vendor is willing to provide maintenance services for the program.

22. The vendor is willing to design the program and use development tools that will minimize maintenance charges.

23. If subsequent translation to additional languages is anticipated, the same vendor can at least design the project to minimize the effort required for translation. Ideally the vendor can also provide the translation services if required.

LETTING THE VENDOR(S) KNOW WHAT YOU NEED—CREATING AN EFFECTIVE RFP

In 1996, we were asked by a local training firm to create a checklist for them to help them ask the right questions of their clients who expressed interest in developing online training. That firm would then bring their client's answers to us so we could develop a quotation for the project. After the checklist was developed it was published in the now-defunct CBT Solutions magazine (article is online at www.caicbt.com/*projest.html*). Shortly thereafter we put it up on our site and called it i-tour Project Estimator (available at www.caicbt.com/projest.html). It has been updated several times since then to incorporate new developments such as Hybrid CDs, and Web delivery. It has been downloaded from our website by hundreds of individuals since that time. Frequently I am pleased to see RFPs that have been created using the Project Estimator as a guide. It helps the outsourcer identify required and desired elements and criteria for the custom development effort. The following information comes from the Project Estimator. Your RFP needs to include the following information:

1. The size, geographical distribution-and makeup of the intended audience

2. Estimated e-learning course duration based on estimated traditional training

3. Intended purpose of the training (product launch, ongoing training, classroom supplement, etc.)

4. The intended platforms (LAN, Web, dialup, CD-based, both Web and CD, existing standards or requirements, etc.)

5. CD quantities required (if applicable)

6. Packaging design needs if a CD is required (artwork and content creation for the CD, jewel case, and mailing envelope, etc.)

7. Identify if high-bandwidth elements are required via a slow dialup connection (indicating a need for a hybrid CD solution)

8. If an Intranet implementation is required, indicate that IT has been contacted to insure necessary bandwidth availability, willingness to support plug-ins and/or external hosting (if necessary)

9. Indicate the desired course completion timeframe

10. Indicate the degree of desired on-site presence of the vendor (initial meeting only, periodic review meetings, all development on-site, etc.)

11. Need for a "pay and play" web-based solution (do you want to sell per-student access to the course via the Internet)?

12. Desired outputs (tracking and reporting). Do you just want completion information or full tracking of responses by date and time?

13. Identify what resource materials already exist (user guides, system specifications, product literature, etc.)

14. Describe the e-learning experience level of the group issuing the RFP (no prior experience, some experience, etc.)

15. Indicate the perceived needs for graphics, photographs, animations, audio and video. Do any of these elements already exist?

16. Will the product initially or eventually need to be translated into other languages?

17. What are acceptable timeframes for client reviews (three days, two weeks, etc.)? This is a significant factor in meeting the desired development timeframe.

18. Will vendor assistance be needed with implementation (technical startup, course administration, promotion, etc.)?

19. Who will be maintaining the program (you or the vendor)? An "easier" but "less powerful" tool may be appropriate depending on the situation.

Keeping Yourself Informed

Your vendor, simply by working with multiple clients, is constantly being stretched to stay at "state of the art" level to provide all clients with optimal solutions. However, you cannot rely entirely on your vendor to anticipate your every need. The vendor will never know your organization and its needs better than you do. Therefore, it is imperative that you attend e-learning conferences and seminars to keep yourself abreast of new developments as only you can in effectively representing your organization. This will enable you to keep your vendor "on their toes" and effectively challenge them to stay focused on your specific needs and to work as an effective partner.

WILL HISTORY REPEAT ITSELF?

In the late 1970s and early 1980s many large organizations invested heavily in elaborate in-house video production studios to create "state of the art" training and marketing videotapes. They hired top-notch video communications personnel who expected to become the firm's in-house Stephen Spielberg. The reality was that there weren't enough projects to keep the studios working at full capacity. "Training videos" were often nothing more than using a $20,000 camera to record a visiting professor's "bobbing head" during a lecture—hardly the type of work the video professional hired on for. The cost of staying "state of the art" was high as the technology changed every couple of years.

Today, organizations with *full-time* needs continue to maintain those studios, whereas those with only *occasional* needs have disbanded in-house production and regularly use the services of external studios, who have highly skilled professionals with state-of-the-art equipment. The studios focus on the technology, whereas their clients focus on their business and the message that needs to be communicated through the video medium. I predict that a similar evolution will take place in the custom e-learning industry once the "pain" of repeatedly building and losing in-house expertise becomes too great.

TIPS AND HINTS

For Hiring

- ➤ Realize that the e-learning team should be comprised of different types of people

- ➤ Don't try to force trainers to become e-learning developers. Know their aptitudes, help them to become e-learning facilitators, and understand how e-learning can enhance their job, not eliminate it.

- ➤ Instructional designers:

  1. Trained instructional designers,

  2. Persons with experience in adult learning theory,

  3. Creative individuals with good speaking, listening, and design skills. Don't confuse current training *delivery* skills with *design* skills.

- ➤ Storyboard writers: need e-learning background and excellent writing skills for on-screen text and graphic descriptions, as well as audio and video scripting.

- ➤ Don't confuse *delivery* of training content with *creation* of training content.

- ➤ Graphic designers need experience in computer graphics for computer display and a realization that they will be working in a production environment.

- ➤ Don't assume that experience creating print-based graphics implies competency for creating on-screen graphics.

- ➤ Author: Plan to have at least one "heavy duty programmer" on the team who is a troubleshooter and can get into the "bits and bytes" of the problem, working with the authoring tool vendor(s).

- ➤ Realize that your team members are individual professionals with widely varying aptitudes and skill sets.

- ➤ Understand that the role of management is to coordinate the development of the project.

- ➤ Have plenty of work for the team. Sell, sell, sell to insure a steady stream of projects.

- ➤ Build ROI-calculating mechanisms that help promote the cost benefits.

- ➤ Send the team members to seminars and conferences.

For Outsourcing

- ➤ Seek out potential vendors you would feel comfortable with as an outsourcing partner.

- ➤ Create an effective RFP that clearly communicates your requirements.

- ➤ Keep yourself informed on the state of the e-learning industry.

RESOURCES

ASTD.org—Buyer's Guide and Consultant's Directory
Brandon-hall.com—Lists hundreds of custom development vendors
caicbt.com—Creative Approaches, Inc
Advice and Tools:
    Off-The-Shelf Courseware Providers
    Cost Justifying CBT or Multimedia
    Outsourcing vs. Hiring Developers
    Selecting a Multimedia Vendor
    Our Recommended "Best" All-Around Authoring Product
    Using Simulations in Training
    Download our Project Estimator

Links:
    Available at caicbt.com/links.html
    Inside Technology Training Magazine
    The magazine for computer-based training, web-based training, electronic performance support and interactive multimedia technologies.

The MASIE Center
International think tank dedicated to exploring the intersection of learning and technology.

Macromedia
Macromedia is the developer of such programs as Flash, Director, and Authorware. The site has downloads available as well as an extensive gallery and product support material.

ONLINE-LEARNING-NEWS
This weekly publication comes to you WEEKLY and it's FREE from VNU Business Media

➤ABOUT THE AUTHOR

Travis Piper is the President of Creative Approaches, Inc. He has spent nearly 30 years in the CAI, CBT, Multimedia, e-learning industry managing projects and learning about the types of people and the culture needed to create e-learning. He was Project Manager of the first CBT staff at Xerox Corporation from 1974–1983. The internal group was created to provide in-house custom CBT development services. In the early 1980s the group was experiencing over 50,000 hours of online training each year. In the late 1970s, to offset peak-and-valley workloads, Piper was instrumental in making the staff an outsourcing resource to other companies. In 1983, Piper formed Creative Approaches. That early start makes the company the world's senior custom e-learning development firm today. The firm has completed well over 250 projects since its founding. He is the recipient of an international award for custom CBT development. He has a Masters of Science degree in Speech Communications from UCLA.

Phone: (800) 964-6299
e-mail: *tpiper@caicbt.com*

CHAPTER 9

LEARNING MANAGEMENT SYSTEMS FOR E-LEARNING

➤**BRAY J. BROCKBANK**

INTRODUCTION

A complete e-learning technology solution is comprised of seven components or technologies that should work seamlessly together. Although each component is an independent tool in the e-learning industry, together they create a complete e-learning solution. E-learning components include: content, collaboration, testing and assessment, skills and competency, e-commerce, Internet video-based learning, and learning management systems (LMS).

An LMS ties the six other e-learning components together in a framework that tracks, supports, manages, and measures e-learning activities. In a nutshell, an LMS is the *"nerve system"* of a total e-learning solution whether the organization is using computer-based training (CBT), web-based training (WBT), document-

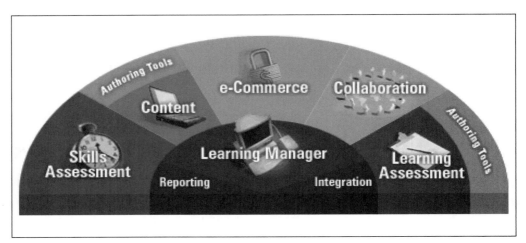

FIGURE 9-1. **LMS**

based training (DBT), instructor-led training (ILT), or blended training methods (BTM) (see Figure 9-1).

Initially, the LMS administrator will configure Web services, user accounts, and discussion software tools, and the instructor will prepare content and tests. Once the LMS is implemented, the administrator will need to physically load courseware and content.

On the technical side, an LMS is a server-based software system that controls e-learning. Learners receive content via a Web browser. Middle-tier application server and back-end database server run the course materials, collaborative tools, and other data essential for learning. Because user access the LMS via the browser the system is easy for administrators, students, and instructors to use. By separating the LMS application logic onto the middle-tier and maintaining course materials, student records, and associated data on back-end servers, organizations can increase the scalability of their LMS solution.

CHOOSING AN LMS

With an estimated 200-plus LMS in the market today, buyers have many providers and options to choose from. When you are considering an LMS you should:

- ➤ First, analyze the organization's current training and learning environment, commitment, technology, and resources.

- ➤ Second, determine what needs must be met by an LMS.

- ➤ Third, what existing IT training (tools, content, etc.) will need to be integrated into the LMS?

- ➤ Fourth, what is the schedule for the deployment of the LMS?

Features

Once these questions have been addressed and answered adequately, then you should only choose from those LMSs that offer scalability, flexibility, interoperability, and extendibility. These four features should be at the top of any LMS requirements list.

Scalability: how well the LMS solution will work when use increases or decreases over time.

Flexibility: allows the LMS processing to be customized to meet business processes without writing additional code.

Interoperability: the ease with which an LMS works with tools and content created by other companies and software packages.

Extendibility: the capability of adding new functionality to current or existing LMS product features.

Hosted LMS

In choosing an LMS, you must decide if you will host the LMS on a company server or have it hosted externally through a service provider. This decision requires some research within the organization. Choices and issues include: behind the firewall, outside the firewall, support, guarantees, security, and so on.

Hosting the LMS internally may require hiring additional staff to maintain and manage the server, hardware, and related technology. Hosting externally may require hosting fees be paid to the external provider on a monthly, quarterly, or annual basis. Options should be discussed with the LMS provider to get a better idea of related costs and limitations of each decision.

Industry Development

Hal Varian, dean of the School of Information Management and Systems at the University of California at Berkeley, once stated that ". . . a technological innovation passes through five main stages as it undergoes industrial development: experimentation, capitalization, management, hyper-competition, and consolidation." (*Forbes*, February 21, 2000). E-learning technologies are no exception. E-learning is currently making the transition from hyper-competition to the consolidation stage.

As is common in most markets, the LMS market is comprised of small, medium, and large vendors. Many vendors are recent start-ups (less than 36 months) backed by large amounts of venture capital. Large LMS vendors include Sun Microsystems, IBM, and Oracle. Microsoft and Cisco Systems are also poised to enter the LMS arena. Other large multinational companies are beginning to develop or invest in LMS vendors and products. Even though many of the big technology companies have jumped in to the LMS market, nobody has captured it—at least not yet.

The e-learning industry is comprised of three vendor segments: technology, content, and services.

➤ **Technology:** This segment includes LMS, learning content management systems (LCMS), authoring tools, training delivery systems, enterprise resource planning (ERP), application service providers (ASP), live e-learning tools, streaming video, EPSS, and testing and assessment tools.

➤ **Content:** This segment includes third-party content providers, book and magazine publishers, enterprises, subject matter experts (SME), government agencies, colleges, universities, schools, training organizations, learning portals, IT firms, and system integrators.

➤ **Services:** This segment includes enterprise information portal vendors, corporate universities, learning service providers (LSP), content aggregators, learning consultants, consulting, professional services, certification service providers, collaboration services, and online mentoring services.

There is some crossover of vendor segments, with several LMS vendors marketing themselves as learning portals, end-to-end solutions, blended e-learning solutions, best-of-breed technology, global learning management solution, integrated learning and management systems, and e-learning infrastructure technology.

Some e-learning vendors are seeking to be a "total e-learning solution" by providing technology, content, and services through acquisition and merger efforts, while others are establishing themselves as one-stop-shops by developing home-grown solutions for all these functions. But the road to offering a complete e-learning solution has been paved with difficulty and failure. The trouble with trying to be a complete solution is that no one vendor is ever likely to be able to offer the best content, collaboration, testing and assessment, skills and competency, e-commerce, Internet video-based learning, and LMS.

Proposed Standards

Many industries, in their infancy, suffer from a lack of "standards." A standard is a documented, generally accepted guideline that has been established and accepted by a board or committee to promote further industry development. To date unfortunately, no LMS or content standards have been established and supported as "de-facto." Proposed or emerging LMS standards are likely two to three years away from being completed. Until then, "plug-and-play" compatibility between proprietary systems isn't very promising—or even probable.

The federal government, a major e-learning advocate, has been pushing for completion of standards for years and remains one of its biggest supporters of the effort. Even though many LMS vendors are beginning to embrace and support emerging standards, the cost of supporting each proposed standard is not only burdensome to vendors but costly to buyers as well. The costs related to supporting several proposed standards increases the burdens to both parties even more. The LMS company may lose its advantage in "low-cost" quick "time-to-market" with its product, while the customer must wait and pay for a product that has many proposed standard specifications to meet. In the end, the extra time and money spent in R&D of several proposed standards would be better spent in meeting the driving needs of the customer.

Those who support the establishment of technological standards for LMSs are growing in number, but still remain a small segment of the overall e-learning market. Vendors who support standards, in general, have *re-engineered* their LMS to support emerging standards incurring significant costs. In addition, vendor content that does not support emerging standards must be *repurposed* to work with LMS standards.

Current proposed industry standards bodies include: SCORM, IMS, LRN, AICC, and IEEE.

Shareable Content Object Reference Model (SCORM)

SCORM is being developed by the Advanced Distributed Learning initiative (ADL). The Department of Defense (DoD) and the White House Office of Science and Technology Policy (OSTP) launched ADL in November 1997. ADL's purpose is to ensure access to high-quality education and training materials that can be tailored to individual learner needs and made available whenever and wherever they are required. One goal of SCORM is to provide a reference model that defines Web-based learning content. You can learn more about SCORM at *www.adlnet.org*.

IMS Global Learning Consortium, Inc (IMS)

IMS is developing and promoting open specifications for facilitating online distributed learning activities such as locating and using educational content, tracking learner progress, reporting learner performance, and exchanging student records between administrative systems. You can learn more about IMS at *www.imsproject.org*.

Learning Resource iNterchange (LRN)

LRN provides content creators a standard for identifying, sharing, updating, and creating online content and courseware. LRN is based on the IMS Content Packaging Specification and helps ensure that content is compatible with a variety of e-learning products and tools. You can learn more about LRN at *www.microsoft.com/elearn/*.

The Aviation Industry CBT Committee (AICC)

AICC is trying to standardize how results are obtained and shared between content and learning management systems. AICC promotes interoperability standards that software vendors can use across multiple industries. They provide a list of products on their website that are AICC-certified and also support the broader standards initiatives, such as SCORM and IMS. You can learn more about AICC at *www.aicc.org*.

Institute of Electrical and Electronics Engineers, Inc. (IEEE)

IEEE ("eye-triple-E") is trying to advance and promote the engineering process of creating, developing, integrating, sharing, and applying knowledge about electrical and information technologies and sciences for the benefit of humanity and the profession. You can learn more about IEEE at *www.ieee.org*.

Cloudy Standards Forecast

Until proposed, emerging standards mature and gain broader support, buyers should beware of vendor claims of being compliant with standards.

There is much misinformation out in the market on emerging standards. Claims of compliance made by vendors can be very misleading and at times blatantly erroneous. There are three levels of standards support: compliance, conformance, and certification.

➤ *Compliance* is the lowest level of standards support and is based on a claim made by the vendor (unchecked by independent party).

➤ *Conformance*, a claim made by a vendor following successful completion of self-testing and validation with an authorized testing suite—with no validation made by an independent third party.

➤ *Certification* is the highest level of support—achieved through successful testing by an authorized, independent, third-party testing firm.

SCORM and AICC have at least three levels of compliance currently being proposed and entertained. To date, SCORM hasn't offered certification, only compliance testing. There is one test for SCORM (1.1) compliance. But even within the SCORM test there are three degrees of compliance. When looking at LMS and content providers, buyers should ask which specifications and tests the product was tested against to be compliant, and more importantly who conducted the testing and reporting of results.

Even though each emerging standard has its supporters, SCORM currently offers the most comprehensive standards approach today—and may prove to be the standard of choice by the U.S. federal government. Then with continued government support, SCORM could become the standard of choice. But SCORM isn't finalized and is still some time away from becoming the de facto standard for LMS products and e-learning content.

With AICC there isn't "one" specification or test for vendor compliance. But to its credit, AICC has a certification process in place, and there are some AICC-certified LMS vendors today (*www.aicc.com*.) But certification doesn't guarantee inherent plug-and-play content. AICC certification, however, does mean interconnectivity or interoperability is close—with minor modification being required.

According to industry reports, over half of all LMS vendors currently support AICC in one form or another. AICC support is also expected to grow as vendors seek interoperability between their proprietary systems and other vendor content, systems, and tools.

THREE TYPES OF LMS

Vendors have primarily taken three separate and distinct approaches in engineering their LMS. The three approaches include:

➤ Proprietary (closed and not easily interoperable with other e-learning components)

➤ Standards-based (supported)

➤ Open architecture systems (interoperable)

Proprietary

Proprietary systems are the largest category of LMS vendors. Vendors who fall under "closed, proprietary systems" offer very limited interoperability—meaning their LMS will not "plug-and-play" with off-the-shelf or customized courseware content or systems. Instead, the LMS closed structure requires that content undergo a "reworking, re-engineering, and repurposing" process to work with the LMS. This re-engineering process requires an extensive amount of time, money, and patience on the part of the LMS provider and buyer.

Even after 18 months or more, many proprietary LMS integrations and implementations are still unsuccessful. These systems require extensive work before the LMS system can go live. In addition, these proprietary systems require lengthy processes to bring together proprietary systems that are already in-house (legacy systems).

Some vendors even go so far in defending their record of failure by claiming that their system is "highly customizable" to meet the needs of their customers—but this required customization is literally what locks the customer into lengthy and too-often failed attempts at system implementation and integration. If the LMS vendor doesn't offer an out-of-the-box solution, then their system is too "customizable" and proprietary to meet the customer's immediate needs—not to mention future growth and needs.

Many of these "proprietary" vendors have adopted the "one-to-three" business model. For every dollar spent on product by the customer, another three or four dollars can be extorted for consulting services. These vendors aren't selling systems (software) so much as selling consulting (services).

Standards-Based

The standards-based LMS is the fastest-growing LMS category. Many proprietary LMS companies are looking to standards to save them from their "lock-in-lockout" systems. They're looking for standards to make their system work with other systems—which they've been unable to do to this point.

Support of standards will bring interoperability or built-in connectivity. But vendors who rely on standards are limited by the quality of the standards—and their product offering is only as good as the standards are. Standards bodies and coalitions are slow to adapt to market needs and demands—and tend to compromise their standards due to panels, experts, hidden agendas, and lengthy discussion processes.

The jury is still out on standards and whether they will ever prove useful. Only a handful of LMS vendors currently support both the AICC and SCORM proposed standards. Visit *www.aicc.org* and *www.scorm.org* for a complete listing of vendors supporting each of their respective proposed standards.

Open Architecture

Very few LMS vendors have open architecture. Many of the problems that the e-learning industry is currently plagued with are a result of the proprietary systems in the market. Many claim system "openness" but fail to deliver on their claim when implementing their system. Truly open LMSs require little effort to connect or integrate with content, collaboration, testing and assessment, skills and competency, e-commerce, and Internet (streaming) video-based learning—whether the tool or content was developed in-house (home-grown), customized, or purchased from a third-party vendor. As e-learning standards are finalized, open architected LMS will likely require little more than minor modifications to comply with such standards. Open architected systems are made to work with proprietary, best of breed, customized, and home-grown content and systems.

The greatest selling point of an open LMS is that it allows organizations to use existing IT systems that are already in place. The philosophy behind open architecture is to have connectivity with "all" solutions and extendibility to new solutions (systems, content, etc.) as they become available. This openness extends to legacy, current and future systems yet to be conceptualized or marketed.

E-LEARNING INFRASTRUCTURE

E-learning infrastructure, for the most part, is built on traditional networking and enterprise infrastructure including networks, web browsers and databases. Applications that organizations use can be divided into three primary sets of technologies: virtual classroom (VC), learning management system (LMS), and e-learning content management system (LCMS).

Virtual Classroom

Virtual classroom (VC) technology was designed to support synchronous collaboration by allowing a live classroom experience to be conducted over the Web. It includes functionality such as:

- Voice over IP (VoIP)
- Video conferencing
- Shared whiteboards, application screen sharing, and live feedback
- Archiving of classes as learning objects
- Interconnectivity with (select) LMS and LCMS providers

LMS

LMS software products include a database of student records with administration and delivery interfaces for learning. LMS products typically provide functionality such as:

- Competency and skills management
- Skills-gap analysis (built into the LMS or as a purchased add-on product)
- Resource management (management of physical resources: computers, rooms, books, etc.)
- Interconnectivity with VC, LCMS, and enterprise applications

An LMS should offer the following tools, features, and functionality out-of-the-box:

Administrator

The administrator tool enables the administrator to set up, manage, document, track, and report information for classes, individual learners, and groups.

An *administrator* can configure all system options; track course cost; establish and modify user-defined fields (UDF's); specify course recertification requirements and notification periods (when the user will be notified); manage transaction logging (log of user events); import existing registration and completion information; add, delete, modify, and import all course information; import current HR data from HRIS or ERP systems; create or import groups and group managers (groups can be set up according to job title, duties, and functions); use full reporting capabilities (report generation), and customize security options with intruder detection and password expiration.

Online Manager

The online manager is a browser-based tool that enables managers to document, track, and report on classes, individual learners, and groups of learners assigned to each manager role (determined by the organization) by the administrator.

A *manager* can manage assigned courses, individual learners, and groups of learners; track course usage; view and print learner reports; monitor learner progress; assign courses and curricula to learners; add and modify learner information; authorize courses as required or as elective; mark course completions; limit managers to only view information (not allowing edits to records); streamline completions; and electronically sign appropriate training documents.

Online Student

The online student is a browser-based tool that the learner uses to register for and launch courses, view assignments, and view course completion information.

A *learner* can: use the simple and intuitive browser-based interface to view the online course catalog, course detail, and schedules, run several personalized reports from within the browser; launch CBT courses from any (Internet connected) desktop with a browser; electronically sign completed document-based training (DBT); provide automatic recertification notification; view only the learner's personal information; view the online course catalog, course detail, and schedules; and cancel registration online.

Connectivity and Interoperability

Connectivity and interoperability are present when an LMS can launch, manage, and measure course activities; launch, track, and score CBT without making changes to the course (repurposing or re-engineering content); launch any type of electronic course or Windows document (.pdf, .doc, PowerPoint presentation, etc.) from the browser; electronically sign completions; automatically check for and install proper snap-ins (required updates, files, etc.) or media players with SmartUpdate; download a course; disconnect from the network and complete the course; then upload the course information to track the learning results.

Automated E-Mail Notification

Automated e-mail notification serves as a reminder of upcoming courses, required courses past due, completed training, course registration, required classes or courses, revisions to required courses or documents, and recertifications to be completed.

Embedded Database

An embedded database (included or built-in) like Microsoft Database Engine (MSDE) may be bundled with the LMS. Small businesses without the need for a large database can utilize MSDE or some other database product to meet their database needs. The LMS should offer the option to still use SQL or Oracle for larger organizational environment needs.

LMS Customization

All organizations have their own particular needs. To avoid being overly "customized,"—the following questions should be asked of the vendor:

➤ How much customization is *required*

➤ How much customization is *optional*

> ➤ How *long* will the customization take

> ➤ How much will it *cost*

An organization can choose to go the route of customization or not. The option to customize can be exercised following the LMS implementation. An organization can test-drive the system to see what, if anything, will need to be customized to make the system a "total solution" to the organizations e-learning needs.

Required (or involuntary) customization can prevent a system from going live as planned. Many customized systems are no more than a set of ingredients. The vendor experiments with the various ingredients to create a recipe for each organization. On the surface this may sound fine, but what happens as the organizations taste (needs) and appetite (wants) change? More experimentation and ingredients are required—with all the headaches included.

If a LMS vendor doesn't offer an out-of-the-box solution, then the organization can realistically expect lengthy customization processes, experimentation, implementation, and integration, all at enormous financial cost. The original premise of an LMS solution was to focus on cost displacement by administering existing classroom training through the Web, focusing on elements such as catalog and registration, resource management, back-office financials, and so on. But when extensive customization and development is required, the e-learning solution has been received with some disappointment.

Re-Branding

Most LMS providers offer re-branding options with their LMS. Re-branding is the ability to change the look and feel of the LMS. Simple re-branding may include the addition of an organization's logo and color preferences. Other options may include layout changes and reorganization of the LMS to better replicate the organizations own Web user interface (UI).

Localization

Since most organizations are operating globally, the LMS should provide the ability to support multiple languages in a single database. It should also be able to support single-byte languages (French, Spanish, Italian, etc.) as well as double-byte languages (Chinese, Japanese, Korean, etc.).

New Market Segment

The LCMS came about for two reasons: first, some LMS customers' needs required the ability to create and manage content; second, the rapid increase of competition and the perceived deterioration of a LMS value proposition—dissatisfaction with LMS installations and the inability to integrate into other enterprise applications. LMS and LCMS are complementary in nature, working together toward a total solution. Each addresses different business constraints. The LCMS was not created to replace the LMS, but rather to serve clients who required the additional capability of content management. The LCMS focuses on reducing time to performance, while the LMS focuses on connecting e-learning components and reducing training administration time.

Because the e-learning space is young and overpopulated, the market is going to see rapid consolidation. LMS and LCMS, content and skills-assessment, virtual classroom, and instructor-led training (ILT) will all consolidate to better meet the changing business market and training needs of organizations. Consolidation will be the only reason many market players survive the onslaught of hyper-competition.

Learning Content Management System

LCMS solutions are a class of software products that include a learning object repository (LOR) with authoring and delivery interfaces for e-learning and knowledge management designed to support the express capture, delivery, and measurement of knowledge in a web-based manner. LCMSs focus on achieving "personalized" (by tailoring training to the users' learning styles) learning on demand (LOD) to drive performance in an organization by delivering content to learners to solve business problems.

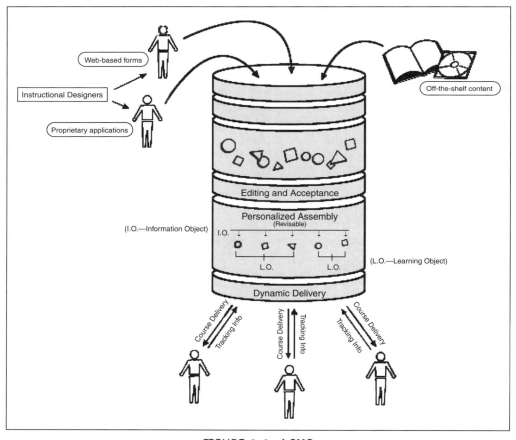

FIGURE 9-2. **LCMS**

Harvey Singh, an LCMS specialist, stated that "learning management systems have focused first and foremost on the administrative aspects of class, student, and instructor logistics." He further stated that LMSs are "not designed to address the issues of interactivity, scalability, reusability, personalization, and the level of tracking capability required with online learning content." Singh argues that the e-learning industry needs a system "designed to help companies collect, organize, manage, maintain, re-use, and target instructional content." ("Learning Content Management Systems: New technologies for new learning approaches," *eLearning Magazine*, February 2001, p. 36).

As seen in Figure 9-2, LCMS is an assembly of software products that include a learning object repository (LOR) with authoring and delivery interfaces for e-learning and knowledge management. LCMS software products are primarily responsible for creating, managing, maintaining, delivering, and tracking Web-based content and provide functionality such as:

➤ Content migration and management

➤ Asynchronous collaborative learning via e-mail and discussion groups

➤ Content reuse and adaptive individualized learning paths based on learning objects (LO)

➤ Interoperability with LMS, ILT, and enterprise applications

➤ Testing and certification

➤ Learning object repository

An LCMS is used to author, approve, publish, and manage learning content or objects. The LCMS combines the administrative and management dimensions of a conventional LMS with the content creation and personalized assembly dimensions of a CMS (content management system).

LEARNING OBJECTS

A learning object (LO) is an object designed for instructional purposes. An LO is simply a piece of content or information. An LO is self-sufficient, providing instruction on a distinct skill or unit of knowledge. It's platform (LMS) independent, and runs on standard Web platforms and operating systems. An LO doesn't require special "plug-ins" or prior application installations.

A learning object also has descriptive meta-data wrapped around it. Meta-data is used to describe what each object contains. Each object is catalogued using subject-explicit meta-data and can be indexed, searched, and reused as required. Typically meta-data includes information about the instructional content—how long the content takes to complete, the language in which it is written (English, Chinese, etc.), and any prerequisite knowledge required to work with the object.

By using LO, employees receive a personalized, just-in-time training experience—increasing time to performance. LO is reusable and resequenceable. The only limitation with LO is that they only provide "one-way" communication of knowledge—from instructor to learner.

Reusable Learning Objects

Typically, an RLO is considered to be a modular building block of e-learning content, the smallest, self-contained, chunk or byte of e-learning instruction possible. Each RLO can be mixed and matched to generate complete, personalized courses, lessons, and instructional events.

A RLO is a collection of reusable information objects (RIO), overview, summary, and assessments that support a specific learning objective. An RIO is a collection of content, practice, and assessment items amassed around a single learning objective. RIOs are built from templates based on whether the goal is to communicate a principle, concept, process, fact, or procedure. Each RIO contains content, practice, and assessment components.

The objective is the instructional objective, or performance goal, that the RLO aims to achieve. The learning activity is the body of the RLO or the instructional strategy that the RLO uses to satisfy the instructional objective. The "assessment" part tests the mastery over the subject matter.

RLOs work individually or in sequence to produce a course. RIOs and RLOs combine in different ways to build custom learning and performance solutions.

Learning Object Repository

Learning object repository (LOR) is a central database used for storing and managing learning content. It is from this point that individual LO are either dispensed to users individually or used as components to assemble larger learning modules or complete courses, depending on individual learning needs.

Instructional production may be delivered via CD-ROM, the Web, or printed materials. Each object produced is reusable—and the integrity of the content is preserved regardless of the delivery platform used. XML provides this function by separating content from programming logic and code.

PRICING AN LMS OR LCMS

Many things need to be considered when looking at the cost of an LMS or LCMS:

➤ Total cost of ownership

➤ System pricing structure

➤ Maintenance

➤ Per-seat, annual licensing fee

Popular LMS vendors include: Docent, Gen21, Knowledge Planet, Learnframe, Pathlore, Saba, and THINQ. A more detailed list of e-learning vendors can be obtained at *www.internettime.com*. Also, LMS and LCMS analyst reports can be purchased and/or obtained at *www.brandonhall.net* and *www.masie.com*.

A GLIMPSE INTO THE FUTURE

As markets and systems like learning management (LMS), knowledge management (KM), business intelligence (BI), customer relationship management (CRM), competitive intelligence (CI), supply chain management (SCM), and others begin to converge, both the LMS and LCMS platforms will likely make the transition towards being a type of universal management platforms (UMP).

Figure 9-3 shows that UMP will provide the infrastructure that enables organizations to pull all of their systems, processes, planning, applications, and pieces together into one system platform. The UMP will offer a truly open system that will connect or integrate all enterprise systems together seamlessly.

Leading LMS & LCMS companies are moving toward a UMP architecture design and philosophy. UMP architecture will likely be based on an open architec-

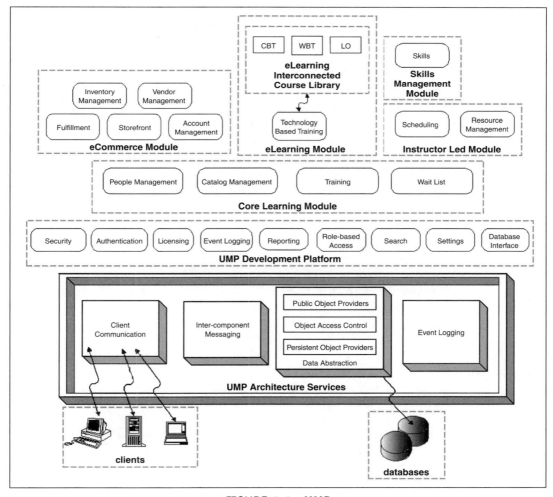

FIGURE 9-3. **UMP**

ture that quickly and seamlessly integrates any content, providing a sophisticated level of automated training administration. Beyond the basic LMS capabilities of managing ILT, e-learning, and skills management, the UMP will also provide a total integration platform that easily interacts with a variety of enterprise systems and truly provides a centralized point of management and access for all corporate needs and initiatives.

Components and Versatility

Because of this "open" design, UMP will be flexible and extensible—allowing the system to be tailored to business processes. The power of the component architecture is harnessed through the creation of modules. A module may be a single component or group of components that satisfy a functional need. Modules based upon the component nature of UMP will allow organizations to choose the modules that best meet their needs, whether these are out-of-the-box modules, third-party solutions, or modules developed by the organization internally.

UMP out-of-the-box components will provide leading LMS functionality with optimal flexibility, scalability, and ease of use to facilitate organizational development. As a knowledge platform, this architecture will allow integrated solutions—by taking advantage of existing enterprise services and infrastructure.

Each component will own its own data (independent, self-contained) and business logic and provide a public interface accessible by other components, the user interface (UI), and reports. This public interface provides other components the ability to use the same interface without regard to its internal operations. A new component will be capable of replacing a similar component in the UMP system without affecting the functionality or operation of any other component. Because the new component supports the same interface as the component being replaced, all other system components continue to work seamlessly and flawlessly.

Component architecture will be the foundation of the system's versatility and scalability. Each component will be easily interchanged with any other component that provides similar functionality. Each component will be capable of extending or adding new functionality to the features of another component. New components will have the ability to modify the functionality of other components without changing the original component code—allowing components to be independent and interchangeable.

Localization

The UI and the product itself will be enabled for localization. The UMP database will support multiple languages in a single database, a single UMP system will be used to support the preferred language of a variety of organizational users (French, German, Spanish, and Italian). Regardless of whether the users are learners or administrators, they will each have their UI display in their preferred language while using a single installation of UMP. UMP will support single-byte languages such as French, German, Spanish, and Italian, as well as double-byte languages like Chinese, Japanese, and Korean.

Development Platform

The UMP will also serve as a development platform. The development platform will provide tools for creating a set of components that provide useful functionality to any application. These components will not be LMS-specific and will be used as building blocks for any organizational application. Programmers will develop applications based on UMP components using the UMP software developer's kit (SDK).

Scalability

Instead of having to deploy an entire end-to-end UMP solution all at once, organizations can implement a basic UMP to start and enable other modules, such as skills management, e-commerce, resource management, or ILT as needed. All of these modules are built upon and shared access to the core UMP components. Each component can be upgraded independently of other components, resulting in less downtime, quicker migration to new versions, and less painful upgrades. System upgradability will be dynamic and painless.

User Interface

The UMP UI layer will use HTML, XML, or similar programming language. This will create browser independence as well as a true "thin" client operation, requiring no plug-ins or downloads. The UI will be simple, intuitive, and designed using scientific human factors principles including customer research and usability studies. The UI content will be presented based on the user's role in the system. A user will be presented with only the tasks they have access rights to perform.

All text will be fully customizable. Organizations will be able to easily change various common strings to match the terminology of their organization. For example, in some enterprise settings, a learner may be referred to as an "employee" while other organizations may use "student" instead. Either way, each organization will be able to easily customize the interface.

Another flexible aspect of the UMP interface will be the simple customization of the interface's look and feel (re-branding). By using industry standard style sheets, an organization will easily customize colors, fonts, and other visual styles through editing the UMP style sheet template. Finally, UMP will use text strings rather than bitmap images in all of its graphical navigation aids, such as tabs and buttons. Because of this design, UMP will be both flexible and extensible, allowing for the system to be truly tailored to business processes. The power of the component architecture is harnessed through the creation of modules. A module may be a single component or group of components that satisfy a functional need. Modules based upon the component nature of UMP allow organizations to choose the modules that best meet their needs, whether these are third-party solutions or internally developed modules (developed by the organization using the UMP SDK).

Transitioning to a UMP

As organizations make the transition from old economy to the new knowledge economy, they will begin to recognize the imminent need for an organizational LMS that will provide an integrated, scalable learning technology platform. Future organizations will be valued according to their ability to learn, adapt, and react.

In the near future, everything in the organization will focus on the management of knowledge, learning, and training. For this reason, the LMS platform will evolve to manage all organizational processes and activities. The LMS and LCMS will become UMP. The universal management platform cometh.

RESOURCES

Readings

Horton, William (2001). *Evaluating E-Learning*. Alexandria, VA: American Society for Training and Development.
Mantyla, Karen (2001). *Blending E-Learning*. Alexandria, VA: American Society for Training and Development.
Rosenberg, Marc J. (2000). *E-Learning: Strategies for Delivering Knowledge in the Digital Age*. New York: McGraw-Hill Professional Publishing.

Websites

www.astd.org
www.brandon-hall.net
www.elearningjournal.com
www.elearningmag.com

www.elearningpost.com
www.elearnmag.com
www.internettime.com

Proposed E-Learning Standard Bodies

www.adlnet.org
www.aicc.org
www.ieee.org

www.imsproject.org
www.microsoft.com/elearn/
www.scorm.org

➤ABOUT THE AUTHOR

Bray J. Brockbank is a marketing, business, and technology integrations consultant. Bray has over 11 years extensive experience in enterprise consulting, management, strategy, technology integrations, organizational development, sales, and marketing. He's also worked in the software, biotechnology, pharmaceutical, educational, financial, and automotive industries. He has written several authoritative articles and papers on e-learning, business, technology, trends, strategy, and leadership development. He is happily married to a beautiful wife with three children. He can be reached by e-mail at *elearningconsultant@yahoo.com*.

CHAPTER 10

DISCUSSION GROUPS AND CHAT: ELECTRONIC TOOLS FOR BUILDING ONLINE COMMUNITIES

➤SAUNDRA WALL WILLIAMS

Communities can be characterized by common interests, frequent interaction, and shared goals and can be defined as interacting populations of various kinds of individuals in a common location or groups of people with common characteristics or interests living together within a larger society. Although these general definitions of community seem obvious, defining an *online* community has not been as straightforward. The widespread use of e-learning has required practitioners and organizations to investigate forming online communities through the Internet as an approach to learning. Developing an online community is a complex activity. Hence, e-learning practitioners within organizations need a definition of online community that will guide practice. In addition, tools that help to promote collaboration and interactivity within the online community are also a requirement for e-learning activities.

As the demand for e-learning continues to grow, the need for tools and activities that promote collaboration and interactivity among participants will also increase. These should allow for sharing of information, information gathering, collaboration, and interactivity. This chapter reviews the definition of online community and two electronic tools that help to build an online community by promoting interactivity: discussion groups and chat.

QUESTIONS THAT WILL BE DISCUSSED IN THIS CHAPTER:

➤ What is an online community?

➤ What electronic tools can be used to build online communities in e-learning activities?

➤ How can discussion groups and chat foster participation and collaboration in e-learning activities?

WHAT IS AN ONLINE COMMUNITY?

E-learning has been criticized that it can foster a sense of isolation and a loss of informal learning in a social context. The building of an online community is the answer to this criticism. An online community is a group of people who may or may not meet together face to face, and who exchange words and ideas through the mediation of computer bulletin boards, discussion boards, chat rooms, or other electronic network mechanisms. Online communities consists of two major elements. These elements, as in a face-to-face world, work together to form the online community. The first element is *people*. In an online community, people interact socially or perform special roles, such as leading or moderating. Although the people may not see each other physically, they tend to define their roles in the online community. The second element is a common *purpose*. This common purpose could be an interest, need for information exchange, learning, or service that provides a reason for the community.

Building an online community as part of an e-learning activity gives participants the opportunity to interact and feel a part of the overall learning process. The concept of community also empowers the participants to own and take control of the learning process.

ELECTRONIC TOOLS TO BUILD ONLINE COMMUNITIES: DISCUSSION GROUPS AND CHAT

How do you build an online community? There is no single method to establish community on the Web; however, there are some tools to help encourage community and foster interactivity and participation. The most effective method for building an online community in e-learning activities is to utilize tools that foster interaction between people. The most common tools for accomplishing to foster interaction are discussion groups and chat sessions. These tools utilize interaction and communication to build an online community.

The remainder of the chapter will focus on using discussion groups and chat as mechanisms to building online community within e-learning activities.

DISCUSSION GROUPS

Online discussion groups can be a powerful tool in the development of critical thinking, collaboration, and reflection. This type of group interaction allows for unrestrained, comfortable, and flexible participation. Discussion groups provide an opportunity for ongoing electronic conversation among a group of people. This forum allows people to communicate about various topics by posting messages and replies to messages under the heading of a particular topic. In addition, they allow participants to express viewpoints by reading other participants' contributions and building on them.

There are several forms of online group message exchange. Those widely used in e-learning are e-mail lists, bulletin boards, forums, and list servs. Although similar in function, each of these methods can be used as a distinct tool for electronic group conversation. Each of these mechanisms for discussion groups can be effective in creating an online community.

Most discussion group software allows participants to browse through the postings before logging in, and once they feel comfortable they can set up their name and submit their own posts. Figure 10-1 shows the American Society for Training and Development (ASTD) E-Learning Community Discussion Board Welcome page. Welcome pages are typical in discussion groups and they give the participants an introduction to the topic to be discussed. The discussion facilitator or the instructor of the e-learning activities can set up the Welcome page. Figure 10-2 shows an originally posted message from the ASTD e-learning Community Discussion Board. The message gives the poster's name (in this case first name only is used), the date and time of the post, and the original message. Figure 10-3 shows the participants of the discussion who responded to the message, and Figure 10-4 shows the mechanism for additional participation or additions to the online discussion.

The types of online discussion groups shown in Figures 10-1 through 10-4 are taking place on a bulletin board. In this example, a message was posted concerning e-learning and leadership and several responses to the original message have been posted. These types of discussions have gained in popularity and are the central component for online communities. Participating in e-learning discussion groups can provide open online conversational spaces around which participants may form some sense of community over time. This community is important to the interaction and collaboration required in e-learning activities.

Most discussion groups are text-based; however, there are applications that allow the insertion of or linking to images, audio-and video files. More options are being added and increased bandwidth will make these more practical in the future. This is important for e-learning development because the new applications will provide a greater range of tools for expression and communication.

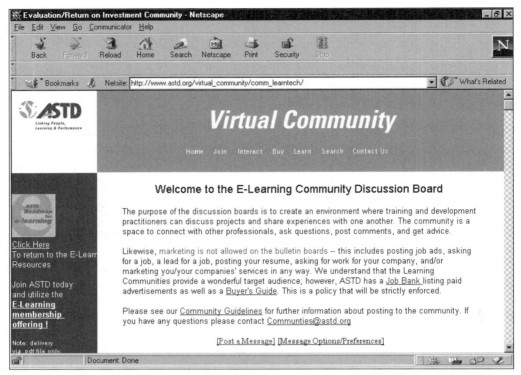

FIGURE 10-1.

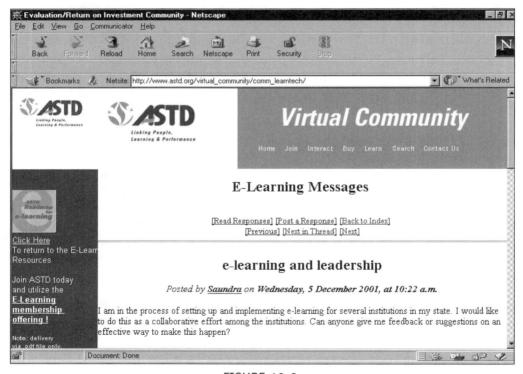

FIGURE 10-2.

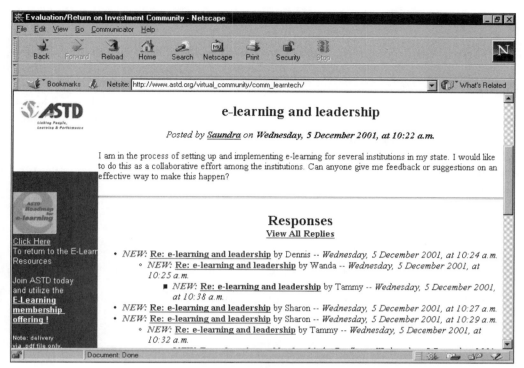

FIGURE 10-3.

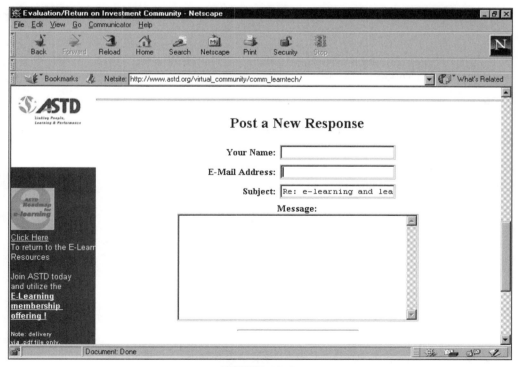

FIGURE 10-4.

Discussion group communication is asynchronous, which means that all participants do not have to be online at the same time. Discussion groups rely on a variety of software applications that provide linear or threaded asynchronous communications capabilities. Linear software presents posts in chronological order and is favored for more conversational and relationship building interactions. Threaded applications allow specific responses to specific posts, splitting off sub-threads as needed, and are often used for distance learning and question and answer applications. Figure 10-3 shows a threaded and a sub-threaded application.

Advantages and Disadvantages of Discussion Groups

There are advantages and limitations to setting up discussion groups in e-learning activities. Regardless of the type of discussion groups on the positive side they:

➤ Allow for the building of relationships over time,

➤ Provide an environment for sharing of ideas,

➤ Can be enhanced with skilled facilitation.

But on the negative side of the coin they:

➤ Can be time consuming,

➤ Are easily open to misinterpretation in the absence of physical cues and feedback (this disadvantage can have major impact for cross-cultural or sensitive discussions), and

➤ Are not attractive to those who have limited reading and writing skills.

The following section reviews the advantages and disadvantages of both threaded and linear discussion groups.

Advantages and Disadvantages of Threaded Discussion

With a threaded system, messages are arranged into topics or "threads". A message will be attached to the message to which it is replying, whether or not it appears in chronological order. Threaded discussion has advantages and disadvantages for use in the e-learning activities.

Advantages

➤ Threaded discussion is good for technical information where people need to be able to find answers to a particular question easily.

➤ Threaded discussion keeps topics neatly organized.

Disadvantages

➤ Threaded discussion can be more organized than the participants. Hence, the participants may lose track of the discussion because it's categorized under the thread from which it originated.

➤ Threaded discussion may be less conducive to social communities.

Advantages and Disadvantages of Linear Discussion

With a linear discussion, each post within a given topic arrives in chronological order. The result is more like a real conversation. Often with a linear system you can read more than one post per HTML page. Linear discussions, sometimes called "conferencing," also offer several advantages and disadvantages.

Advantages

➤ Linear discussions are appropriate for social conversation and in-depth discussion of important issues, particularly in learning activities.

➤ Linear discussions are more conducive to displaying conversation the way people really talk. This is especially important for group work, interactions, and collaboration.

➤ In linear discussions, participants can often see a number of messages on one HTML page.

Disadvantages

➤ Linear discussions are difficult to reach resolution or conclusions.

➤ Linear discussions are difficult to acquire specific reference information if needed for future reference.

➤ Linear discussions can also become confusing if different people want to discuss different topics.

CHAT

Chat rooms bring instant interactivity to e-learning activities. It allows for real time conversations using a low-speed Internet connection. Chat, also referred to as "text-conferencing," allows for simultaneous communication by people who are online at the same time and typing messages to each other. Chat can be done in "public rooms," open to anyone, or "private rooms "where only those of the community (e-learning course) can enter. Chat is not just a social tool, as it can be used for one-to-one meetings, brainstorm sessions, and other work or education-oriented applications. Figure 10-5 shows an example of chat within an ASTD learning community.

Similar to discussion groups, chat can also be an effective tool for online collaboration and learning. Chat can provide an online experience that can be helpful for building social relationships and working on activities in small groups. Chats also bring more anonymity than a discussion group. Participants can come into a chat room, give themselves any name they like, and talk to other people with similar interests. Good chat allows for one person (or more) to act as a moderator so you can have facilitated chats and control the room. Once chat room is set up in an e-learning activity it can be used for a variety of activities, including

➤ regular chat sessions,

➤ informal meetings,

➤ people coming and going as they please to discuss various topics in the course,

➤ protocol and nonprotocol meetings,

➤ informal socializing and "Get to Know" sessions,

➤ question and answer sessions,

➤ guest speakers with audience interaction,

➤ guest speakers with moderated interaction,

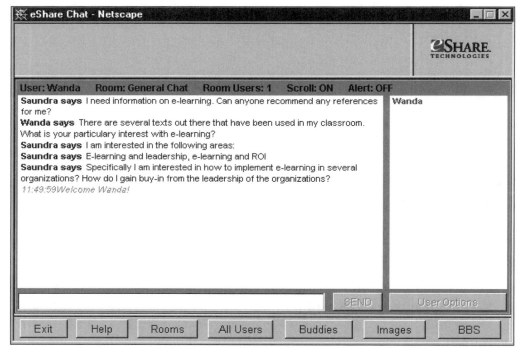

FIGURE 10-5.

> brainstorming, troubleshooting, and problem solving sessions, and

> study group meetings.

Advantages and Disadvantages of Chat

Chat offers some unique online interaction features. It can be a useful teaching tool used in combination with asynchronous discussion groups. Chat is effective for small group meeting where decisions can be made and details arranged. The advantage is that for a very low cost, participants can gather and interact with a small group. The major disadvantage is that participants must be able to select a time where everyone can be online at the same time. This simultaneous activity becomes increasingly difficult as e-learning expands to include global participants. Other advantages and disadvantages of chat include:

Advantages

> Effective for meetings where you want to come to a conclusion with everyone,

> Can have a real-time discussion,

> Can have a guest speaker to answer questions,

> Can log the transcript to be posted later.

Disadvantages

> Difficult to schedule a time if you have users around the globe and

> Sometimes inexperienced chatters have difficulty keeping up with the pace.

TIPS AND HINTS FOR FACILITATING DISCUSSION GROUPS AND CHATS

Discussion groups and chats when used in an e-learning activity will require a moderator/facilitator. The instructor of the e-learning course or a course participant can assume the role of moderator/facilitator. The following strategies will help when moderating/facilitating online discussions or chats.

> Plan the discussion group or chat agenda.

> For chats, ensure there is a good chat host (instructor/facilitator) who can help bring order to a group of people who are talking outside the agenda. Agendas or using clear, focused questions are some approaches to consider.

> The moderator/facilitator must be prepared to deal with silence during the chat.

- ➤ Each person should use people's names to address and respond to their comments so they know you "heard" them.

- ➤ Consider starting the e-learning chat with a practice session. The practice session will give the participants opportunity to become familiar with how the chat will work.

- ➤ Use open-ended questions to initiate thinking and encourage collaboration and interactions among the participants.

- ➤ Clarify meanings of words and phrases through paraphrasing and summarizing.

- ➤ If a participant is "silent," send an individual message to ensure reasons for nonparticipation.

- ➤ Provide prompt, timely and thorough online feedback to questions and assignments.

- ➤ Use online introductions and icebreakers. An example is to allow participants to create personal web pages.

- ➤ Establish ground rules and expectations of participants.

- ➤ Ensure that comments from participants are built on ideas.

- ➤ If someone becomes distractive, distract the participant in private messages via e-mail or instant messages.

- ➤ Involve all participants in the discussion in a positive way. Set rules and standards for good "netiquette" within the discussion groups and chat rooms.

SUMMARY

Although online communities are essential for interaction and collaboration within e-learning activities, building an online community is not a simple task. Discussion groups and chat are tools that enable participants to participate in conversations via an electronic medium, and they also help to develop online communities. This chapter reviewed these two tools as mechanisms for building online communities.

RESOURCES

Readings

Blount, R. (2001). How to build an e-learning community. *E-learning, 2,* 18–23.

Driscoll, M. (1998). *Web-Based Training: Using Technology To Design Adult Learning Experiences.* San Francisco: Jossey-Bass.

Horton, W. (2000). *Designing Web-Based Training.* New York: Wiley.

Lee, W., Owens, D. (2000). *Multimedia-Based Instructional Design.* San Francisco: Jossey Bass.

Palloff, R., and Pratt, K. (1999). *Building Learning Communities in Cyberspace: Effective Strategies for the Online Classroom.* San Francisco: Jossey-Bass.

Rosenberg, M. (2001). *E-Learning: Strategies for Delivering Knowledge in the Digital Age.* New York: McGraw-Hill.

Williams, S., Watkins, K., Daley, B., Courtenay, B., Davis, M., and Dumock, D. (2001). Facilitating cross cultural online discussion groups: Implications for practice. *Journal of Distance Education, 22,* 151–167.

Websites

E-learning (*http://www.elearningmag.com*)

Online Community Resources (http://www.fullcirc.com/commresources.htm)

Online Community Toolkit (http://www.fullcirc.com/community/communitymanual.htm)

Online Learning (http://www.onlinelearningmag.com)

➤ABOUT THE AUTHOR

Saundra Wall Williams, Ed.D. is Vice President of Administration for the North Carolina Community College System. Dr. Williams is responsible for information technology, human resource development, planning, research, program auditing, staff training, and organizational development functions. Dr. Williams is also an Adjunct Research Assistant Professor of Adult and Community College Education at North Carolina University. Her specialty area is training and development. Dr. Williams was also named a Cyril O. Houle Scholar in Adult Education and serves on the editorial board for the *Journal of Workplace Learning.* Previously, Dr. Williams worked for twelve years in business and industry for Nortel, Broadband Technologies, and Syntel. Dr. Williams has an undergraduate and masters degree in Applied Mathematics and an Ed.D. in Adult Education, all from North Carolina State University.

**YOUR E-LEARNING QUESTIONS
ANSWERED BY THIS CHAPTER**

➤ Is e-learning effective for all
levels and types of learners,
particularly those with low
literacy levels?

➤ What are the minimum
technology requirements for
effective e-learning?

➤ Can e-learning be designed so
there is no need for downloads?

➤ What technical or other
problems can be anticipated and
avoided when getting started
with e-learning?

➤ How do I pick the best
e-learning tools, software,
platforms, and so on?

CHAPTER 11

BANDWIDTH BE DAMNED: WHY ONLY LAZY TRAINERS WORRY ABOUT BANDWIDTH ISSUES

➤JOHN HARTNETT

One of the most widespread, pervasive, and downright viral of all e-learning myths is the mistaken idea that bandwidth problems are holding back the quality of e-learning. People say, "Online learning would flourish if only we had more bandwidth. If only we could return to the good-old-days of CD-ROM training using audio that just repeats the onscreen text and video clips of jumpy, stuttering talking heads, then most of our technical problems would go away and e-learning would finally catch on."

The reason for this myth is that most people think that impressive e-learning means big-screen graphics, audio and video content, and big file sizes, which, in turn, means hassling with browser settings and lots of waiting around for pages to download. Much of the time, they're right about the browser setting and the long downloads. But with a little creativity and hard work you can get the large-screen experience learners want and still keep the download times and plug-in hassles to a minimum.

The trick is to *optimize* your graphics and to *design* your training for the web so that your pages look good and work fast.

DESIGN FOR THE WEB

Designing for low bandwidth requires you to make creative choices early in your process that will lead to attention-getting graphics that naturally have small file sizes. To design for low bandwidth, you should:

➤ Use a visual hierarchy to direct the eye

➤ Crop graphics for maximum caching

➤ Don't use a graphic where text will do

➤ Use large areas of web-safe solid colors

➤ Use illustrations instead of photographs

➤ Design for interactivity

Let's take a look at each of these.

Visual Hierarchy

Let's play graphic designer for a moment and talk about how to build a visual hierarchy. By "visual hierarchy" all I mean is that pages should be designed so that the user's eye is drawn to the most important thing on the page first, then the second most important thing and so on. If the most important thing is a start button, we ought to design the page so people are drawn to that button. If the most important thing on the page is a list of the four steps for filling out an online form, the page should draw the eye to that.

There are three ways to draw attention to something—contrast, color, or size. It's not too difficult to imagine how to use contrast to draw the eye. For example, a black dot in the middle of a white page has plenty of contrast, so your eye goes straight to it. Likewise, if everything on your page is a shade of blue and there is an orange button on the page, the button will get the most attention. Contrast and color are features of your design that have no effect on file sizes.

To use size to draw the eye, you just make the featured image a lot bigger than the other images around it. Put a great big round button the size of your fist in the middle of the page and it won't matter too much what color it is or how much contrast it has. Users will still go straight to it.

But using size to draw attention to something has a huge drawback. Graphics that are large on the screen will usually be large on the hard drive as well. Pages designed with large splashy graphics, even when compressed, will usually end up choking the user's modem. The way to get large visual size without large file sizes is to:

➤ Design with large areas of light-colored, web-safe colors that the browser can easily create on the learner's screen for you (sparing the use of real graphic files that have to be downloaded)

➤ Try to tile a small graphic in a frame, background, or layer rather than using a larger graphic to fill a page

➤ Fill HTML table cells or DHTML layers with colored backgrounds rather than graphics

➤ Layer small illustrations over colored backgrounds for a much larger effect

Crop Graphics for Maximum Caching

Another way to build fast pages is to crop your graphics for reuse and maximum browser caching. A cache works by storing the most recently downloaded image and web page files in the memory. When the browser needs to access a web page, it first checks to see if the file is in its cache before downloading it again. Users experience a significant increase in performance if the browser can access the same file from the cache much faster than downloading new files over and over again.

For example, let's say you want to include your company logo at the bottom of your WBT pages. If you use a large version of the logo on your menu pages and a smaller version of the logo on your content pages, you'd have two different graphic files that would each have to be downloaded. No matter how well you optimized them, you'd have twice the graphics you really needed, doubling the download time.

Similarly, if you laid out your pages so that the company logo had a different background in each lesson, you'd get many versions of what is essentially the same graphic. As you're going from design to production, look for ways to use the same-sized graphic with the same file name over and over again. In the case of a logo file, for example, it might be better to make a slightly larger file with a little more white space around the logo, if you could then use that same file on ALL your training pages. This would mean only one download, then the browser would cache that logo and redisplay it instantly on later pages.

Taking advantage of caching is particularly important for user interface graphics. No self-respecting developer would load all new interface graphics for every page. But this trick also works for content graphics. Let's say, for example, you're going to walk the user through the steps for filling out an onscreen form. You could show a screen capture of the form with the first field highlighted in a red box, then show another capture with the next field highlighted, and so on. If you did, you'd end up with four or five different large graphics that all needed to be downloaded.

Instead, crop your content graphic so that the user sees the first screen capture, then display a separate red arrow to the side of the screen capture, pointing at the first field. Then as the student went from step to step in the lesson, you could move the red arrow and point it at the next field, and so on. This way you'd accomplish the same learning objectives, but with only one graphic of the screen capture and one graphic of the red arrow to download.

Don't Use a Graphic Where Text Will Do

On most web pages, over half the graphic files are actually text. The text is set in a graphic file because the designer wanted to be sure the text looked exactly as intended. Until recently, browsers did a terrible job of displaying text. They only understood a few of the most boring fonts and only displayed these fonts in a few of the least useful sizes.

If your learners have 4.0 browsers or better, however, you may have the capability of using style sheets. This means you aren't limited to the four or five standard fonts and sizes of type. Style sheets (actually called Cascading Style Sheets or CSS for short) allow you to assign a font, font size, color, and style to any definition. You might decide, for example, that all top-level headlines (tagged <H1> in HTML) will be displayed as blue Helvetica 18 point bold. Using CSS tags to display your text will greatly reduce the number of graphic files per page.

CSS does have a few disadvantages, though. First, different browsers interpret CSS tags in different ways, so if your learners have lots of different browsers, you may want to avoid CSS. Second, CSS still won't give you the opportunity to track or kern your text so it looks its best. If you're the kind of designer who just can't let "loose text" out into the world, CSS won't help you a bit. Third, in order to display the text accurately, the learner's system must have the font you are calling for in your tag. You'll have to restrict yourself to fonts you KNOW will be on the user's system, otherwise the browser could substitute who knows what for your lovely Goudy. So if you can count on your user's browser and fonts, and your designs can tolerate the common fonts found on most users' systems, CSS can eliminate tons of graphic files. Obviously, if you are designing e-learning for internal employees where you have a lot of control over the configuration of the computers, this is a terrific option.

Use Large Areas of Web-safe Solid Colors

When making your designs, you'll have a lot easier time if you use web-safe colors. Choosing web-safe colors (any of the 216 colors that all browsers on all systems will display exactly the same way) lets you set the browser's background color to match your on-screen graphics. This means you don't have to use graphics everywhere on your page; you can position a graphic over a colored area of the background and no one will be able to tell where the graphic ends and the browser background color begins.

There are many examples of this out on the web. A friend of mine who is also in the design business has a giant letter "Z" surrounded by a circle and two large colored panels as the background of her website. The design takes up the entire screen and is impressive in its size and simplicity. The beauty of the design, though, is that it takes only 3K to splash that screen with color. Another well-known example of this type of design is Lynda Weinman's site. Her site opens with a large illustration of herself (it IS her site, after all) over a bold background color. The color is not a graphic at all, but a color setting for the HTML page, while the image of her that takes up most of the screen is less than 10K.

Use Illustrations Instead of Photographs

If the design of your site depends on the kind of full-screen, sharp photography you see in Nike commercials, no amount of optimization or tricks will save you. You will end up choking your user's modems for sure. But if you could use an *illustration* of a runner on your site, it is relatively easy to compress the image to something manageable. Likewise, if your photography can afford to be a little "artsy," that is, blurry or out-of-focus, you can get away with optimizing a large image down to nearly nothing. On a recent WBT site of mine, I tried to use a very rich collage as background image for a laboratory safety training course aimed at college students. The image was gorgeous (deep-blue beaker superimposed over acid crystals and a periodic chart), but took up a whopping 70K all by itself. I was lucky in that, as a background image, it didn't have to be sharp and clear. I was able to optimize it down to 12K in Fireworks and still live with the effects. The client actually thought the gentle blur in the background was intentional.

Design for Interactivity

Designing for interactivity is probably the easiest, least technical, and most efficient way to design training for low-bandwidth environments. Designing for interactivity means focusing your instructional design on how people interact with the content, rather than on the multimedia mania that pervaded the CD-ROM era.

Let's say you have to train your users to recognize the four parts of a URL. (URLs are the web addresses of most web pages.) You could present a short animation or video clip that highlighted each part of the URL. ("HTTP:// stands for Hypertext Transfer Protocol. This begins all web URLs . . . "). The animation or video, even if streamed, would probably take a couple of hundred kilobytes. On the other hand you could design an interaction where users have to assemble a URL out of each piece. Let's say your users have to drag each section of a standard URL in the right order into the address section of a browser window. Learning takes place as users discover on their own that the http:// only fits at the beginning of the URL, the .com only fits at the end, and so on. The result is a low-bandwidth page that is more effective than its high-bandwidth alternatives.

Highly interactive instructional design is not a low-bandwidth compromise that has been imposed on trainers. It is a better way to design e-learning that just happens to require less bandwidth.

Design alone, however, will not get you to the "lowest" level of low bandwidth design. You must also optimize your graphics for your learner's environment.

COMPRESSION VERSUS OPTIMIZATION

To understand optimization, you first have to understand compression. Graphics purists will point out that there is a difference between compressing an image file and optimizing it. That's because saving an image in one of the common web formats compresses it automatically, but doesn't optimize it.

All the web file formats take advantage of the fact that describing an image with a formula is much more efficient than describing it one pixel at a time. Think of it as the difference between defining an image of a blue square as "a 200-by-200 grid of blue pixels" rather than defining it as "one blue pixel, one blue pixel, one blue pixel," and so on. A bitmap image (like a Windows .bmp file, for example,) describes itself one pixel at a time. It is an uncompressed file format. Just saving your usual bitmap image in one of the common web file formats alone will compress it by 50 percent or more.

Different web file formats use different formulas to compress the information required to recreate the image. Each has its own advantages and disadvantages.

For photographs, you should almost always use JPGs. JPGs can support millions of colors in a single image. The other advantage of JPGs is that they are really good at compressing images with gradations. The main disadvantage of JPG compression is that it is a *lossy* compression format. This means you lose a little information when you save an image as a JPEG file.

For artwork and illustrations, you should almost always use GIFs. GIFs are limited to 256 colors, which is usually enough for flat art, but not for photography. GIF compression is *lossless*, meaning it doesn't lose any information during compression. The trick to optimizing GIFs is to choose as few colors as you can live with. Flat-color buttons and artwork can often be reduced to less than 32 colors and still look good.

The newest web file format is the PNG (pronounced "ping"). PNG is the least-used compression format, mainly because it's the newest, and browser support for it has been inconsistent. The advantage of the PNG is that it can support millions of colors, like a JPEG, but it's also lossless, like a GIF. PNGs can also store information to help them compensate for the brightness of different displays in different operating systems. The problem with PNGs is that not all browsers support them properly.

Saving your images in one of the web file formats compresses them automatically. So anyone making e-learning for the web is already compressing their graphics. But to design for low-bandwidth you must optimize your images as well. This is the step most lazy designers skip.

Optimizing your graphics is an easy, painless process if you have the right tools for the job. The right tools, in my opinion, are Macromedia's Fireworks or Adobe's ImageReady. If you design your training interfaces or content graphics in Adobe Photoshop or any of the other "standard" design or graphics programs, you'll usually end up with relatively huge file sizes. Even though Photoshop has a special setting allowing you to save an image for the web, when you export an image from

Photoshop and save it as a GIF or JPG, you'll always get a bigger file than if you use a program designed for the web.

Both Fireworks and ImageReady work pretty much the same. I have and use both, but I'm slightly more familiar with Fireworks, so I'll talk about it for now.

To optimize an image using Fireworks:

➤ First, open the image you have created in whatever software in Fireworks. The program can open Photoshop files directly, saving you the trouble of saving your designs as GIFs or JPGs. Fireworks and ImageReady will also open most other graphic formats as well.

➤ Choose File, Export Preview to open the Export window. In the old days of web graphics design, you had to export a GIF out of Photoshop, open a web browser, and look at your file to see how ugly it was. With Fireworks, the Export window lets you experiment with different settings and see the file size and what the file will look like ahead of time. This way you can try using different color palettes, fewer colors, different file formats, dithering, and optimization and see what the file will look like in the browser window and how big it will be when you export it.

➤ Use GIFs with adaptive palettes. For illustrations and artwork, your best file size/image quality combination will usually be a GIF with an adaptive palette and the minimum number of colors you can live with before the image starts to look bad. Dithering usually makes things worse, so I recommend against it.

➤ Use JPGs reduced to 30 to 70 percent of their original size. For photographs or images with gradations of color, your best file size/image quality combination will usually be a JPG with a quality setting between 30 to 70 percent. Most of the images I've tried at 70 percent look nearly identical to 100 percent, so your only limit here is when the image starts to look blocky or grainy. If you're like me, you'll be amazed at how much smaller a JPG of 30 percent quality will download.

➤ Save your file. There are many more options for slicing images, exporting HTML, creating automatic rollover tables, and the like. For now, we'll concentrate on the images and their file sizes.

What are we shooting for in file size? My rule of thumb is that no single graphic should be larger than 12K and no page should contain more than 60K total for all images. Sound impossible? Using optimization and good design, I've delivered over a dozen highly interactive, visually rich courses in the last year that fit on a single floppy disc. Most of my buttons are 1K. Most of my headline graphics are 1K each.

I'll let you in on two optimization secrets that will save you a lot of time. First, in case it isn't obvious, you would save yourself a lot of time and trouble optimizing graphics if you designed your pages in Fireworks or ImageReady from the beginning. Get rid of Photoshop or Illustrator or any other graphic dinosaur that is made for print work, and choose a tool that is made for the web.

Second, remember that graphics that overlay must use the exact same optimization settings. Say for example you have a button that lies over a colored background. Say also that for whatever reason, you decide that the image of the button contains a few pixels of the background. The user has no idea where one image ends and the other begins. But if the two images are optimized using different settings, there will be small differences between the background color in the button image and the background color in the image that lies behind it. The color may be off by just a little bit so that you end up seeing the edge of the button. If both the button and the background are optimized using the same settings, all the colors will be identical.

Optimizing graphics and designing properly for the web can transform just about any bloated WBT program into an elegant online experience regardless of the infrastructure. It's not a lack of bandwidth that is holding back e-learning. It's a lack of effort and imagination.

RESOURCES

Readings

Siegel, David. *Secrets of Successful Web Sites : Project Management on the World Wide Web.* Indianapolis, IN: Hayden Books.

Website

Online Learning magazine (www.onlinelearningmag.com).

➤ABOUT THE AUTHOR

John Hartnett is President and CEO of BlueMissile, a Minneapolis-based e-learning design and development company. He is an internationally known expert in the field of web-based training design and teaches many web and e-learning classes and seminars for companies and organizations all over the world.

As Technology Editor for *Online Learning* magazine, he writes the popular monthly column, "Nuts and Bolts." John's book, *Making and Managing Online Learning* will be available soon from Stylus Publishing.

Recently, he was Master of Ceremonies at the Influent Technologies *WBT Producer's Conference 2001* and a Keynote Panelist at *Online Learning 2001.* He was also a Featured Presenter at *Training 2002* in Atlanta and a judge for *Inc. Magazine's* annual Web Awards.

CHAPTER 12

WEBCASTING

➤**MIKE FINK**

INTRODUCTION

In the short time since the "e" was attached to "learning", e-learning
has evolved from simple online textbooks to complex content delivered via a variety of enhanced media with interactive capabilities. A
new vocabulary to describe these developments has evolved (and
continues to evolve). The latest catch-all phrase for updated and upgraded delivery of content is rich media. Rich media encompasses
graphics and effects, computer-generated animation, and highly sophisticated audio/video. It is accessible to PCs through the intranet
or internet via Webcasting. Rich media also includes a variety of
methods for real-time communication and interactivity between
teacher and student—no matter where they are located across the
globe.

It wasn't until technology advancements increased the capacity or bandwidth of the IT infrastructure and the Internet itself, that rich media could be delivered online. New compression algorithms make video more accessible and have greatly improved the picture and sound quality. Content developers are applying the latest technology to time-tested principles of instructional design to create a new standard in effective education. Retention rates are significantly improved when the learner is presented with both audio and visual stimuli—the higher the quality, the better the retention. Mirroring the dynamics and interactivity of an instructor-led class, e-learning involves the learner, stimulates participation and, ultimately, the thinking that goes with true understanding.

These developments in rich media place an added responsibility on the educator. Content alone will not carry the educational process; *how* it is delivered is quickly becoming as critical as *what* is delivered. In addition to creating the most effective content and instructional design, the development team now must think in terms of the accompanying media and, to some degree, function as producers, directors, and visual designers. Becoming a full-fledged media specialist is not required, but content developers must master the media's basic concepts, language, and hierarchy of tasks in order to communicate with the team that is doing the actual production. It is important to remember that content is still king and the slickest online production will not compensate for poor teaching.

TECHNICAL CONSIDERATIONS

Online delivery of educational materials is a collaborative effort. The technical considerations for the deployment of e-learning initiatives require the expertise and knowledge of a diverse team. Although Education and Professional Development departments often spearhead the initiatives, cooperation and participation is needed from internal and external sources including IT, production experts, developers, and Human Resources in order to coordinate and integrate new and existing technology with content and the requirements of production.

Technical considerations encompass IT infrastructure, new and existing software, and the equipment required for producing a program. The bottom line is to think in terms of what is possible in the organization's environment while maintaining the highest degree of quality. No matter what the content, the audience is composed of highly sophisticated television viewers. They are used to network quality production and crisp, clean picture. Although users are often fascinated with new technology, they tire quickly of poor quality Internet broadcasts of low visual interest.

Be Sure That Your IT Infrastructure Can Handle Your E-Learning Initiative

Before you creating the e-learning program, however, you must consider the technical aspects for the delivery of the final program over the Internet/intranet. Collaborate with the technology team to review the existing technology infrastructure including the organization's array of software, hardware, and tools that are loaded onto PCs and the network. In this way, you will be able to assess the total capability of the system and determine what media can be effectively delivered through that system and, most importantly, how the program should be written and designed. An inventory of the organization's IT capabilities must go into the planning of any script. For example, a program that uses an audio track will not work on a PC that doesn't have a sound card.

When evaluating technology for eLearning initiatives, always consider how that technology will integrate with the existing infrastructure and how it will interact with or replace legacy systems. Many large companies have deployed enterprise software like SAP and PeopleSoft for their HR functions. The technology purchased for a Learning Management System (LMS) must therefore have the capability of sending and receiving data from these systems.

Software for Webcasting

There are many software products on the market that allow you to "broadcast" or Webcast audio and video over an intra- or Internet infrastructure.

Most video sources must be converted to an MPEG format for distribution. MPEG is a compression format that permits streaming video Webcasting that requires less bandwidth than uncompressed video files. The conversion process is usually performed by IT or an outside supplier.

You can Webcast audio and video in either a synchronous or asynchronous learning event. Synchronous transmission is a live event that takes place in real time. It can be one way—from the presenter directly to the user—or it can be interactive. Asynchronous transmissions are prerecorded and available to the user on demand. These prerecorded events can also be programmed to include various types of user interaction. Often, a synchronous learning event is recorded and made available on demand for review or for a larger audience. This process broadens the potential reach of the event and lowers the development and broadcast costs when calculated on a per-user basis.

Leverage Underused Equipment Already In-House

E-learning initiatives can often leverage technology brought into companies for other business purposes. By repurposing technology, costs can be spread over several departments. Using this concept and investigating technology that has already been deployed, the Education and Professional Development Department eliminates the need to purchase some software and the need to alter or add to the existing IT infrastructure Video conferencing software is a prime example of this. One global Financial Services company invested significant budget dollars in an extremely high quality video network for morning analyst meetings. Although the system was also used for video conferencing, this hardware/software combination was underutilized for a portion of the day. When the education department began using the system for both synchronous and asynchronous course delivery, IT, the business units, and education all benefited. Costs were amortized over several departments and the investment produced additional tangible gains for the company.

Invest in Quality Production Equipment

The quality of the video and audio equipment used for Internet production is the most overlooked aspect of technology involved with producing e-learning. Companies invest millions in hardware and software to insure a complete solution for their e-learning needs and then produce video segments with a home video camera or an inexpensive desktop camera. Certainly you don't need full broadcast quality equipment, but you should use high-end industrial cameras and the finest audio equipment that your budget cab allow for. High quality, high-resolution digital cameras are available at modest cost ($ 3,000 to $ 5,000 range). Their use will enhance the look and feel of any education module, and even with signal disintegration that is normal over the net, they will produce a solid picture acceptable to a sophisticated user.

High-quality audio equipment is also essential for both video and audio only Webcasts. If internal departments are going to produce synchronous education Webcasts or virtual classroom productions, audio quality is critical. You should use a mix of directional microphones, lavalier microphones, and radio frequency (RF) mikes available to cover all possible situations. It is also a good idea to own a small audio mixer to control sound when more than one microphone is in use during a production. As is true with video signals over the net, audio quality disintegrates when it is transmitted and that is compounded by small, low-quality speakers at the desktop.

Adopt Technical Standards for Better Content Management

There has been a significant movement towards the adoption of technical standards for content management. Both content developers and corporations are adopting these standards. SCORM (Sharable Courseware Object Reference Model) and IMS (Instructional Management System) are the most widely accepted content standards systems. These systems enable content to be broken down into smaller units, called Learning Objects, that can be strung together into a customized course or accessed individually by the learner. Content Management Systems (CMS) control the distribution of learning objects. Deploying CMSs and the adoption of these standards have increased the use of rich media segments within courseware. Educators and developers are inserting video and audio files into courseware to enhance the presentation of content and to stimulate interest of learners. Rich media segments wrapped as Learning Objects place less strain on bandwidth and infrastructure while enriching the educational experience of the learner. Adopting Content Management Standards will impact the instructional design, development, and creative processes.

WEBCASTING—THE PROCESS

A number of common formats and types are available for Webcasts including:

- ➤ Audio used with a series of timed graphic screens
- ➤ Audio linked to PowerPoint slides
- ➤ Conference calls employing online graphics and/or PowerPoint
- ➤ Video window over static or changing graphics
- ➤ Full-screen video
- ➤ Virtual Classroom

Audio used with a series of timed graphic screens. This is a relatively simple Webcast format. Graphics are created and strung together in a sequence and timed to sync up with the audio. Animated screens can be included in this format. In this way, the audio and the visuals are linked for simultaneous Webcast.

Audio Linked to PowerPoint Slides. PowerPoint can be used as the graphic generator and "synced" to prerecorded audio in the same way as timed graphics. PowerPoint has this capability built in and is easily activated for either presentation or Webcasts.

Conference calls using online graphics and/or PowerPoint in a similar way. The audio in this format is usually live and the graphics may either be pre-timed or manually changed during the Webcast. These Webcasts often include one or more Question and Answer segments in which the presenter interacts with the audience.

Video window over static or changing graphics. This format divides the real estate of the screen between a live or pretaped video sequence and preselected graphics. The video usually appears within a frame or window and occupies a relatively small portion of the screen. This common format requires little bandwidth and is reasonably flexible in look and feel and can even be personalized to meet corporate logo standards.

Full screen video. This is rarely available within corporations because it requires either enormous bandwidth or a costly virtual private network. This format comes closest to broadcast-quality Webcasting. Some full-screen video software packages combine this capability with video conference and split screen options and are used for a variety of Webcast events.

The Virtual Classroom format. This format is a live, synchronous presentation using software packages that usually split the screen real estate into at least four separate components. There is a window for the live instructor, one for graphics, one for the class register, and one for either live interaction or e-mail/chat functions. This format attempts to simulate an instructor-led classroom experience. The Virtual Classroom is the most robust webcasting format with software packages that typically include the ability to display prerecorded video and audio.

In each of these formats the design of the graphics and/or PowerPoint slides is critical. Most PowerPoint presentations do not transfer well to either video or Webcast formats. With too much text and too many lines of copy, they are generally too "busy" to be readable. PowerPoint graphic illustrations are generally not bold enough to be effective. It is always best to keep graphics simple and the text fonts consistent and highly readable. Keep text to a minimum so it doesn't compete with what the learner is listening to and viewing.

The Benefits of Webcasting

➤ Gets a message out simultaneously to a large, diverse population.

➤ Effective both for scheduled courseware and for getting information out when speed to market counts.

➤ Formats can also be recorded for asynchronous delivery and/or archived within most IT infrastructures for on-demand use.

➤ Requires sound instructional design.

➤ Can also be part of blended learning solutions.

A blended learning solution generally combines online delivery of content with instructor led sessions. The blended learning approach shortens the length of the instructor-led sessions by delivering either prework online or providing access to base knowledge that is required for increased productivity in live sessions. Blended learning solutions are economically beneficial because they combine inexpensive content delivery which permit shorter instructor-led programs and less expenditure for travel and expenses.

MARKETING THE PROGRAM

How the program is announced and marketed is an important part of the planning process. The best program in the world will mean nothing if no one knows when and where it's playing, or it doesn't create enough interest for people to sign up. All announcement and sign-up information sent to potential participants must be accurate and thoroughly checked before distribution. One company did a fabulous job of building interest in a Webcast event designed to train employees on a new product line. This training was of significant importance and value to both the employees and the company. After the buildup, a final e-mail announcement was sent which posted an incorrect telephone number for dial in access. Disaster is a mild description for the outcome. "The devil is in the details." That cliché is true for all aspects of Webcast production.

PREPRODUCTION, PRODUCTION AND POSTPRODUCTION

Education and Professional Development Departments are typically the producers of educational Webcasts. In some cases, an internal production team will do the hands-on production. In other situations, the departmental team functions as "the client," with responsibility for coordinating and approving production elements provided by an outside supplier. In either capacity, the producers must understand the three basic phases of production: Preproduction, production, and postproduction.

Preproduction is the vital planning stage where all of the content and design elements are solidified. Thorough preproduction will insure the success of any program, whether it's "live" or prerecorded for later net-based delivery. Production is broadcast or Webcast of the actual live event or the recording of material for later use. Postproduction is either the editing process and/or the preparation of the Webcast material for asynchronous delivery. Each facet of the production process requires planning and specific skill sets to create a successful education event. Whether serving as the internal producer or the client, the "producer" must be involved in all of the decisions that comprise the production and distribution of the program.

For educators, the process of making a program begins even before the preproduction phase. The purpose and objectives of the training are determined. Once these goals are established, content is reviewed and targeted to the intended audience. To accurately target the needs of the learners, it is important to ask a number of questions about them. What is their educational level? Are there cultural differences that should be addressed? What base line knowledge will they come to the session with? How sophisticated are they and in what kind of environment will they be viewing this program? Will the program require an online assessment or certification? Once these determinations are made, the producer can set a rough timeline, develop a preliminary budget, select the appropriate Webcast format, look at and bid out to outside suppliers, if necessary, or if done in-house, communicate the plan to the appropriate internal staff. Any and all internal clients for the project should be notified of the process and completely involved in the decision-making. Except for the Webcast elements, this is no different than planning any training or education event.

Preproduction

The producer is now ready to gather the Webcast team to create production specifications and a production concept. After a review of the decisions made, a line item document is created to guide either the internal Webcast production process or define the RFP specifications for outside suppliers. This document should be as specific as possible and cover all of the predetermined elements of the project. Review this document with the internal client if there is one as a final "sign off " to this stage of Preproduction.

If the project is going to be fulfilled by an outside supplier, include the appropriate, proscribed legal language and a Non-Disclosure Agreement (NDA) with a Webcast project description into your RFP. Separate the budget categories into the three segments of the project—(1) preproduction, (2) production, and (3) postproduction. It is also a good idea to set up a conference call to answer bidders questions regarding the specifications in the RFP. Include as many specific final delivery dates as possible, such as scheduled date of the Webcast, at the end of the budget section. Allow a reasonable time for supplier response. When you make your selection the quality of the response should be combined with the proposed budget to determine the company awarded the project.

The Creative Approach

Preproduction now moves forward to determine the creative approach. The most abstract and subjective area of the process, the creative approach, is tied to the somewhat nebulous phrase "production value." Production value is what is added to the content to bring it from textbook to media-enhanced programming and involves such creative touches as the look and feel of the program, its theme, and the "hook" by which the audience is drawn to the message. One hard and fast rule: keep the creative approach in line with the prevailing corporate identity, image, and overall culture. When shaping the creative approach, always weigh the cost of any production value against the effect it will have on the program's success for learners. If a proposed creative idea doesn't enhance the learning process, don't use it. Never allow the creative aspects of the program to overshadow the message.

Script and Storyboard

Scriptwriting is the most critical aspect of the preproduction process. The script equals the content. A script can be a word-for-word rendering or it can consist of speaking points. In any case, a detailed outline is critical to insure accuracy and complete coverage of the content—delivered by an "on-air" speaker within the specified time of a video presentation or Webcast. A script isn't simply a spoken textbook; "dialogue" is very different from written language.

Scripts also differ from written text because they include visual material. An effective graphic, picture, or animation can eliminate the need for a detailed description. Allow the visual side of audio/visual to "speak for itself."

How the script is set up and written depends very much on who will deliver it. In broadcast television, "casting" of the "on-air talent" is vital. In educational media, the same is true. Instructors vary widely both in teaching technique, style of delivery, and experience. Some highly skilled instructors have been known to freeze on camera; successful teachers lose their charisma the instant the camera rolls. Since there is sometimes no choice about who will deliver the class, advance preparation is key. How the on-camera talent teaches should be well known before production begins so their individual teaching techniques can be accommodated and/or enhanced.

A script can be written using a number of methods. Again, it depends on the content, how it is delivered and to whom and by whom. Some examples: a scriptwriter can begin at square one, researching content, building an outline, and developing the script. A subject matter expert can develop a script from an existing content outline. A regular instructor-led class can be transcribed, then reshaped into an "on-air" script. In all cases, the script should be written or overseen by a person knowledgeable in audio, video, or Webcast production in order to integrate the audio and visual elements into the final program. Scripting provides a vehicle to unify dialogue, graphics, and shooting design into an integrated format.

Because the audio and the visual portions of a program work together, the script is split into the audio side, which includes dialogue, voice-over, and even music and sound effects, and the visual side, which comprises the video picture, graphics, and/or a description of the action.

A storyboard can be extremely useful in visualizing and designing the program. A storyboard is a series of simple drawings or thumbnail pictures placed next to accompanying dialogue. Storyboards are a particularly valuable tool for people with little Webcast or video production experience. A storyboard template can be found in Appendix 12-A.

Graphics

As a visual medium, Webcasts and video programs depend heavily on graphics. Graphic approach and design must be coordinated with script elements to enhance and/or clarify messages and learning points. Graphics should be designed to introduce and/or reinforce content. They should be designed to add production value and visual interest, but should never be used indiscriminately. Graphics should always have communication and/or educational value; simple and straightforward graphics are the most effective.

Video Webcasts afford the opportunity to utilize dynamic graphic elements by creating builds, reveals, and video animation. **Builds** are text or illustrations that grow on screen as the content is being discussed. A good example of a build is seeing the frame for a car on screen and watching as the wheels, interior, and exterior are added to complete the whole. **Reveals** are usually text that is set up in a linear progression that the viewer sees line by line as the content is described. **Video animation** can be as simple as a logo spinning and growing until it fills the screen or as complex as creating a cartoon character that illustrates a learning point and is seen in full motion.

Graphic design should be consistent within a program and aligned with corporate standards, including logo placement, font, and type size. Corporate branding requirements should always be a part of the approach and graphic designers should receive a package illustrating these requirements. Most companies have a logo standards guide that is supplied to all internal and external producers. It is important to remember that PowerPoint slides must be redesigned and reformatted for Webcasting and video. If all of the information on a PowerPoint slide is necessary to highlight a message, the slide usually must be redesigned as a build, a reveal, or broken into a series of slides.

Reviewing the production Plan and Scheduling

Before moving forward with the production process, all script and production elements developed so far should be reexamined to make certain that the concept and the planned Webcast format will fulfill the goals of the program. It is easy to "fall in love" with a creative idea and production concept and ignore the potential effectiveness for the learner in terms of retention and communication. This is a milestone for the Producer and client to agree on all key factors in the planning process. The process now changes from concept and planning to production and reality.

A time line is a essential part of this review. You must be sure that the production concept is doable within the allotted times specified for each aspect of production and that the Webcast/delivery dates are realistic.

If you have chosen to use an outside supplier, RFP responses should now be in-house. Choose the supplier that best fulfills all of the elements of the Webcast production concept. Suppliers should not be chosen on price alone. Creativity, alignment with production concept, and past performance should be considered along with price. It is not unusual for the Producer and client to use an RFP response as a starting point for production—not a final process document. The chosen supplier generally has not been involved in every aspect of the preproduction process and will need guidance to understand and implement the Webcast concept.

Team Meetings

The process moves forward with a creative concept/preproduction meeting with the entire team. This meeting sets the stage for production. It should include any of the following people:

- ➤ Internal Client
- ➤ Producer
- ➤ Director
- ➤ Scriptwriter
- ➤ Graphic Designer
- ➤ Production Manager or Supplier contact
- ➤ On-camera presenter (if internal)

If you are planning complex video segment(s), the meeting may also include the set designer, lighting designer, camera operator, and video editor.

All aspects of the Webcast production should be discussed at this meeting and a common understanding of the education/training objectives and the look and feel of the program agreed upon. Define responsibilities for the duration of the production process and assign action items for accomplishing preproduction elements. Establish communication channels and sign-off responsibilities.

Choosing a Location or Studio

For economy and realism, corporate Webcasts with on-camera presenters and video productions are often shot on location rather than in a studio. The location can be as simple as an office or classroom or as complex as a manufacturing facility or the trading floor of a financial institution. In every instance, the location must be "scouted" to make certain it meets production requirements such as Internet access, sound quality, low ambient noise levels, and adequate electricity. Plans can also be made for the placement of the camera, lighting, proposed entrances and exits, and so on. This should be done even when the location is familiar—for example an often-used classroom—because the room will look quite different through the selective eye of a camera lens.

Plans for additional props or set dressing to make a bland room more visually interesting can be made as well. If the producer and/or client cannot personally visit the location, photos should be presented to them for approval. Too often the description of an ideal location and the reality do not match. This physical inspection process eliminates surprises on the day of the production or Webcast.

If a professional, external production facility/studio is required for prerecorded video segments, it too should be visited to determine whether it is adequate for the production design. The studio should provide camera and lighting equipment, along with facilities for handling the production team and the on-camera talent. An inventory of equipment can be checked and, if needed, additional equipment can be ordered. It is also a good idea to go to the studio to accurately gauge travel time for the Webcast team, cast, and crew. It is inefficient to use a facility that requires the on-camera talent to travel for several hours before beginning a difficult day. By checking the studio in advance, adjustments can be made that eliminate potential problems on the days of the shoot.

Casting

The first casting decision is whether the Webcast or video requires a professional actor or an internal subject matter expert. The selection of the presenter/talent for education Webcast events is often predetermined. In this setting, the person most qualified to be the presenter is the instructor or the subject matter expert. However, the services of professional actors are sometimes required.

Professional actors are trained to play a variety of roles, so it must be determined what physical attributes are required for the role as well as the desired voice quality. The best process for choosing a professional is to videotape an audition session in which several actors read on-camera from the actual script. Pictures and resumes can be deceptive—even experienced directors can be fooled by a good glossy photo and an impressive list of credits. It is important to meet the actors and watch them in action—for example, how they take direction and how they move. This is a delicate process and should be done with great care. Brilliant planning combined with a brilliant production design will not insure success if the wrong on-camera talent is selected. When possible, these same criteria should be applied to an internal on-camera talent. If there is no choice regarding the internal on-camera talent, this process permits planning strategies that will overcome any shortcomings.

Rehearsal

Another area that is most often neglected in corporate Webcast and video production is rehearsal. Rehearsal of professional and amateur on-camera presenters is essential. Rehearsal allows the producer or director to improve performance and fulfill the production concept. It gives the on-camera presenter more confidence in the presentation and a greater command of the script. This confidence will show on the final Webcast or video. Even seasoned professionals rehearse before ever going in front of the unforgiving eye of the camera. This is an inexpensive way to insure greater quality in performance. One technique that is particularly helpful with amateur on-camera talent is to tape a rehearsal (home video quality), review the tape with the talent, and devise a plan to maximize strengths and minimize weaknesses in presentation.

Wardrobe

Select the presenter's wardrobe and test it on camera before you shoot or go live. Colors and patterns often have a different look on camera. The lower the resolution of the camera, the more critical wardrobe choices are. Always avoid tight patterns (herringbone, small checks) and overly bright colors. If at all possible, see the presenter wearing the clothing on set and on camera to evaluate the overall look. Several outfits should be available to select the best on-camera choice. Wardrobe projects corporate image and the tone of the program. Keep the wardrobe selection consistent with the content, the corporate culture, and the corporate image. Many internal education programs are shared with external clients and you want the proper image to be projected.

Final Preparations: Check/Recheck

The final point-by-point review includes review of the completed script or speaker notes. During this last review before production: check for accuracy of the content, the flow of information, and the overall timing of the program. Perform this process again if any changes are required after this review.

Evaluate the process to this point to make certain the anticipated milestones have been reached, the project is still on schedule, and the delivery dates are not jeopardized.

With the preproduction process completed, the real challenges begin to unfold. Whether you are shooting video segments or going live with a Webcast, there are important responsibilities and checks to be made before the "live" action begins. Either on location or in the studio, check to see that all of the details are consistent with the production design and plan. Look at the room, set, staging area, props, and set dressing using the video camera and the TV monitor. Now is the time to make any adjustments necessary in the look and feel of the set and what the viewer will see. Always check these details after lighting has been completed.

Members of the team should check graphics for design and accuracy and against the script for approximate timing. This is less critical if the graphics are going to be edited into a prerecorded video segment of the program in postproduction. If they are going to be a part of the live Webcast or "cut" in live, they must be perfect at this point in the process.

Graphics

Whether you are producing a live Webcast or shooting video segments, graphic material is usually prepared as a separate unit. For live Webcasts the graphics are either rolled into the program or preset within the software package being used. There is generally a window or portion of the screen real estate set aside for PowerPoint and graphics.

Production

Makeup and Hair

If the presenter appears on camera, some makeup is usually required. Even if the makeup is only a light powder to eliminate the skin's natural shine, makeup must be seen under lights (if you are using them) and checked on camera. For video, the type of lighting instruments and color gels used will change the color of makeup and the look of the presenter. For multiple Webcasts or several days of shooting video, this should be done every day prior to going live or rolling tape. Makeup can compensate for normal changes in skin tone from day to day caused, for example, by the presenter being tired or having been out in the sun. This is especially true for video as you want to create a consistent look, because the final edit may be a combination of sequences from different shooting days.

Before Going "Live"

The producer and the client should be on-location at the Webcast shoot to observe the entire process. Whether the program is a live Webcast or is being shot for later delivery, the client, producer, or producer's representative should be present during the entire production process. A video shoot is a very complex and busy operation and someone with authority and objectivity is needed to keep the process running and on target. Even in the case of a video shot for asynchronous delivery, the notes taken during live presentations can impact the editing of the taped version. For example, the program may need to be shortened for later delivery, or certain time and date references may need to be eliminated.

The Shoot

When you are doing a live Webcast, what you see is what you get. In a video shoot, you have the ability to reshoot sequences to improve the presentation or to correct mistakes. When it appears that a video sequence is good and it is "a take" or approved, review the tape to double-check it for quality and technical problems, and to recheck that what was seen live actually appears on the tape. It is not unusual to feel that a sequence is "perfect" and then review the tape to find a key word has been left out or that the presenter has stumbled on a key point. This on-set double-check avoids problems and expense in postproduction. Even after a careful preproduction review process, minor dialog changes may be required on the set. These usually become apparent when reviewing selected takes. The Producer and the presenter can usually rectify the problem quickly on the set with a minor word change or minor rewrite. Sometimes this occurs because the presenter cannot read a particular line(s) comfortably; a small change can smooth the delivery.

At the end of each production day, review the progress of the shoot. Try to anticipate schedule changes, the need for a longer shooting day to make up lost ground, and so on. If this is done daily, there are no surprises and, if necessary, additional shooting schedules can be set and locked in for talent, studio, and crew.

If you have recorded a live Webcast for later on-demand viewing, carefully review the tape to make sure it does not require editing and that it meets the standard you have set for the program.

Postproduction

If you have shot video segments, have the studio or supplier transfer all camera master tapes to VHS cassettes with visible time code. The time code (SMPTE) is a digital read out of the hours, minutes, seconds, and frames that measure the tape footage. Visual time code looks like this and can be superimposed over a live picture:

01:22:56:24

It appears on the screen and serves as an edit reference and computer editing cue point. Sometimes it is desirable to produce cassettes with only the selected takes. This cuts the viewing time and still provides a visual reference to the camera masters for additional needed footage. When you receive the time coded cassettes, you are ready to begin the pre-edit. This process sets the stage for the on-line edit. A "paper edit" is the end product of this viewing of the footage. A paper edit is a timed, sequential layout for the editor. During this review the producer and the client determine the order of the content—which scenes are used in the final edit and the placement of all graphic and animation material. Unless a timing point is critical, editing notes need not be calculated to the frame—the second is close enough for the editor. A template should be used for these editing notes that identify the time code and the visual or word cue. Voice-over segments should also be noted in this review. The more precise these notes are, the less confusion the editor will have cutting the final product. Careful and accurate pre-edit notes insure less time in the on-line edit suite and can have a positive impact or the budget.

The supplier/editor should be able to construct a rough assembly and/or a rough cut from the pre-edit notes. The viewing copy of the assembly/rough cut should also be produced with visual time code for reference. This cut should contain all chosen footage in proper sequence and indicate all graphic sequences precisely where they will appear in the final product. A review of the rough cut should concentrate on sequence and content. Notes to the editor should include any sequence, "take," and placement changes.

Music

Many education and corporate videos use music at the opening and closing of the program to project the image of the company and feel of the program. Be careful with the addition of music for web-delivered programs, as you are likely to stretch the bandwidth of your infrastructure with too much digital information when you combine video, voice, and music. If you have the bandwidth capability, music may be used as a bed (background) to enhance production value and help the pace of the program. This is the responsibility of the sound editor but requires approval from the producer and the client for both the type of music, placement, and mix.

Graphics

For video segments, complex graphics are often created as a separate reel. These graphic sequences are cut into the program during the final on-line edit. Before the on-line edit, these graphics should be reviewed and approved. The graphics that are to be created during the final edit should be committed to paper or electronic media at this point and checked for accuracy and placement. All on-line edit suites have electronic character generators that can be used to add text or change a pre-planned graphic. One reason to have graphics created before the on-line edit is budget. The preparation of the graphics reel is generally charged at a much lower rate than the studio charges for on-line editing.

Editing

With all of the prework executed for the on-line edit of video sequences, the program is now in the hands of the video editor. Either the producer or the client should be present at the edit or arrange for segments to be viewed as they are completed. Often in the final edit layers of video are built into sequences to achieve proper timing, sound, and/or graphic effects. It is costly to move ahead with the on-line edit without sequenced approvals either on site or soon after video segments are completed. If the producer and/or client are present at the edit, these approvals are done in real time and the final product needs only a cursory review. If the approvals are to be given after segments are cut, a time-coded cassette should be provided if reference points are necessary for fixes in the final cut. Whenever possible, be at the final on-line edit for input and budget controls.

Once the on-line edit is completed, screen the final product very carefully. This is a necessary review to make sure that all changes have been made and/or the final composite cut reflects the approved program. It is also a necessary quality control viewing to check the audio mix, tape master quality, and all visual elements. When this cut is approved, the video segments are ready for inclusion in a web-based learning program. The studio or a programmer should meta tag the video segments as separate learning objects. This process permits them to be reused easily, called up by a learner through a knowledge management search engine, and keeps the size of your on-line course manageable. You will probably have the edit studio create an MPEG conversion after the final approval. A template for video edit notes can be found in Appendix 12-B.

THE FUTURE

The most exciting aspect of the Internet and the future of Webcasting is the knowledge that it is in a constant state of flux. Technology is changing, quality is improving, and the options are growing every day. However, there is a security in knowing that the basics of production, instructional design, and effective teaching

ACTION: _____
_____
_____

AUDIO: _____
_____
_____

COMMENTS: _____
_____
_____

ACTION: _____
_____
_____

AUDIO: _____
_____
_____

COMMENTS: _____
_____
_____

ACTION: _____
_____
_____

AUDIO: _____
_____
_____

COMMENTS: _____
_____
_____

APPENDIX 12-A. **STORYBOARD**

Program Title: _____
Producer: _____
Date: _____

REEL NO.	TIME CODE	AUDIO	VIDEO
00	In-00:00:00 Out-00:00:00		
	In- Out-		
	In- Out-		
	In- Out-		
	In- Out-		
	In- Out-		
	In- Out-		
	In- Out-		
	In- Out-		
	In- Out-		
	In- Out-		
	In- Out-		
	In- Out-		
	In- Out-		
	In- Out-		
	In- Out-		
	In- Out-		
	In- Out-		
	In- Out-		
	In- Out-		
	In- Out-		
	In- Out-		

APPENDIX 12-B. **VIDEO EDIT NOTES**

remain constant. The principles outlined in this guide can be applied to technology and Internet delivery of education regardless of the software package or bandwidth expansion.

RESOURCES

Reading

Zettle, Herbert, (Dec. 2000). *Video Basics* 3rd. Edition. San Francisco: Wadsworth.

Website

http://www.internetcaster.co.uk—Airscape's Webcasting Directory—complete source material guide ranging from suppliers to newsletters.

➤ABOUT THE AUTHOR

Michael Fink is the executive vice president of VOICE. He is an e-learning and communications consultant, specializing in corporate education and professional development and training. Prior to becoming executive vice president, Mr. Fink worked as a consultant for UBS AG, where he was responsible for developing strategy for global e-learning initiative. He was also consultant, producer, and director of global education programs, including global webcasts, at UBS Warburg.

Mr. Fink has also developed and presented seminars and programs for several companies, including "E-learning—Passport to the Present" for Dearborn Financial Services, "Linking Technology to Business Solutions" for Ernst and Young LLP, and "The Blended Learning Seminar Series."

CHAPTER 13

LEARNING PORTALS

➤**CURTIS KANAHELE**

*Author's Note: A special thanks to Trey Mooney, Director of
Product Management at Learnframe, Inc., for his tremendous
contribution to this chapter. His insights on the e-learning industry have been invaluable in preparing this work, and he has
been an essential sounding board for the ideas and concepts presented here.*

INTRODUCTION

The World Wide Web has revolutionized nearly every industry.
Some industries have quickly adopted Internet technologies and
others have changed at a slower pace. The education and training
industry is just beginning to develop effective models for applying
Internet technology to its work.

Learning portals have been on the forefront of the industry's adoption of the Internet. Learning portals can combine many complementary e-learning features together into an effective learning solution, one that can manage the flow of learning that adults follow in their quest for personal and professional improvement. This flow of learning, which I refer to as the learning cycle, includes phases of needs assessment, preparation, learning, and evaluation. Although learning portals may be varied in their characteristics, the full-service learning portal is designed to fully support the learning cycle of adult learners.

In this chapter, I discuss learning portals and the features that support the learning cycle. I give examples of viable products—highlighted in italics—that exemplify these elements. Finally, I provide a decision-making guide that compares learning portals to internal learning management systems, outlines criteria for decisions between building versus buying a learning portal, and specifies what to look for when purchasing learning portal services.

WHAT IS A LEARNING PORTAL?

Anyone who has paid any attention to the Internet and the World Wide Web during the past few years has heard the term "portal" used to describe a variety of websites. Although the term portal can be defined as a gateway into a particular domain, the use of the word portal on the Web has become incongruent. At the dawn of the World Wide Web, sites such as *Yahoo!* and *Lycos* were described as portals that led the public into an organized view of the mountains of information on the Internet. As information broadened on the Internet, websites popped up that supplied information focused on particular subjects, industries, or vertical markets.

Corporations and organizations broadened the concept of portals by creating centralized websites where employees and other interested parties could obtain corporate information. The corporate portal has opened an entire market for enterprise vendors who create enterprise information portals (EIP).

Another trend in portal development is personalization. Website developers initially built the ability to customize views of their portals—based on consumer interest—to attract and retain more users. This has been expanded to include the ability to customize information. Member-oriented sites, including most corporate portals, now provide customizable views that supply personal information to their users.

All of these developments have given rise to the learning portal. A learning portal is a gateway to learning. It is a specialized portal leading to all of the learning resources available to the target user population. Learning portals are the epitome of e-learning. They deliver on e-learning's promise of "just-in-time learning" and "learning on demand." In other words, learning portals allow users to learn just what they need to learn, when they need to learn it, and from wherever they can learn it, and, to some extent, how they can choose objects in the order they desire, chunked as they want, or perhaps choose between different ways to learn the same information?

Learning Portals Applications

➤ Corporate university

➤ Online extension of academic institution

➤ Industry focus

➤ Courseware delivery

➤ Product training

➤ Learning content aggregator

➤ Learning service provider (LSP)

The term learning portal has been used to describe a variety of portal applications that serve different user populations.

The corporate university has been the most popular application of the learning portal. Also referred to as an internal portal, the corporate university is the central point of learning for employees throughout the corporation. For example, the Thomson Corporation has established an online university to service their 40,000 employees in 300 companies across the globe. Other corporations, such as Chevron, General Motors, and Motorola, joined a consortium for e-learning using the learning portal *LearnShare*. Figure 13-1 provides a list of applications and the purpose for which they are most effective.

Online Extension of an Academic Institution

Traditional and nontraditional academic institutions are also offering learning portals to their target audiences. Michigan Virtual University, with its IT Training Initiative, is delivering e-learning to 850,000 students, teachers, and staff throughout Michigan. Western Governor's University covers a broader area. The governors of several western states founded the online university to offer competency-based degrees to students wherever they are.

Industry Portal

Some learning portal developers have focused their gateway to learning on a specific industry. These are often nonprofit organizations offering discounts on industry-specific content to members. The Society of Manufacturing Engineers (SME) and the American Society of Employers (ASE) are two associations that offer their members e-learning in topics applicable to their respective industries.

Courseware Delivery

For courseware developers, the Web is a natural delivery mechanism for their web-based content. Courseware developers such as *SmartForce* and *DigitalThink* produce a catalog of their respective courses for corporations and individuals alike to access learning online.

Product Training

Manufacturers of products other than courseware have also capitalized on the Web infrastructure to deliver training. Software and hardware manufacturers, such as Lucent and Compaq, have designed learning portals to educate their customers, resellers, and support channels on their products. This method of education is especially useful for customer training at the early stages of product adoption.

Content Aggregators

Learning content aggregators manage a different type of learning portal. Aggregators maintain a wide selection of learning products from a variety of vendors that are purchasable on the Web. Learning items from aggregators are primarily shipped to the customer and are not taken online. Pure content aggregators, such as *Trainseek*, are harder to find these days. Without a clear business model, many of the large learning content aggregators fell victim to the decline of the Internet economy in 2000.

Learning Service Providers

Finally, the learning service provider (LSP), a variation of the application service provider model, is ideal for hosted e-learning solutions. Learning companies who have assembled a wide variety of online content, such as *Learn.com* and *Learn2.com*, combine e-commerce with learning to make e-learning available to a large target audience of learners.

These learning portal types include a broad range of e-learning features. Notwithstanding this breadth, by considering audience and purpose, we can identify shared features across many of the learning portal applications. The chart in Figure 13-1 compares the typical features of learning portal applications.

THE LEARNING CYCLE

From these mutual features, we can identify key elements that learning portals must have to afford users a rich learning experience. These elements follow a learning cycle of assessment, preparation, learning, and back to assessment. The learning cycle supports the notion of lifelong learning, in which responsibility "for the learning process shifts from institutions to individuals" (Commission on Technology and Adult Learning, 2001). That is, a lifelong learner is an individual who seeks to continuously improve her- or himself in an assessment-preparation-learning cycle spiraling upward toward greater knowledge and skill levels. Figure 13-2 provides a graphic of the cycle for you to follow.

	Knowledge/Skill Assessment	Offline Content or Instruction	e-Commerce	Community	Courseware Launching	Learning Evaluation
Corporate university	Sometimes	Often	Rarely	Often	Sometimes	Sometimes
Online extension of academic institution	Sometimes	Usually	Rarely	Sometimes	Sometimes	Sometimes
Industry focus	Sometimes	Often	Usually	Often	Usually	Sometimes
Courseware delivery	Rarely	Rarely	Usually	Sometimes	Usually	Sometimes
Product training	Sometimes	Sometimes	Usually	Sometimes	Usually	Sometimes
Learning content aggregator	Sometimes	Usually	Usually	Rarely	Rarely	Rarely
Learning Service Provider	Sometimes	Rarely	Usually	Sometimes	Usually	Sometimes

FIGURE 13-1. **LEARNING PORTAL APPLICATIONS AND THEIR FEATURES**

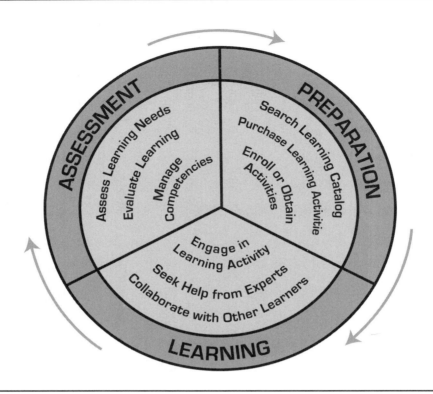

FIGURE 13-2. **LEARNING CYCLE**

Assessment

The best place to enter the learning cycle is at the assessment phase by assessing the needs or goals of the learner. Adult learners are motivated by goals. Whether the goals are initiated internally by the learner or externally by another entity, they are typically related to qualifying for a job (note that I am using the term job here loosely—it could mean a task for a person's current position or it may mean an entire job position, current or prospective).

Assessing an individual's learning need starts with an evaluation of his knowledge or competencies. This knowledge assessment is then compared with the competencies required for the job. A comparison of the competencies that are currently possessed by the learner and those that are required for the job results in prescribed learning that would ultimately eliminate his competency deficiencies.

Preparation

Once the learning need is assessed, individuals make preparations for fulfilling their learning needs. They make a plan from the list of learning activities that would best meet their needs. Learning resources may come in a variety of forms and they may have been created for specific learning styles. The right learning resource must be chosen to make learning effective for the individual. During the preparation phase, the appropriate learning resources are purchased or otherwise obtained. Any enrollments in instructor-led or self-study courses are also made at this stage.

Learning

Once preparations are completed, the learner may enter the principal phase of the learning cycle, learning. The learner engages in learning activities to build knowledge and develop competency. Ideally, the learner has access to help from experts in the subject matter. Moreover, it is most beneficial for a learner to be able to interact with other learners on the same subject in a collaborative effort to understand complex concepts and to share diverse perspectives on the subject. Such interaction not only broadens the learner's knowledge, it expands his view of the subject's applicability in the real world.

Back to Assessment

Following learning, evaluation is essential in developing competency, for without testing an individual's learning there is less motivation for retention and internalization of learned concepts. Like learning activities, assessment and evaluation may come in a variety of forms, each with its advantages and disadvantages (see Chapter 26, Methods for Evaluating E-learners).

A revolution of the learning cycle is completed when a learner's increased competency is verified via evaluation and then added to his competency profile. The cycle may then continue into another learning needs assessment. This assessment might compare the learner's higher competency level with a more challenging job, or the individual may focus on improvement of a different competency.

THE FULL-SERVICE LEARNING PORTAL

The full-service learning portal supports the learning cycle with various components of e-learning. Some of these components are core to the learning process and are essential to a full-service learning portal. Additional features may enhance the learning experience within the portal. All components of a full-service learning portal are well-integrated with smooth transitions for the user from one component to the next. Figure 13-3 provides a graphic of the full service learning portal.

Core Components

Within the full-service learning portal, there are several components associated with each phase of the learning cycle. The assessment phase is composed of components for knowledge assessment, competency assessment, and learning evaluation. The preparation phase contains learning catalog, e-commerce, and enrollment components. The learning phase comprises learning activity, expert forum,

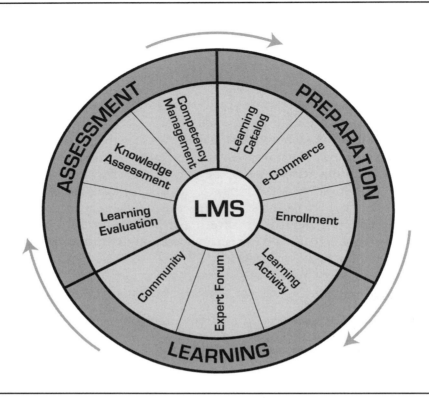

FIGURE 13-3. **FULL-SERVICE LEARNING PORTAL**

and community components. Central to the full-service learning portal is the learning management system (LMS). The LMS provides the infrastructure to tie all of the learning portal components together into a cohesive system (see Chapter 9, Learning Management Systems for E-Learning). It is "the most important foundation of e-learning" (Hall, 2000).

Assessment

The best way to begin in the learning cycle is with need assessment. Two core components assess learning needs: knowledge assessment tools and competency management systems (CMS). Although knowledge assessment services, such as the *Brainbench Test Center*, are primarily used for postlearning testing, they may also be used for prelearning knowledge assessment. These knowledge assessments can then be used as competency input to a competency management system. A CMS uses profiling to map individual competencies against defined job roles to identify learning needs through gap analysis. Here is how it works (see Figure 13-4).

First, standard levels of competency for a job are predefined as skills, knowledge, and/or experience that are required for the job. Then an individual enters competency information for himself into the CMS. These competencies may be validated or adjusted by supervisors and peers.

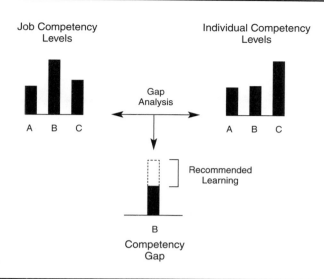

FIGURE 13-4. **COMPETENCY ASSESSMENT**

The CMS performs a gap analysis between the competencies possessed by the individual and the competencies necessary for the job. The result is a list of recommended learning activities that would aid the individual in meeting the requirements of the intended job. Ideally, the list is organized into a personalized curriculum or learning path that guides the individual through his personal/professional development. In Figure 13-4, the individual has enough of competency A to do the job. He exceeds in competency C over the level required for the job, but he lacks in competency B. As a result, the CMS returns a recommendation for learning that should help the individual to close the gap. Systems that effectively manage competencies in this way are available from vendors such as *SkillView* and *SkillScape*.

Preparation

Following a needs assessment, the full-service learning portal prepares the learner's personalized curriculum by matching recommended learning activities with learning resources available in its catalog. A rich catalog contains learning content developed for various delivery methods and it offers learning content from multiple vendors—for example, the *Learnframe Learning Center* catalog has online courses developed by *NETg, SkillSoft, NIIT, Element K*, and many other vendors. Variety is especially important in courseware because each course vendor has different perspectives and goals in their instructional design; they also focus on different skill sets (i.e., IT, soft skills, etc.). Therefore, it is important for a learning portal administrator to carefully manage his learning content offering.

In addition to self-study courses, a full-service catalog includes instructor-led courses, be they online—through systems such as *Interwise Millenium*—or in the classroom. A blend of classroom training and online learning is the current trend for effective organizations. Full service catalog contents might include:

- ➤ Interactive media

- ➤ Books and other documents

- ➤ Audio

- ➤ Video

- ➤ Online recorded instruction

- ➤ Instructor-led classroom

- ➤ Instructor-led virtual class online

- ➤ Lab exercises

- ➤ Assessments

The full-service learning portal provides for a blended package of learning. With its complement of learning media and methods it is like a supermarket that not only offers groceries, but also nonfoods, optical services, video store, banking, dry cleaning, and other nongrocery services.

The key to a rich catalog that motivates consumers to buy is not the number of items in the catalog, but learning activities that have relevance and quality. The competency assessment component helps in identifying learning that would be relevant to the user. However, the actual courseware and other learning activities must (1) include the right concepts, exercises, and organization, and (2) be of sufficient quality that contributes to the learner's success. Relevance and quality are vital to e-learning.

Also key to commercial learning portals is e-commerce. E-commerce in a learning portal enables a learner to purchase learning resources from the catalog. Knowledge commerce describes the union of knowledge acquisition and e-commerce. It is the bridge between purchasing learning resources and engaging in learning activities online. Various business models have been used to implement knowledge commerce. The obvious model is to set a price per course, or learning activity; this allows the learner to access a single online activity at will. Another popular model is the all-you-can-eat subscription model, where learners can engage in a number of learning activities for a set fee per time period (e.g., per month). Pay-per-view is another method for selling e-learning.

Once a user locates and purchases online activities, the LMS of a full-service portal "enrolls" the user in the course or other e-learning activity and adds it to the user's learning path within the learning environment. This operation completes the phase preparatory to learning.

Learning

The learning environment is the area of the learning portal that is the culmination of assessment, preparation, and personalization for the learner. It presents the user's personalized learning plan, along with other resources, to assist him in learning. From here, the portal LMS launches online courses and other e-learn-

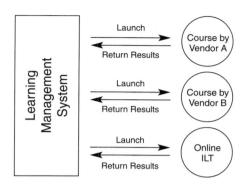

FIGURE 13-5. **FULL-SERVICE LMS**

ing activities, such as online instructor-led training (ILT). Progress within these activities is tracked and the LMS retrieves scores or evaluations resulting from learning sessions.

In Figure 13-5, you can see that the LMS of a full-service learning portal is able to track progress and retrieve scores from any number of vendors. *Learnframe's LMS*, for example, launches and tracks courses and other e-Learning activities from more than 50 different vendors. Such an LMS affords maximum flexibility in preparing curricula for a portal's target learners. A full-service LMS manages courses by arranging class schedules and instructors, tracking student registrations and learning progress, and providing reports at the organization level of a learning portal.

A full-service learning portal augments online instruction with interactive communication. Interactive communication in a learning community with an instructor or subject matter expert, as well as with other students, is an important aspect of online learning. Because learning is increased with collaboration on a subject, learning portal communities may also include a company's partners, vendors, and customers. Perhaps the best organizational learning communities are those that mirror workplace communities (Beer, 2000).

Communication online is facilitated by collaboration tools such as *Centra's Symposium*, and by discussion forum tools such as *ChatSpace's WebBoard*. These tools provide expert forums and learner communities through which learning is fostered. In addition to tools, services such as *KnowledgePool's e-Learning Service* maintain a staff 24 hours a day, 7 days a week to answer questions and facilitate discussion among learners regarding online course materials.

Back to Assessment

The learning cycle continues when learning from the various learning activities has been evaluated. Supplemental to course scores retrieved by the LMS are predefined assessments and evaluation engines. Predefined assessments are tests that assess learning in a particular subject or course of study. For example, certification tests on Microsoft Windows operating systems are offered from companies like *Measure Up*. Evaluation engines, such as *Questionmark's Perception*, give curriculum developers the flexibility to create tailored assessments outside of predefined courses. After the learner has completed the evaluation, the full-service learning portal feeds the scores into its competency management system for further assessment and subsequent learning.

THE LEARNING CYCLE IN PRACTICE

Now that I have described the core components of the full-service learning portal, I can walk through a scenario of the learning cycle in the context of a learning portal. As an example, consider the steps that an information technology (IT) specialist takes to achieve a technical certification.

- ➤ *Knowledge Assessment*—the IT specialist takes a preliminary test to evaluate her knowledge in the area of certification.

- ➤ *Competency Management*—the IT specialist enters the results of the knowledge assessment into a competency management system. A gap analysis is performed comparing her knowledge with the competency required for the certification. A recommended curriculum of learning activities is produced by the portal's CMS.

- ➤ *Learning Catalog*—the IT specialist selects several online courses, synchronous learning events, and texts that fall under the recommended curriculum.

- ➤ *Commerce*—using the portal's e-Commerce options, the IT specialist purchases the selected learning activities.

- ➤ *Enrollment*—the IT specialist is enrolled in the online courses and synchronous learning activities by the portal's learning management system.

- ➤ *Learning Activity*—the IT specialist employs the learning items that she has purchased to learn about the area of certification. During her use of online courses, her progress is tracked and the results from online quizzes are stored into the portal's LMS.

- ➤ *Expert Forum*—using the portal's certification forum, the IT specialist asks a subject matter expert questions generated from her learning.

- ➤ *Community*—the IT specialist also discusses technical concepts—through the portal's discussion forums and chat sessions—with other learners who are seeking the same certification.

- ➤ *Learning Evaluation*—the IT specialist uses online sample exams and labs to test her grasp of the new concepts that she has learned.

➤ *Knowledge Assessment*—the IT specialist takes the certification exam at a testing center.

➤ *Competency Management*—the successful completion of the certification is entered into the IT specialist's competency profile, potentially qualifying her for a promotion.

This example has shown how effective the learning cycle can be with the core components of a full-service learning portal. The benefits of a learning portal can be further enhanced with additional portal features.

ADDITIONAL PORTAL FEATURES

There are many other features that either improve the effectiveness of the portal or meet particular learning needs of the target learners. The addition of these features is only possible because a full-service portal is capable of integrating various components into a cohesive system that will increase learning on the website. They include:

➤ Branding/customized look

➤ Recommended learning based on learner interests

➤ Continuing education units

➤ Integration with corporate systems

The desire to have a learning portal look a certain way is typical of organizations that seek to add a portal to their employee development offering. Flexible learning portals allow an organization's implementation of the product to be customized, conforming to the organization's brand or unique look and feel. Some learning portals allow for minimal changes, such as the addition of a logo and the selection of predefined color sets. Other learning portals provide complete flexibility in customizing the learner experience. The Learning Centers at *ElementK.com* and *Learnframe.com* offer flexible, customizable portals to organizations needing a specific look and feel.

An important feature for commercial learning portals is a system for recommending learning activities to customers based on their interests. These portals enable learners to identify the subjects that they are interested in. The system will then present the most popular learning products to the customer as an enticement to acquire additional learning. This is similar to the product recommendations given at *Amazon.com*.

Anything that would help potential customers feel good about making a purchase adds value to a commercial learning portal. Recommendations may be augmented by content evaluation. Ratings by other learners who have already used the learning content may give prospective buyers the comfort they need before paying a significant price for learning products. Such recommendations build customer loyalty and increase brand equity for the learning portal.

In some learning portal applications, learners may be interested in receiving continuing education units for academic certificates and degrees. This is only available from those courseware vendors and portal providers who have agreements with accredited academic institutions that map online learning experiences with academic requirements. *UserActive* is one such learning portal that has partnered with the University of Illinois to credit online learning toward technical certificates.

For corporate learning portals, the integration of the portal with other corporate systems, such as financial and customer service systems, is vital for corporate processes. These companies build links between the commerce engine of their learning portal and their financial system to manage customer accounts and produce accurate corporate sales data. A full-service learning portal infrastructure is capable of seamlessly transferring data to other systems with little development effort.

FORESEEABLE FUTURE

Like any industry influenced by technology, it is difficult to predict the future of e-learning. However, the trends suggest that learning portals will evolve with greater personalization and intelligence. Learning portals of the future will know all about its users—their knowledge, skills, certifications, learning preferences, personality, and so on. With this "knowledge," portals will be able to intelligently personalize the user's experience, for the more individualized a user's experience is, the greater the impact of the learning is on the user. Rosenberg (2000), a key proponent of e-learning stated, "In an era of specialization, each individual needs a customized learning plan. The old "spray and pray" approach to training—i.e. "spray" it out to everyone and "pray" that it sticks—is an anathema to where organizations are headed."

The most obvious form of personalization is the look and operation of the portal. Colors, layout, navigation, and interaction heuristics could be changed dynamically according to the learner's preferences. The site may also adapt to the learner by replacing default behavior with options that are frequently selected by the user.

Noncourse content—such as text, articles, graphics, and so on—would adjust not only to a learner's preferences, but also to a learner's role. For example, a manager would see text related to leadership, while a network engineer would see articles on information technology. Intelligent search agents would seek information on the Internet and in vast databases to locate content applicable to the learner's needs. Collaborative filtering might also be employed so that a network engineer would see articles that other network engineers found interest in.

Online courses may be personalized as well. The e-learning industry's move toward reusable learning objects will enable learning portals to create custom courses dynamically. Custom courses will be assembled based on learning needs, learning styles (e.g., visual, auditory, kinesthetic), roles, business needs, and other personal learning preferences. Moreover, course delivery methods and formats may also be personalized. The learning portal, for example, will know that a particular learner uses a Web client and a PDA; as a result, the portal will deliver courses that support the learner's preferred platforms.

Personalization and intelligence are the next frontiers of e-learning. Economic and competitive factors are pushing the e-learning industry to provide learners only what they want and need to learn, when they need to learn it, and in a form that will make them most effective in their acquisition of knowledge and skills.

TIPS AND HINTS

Here is what you should know about learning portals:

➤ A learning portal is a gateway to learning for a particular population of learners.

➤ Although learning portal applications vary widely in their features and functions, there are several features that are shared among many of the portals. They are knowledge and skill assessment, offline content or instruction, e-commerce, community, online courseware launching, and learning evaluation.

➤ The learning cycle is a supporting element of lifelong learning that includes phases of assessment, preparation, and evaluation.

➤ The full-service learning portal supports the learning cycle with various components of e-learning.

➤ Core components of the full-service learning portal that support the assessment phase are knowledge assessment, competency management, and learning evaluation.

➤ The full-service learning portal supports the preparation phase with a learning catalog, e-commerce, and enrollment components. A rich catalog contains learning items from a variety of delivery methods.

➤ Components for the learning phase include learning activities, expert forums, and online community discussion groups.

➤ The heart of the learning portal is the LMS. A full-service learning portal is built around an LMS that can launch and track online courseware from a variety of courseware vendors.

➤ Beyond the core components, additional features enhance the learning experience on the portal. Beneficial components are customized look and feel, recommendations for learning, continuing education units, and integration with corporate systems.

➤ Learning portals are evolving to meet the personalization and intelligence needs of learners. In the future, learning portals will adjust learning content, information, and the learning environment according to the users' knowledge, skills, certifications, learning preferences, personalities, roles, interests, and learning devices.

DECISION MAKING GUIDE

This guide is intended to help managers, educators, and learning professionals make decisions about learning portals. It will compare learning portals to internal learning management systems, outline criteria for decisions between building versus buying a learning portal, and specify what to look for when purchasing learning portal services from an LSP.

Choosing an E-Learning Solution

When faced with a decision between a learning portal and internal LMS options, there are many criteria that should be considered. The chart in Figure 13-6 identifies some of the criteria that differentiate learning portals from learning management systems built for intranet use at enterprises and small-to-medium-sized organizations.

Typically, an e-Learning solution is positioned to be attractive for a particular company size. An enterprise LMS is targeted for the Global 2000 companies, whereas a small business LMS is priced for small to medium-sized organizations. A commercial learning portal, hosted by a learning service provider (LSP), is frequently considered to be a solution for smaller companies and departmental workgroups. However, commercial learning portals are becoming more attractive for larger organizations whose e-learning strategies are evolving. Many of these or-

Product Feature	Learning Portal	Small Business LMS	Enterprise LMS
e-commerce	yes	no	no
Reporting flexibility	low	medium	high
Content variety	high	low	medium
Custom content support	low	medium–high	medium–high
Network scope	Internet	Intranet	Intranet
Accessibility	high	low–medium	medium–high
Security of sensitive data	low	medium–high	high
Customizability	low	medium	high
Interoperability	low–medium	low	high
Other Considerations			
Cost of deployment	low	medium	high
Time to deployment	low	medium	high
IT infrastructure needed	none	low	medium–high
IT expertise needed	none	low	medium–high
Courseware maintenance	none	medium–high	medium–high

FIGURE 13-6. **COMPARING E-LEARNING SOLUTIONS**

ganizations have chosen to start with a learning service provider with the intention of migrating to an internal learning management system. A commercial learning portal offers organizations that are just entering into the realm of e-learning a solution with a minimum set of technology requirements: a client with a browser and a connection to the Internet.

Build Versus Buy

Organizations that have chosen to implement a learning portal may be faced with the decision to build their own portal or contract portal services from an established vendor. The primary benefit to building a portal is control over such things as portal features, product functions, financial transactions, customer data, choice in technology and infrastructure, and so on. The biggest drawbacks in building a portal are cost and time-to-market. There are many considerations in building your own learning portal (Figure 13-7).

The following is a list of costs in building a learning portal:

➤ Infrastructure

Hardware

Servers
Firewall
Data storage
Redundancy (load balancing)

Software licenses
Operating system
Web server
Monitoring software
Courses and learning content

➤ Software development

➤ Web design costs

➤ System integration
Payment processor
Merchant account

➤ Maintenance
Course and learning content maintenance fees
System administration
Portal administration
Webmaster

The benefits to buying services from a learning service provider are: faster deployment, lower startup costs, leverage of vendor's ASP expertise, and existing

Category	Criteria
Full-service features	Does the portal support the Learning Cycle by incorporating Learning Management System, Knowledge Assessment, Competency Management, Learning Catalog, e-Commerce, Enrollment, Learning Activities, Expert Forums, Community, and Learning Evaluation components into a cohesive system?
Usability	Is the user interface of the portal easily navigatable and intuitive? Can it be used without reading help text?
Branding	Can the portal's look and feel be customized for each organization? Can custom text and Web pages be added? Can this customization be modified by a customer?
Administration	Does the portal offer you remote management of your organization's people, catalog, and learning records?
Rich catalog	Does the portal offer a rich catalog with learning activities of all types of delivery methods and from a multitude of vendors? Is blended learning offered? Are the courses relevant and of high quality?
Standards support	Does the portal support e-Learning standards such as AICC, IMS, and SCORM?
Custom content	Can custom content be added to the portal's catalog? How much time is required to do so?
Infrastructure	Does the portal ensure security (redundant components, data backup, precautions against attacks)? Is the system scalable to support the number of users expected? Is the product Web-based or just Web-enabled?
Interoperability and connectivity	Can the portal be connected to your existing systems to which data must be exchanged? Does the portal support standard data exchange formats such as XML?
Customer orientation	Is the portal designed to support your target market? Does it support B2C, B2B, or B2E (business to employee) business models?
Vendor ability	How long has the portal vendor been in the business of developing e-Learning solutions? How long does it take to deploy a new customer?
Service level	Does the vendor guarantee a minimum of 99.5% uptime?

FIGURE 13-7. **CONSIDERATIONS IN CHOOSING A LEARNING PORTAL**

bank services. The primary drawback is that there is less flexibility in customizing the learning experience than what a company would have by building its own portal.

Selecting a Learning Portal

If the choice is to contract services from an LSP, then there are important criteria for choosing the right vendor. The chart in Figure 13.7 suggests what to look for in a learning portal.

I conclude with the notion that the learning portal is the "face" of an e-learning strategy. Learning portal users—be they employees, customers, or partners—will assess the quality of your learning program based on what they see and experience on the website. All components, features, and information should be carefully planned and orchestrated to ensure the successful presentation of the e-learning initiative.

RESOURCES

Readings

Beer, V. (2000). *The Web Learning Fieldbook: Using the World Wide Web to Build Workplace Learning Environments*. New York: Jossey-Bass.

The Commission on Technology and Adult Learning (June, 2001). *A Vision of E-Learning for America's Workforce*.

Rosenberg, M. J. (2000). *E-Learning: Strategies for Delivering Knowledge in the Digital Age*. New York: McGraw-Hill.

Additional Readings

There isn't much in the way of reference information on learning portals. However, there is a great deal of information on e-learning and Internet portals in general. Much of the information contained in resources on these related topics will apply to learning portals.

Delphi Group (2000). *Need to Know: Integrating e-Learning with High Velocity Value Chains*.

IDC (March, 2000). *Hosted Learning Management Solutions: The Impact of the ASP Model on the Learning Industry*.

Morgan Keegan & Co. (July, 2000). *eLearning: The Engine of the Knowledge Economy*.

Sun Trust Equities (March, 2000). *e-Learning and Knowledge Technology*.

The Web-based Education Commission (December, 2000). *The Power of the Internet for Learning*.

WR Hambrecht & Co. (March, 2000). *Corporate E-Learning: Exploring a New Frontier*.

Websites

e-Learning Magazine (Online Magazine).

Hall, B. (2000). *e-Learning: Building Competitive Advantage Through People and Technology.* http://www.forbes.com/specoalsections/elearning/

Learning Circuits (Online Magazine).

LGuide (e-Learning Research and Consulting).

Online Learning Magazine (Online Magazine).

Online Learning News (Online Magazine).

Training Magazine (Online Magazine).

➤ABOUT THE AUTHOR

Curtis Kanahele has more than 15 years of experience in the systems development life cycle and is pleased to be part of the e-learning industry. Mr. Kanahele is the Director of Software Development at Learnframe, where he manages the development of learning management and knowledge commerce systems. He also oversees interoperability development for Learnframe learning management systems for integration with third-party courses and e-learning systems. Before Learnframe, Mr. Kanahele worked as a systems consultant, product manager, product support engineer, quality assurance engineer, and software engineering manager. He teaches IT courses at the University of Phoenix Online campus and is a Certified Novell Instructor. Mr. Kanahele received a Bachelor of Science degree in computer science, a Master of Science degree in information management, and a Master of Business Administration degree.

CHAPTER 14

MAKING THE INTERNAL/EXTERNAL DECISION

➤PATRICK M. HENTSCHELL

INTRODUCTION—WHAT IS OUTSOURCING?

In basic terms, outsourcing is when one company requests the services of another to perform a specific task they either do not want to do or are unable to do. Unless your company is self-contained, the decision to outsource will have to be addressed sooner or later.

The type of service or work to be outsourced varies from company to company. Outsourcing can include professional services to perform accounting activities like payroll, billing, taxes, and so on, or general contracting for the construction of buildings or additions to an existing structure. Since the focus of this handbook is on e-learning, the outsourcing considerations addressed in this chapter will primarily address e-learning and training-related decision-making.

When it comes to training, most companies have some form of training support function. Depending upon the size of the company, this support can vary from internal development of all training needs to the coordination of training from external sources. The latter outsources everything, while the other approach develops and delivers all their training needs. As delivery approaches evolve with new delivery technologies such as e-learning and technology-based training (TBT), the need to outsource becomes inevitable.

WHEN SHOULD YOU MAKE THE OUTSOURCING DECISION?

The earlier you make the decision the better. The decision to outsource e-learning as a solution for a training need involves many factors. Unless you can do the job internally, or you already have an existing vendor in mind, time is one of the more critical factors.

Additional factors that contribute to the need to make an outsourcing decision involve the proposed delivery solution, target audience, and anticipated delivery date. Essentially, these elements determine the project scope. Depending upon the capabilities and experience of your training department, the need to work with an outside vendor becomes more and more of a consideration.

Typically, important decision-making information regarding an e-learning solution, the target audience and delivery date is determined as a result of a fairly rigorous front-end analysis. Through the conduct of an effective analysis involving a needs assessment and task analysis, decision criteria is collected that outlines the scope of the project.

From the results of a good needs assessment, it may be determined that training is not required and alternative solutions should be considered. Most likely though, some form of training solution is already being considered and the results of the analysis provides the background information necessary to scope the project.

The following identifies some of the information you can uncover as a result of a thorough front-end analysis:

- If training is needed

- Training goal(s)

- Target audience profile

  - Skills and characteristics

  - Reading level

  - Average age

  - Primary language

- ➤ Geographic location
- ➤ Number of trainees
- ➤ Computer literacy
- ➤ Corporate training goals
- ➤ Delivery approach
- ➤ High-level presentation strategies
- ➤ Content breakdown
- ➤ Media requirements
- ➤ Technology delivery requirements
- ➤ Current organizational technology capabilities
- ➤ Budget and schedule constraints
- ➤ Audience receptiveness to technology
- ➤ Identify Subject Matter Experts (SMEs)
- ➤ Stability of the content identified for training
- ➤ Current delivery approach
- ➤ Status and quality of available content

Using the results of a comprehensive front-end analysis, you will be able to knowledgeably address the various considerations that help formulate your outsourcing decision. Without this information your decisions may negatively impact the success of your e-learning project.

WHAT ARE THE CONSIDERATIONS YOU NEED TO MAKE A DECISION?

To make an informed decision, you need the front-end analysis information and some additional information based on the goals and business direction of your organization. Four basic considerations (see Figure 14-1) can be used to help guide your decision-making:

- ➤ Business
- ➤ Personnel
- ➤ Technology
- ➤ Content

Business | Personnel

Technology | Content

FIGURE 14-1. **FOUR BASIC CONSIDERATIONS**

These considerations, outlined in the following sections, are key factors that need to be addressed as you formulate your outsourcing decision. E-learning solutions are typically complex with a diverse set of requirements involving a variety of skills and talents. Depending upon your organization's experience and capabilities, your outsourcing needs may vary. Using your analysis information in conjunction with the four considerations, you will be able to determine if and/or how much outsourcing is required for your e-learning project.

Business Considerations

The decision to develop an e-learning solution internally is a major initiative depending upon your organization's business goals and core competencies. If technology-based training is not an area where your organization has expertise or a desire to pursue, you need to take a hard look at the outsourcing option. The requirements to enter into the e-learning arena are costly with a steep learning curve.

A consensus among your various management levels is a key component if you want to succeed with an e-learning initiative. A comprehensive team is required to successfully design, develop, and deploy these types of solutions. If an agreement can be obtained to support an e-learning team, the need to outsource is minimized. If only a partial agreement is secured, then you may be able to internally develop certain elements of your project and outsource the rest. If this is your first e-learning project, this approach will minimize the risk and allow you to grow and gain experience in this arena.

Deciding to enter the e-learning market, even if it is to develop internal training, is a big decision that requires long-term commitment. Once the course is developed, it will have to be maintained and modified as the content changes. Upgrading and maintaining your delivery environment is costly and difficult to keep up with as the technology continues to rapidly change. The return on investment (ROI) should be thoroughly examined with regard to increases in productivity, reduced downtime, and the potential for improved employee retention.

Before you decide to develop a solution internally, you need to know if your training requirements, upper/lower management, and the business commitment are there to support your team.

Personnel Considerations

Outsourcing an e-learning initiative is highly dependent upon the capabilities and experience of your staff as well as the skill set of your team. You may have a highly experienced team for instructor-led training (ILT); however, this skill set does not encompass the design and development requirements of an e-learning project. Teaching skills do not always translate to technology-based design skills.

Typically, not all organizations have the broad-based skill set necessary to effectively handle all of the various aspects of an e-learning solution. Listed below is an example of an e-learning design and development team with experience in the following areas:

➤ Computer technology (hardware, software, programming, and the World Wide Web)

➤ Instructional systems design (ISD) (hopefully with a background in technology-based training such as computer-based training (CBT) or electronic performance support systems (EPSS))

➤ Graphics (preferably experienced in web site design, animation, and instructional graphic development)

➤ Content specialists (preferably experienced with education and training)

You should also have personnel with strong project management skills in technology and training-based programs. Depending upon the design requirements of an e-learning solution, additional expertise may be required in specialty areas such as video, photography, or audio production.

If your team does not contain the expertise to address the various areas for your e-learning solution, outsourcing the areas where you are lacking experience or necessary skill set may be the solution. If you do not intend to outsource, then you will be obligated to hire what you need or train staff members in the areas required. In most cases, because time is a critical factor, it does not make sense to retrain or hire new staff.

If resources are hired it is important to ascertain if their skill set can be used for future projects. If not, then these are areas where outsourcing provides the necessary resources you need to get the job done.

Finally, another important consideration regarding your existing personnel is their receptiveness to the idea of e-learning. Many organizations have a strong ILT staff. Occasionally, they feel threatened by technology-based training solutions. It is important to gain their support if you intend to use their knowledge and experience on the team.

Technology Considerations

Frequently, the need to outsource is necessary based on technology. Staying abreast of the technological advances in e-learning is no less than overwhelming. In fact, companies and industries in the e-learning business have a difficult time.

Based on your analysis information and a solution design, you can take an honest look at your technology capabilities against the requirements and decide if you are capable of accomplishing the task. At a minimum you will need to answer the following technology questions:

➤ How complex is the solution? (Text & graphic-based, synchronous learning, high interactivity, student tracking and registration, etc.?)

➤ Does your company have the infrastructure to develop and host it?

➤ Does the target audience have the platform to receive it?

➤ What bandwidth is needed to deliver it effectively?

➤ Is it necessary to comply with a national or world standard? (SCORM, AICC, etc.)

➤ Will you be able to support it if upgrades and modifications are necessary?

➤ What if you want to migrate toward a more advanced technological solution? Are you willing to continue to stay in the technology race?

➤ If you need to upgrade your infrastructure, do you have the time? Budget?

Technical expertise can be hired and the business case can be justified, however, if your technology capability requires an extensive upgrade you may opt to outsource certain aspects of your e-learning solution.

Typically, e-learning solutions are very unique for each company. Once you have established a technology base line and decide at a later date to handle the technical aspect of an e-learning solution, you can use your first project as a springboard for your next initiative.

Content Considerations

Your analysis results will provide you with a great deal of information about the subject matter to be trained. Based on this information and some additional design work, you can determine the instructional and technical complexity of the e-learning solution.

Using adult learning theory and solid instructional design principles, instructional delivery strategies and media need to be identified based on the content and the instructional objectives. This information in conjunction with target audience characteristics like geographic location and size should be used to help specify the technology delivery environment.

In the case of e-learning, this information helps specify the technical complexities required by the system to effectively deliver the content. The more capable the delivery environment is in presenting the content based on ISD principles, the more effective the learning will be.

The impact of instructional delivery strategies, media, and audience characteristics on technology-based delivery requirements are worthy of a whole new article. However, some of the considerations that can help you with an outsourcing decision are identified below:

➤ Will audio or video be required?

➤ Does the content require detailed or extensive use of graphics?

➤ Is the content based on application training?

➤ What is the learning level of the content? (Fact, concept, etc.)

➤ Is simulation or a high degree of interactivity required?

➤ Are realistic scenarios required?

➤ How stable is the content?

➤ Is an instructor required (i.e., synchronous learning)?

➤ Is collaboration with other students and/or an instructor important?

➤ How much content is there? (1 hour, 10 hours, etc.) Will there be more in the future?

➤ What types and levels of feedback are required?

➤ Will you need student tracking and scoring?

➤ Is certification testing a requirement?

➤ How elaborate is your learner comprehension and test strategy?

➤ Is online registration required?

As you can see, the instructional aspects of the content have a major impact on the delivery requirements of not only an e-learning solution but any solution.

Unless you have the results of an analysis outlining the instructional requirements of the content and target audience, you cannot properly identify the most effective delivery approach.

Properly, evaluating the training requirements of your project will guide you in making the right decision to deliver your content using an e-learning solution. One mistake to avoid is to rollout an e-learning solution just for the sake of technology.

OUTSOURCING OR INTERNAL DEVELOPMENT—BENEFITS AND DRAWBACKS

This next section is provided to function as a job aid that you can use to help determine if outsourcing some or all of your e-learning requirements are right for your organization. Before you begin your e-learning project, objectively review the benefits and drawbacks associated with internal development and outsourcing. The items identified in Table 14-1 and the information discussed in this chapter should help you make informed decisions regarding how you want to proceed with your e-learning project.

TABLE 14-1. **Internal development versus outsourcing**

Benefits	Drawbacks
Internal Development	
Better customization of content	May have to hire resources to cover all aspects of a project
Local control of project and resources	May encounter delays in order to get up to speed
May benefit other training initiatives	Additional equipment and space may be required
Easier to update content	Resources may not be dedicated to the project
More control over costs and expenses	Retraining may be required
Proprietary information remains in-house	Potential exists that leading-edge talent may leave the company
Increased flexibility over content, schedule, etc.	Solution may lack important elements due to lack of experience
Broadens company capabilities	Developers/SMEs may be too close to the content and slow down the project
May open up new business opportunities	Newer technologies threaten job roles and existing environments
	Upper and lower management support may be difficult to obtain
	More risk depending upon experience
	Lacks fresh perspective

TABLE 14-1. *Continued*

Benefits	Drawbacks
Outsourcing	
Can be contracted as a fixed cost	Vendor may use proprietary software/hardware resulting in a single source for continued services
May provide a learning baseline for future projects	Relationship can be strained and degrade
Eases resource recruiting needs	Vendor may not be financially secure
Minimizes risk if using reputable vendor	Experience and capabilities may be over sold
Jump starts project with experienced developers	Costs can escalate if problems arise not accounted for in the contract
Vendors typically strive to ensure total customer satisfaction	Vendoe not familiar with content and culture
Allows company to focus on "core" business goals and objectives	Contracting process may increase project schedule
Vendor may have commercial off-the shelf (COTS) courseware	May require higher level management support
Additional services and products may be available from the vendor	Difficult to select the "right" vendor
May get lower costs with volume discounts	Company proprietary information is revealed to outside source
Gain access to leading edge experience and knowledge	May involve more than one vendor to effectively develop your solution
Brings fresh insights	Some education of the customer may be required to get them up-to-speed
Vendor can provide whole or partial solution	Vendor may try to "push" something you may not need or want
Increased chances for success	
Vendor experience may uncover new training opportunities	
Typically uses proven technologies and delivery approaches	

GUIDELINES FOR CONSTRUCTING AN RFP

If outsourcing is deemed necessary for your e-learning project, then you need to decide who is the best vendor to do the work. In most cases, this is accomplished using a document called a Request for Proposal (RFP). The RFP process is not as easy as one would like it to be. However, this section will attempt to provide you with some guidelines and helpful information to make the RFP process and outsourcing decision easier.

Vendor Selection Process

As you can imagine, outsourcing and subcontracting have been going on for a long time. A proven process has evolved that facilitates this process. Essentially, the steps of this process helps companies select the most capable vendor to do the job. It also helps identify vendors that suit your organizational culture resulting in a good working relationship for short- and long-term needs.

As you may already know, there are a multitude of vendors ready and willing to assist you with your e-learning project. Not all vendors are alike. Some have distinct areas of expertise and others have broad areas of experience and skill sets. A four-step process is described here to provide a basic structure for you to follow as you venture into the outsourcing arena. The four basic steps of this process are:

1. Construct a Request for Information (RFI) and distribute

2. Review RFI submittals and select three to five finalists

3. Construct an RFP and distribute

4. Review and select the vendor

Step 1: Constructing an RFI

The RFI phase of the vendor selection process allows you to sift through the numerous vendors on the market. It will help you identify vendors with the capabilities and work ethics that match your organization and training goals.

The objective of the RFI phase is to identify a finite number of venders (no more than five) that you are happy with and would like to have submit proposals for your project. At the RFI level you need to collect background and capability information about the prospective vendor. Create a form or outline they can use to provide company-specific information. Questions you ask may be unique for the specific project you have in mind as well as some basic background checks. Some of the typical questions for an RFI include:

> ➤ How long have you been in this line of business?

> ➤ What are your long-term goals?

> ➤ What are your capabilities to perform the type of project we plan to propose?

- Are there other areas or capabilities that we should know about?

- What type of resources do you have?

- What are the names of some of the clients you have worked for?

- Can you provide reference names and numbers?

- How stable is your company's financial status?

- What other experience do you have in this area?

- Can you provide resumes of your key individuals?

- What is your cage code (security information/Dunn & Bradstreet rating)?

In addition to requesting this information on your form, you should provide the vendor with some high-level information about your organization and your goals for the upcoming project. This will provide them with a framework that will help them construct their responses.

Optimally, you do not want to make this a long drawn-out affair. Be sure to take into consideration what is being asked of the potential vendor. Constructing a response to an RFI takes valuable time and money without any firm commitment of a contract award. If possible, provide some submittal guidelines that limit the page count and number of examples or resumes. The more structure you have for your RFI responses the more time you will save during your review process.

Distribute your RFI using a variety of venues such as trade magazines, conferences and trade shows, seminars, networking contacts, and so on. Contact other companies that are using technology-based solutions to find out which vendors they have successfully used.

Once you have collected this information you will have the information you need to create a short list of vendors for your current project and ones that may be desirable for future projects.

Step 2: Review RFI Submittals

You need to ensure you have accounted for an RFI phase in your project schedule. Selecting a vendor with little or no time to evaluate their capabilities can seriously affect the success of your project.

If you provided enough guidance to the vendors during your RFI phase, reviewing the responses should be a fairly straightforward task. All of your RFI submittals should be similar in size and vendor information. Read through the RFIs and select the ones (no more than four or five) that fit your project needs and organizational work ethic.

Carefully review the responses to see if the vendor took the time to respond specifically to your RFI guidelines. Look for clues that might suggest they visited your website to learn about your organization and "tailor" their response to your organization.

In addition to the RFI document you may decide to have brief interviews with selected vendors to discuss follow-up questions and observe demonstrations to refine your search criteria. You will also glean additional information as you work with each vendor through the RFI process and that will help determine how well a working relationship might transpire. "Good feelings" about a particular company can go a long way to making your project a success.

Step 3: Constructing an RFP

Similar to the RFI phase, only more importantly for an RFP, the more direction and thought put into the response criteria the easier it is to review and select a vendor. Responses to your RFP should be limited to the "short list" of vendors selected as a result of your RFI process.

Essentially, the RFP outlines the details and requirements of your e-learning project. Selected vendors respond to the RFP providing detailed information on how they plan to design, develop, and deliver the e-learning requirements you are outsourcing.

Basically, the RFP outlines your agreement with the vendor for their services. It also provides a baseline for contractual agreements like costs, payments, contract changes, and termination if they are required. Table 14-2 identifies the various format items and sections of a comprehensive RFP and provides a brief description of the sections. Feel free to use the table as a resource to help you construct an RFP. Additional sections or information may be needed depending upon the specifics of your organization or e-learning project.

As you can see, an RFP can be fairly complex and detailed. The table only provides a list of recommendations for an RFP. Depending upon the unique needs of your e-learning project you may need additional sections or items to help you with the selection process.

Once you have developed an RFP format you feel addresses the needs of your project, distribute it to your "short list" of vendors so they can construct their proposal. With a little effort your format can be reused so you can use it for future projects.

Having a format that details the specifics of your project and how your vendor plans to approach it with their proposed solution is extremely important for the success of any project. It also lays the foundation for the day-to-day working relationship with the winning vendor once you have made your final selection.

Step 4: Selecting the Vendor

After you receive the responses to your RFP you are ready to evaluate the proposals. Hopefully, this will be simplified if the vendors followed the RFP guidelines outlined for proposal submittal.

Proposal review should evaluate the vendor responses to determine which one matches your project with the approach you deem most effective and meets your budget. You need to be receptive to original thinking and new approaches. Some

TABLE 14-2. **Suggested RFP Sections/Items**

Section/Item	Description/Purpose
Page count	Recommending a page count maximum/minimum helps level the playing field and minimizes the time required to review the submittals.
Response format	If paper-based or soft-copy proposals are desired it is beneficial to specify what word processing software is to be used. Also, items like spacing, font size, etc., are helpful items to specify to keep things consistent.
Cover letter	Suggesting that a cover letter accompany the proposal helps maintain the communication link between the vendor and your organization with the primary point of contact for this proposed effort.
Required sections	Providing a rough outline of your outsourcing requirements that you feel must be addressed helps structure all of the proposals so that you can evaluate them based on some common factors.
Proposal due and reply dates	Setting a due date for responses will help you keep on schedule with your project and put some boundaries around the proposal review cycle. Letting participating vendors know the status of the award will allow them to look for other opportunities if necessary and not waste any additional time and resources.
Project due dates	This information allows the vendor to develop a project plan based on your time limits.
Executive summary	This section provides a synopsis of the vendors understanding and approach for management personnel that only need an overview of the submittals.
Understanding of the problem	This section allows the vendor to explain how they understand your needs and where their solution fits that need.
Project approach	The vendor provides a detailed description of their approach they plan on using to address your needs. It should include the technologies, strategies, instructional design approaches, methodologies etc. they plan on using to do the work.

(continued)

TABLE 14-2. *Continued*

Section/Item	Description/Purpose
Project plan	A high level project plan at the proposal stage is important to see how the vendor plans to meet your deadline. A more detailed plan can be provided at a project kick-off meeting. Items that should be addressed include: milestones, quality control, testing, deliverables, etc.
Project team and qualifications	It is important to get some background on the key players (managers and performers) the vendor plans on using for your project.
Required deliverables	Having the vendor identify the deliverables they plan on providing as they design and develop your solution is important. This will help you evaluate the vendor's approach and give you the opportunity to see what you will be receiving for your money.
Cost and payment information	This section identifies the costs like labor, travel, supplies, etc., the vendor plans on expending to accomplish the task. The resulting figure includes their profit and is the proposed cost to you for the job. Payment information includes contact information and payment schedules as deemed appropriate.
Assumptions and agreements	This section takes into account various factors that have been discussed or implied during the proposal process. Some items include what resources will be supplied by your organization, formats for media elements, maintenance agreements, on-site requirements, etc.
Signatures and points of contact	It is important to have signatures of individuals with authority to assign company resources to a project. It is equally important to have names and numbers of individuals who can be contacted in case of financial and project specific questions.
Terms and conditions	Legal rights and responsibilities between your organization and the vendor are outlined in this section. Typically companies have a "core" set of Terms and Conditions (Ts & Cs) they include with their proposal submittals.
Additional information	As appropriate, attachments and other project related information, not included in the above sections, could be provided here.

vendors have unique strategies and capabilities that set them apart from other vendors. Some of these approaches can result in time and cost savings.

Look for responses that are clear and specific that address your particular training need and delivery environment. Try to "read into" the proposed solution to see if the potential for "scope creep" exists. Sometimes, additional funding or tasking may be necessary, however, you want to make sure it is absolutely necessary and essential for the success of your project.

If your e-learning project is complex, you may want to allow participating vendors the opportunity to ask questions prior to final proposal submittal. This allows the vendors a chance to get more detailed information and "fine-tune" their responses.

Depending upon your time constraints you may ask the vendors to make an oral presentation of their proposal. This allows you and the prospective vendor the opportunity to have an open dialog to ask and answer questions. It also gives you some insight on how your relationship with a potential vendor might develop if their RFP is selected.

Occasionally, if the project is complex and potentially difficult, some organizations will provide a nominal stipend to the short list of bidders to offset some of the cost to construct a response. As you can imagine, the resources necessary to develop a well thought out proposal takes a fair amount of time and resources.

Finally, from the responses you receive and the "feelings" you get as you work through the RFP process you will select a preferred vendor. Based on their response to your RFP, a more formal Statement of Work (SOW) can be produced that outlines the tasks they are going to perform, items to be delivered, and schedule and cost that is more contractual and legally binding.

If you were careful in constructing effective guidelines and made your vendor selection based on the various phases of the process including the RFI phase, you will be well on your way to a successful project.

SUMMARY

As you can see, a formal proposal process can be lengthy and needs to be accounted for in the planning stages of your project. Variations of this process can be used based on your individual company and e-learning needs.

The more effort you put into the design of clear and constructive guidelines for your RFI and RFP responses, the closer you will be to identifying a vendor that will address the unique requirements of your e-learning project. Adhering to the entire RFI/RFP process may be difficult depending upon your training delivery date. However, your ability to follow the process to some degree will help your vendor selection process and contribute to the success of your e-learning initiative.

The days of conducting "business on a handshake" may be long forgotten or abandoned. Regardless, the RFI/RFP process is an accepted business practice that works in the best interest of all parties concerned.

RESOURCES

Readings

Cowan, S.L. (2000). Outsourcing Training. Alexandria, VA: *Info-Line, ASTD.*

Components of a Typical RFP. Instructional Designs, Inc.

Field, T. (1997). An outsourcing buyers guide caveat emptor. *CIO Magazine, CXO Media, Inc.*

Mielke, D. (1998). Put it in writing. *Network World, Inc.*

Morris, B. (1998). How to write a request for proposal for a web project. *INT Media Group, Inc.*

Romero, J. (2001). The Art of the RFP.

➤ABOUT THE AUTHOR

Patrick Hentschell has been working in the multimedia industry for more than 15 years as an instructional designer and project manager. As a professional he has worked for some of the industry's giants that include IBM and General Electric. He has worked with a variety of institutions that include manufacturing, government, banking, insurance, and public education. His experience developing technology-based courseware ranges from military equipment troubleshooting and repair to software application training for end users and performance support.

Mr. Hentschell received a Master's degree from Michigan State University in Instructional Systems Design, a Bachelor's degree in Mathematics from Saginaw Valley State University and an Associate's degree in Commercial Photography from Lansing Community College.

CHAPTER 15

CLICKING WITH VENDORS—WHAT TO ASK YOUR E-LEARNING VENDOR BEFORE YOU GET INVOLVED

➤**JOHN HARTNETT**

Let's face it, the only thing expanding faster than the number of learning management systems is the number of training companies courting your company's dollars. Every day it seems there's a new suitor on your doorstep pushing to do your web-based training (WBT) project. Partnering with an online learning company is a little bit like a marriage. So before you tie the knot, here are some suggested discovery questions for your WBT prenuptial agreement.

IS THIS THEIR FIRST TIME?

In the eighteenth century, virginity may have been a marital asset, but in the information age, it's grounds for calling off the wedding. Funny as that may sound, many training companies are trying to bankroll their expertise in CBT or database design into the web realm. This doesn't always work well. Make sure your training company has experience. Make sure that it's done a few WEB projects before. Ask to see samples of its work—both screen designs and working models of programs it's delivered. If a company can't show you any working samples, that is, WBT programs that real students are using and that a client paid real money to have developed, think twice about their level of experience. Granted, most companies will have some trouble showing you training samples from corporate intranets. This is understandable, as many clients don't publish their WBT programs on the World Wide Web, and many don't want to give outside companies access to their internal training programs. But to be fair, any WBT vendor worthy of an RFP should have something to show you—either on their site or as a working sample.

You're probably asking yourself, why would any e-learning company not have a presentable sample of training? They could be a back-end database development company trying to move into the e-learning market. Or they could be an LMS vendor trying to launch a "Custom Content" division. They could be a content creation tool or computer hardware vendor trying to expand their offerings. Or they could be a company known for their library of off-the-shelf training trying to use custom work as a leader into their catalog. Whatever the reason, make sure your project isn't their guinea pig.

ARE THEIR SAMPLES INTERACTIVE?

Similarly, when your prospective partners show off their WBT play list, take a close look at the level and nature of interactivity the students were forced to endure. Lots of new WBT companies are making a living translating self-study guides to the web, only to have students "read and click" their way through the course. Good WBT uses a variety of interactions tailored to the content and the computing environment to keep the students engaged through the course.

But interactivity alone still is not a good enough sign that you've met your one and only love. If a company seems to specialize in asynchronous web-based courses, they may not be a good candidate for a highly interactive open-ended learning simulation. Likewise, companies that do nothing but simulations may not be right for your five asynchronous courses on human anatomy. First make sure their samples are interactive, then make sure the type of interactivity matches the training you expect to do on the web.

ARE THEIR DESIGN SKILLS UP TO THE INDUSTRY STANDARD?

I'm not even talking about minimum stuff here like consistent use of shadows and colors, fast downloads, cross-browser support, and JavaScript rollover states to buttons, and the like. Everyone will probably be up to speed on these basic skills. You should, however, also expect screen design that takes the user into account, visual balance, minimum user scrolling, and other "aesthetics." The industry standard for training screen design is rising daily. You shouldn't have to settle for a long list of text links along the left side of the browser and a small white content area with a single content graphic. Well-designed e-learning uses interfaces that support and extend the training content, or at a minimum do no harm. Every day another talented graphic designer or art director makes the switch to the web. Make sure your WBT partner's designers aren't just making pretty pictures that don't work, or functional pictures that aren't pretty. You have a right to pretty pictures that do work and, above all, enhance the training experience.

DO THEY HAVE THE BASICS?

What are the basics? Well, for starters, do they have a home page? This is one of those no-brainers that really sets me off. How can an e-learning partner even hope to do your web work if they don't have a home page of their own? But this happened to me just a few months ago. At a kickoff meeting for an e-learning storefront site (i.e., that is, a World Wide Web site where training will be offered for sale), one of the chief architects of the site didn't even have an e-mail address. Why? Because he was partnering with a larger company to gain credibility. Prior to this project his main experience had been in academic consulting on print-based projects. Similarly, and I know I may sound like a snob here, if your e-learning partner's e-mail address ends with "aol.com," "yahoo.com," or "hotmail.com" I suggest you leave them at the altar. They're not good enough for you.

ARE THEY "ONE-TOOL TOMMIES?"

The best WBT companies aren't tied to a particular technology or a particular set of tools. Each web language that allows for learner interactivity has its advantages and disadvantages. A company that uses nothing but Flash for all animations is not going to work for you if your IT department bans all plug-ins. Similarly, a company that develops everything in Java is going to miss the simplicity and easy maintenance of a JavaScript solution. A company that hosts all training in a Unix environment will have a hard time on your Windows NT servers if you're going to require ActiveX controls. The best WBT partners use a mix of tools, languages, and techniques to match the program to your learning environment.

This is a particularly frequent problem for the "Custom Content" divisions of companies that sell enterprise-level LMSs. Companies who get most of their revenue from a hosted learning management or content creation system naturally tend to steer you to that solution. No matter how "custom" the content may start out, in the end it is going to be hosted on their servers using their preferred technologies. Consequently, you're project is going to get steered to the technologies that work best with their hosting environment. It is far better, in my opinion, to choose a technology-neutral vendor who will put your needs before their own.

DO THEY WANT CHILDREN?

Once your e-learning project is born into the world, it will have to be hosted somewhere. You have three basic choices: your servers, your vendor's servers, or an outside source. If your potential e-learning vendor can't accommodate the hosting plan that will work best for you, find another who will. But even if you do find someone whose child-rearing philosophy agrees with yours, you still might want to stick with a vendor who has the flexibility to host training anywhere you desire. This way as your needs or your IT department involvement changes, your training will be able to stay or move to where you need it.

ARE THEY POPULAR WITH THEIR FRIENDS?

In Arthur Miller's play *Death of a Salesman*, Willy Loman frequently admires salesmen who he thinks are "well-liked." I'm not suggesting that your e-learning vendor has to win a popularity contest. But I am suggesting that the best e-learning vendors have a presence in the industry. Do they present at trade shows and conferences? Are they publishing articles in the industry? Are they known to journalists or often-quoted in other publications? Do they speak at ASTD or technology-training association functions? The e-learning learning curve is fairly steep on the development side. Think twice about placing your trust in a lone-wolf e-learning vendor with no visible means of support.

ARE THEY "TRAINERS," "TECHNICIANS," OR BOTH?

Sometimes it seems like every training company and authoring tool manufacturer with access to Dreamweaver is suddenly in the web-based training development business. Trainers know how learners learn, but they don't usually know how to make websites that work. Likewise, Internet Service Providers and custom software companies are pumping out websites and text-based training programs using tired engineering paradigms—if it doesn't crash, it must be good. Engineers know how to produce software, but they don't ask the same questions training people ask— what are the learning objectives, what's easy to use, what will attract attention, what do we want to get people to do, what will they remember?

Most e-learning vendors started on one side of the fence and added the other later. Some companies started from the front-end (user interface and instructional design) and added the back-end learning management and technology expertise later. Other companies started from the back-end technology engineering and added user interface and instructional design expertise later. There's nothing inherently wrong with either growth path as long as the adult child of the union has a balanced personality. Think of it as an Apple versus Microsoft rivalry. Although the companies started worlds apart, now that they're both mature it's amazing to see how much OS X (the latest operating system from Apple) and Windows XP (the latest from Microsoft) actually have in common.

The best partners for your WBT project will have a combination of training and technical expertise. E-learning is both an intellectual event and a piece of technology. The best partners for you will be those that can appreciate both sides of the equation.

DO THEY OFFER FULL-FEATURED SYSTEMS ENGINEERING?

Training smarts and Internet expertise alone are fine for a stand-alone training piece. But what if you want courses that reconfigure themselves automatically when the learner logs in? What if you want centralized content and student record-keeping for 40,000 students scattered all over the world? What if your test questions need to be reevaluated based on the number of learners that get the questions right or wrong? What if you want the interaction questions to appear in a random order each time someone sees the page? This is complicated stuff. Most newly minted WBT companies just learned their keyboard shortcut commands last week. They certainly don't have the depth or talent to tackle today's top-rated database technologies. If your project is broad in scale, or could grow that way, make sure your training partner has someone around who knows this stuff.

WILL THEY STAY CLOSE TO HOME?

Lately, the e-learning world seems to be enjoying a huge influx in overseas developers. Now there isn't anything right or wrong about using overseas developers to get your e-learning done. Several of the top e-learning companies have over half of their developers in India. In fact, one company that claims to be the largest e-learning development company in the world is based in India. You need to ask how the overseas personnel will fit into the overall project plan. Make sure you are comfortable with the project management procedures and communication methods your vendor will use to route the work back and forth across the oceans.

WILL THEY PLAN FOR THE FUTURE?

One of the promises of the Internet revolution is to cut unnecessary waste. It makes no sense to have your e-learning company produce all new graphics for your program and then be unable to use those new assets in your other training materials: instructor guides, PowerPoint presentations, advanced training courses, or anything else for that matter. Make sure your WBT partner is adept at reusing your existing assets and creates images and saves them so they can be used again. Specifically, make sure they use stock photos with liberal reusage rights (royalty-free being the best), and saves copies of important imagery at print-quality resolutions (onscreen images are fine at 72 dpi, but laser printers need at least 300 dpi. Real printing, like for a poster to display behind an instructor or a four-color self-paced training guidebook, will need even higher resolution.) Make sure any talent they use for photography signs permission letters that clear you for web distribution. It does you no good to pay for a model's time (even if it is only fifty bucks to the good-looking guy who works on the floor below you) only to find you can't legally "repurpose" that photograph when the course graduates from your company intranet to an Internet-based training site. Experienced WBT developers are adept at obtaining clear rights to their work and your materials. If you're only going to do online learning, this isn't as much of an issue. But if you're going to use blended learning approaches, you'll need assets that can travel easily from medium to medium.

DO THEY HAVE A BALANCED PLAY LIST?

Look for companies that have experience in different kinds of training and working with different kinds of companies. Have they done both software training and soft skills training, for example? A company that has pumped out a hundred WBT programs dedicated to using Microsoft Word and Excel may not be the best choice for your sales training simulation course. Similarly, a company that does almost all of its work for one company or one industry doesn't have the breadth of clients to know your industry standards. Look for a balance in their client lists: government, health care, Fortune 500, and others. Stay away from ad agency "new media" departments whose primary expertise comes from their one big print or TV client who threw them a web bone to keep the new media people from bugging the account execs. Likewise avoid game developers and Hollywood special effects houses that do a couple of training projects a year "just to pay the bills." Similarly, I'll repeat my earlier advice. Avoid the "custom content" divisions of large LMS companies who have experience in only one technology environment.

DO THEY WORK "TIME AND MATERIALS, ESTIMATE NOT TO EXCEED," OR SOMETHING ELSE?

There are many different ways of billing clients. Make sure you are comfortable with the way your web-based training company wants to work with you. Do watch out for seemingly innocent licensing agreements that sound inexpensive but add up fast. Companies that charge little or nothing up front sometimes have per-user charges that can run your total costs into the hundreds of thousands of dollars. Also ask about incidental expenses. Postage, courier fees, disk duplication, and hosting fees aren't a lot of money, but be sure you understand up front just who is paying for what on your date. This will allow you to effectively compare your bids.

HOW MUCH DO THEY WANT UP FRONT?

Some robber barons are asking for 75 percent due on receipt of a purchase order. Do yourself a favor—keep a little something for yourself until the job is over. It's fair to give a training company something to get going, but try to limit your marriage dowry to no more that a quarter or a third of the estimated budget.

DO THEY HAVE ANY FRIENDS?

I'll let you in on a little industry secret. No one person can create world-class training anymore, just as no one person can create state-of-the-art film. Web-based training demands too many competing talents. You need a balanced team of eagle-eyed art directors, willow-worded writers, code-crunching developers, whipped-up instructional designers, and animal animators to make each element of your

WBT project world-class. And the whole is nothing more than the sum of its parts. Want world-class? Then make each element in the program world-class. Even in a small company like mine, I act more as a symphony conductor than a solo musician. Almost every project I do requires bringing in interface design specialists, Flash animators, Java programmers, and HTML gurus to round out my expertise, extensive as it may be.

Sure, you're asking, but what about those "Web Training in a Box" programs I saw at the last ASTD conference? They promised I could do WBT right on my desktop. Well, you can. Just like I can take my video camera outside and shoot "Star Wars Phantom Menace" in my backyard. Video cameras don't make you George Lucas any more than word processors make you Ernest Hemingway. Nor do WBT authoring tools or content creation systems make you an e-learning developer/producer. Remember, it wasn't just James Cameron who made *Titanic*. It was the whole production company—computer-generated effects teams, Celine Dion's overwrought solos, and, of course, Leonardo DiCaprio's boyish good looks.

Even if you decide to design and develop your training in-house, get some help along the way. That help can come from books and articles, seminars and classes, or even hiring a trusted soul who has been down the aisle before to walk you through your first project.

ARE THEIR PEOPLE COMMITTED TO YOU?

While we're on the subject, be sure to monitor the number of freelancers that end up on your project. There's nothing wrong with freelancers, per se. All e-learning vendors use outside help from time to time. This helps keeps ongoing costs low while allowing them to bring in a lot of help to keep projects on track when things pile up. But if you're seeing more fresh faces than familiar ones, think about going with a more established vendor.

ARE THEY COMPATIBLE? ARE THEY CERTIFIABLE?

Be sure to check out your vendor's relationship with emerging standards. If standards such as SCORM, IMS, and AICC are important to your organization, pay very close attention to your vendor's standard status. It's relatively easy to declare yourself AICC compatible, for example. To be AICC certified, you have to go through a much more rigorous and objective process. If standards are important to you, make sure they're important to your vendor as well.

WILL THEY SIGN A PRENUPT?

Chances are if you carefully screen your e-learning suitor, you'll train happily ever after. But just in case things don't go well, it's wise to plan the breakup before the marriage. When the project or the relationship is over, who gets custody of the code for your courses? If your e-learning project uses library code from the vendor's other projects or products, do you own that code or do you have to license it? Once the relationship has ended, how will you handle maintenance on the projects you did together? Is it included for a period of time under a maintenance contract, or do you have to pay more for ongoing changes and enhancements?

Figure 15-1 is a checklist for you to use when selecting e-vendors:

☐ **Is this their first time?**

☐ **Are their samples interactive?**

☐ **Are their design skills up to the industry standard?**

☐ **Do they have the basics?**

☐ **Are they "one-tool Tommies?"**

☐ **Do they want children?**

☐ **Are they popular with their friends?**

☐ **Are they "trainers", "technicians" or both?**

☐ **Do they offer full-featured systems engineering?**

☐ **Will they stay close to home?**

☐ **Will they plan for the future?**

☐ **Do they have a balanced play list?**

☐ **Do they work "time and materials, estimate not to exceed," or something else?**

☐ **How much do they want up front?**

☐ **Do they have any friends?**

☐ **Are their people committed to you?**

☐ **Are they compatible? Are they certifiable?**

☐ **Will they sign a pre-nupt?**

FIGURE 15-1. **CHECKLIST FOR CHOOSING E-LEARNING VENDORS**

RESOURCES

Reading

Siegel, David. *Secrets of Successful Web Sites : Project Management on the World Wide Web.*

Website

Online Learning magazine
www.onlinelearningmag.com

➤ABOUT THE AUTHOR

John Hartnett is President and CEO of BlueMissile, a Minneapolis-based e-learning design and development company. He is an internationally known expert in the field of web-based training design and teaches many web and e-learning classes and seminars for companies and organizations all over the world.

As Technology Editor for *Online Learning* magazine, he writes the popular monthly column, *Nuts and Bolts*. John's book, *Making and Managing Online Learning*, will be available soon from Stylus Publishing.

Recently, he was Master of Ceremonies at the Influent Technologies *WBT Producer's Conference 2001* and a Keynote Panelist at *Online Learning 2001*. He was also a Featured Presenter at *Training 2002* in Atlanta and a judge for *Inc. Magazine's* annual Web Awards.

YOUR E-LEARNING QUESTIONS
ANSWERED BY THIS CHAPTER

➤ Are there ways to reduce
e-learning development time?

➤ How do we make e-learning
interesting?

CHAPTER 16

DESIGNING ASYNCHRONOUS LEARNING

➤LARRY ISRAELITE AND NANETTE DUNN

In a song released in 1980, Billy Joel described the ebb and flow of the pop music industry of the 1970s. And, in the end, he concluded that not all that much had really changed: Even called by a different name, rock and roll was still rock and roll.

Although Joel's target was the pop music industry, he might as well have been writing about the learning industry. Regardless of what we call things, the way we go about constructing products and programs that facilitate learning hasn't changed all that much in the past 30 years. And as Billy Joel expresses in his song, new names for old (but not necessarily invalid) ideas and approaches don't make those ideas different. It only means that we talk about them differently. And, sometimes, we even talk ourselves into believing they aren't the same, often at the expense of those who rely on us to create useful and meaningful learning products.

What does this have to do with e-learning or the design of e-learning? The answer is simple. As an industry and/or, perhaps, as a profession, we have stopped looking back—we have forgotten our roots. For some reason, we have chosen to ignore what we know about how people learn or how to design products intended to enable learning. We have approached the design of e-learning like it is something new and unique; like we have never designed instruction that is delivered using computer technology, or over a network, or that included a blend of individual (asynchronous) and group (synchronous) activities.

The other problem is that we continue to be enamored of technology. For years and years, we have allowed ourselves to be seduced by the lure of educational elixirs. The list is long—programmed instruction, instructional television, computer-based training, interactive video, multimedia, and now the Internet. Perhaps it is our ongoing affinity for toys. As children, we always loved receiving gifts of new toys. Sometimes we even played with them for a few days. But in many cases, they soon were relegated to the back of the closet, and we went back to our old standbys. We played with the toys that continued, over time, to bring us enjoyment.

As each new generation of learning technologies was introduced, the same thing seemed to happen. We enthusiastically embrace them, we play with them for a while, and then, when the technologies don't deliver on the overstated promises of learning and/or economic impact, we return to using the methods, tools, and technologies that have served us well in the past.

With this as a context, the topic of *designing for asynchronous learning* is, for the most part, the result of the emergence of the web as the latest teaching toy. Most learning professionals define asynchronous learning as learning products than can be used anytime and anywhere. But it's not like we haven't designed anytime/anywhere instructional products before. If fact, we have done it for years—paper-based self-study courses, early computer-based training, and even CD-Rom-based multimedia programs of the 1990s. Clearly, the web adds some technology resources that expand the media choices that need to be considered during the design and development process. But, by itself, the web is not an instructional device. It is, in its purest form, a tool that enables the effective and efficient distribution and storage of data. At the same time, and not insignificantly, it also is an extremely effective communication device, not unlike the telephone, that provides access to others in a way that simply wasn't possible before. But the instructional design process itself is not new. And the availability of the web should not influence how we go about the process of creating instructional products, other than providing instructional designers with some additional options when contemplating media.

We also should note that there are today two different models of asynchronous learning in the marketplace. The first might be referred to as the university model, which takes its name from the institutions of higher learning that have discovered that the web provides a great opportunity for expanding both the number and types of learners they can serve. The second approach, which might be called the corporate model, is used to improve the effectiveness and cost efficiency of corporate training and to create databases of useful information that can be rapidly accessed and used after training has been completed. The corporate model is the one we will address here.

LEARNING OR TEACHING

In her book on the Psychology of Learning for Instruction (Driscoll, 2000), Marcy Driscoll defines learning as, "a persisting change in performance or performance potential that results from experience and interaction with the world." Robert Gagné (Gagné, 1985) offers an alternate definition when he states that: "Learning is a change in human disposition or capability that persists over a period of time, and which is not simply ascribable to processes of growth." In each case, learning is described as an individual act. It is, by its very nature, an asynchronous act.

Each of us learns every day—anytime, anywhere, under a variety of conditions, with a variety of outcomes. We learn by ourselves; we learn when others are present. Sometimes other people interfere with learning. My children tell me that their teachers (and their parents), for example, often are obstacles to learning. We all have different learning styles. But to say we have learned is to say that we, individually, have changed somehow, which is, in the end, learning, something we do by ourselves.

Teaching, on the other hand, is a different matter altogether. Teaching is a process that, we hope, enables us to learn. That is to say that effective teaching provides some or all of the stimuli necessary for creating the "persisting change in performance" or the "change in human disposition or capability" referred to by Driscoll and Gagné. And we believe that it is teaching, and not learning, that can be either synchronous or asynchronous. Teaching can occur with groups and individuals, together or apart, all at once, or one at a time. So while the topic we will address here is asynchronous e-learning, we think it is important to keep in mind that there are some fundamental differences between learning and teaching, and what we really are offering is a way to think about the design and development of asynchronous teaching that enables learning—a subtle, but important distinction.

The challenge we face in discussing the design of e-learning is that it could evoke an unintended debate about theories of learning and instruction that:

➤ Would be difficult to resolve in a book devoted solely to that topic, never mind a single chapter;

➤ Make this chapter more theoretical than practical, which would, we believe, negate the goal of providing a useful job aide to learning professionals trying to make sense of what is already a confusing and frustrating problem—how to effectively use technology to enable learning.

We have tried, therefore, to present an approach that is learning theory neutral. We will, however, try to illustrate the way in which our approach can be used with the more common approaches to the design of instructional (or teaching) activities.

DESIGNING E-LEARNING

When designing classroom teaching material, the primary delivery medium is the teacher. We support the teacher by creating lesson plans and guides, PowerPoint presentations (remember overhead transparencies?), exercise sheets, and other adjunct instructional aides. The teacher has the responsibility for engaging participants in a variety of instructional activities, each intended in some way to facilitate learning. Even though the teacher cannot assure that learning occurs, she can provide learning support, some of which should been created as part of the instructional design, but some of which comes from simply observing what is going on in the classroom.

With asynchronous e-learning we face an entirely different problem. In this case, the instructional product itself is solely responsible for facilitating, or enabling, learning. This is not to say that learners don't take an active role; of course they do. But the design of the program must address all of the various types of support required to provide a meaningful and effective learning experience. And this is the challenge faced by individuals who are responsible for building learning products whose primary delivery medium is the web. The remainder of this chapter will contain a frame of reference for designing and developing asynchronous e-learning. We do so with the assumption that an appropriate instructional design methodology is already being applied. For reference, we recommend that the reader consider texts like *The Systematic Design of Instruction* (Dick, Carey, and Carey, 2000) or *Designing Web-Based Training* (Horton, 2000).

We believe that most e-learning products (asynchronous or otherwise) contain four basic elements or building blocks that are combined in a variety of ways to achieve the desired outcome, depending, of course, on the content, the audience, the objectives, and the available technologies. These building blocks of e-learning are as follows.

1. **Presentation** contains information about the learning context (i.e., the relationship between the skills to be learned in this program and those that have been acquired previously), content (information to be learned), instructions, or other information the designer wants to directly convey to the learner.

2. **Elicitation** requires learners to make a response that indicates understanding of content or to take an action in response to stimuli presented on the screen. Elicitation building blocks are developmental in nature and, as such, scores or results are neither tracked nor stored.

3. **Evaluation** measures the degree to which learners have mastered the relevant content. In some situations, elicitation building blocks can serve

this function, but with evaluation building blocks scores or results are typically stored for further reference.

4. **Collaboration** enables asynchronous interaction with an instructor, other learners, supervisors, or anyone else who might contribute to the learning experience.

Building blocks are not designs themselves. Rather, they represent the ways in which information can be presented to the learner in order to increase the likelihood that learning will occur. The design of the learning experience is the process through which these building blocks are selected, sequenced, and, of course, populated. It is important to note that we are not prescribing a methodology. Some people might prefer to lead with elicitation and follow with presentation, making collaboration available at all times. Other might take a more traditional route with several sequences of presentation, elicitation, collaboration, and evaluation. We do not have a position about which is better; both can be effective, as can any other combination. What we are saying is that most asynchronous e-learning programs will comprise some combination of the building blocks we have identified above.

It is important to remember that a building block is not the same as a screen, as a building block can comprise one or more screens, depending on the outcome they are intended to achieve. In addition, building blocks are not media specific. They can include audio, video, text, graphics, or any combination of these and other media. Building blocks simply represent a way of thinking about how to construct e-learning experiences.

THE BUILDING BLOCKS

Following are detailed explanations of some of the ways in which building blocks can be used in the design and development asynchronous e-learning. However, these are examples and in no way represent the only ways in which building blocks can be applied.

Presentation Building Blocks

Presentation with a purpose is essential. Content that looks good but which isn't organized to enable learning is of little value. Think of the learner asking these questions about the learning environment: Why should I learn? What is the content? How do I learn it? How will I know if I have learned? Presentation building blocks set the context for the answers to these questions.

Presentation building blocks can be used to:

➤ Communicate the learning context and provide directions

➤ Motivate the learner

➤ Present content

➤ Provide feedback

TABLE 16-1. **Presentation building blocks**

Purpose	Instructional Outcomes	Examples
Communicate the learning context or provide directions	➤ Put learners at ease and set expectations ➤ Provide guidance about the processes or strategies required to engage in the e-learning experience. ➤ Relate content to job or strategic initiatives	➤ Welcome e-mail ➤ Agenda/Map
Motivate the learner	➤ Create tension and demonstrate need ➤ Answer questions	➤ Home page/welcome screen
Present content	➤ Introduce concepts, processes, models, tools, or other instructional informatiom	➤ Interview or news story ➤ Slide show or video ➤ Articles or other written material
Provide feedback	➤ Assess current challenges to determine individual goals or focus ➤ Summarize key points ➤ Review	➤ Dialog boxes ➤ Self-assessment ➤ Resources

Table 16–1 contains more detailed descriptions of the building block examples. Once again, it is important to remember that these are only illustrations of the ways in which presentations can be used effectively in an asynchronous e-learning product. There are many other ways that presentations can be an effective technique.

Welcome E-mail

There is enormous motivational value in welcoming learners to the teaching experience and gaining their attention. A welcome e-mail from the instructor or an organizational leader can set a tone that is hard to replicate. The welcome e-mail may include a basic description of the course, why it's being offered, and the learning objectives. The welcome email establishes a connection between the instructor and the learner, which sets expectations and provides guidance about the processes or strategies required in the e-learning experience. We mentioned earlier that a building block isn't necessarily a screen within an e-learning product. In this case, it is an e-mail that might be sent by an executive before learners even begin participating in the learning experience.

Home Page/Welcome

One of the first presentations learners encounter might be a home page or a welcome screen. The structure of the screen is important in that it might be used for navigation during the remainder of the course and should be designed to ensure that learners don't become so frustrated they choose not to participate at all. A home page sets the expectations for what's in the course by listing program content. It also should answer basic questions such as how long it might take to complete the program and how to find help if it is needed. Perhaps most importantly, the home page should entice learners to engage.

Agenda/Map

Agendas or maps are a form of presentation that suggests a path through the teaching and learning experience. They can act as a syllabus to help learners keep track of where they are and where they want to go.

> ➤ Numbering items on an agenda often suggests to the learner that activities need to be completed in sequence, while bulleted items do not.

> ➤ The agenda or map may include references to several elements of a blended solution, such as a synchronous web session or a classroom meeting.

> ➤ They also can present a micro view of the individual course and/or a macro view of the course within a larger curriculum.

Interview/News Story

The interview/news story is a place within the course that acts a little like a research area or newspaper. The learner is presented with current research on the course topic and might read or hear reactions from organizational leaders or industry experts. This is a place to make a direct connection between the subject matter in the course and its uses on the job.

Slide Show or Video

Slide shows, with or without audio, provide a way to demonstrate skills without the use of video. Still shots are sequenced and aligned with text scripts to show the learner by example. The text and audio, if used, are identical. Learners that do not have access to audio should not miss any content by not being able to hear the presentation. Streaming video can be used as a replacement for slide shows, but it is critical to make sure that the intended audience will have access to a network that allows video to be used.

Dialog Boxes

Dialog boxes provide feedback for learners as they complete elicitation building blocks (described in detail later in the chapter). The text answers questions such as, "Did I do this right?" or "What did I do wrong?" Dialog boxes also can be used to guide learners to the next section of their learning experience.

Self-Assessments

In a classroom, instructors can gauge who understands and who doesn't and then make appropriate adjustments to the lesson. Online, learners are their own mentors to a certain extent. Self-assessments help learners determine where they are in the learning process. These often come before an elicitation building block and answer the question, "What do I know now?" When the learner has the answer then he or she can decide, "What do I need to know next?"

Resources

The resource area within an online course is similar to a mini-library with material directly related to the subject matter of the course. Examples of information to include in the resource area are book titles, articles, websites, job aids, presentations, and so on. References to the resource area can be included throughout the course such that the learner is trained to use it and will be inclined to do so on-the-job.

Both research and personal experience tell us we can listen to a teacher talk for hours and never learn a thing. Similarly, we can look at screen after screen of information, and it doesn't mean we were engaged in a learning process. Presentations in an asynchronous e-learning environment aren't all that different from classroom presentations. Active participation keeps learners engaged by stimulating the recall of prior learning or introducing new stimuli. This provides the motivation people need to meaningfully engage in a learning experience.

Elicitation Building Blocks

Elicitation building blocks can require learners to:

> ➤ Select or construct a response that requires understanding or application of previously taught content.

> ➤ Take action in response to stimuli, without having previously seen or reviewed relevant content or information.

While these applications of elicitation may sound the same, they are, in fact, different.

In the case of the former, the focus is on practice, typically after the learner has experienced one or more presentation building blocks. Learners demonstrate their ability to perform learning objectives by taking what they learned and applying it to real-life scenarios. For instance, we may ask learners to choose the best response to an objection offered by a customer. Learners also may be asked to apply a new process for facilitating a team meeting on-the-job and then have a discussion with their supervisors about what happened when they did.

When learners take action in response to stimuli, they are engaged in a form of discovery learning or, perhaps, a simulation. Learners are presented with information or a scenario and then asked to initiate a response by typing, dragging and dropping, comparing and contrasting, or some other form of original input. Based on learner input, additional stimuli are provided, and the cycle begins again. This continues until a natural conclusion is reached or until learners and/or the program itself determine that the use of other building blocks would enhance the overall quality and effectiveness of learning experience.

Table 16–2 contains more detailed descriptions of the building block examples. They are only illustrations of the ways in which eliciting a response from learners can be used effectively when designing asynchronous e-learning products.

Virtual Brainstorm (Flipchart)

We spend a lot of time in meetings. Often we are asked to brainstorm ideas and write them on a flipchart or whiteboard. The virtual brainstorm offers a "flipchart" with the same functions as the life-size version, but in reality it's a graphic on the screen. A question is posed to a small group of people (four photos of people). Learners click on a photo to read/hear what the person has to contribute to the group discussion. The group member's comment is automatically transferred to the flipchart. After learners hear what everyone in the group has to say, they are presented with a text box on which they can add their own comments to the flipchart. This building block allows the learner to dig more deeply into a concept that is open to various interpretations or applications.

Skeptic's Corner

This is an instructional technique for replicating the richness of classroom discussion in an asynchronous program that may or may not make use of threaded discussions or any other technology that links learners together. This building block comprises three sections. First, learners receive an on-screen message indicating

TABLE 16-2. Elicitation Building Blocks

Purpose	Instructional Outcomes	Examples
Select or Construct Responses	➤ Apply concepts ➤ Respond to examples ➤ Plan job application	➤ Virtual brainstorm ➤ Skeptic's corner ➤ Create an action plan
Take action in response to stimuli	➤ Discovery learning ➤ Simulation	➤ What would you say? ➤ What happens next ➤ You're the boss

that the classroom cynic has a comment to make. After reading the comment, learners construct a response based on their own opinions and experiences. This is then followed by the response an instructor might make were this conversation happening in a classroom rather than online.

For example, in a an asynchronous program on collaboration, the skeptic might say: *"You can't teach collaboration. Either you can work with other people or you can't!"* One learner might respond by writing: *"I agree. I've worked with plenty of people who couldn't find a way to work well with people who were different than they were."* The virtual instructor would follow this entry with the comment: *"Research actually shows that collaboration is a trainable skill, not a trait. So while there may be people who have a difficult time collaborating with others, usually this is because they don't know how, or, more often, because there are no incentives to make them want to collaborate."* In some settings, a link to a threaded discussion is provided as a way to create a broader conversation about the topic.

Create an Action Plan
This building block enables learners to internalize and reflect on what they have learned. Further, action plans provide a concrete format for determining how new knowledge and skills can be applied on-the-job. Learners generate ideas for creative ways to apply new skills, which are then discussed and clarified with learners' managers. In their most robust form, action plans are implemented, with the results reported to and, once again, discussed with managers.

What Would You Say?
The "what would you say" building block is an interesting way to elicit performance by asking learners to react to some information that has just been presented to them. For example, suppose learners were introduced to a model for handling objections in a sales situation. First, a scenario is presented (the stimulus). Learners are asked, "What would you say?" and a text entry box appears on the screen. Learners enter their responses and "submit" them. The feedback is an expert response to the scenario, listed side by side with learner responses. This strategy works well when the goal is to have learners respond to the scenarios they will encounter when applying the skills they are learning in the course on-the-job.

What Happens Next and You're the Boss
These building blocks are variations on a critical theme in eliciting a response from learners. In each case, learners are asked to consider the situation with which they are presented and, in most cases, select the best decision from those that are presented. In the case of "what happens next," decisions tend to be procedural—what work task or process element would make most sense, given the data available. With "you're the boss," decisions tend to focus on how to apply human resources to solve business problems. Although the structure of these two building blocks is similar, the information needed to make the required decisions is much different.

Elicitation building blocks use both "figure it out" and "try it out" discovery activities. Sometimes we try things out in order to figure them out. Discovery is precisely what the elicitation building block allows the learner to do. In *The Psychology of Learning for Instruction*, Driscoll quotes Jerome Bruner, a prominent cognitive learning theorist: "Bruner defined discovery as `all forms of obtaining knowledge for oneself by the use of one's own mind' (1961, p. 22). Discovery teaching generally involves not so much the process of leading students to discover what is 'out there', but rather, their discovering what is in their own heads." (Driscoll, 2000).

In contrast to the presentation building block, the elicitation building block allows the learner to act, to respond to stimuli rather than simply recall or identify content. This is a time for exploration and discovery for the learner and they should have access to guidance without fear of judgment, grading, and scores. The result is a teaching experience in which both comprehension (figure it out) and application (try it out) are the desired learning outcomes.

Evaluation Building Blocks

The main instructional purpose of evaluation building blocks is to measure the degree to which learners have mastered the content. In other words, did learners learn what they were supposed to learn? Unlike the examples provided in the elicitation section, which were developmental in nature, the specific purpose of evaluation building blocks is to test the learner. Learner responses are judged, scored, stored, and progress is measured. Because the actual structure of evaluations can be identical to the structure of the examples provided in the section on elicitation above, we have not provided additional examples here. We do, however, offer some questions that must be addressed when constructing evaluations for asynchronous e-learning products.

When creating an evaluation building block consider these questions:

➤ Is an evaluation appropriate, given the audience and the content?

➤ How much time do we allow for the evaluation? Will the evaluation "shut off" if the time is exceeded?

➤ How many times can the evaluation be taken?

➤ Do we allow learners to go "back" to look for answers or change answers?

➤ How many questions are appropriate?

➤ Are questions aligned with the learning objectives?

➤ How will the evaluation be scored? Numerical? Pass/Fail?

➤ Is feedback provided at the end of the evaluation? Can learners link directly back to the area of the course that covered questions they got wrong.

➤ Who has access to evaluation scores? Learners? Supervisors?

The answers to each of the questions are directly related to the culture of the organization in which the evaluations will be implemented and to the technical feasibility of implementation. One organization may insist supervisors get a printout with numerical scores and the time it took learners to complete the evaluation. Other organizations may prefer scores be pass/fail and kept confidential. The actual design of the learning product and the system through which it is delivered may not make it possible to record certain types of scores and send data to particular places. You must identify key stakeholders in your organization and partner with them to determine what works best for learners and the organization, and what is actually possible.

Collaboration Building Blocks

The possibility of collaboration in asynchronous teaching is what differentiates web-based products from earlier computer-based training products. Collaboration enables two or more people to work together in support of their learning. In classrooms, this happens all the time through the use of discussions, small group work, team assignments, and many other techniques with which we are all very familiar. However, this form of collaboration tends to be synchronous—people working together in real time. And there is a chapter in the book devoted to designing technology-based synchronous learning. In this chapter, however, we are focused on a different issue—how to take advantage of the value of collaboration, but in such a way that people can work together at different time, or asynchronously.

Asynchronous communication (and collaboration) is hardly new to us. We actually use it all the time; we send letters and e-mail (all right, we used to send letters), we leave notes, we use voicemail. Although using asynchronous tools might slow collaboration down, it certainly does not eliminate it, nor does it eliminate the value that working with other people can create. So the question, then, is how can collaboration be used in an asynchronous teaching context?

Collaboration building blocks are intended to:

➤ Facilitate interaction between and among other learners, instructors, coaches, mentors, supervisors, and anyone else who might add value to a learning experience.

➤ Result in a repository of opinions, insights, documents, job aides, and tools that can be used during and after learning.

Table 16–3 contains a description of the instructional outcomes for which collaboration building blocks can be used, along with some examples of how we have used them in e-learning products. Following are more detailed descriptions of the building block examples provided in Table 16–3.

E-mail Assignments

E-mail assignments can be used as a replacement for the individual coaching and feedback that learners typically receive in the classroom. Learners are asked to complete worksheets, analyze data, create presentations, or perform other tasks

TABLE 16-3. Collaboration Building Blocks

Purpose	Instructional Outcomes	Examples
Interact with others	➤ Observe and evaluate ➤ Share reactions and insights ➤ Provide participant feedback ➤ Discuss continued job application ➤ Discuss continued learning progress ➤ Assess impact of new ideas	➤ E-mail assignments ➤ What do you think? ➤ Discussion board
Create a repository	➤ Gather and document best practices ➤ Create or provide follow-on learning events	➤ Document repository

that directly relate to learning objectives or desired outcomes. The assignments are sent to a facilitator who provides feedback, suggestions for improvements, or other information intended to help learners improve their understanding of program content. Assignments can be collaboratively, but asynchronously, worked on by several learners using a variety of web-based tools, and the results can be posted to a repository for further use and reference.

What Do You Think?
This building block encourages learners to react to a situation and then learn from the reactions of others. For instance, learners may asked to complete a learning styles inventory in order to help them better understand the conditions under which they most effectively learn. Then they would click on a "compare" button to see how their results compare with those other learners who have also completed the survey This, in turn, might lead to a threaded discussion about how learning styles might influence work effectiveness. Another form of the "what do you think" building block would be to integrate opinion polls into a learning experience. This strategy is especially effective for topics that don't have definitive right or wrong answers.

Discussion Boards
Discussion boards are quite flexible and can be used for a variety of purposes. For instance, they can be used at the start of a program to enable learners to share in-

formation about their roles and the things they hope to gain from participating. They can be used to share best practices or to post responses from peers, the facilitator or other experts to questions raised in the program. In many ways, the challenges faced when attempting to use discussion boards effectively mirror those in e-learning in general. It is a mistake to assume that people will be active participants simply because discussion boards are available. Their use must be carefully planned, they must be directly linked to learning activities and outcomes, and they must be perceived as beneficial because of the quality and relevance of the information they contain. Finally, experience has shown that the level of participation in discussion boards varies greatly. As a result, there must be sufficient numbers of learners to ensure that there will be sufficient fresh content, opinions, and perspectives.

Document Repository

A document repository provides a method for storing work products that are created during and after participation in a learning experience. In organizations that already have working knowledge management systems, this building block may simply be a reference to that system. When such systems don't exist, a repository can create a context for sharing and collaboration between and among learners, something that can greatly enhance the degree to which people continue to learn after the formal or structured portion of a program has ended.

The goal of building collaborative activities into asynchronous learning experiences is to provide a way to engage others in what might otherwise be an individual activity. Even though we have provided examples that may require special technologies, collaboration can require little more than access to e-mail and some form of shared or common folder or directories. The challenge is to creatively take advantage of the technologies that are available.

CONCLUSION

So what should the reader make of all this talk about rock and roll, learning, teaching, and building blocks? We think the answer is simple. Instructional designers have known for years how to create effective asynchronous teaching products. But for reasons that we don't quite understand, the introduction of new technologies causes some sort of design amnesia to set in. Suddenly, there are new words to describe and new rules to guide the work we have done for years. And everyone gets confused.

We believe that the four building blocks—presentation, elicitation, evaluation, and collaboration—are the foundation on which effective asynchronous e-learning can be based. We have attempted to present examples of how they can be used to weave together instructional designs that result in learning. We encourage people new to the field of instructional design to read the books we referred to earlier and, above all else, seek out the advice of those who have done this before. As Billy Joel suggests so eloquently in his song, you can make up all kinds of fancy new names, but that doesn't mean you've invented anything new. New technologies and new names notwithstanding, all we are talking about here is that application of a few principles of learning and instructional design, and that is not new at all.

RESOURCES

Readings

Dick, Walter; Carey, Lou; and Carey, James O. (2000). *The Systematic Design of Instruction*, fifth ed. Boston: *Allyn & Bacon.*

Driscoll, Marcy (2000). *Psychology of Learning for Instruction.* Boston: Allyn and Bacon.

Gagné, Robert M. (1985). *The Conditions of Learning*, fourth ed. New York: Holt, Rinehart and Winston.

Horton, William (2000). *Designing Web-Based Training.* New York: John Wiley & Sons, Inc.

➤ABOUT THE AUTHORS

Larry Israelite, Ph.D. is a senior vice president of Product Development for The Forum Corporation and FT Knowledge Company. Dr. Israelite is responsible for assembling The Forum Corporation's traditional and technology-based product and service offerings into targeted learning solutions for its customers. He has over 20 years of experience in the creation of technology-based learning products.

Prior to joining Forum, Larry served in a variety of training management positions at John Hancock Financial Services, Oxford Heath Plans, and the Digital Equipment Corporation. Larry holds a Bachelor of Arts in Theater from Washington College. His graduate degrees from Arizona State University include a Master of Science in Instructional Media and a Ph.D. in Instructional Technology.

Nanette Dunn is an Instructional Designer at The Forum Corporation. She designs and develops learning solutions for classroom and technology-based delivery. Her recent research explores the use of collaborative tools for online facilitation and the intersection of desired learning outcomes with media selection strategies.

Prior to joining The Forum Corporation, Nanette worked as an Instructional Designer for John Hancock Financial Services, Inc. There she created product and technical training programs. Her work in the financial industry allowed her to hold Series 6, 63, 26, and Life Accident and Health licenses.

Nanette holds a Bachelor of Arts in Anthropology from Mount Holyoke College and graduated Summa Cum Laude with a Masters of Education in Instructional Design from the University of Massachusetts.

CHAPTER 17

GETTING READY FOR SYNCHRONOUS E-LEARNING

➤JENNIFER HOFMANN

AN INTRODUCTION TO SYNCHRONOUS E-LEARNING

Anyone involved in the training and education arena during the past couple of years has probably heard the term "synchronous learning." It's obviously a trendy delivery method that's all the rage. But what is it, really? The most common definition is some variation of the following:

> **Synchronous Learning**—This term refers to instruction that is led by a facilitator in real time. Examples of synchronous interactions can include traditional instructor-led classrooms, conference calls, instant-messengers, video-conferences, whiteboard sessions, and synchronous online classrooms/classroom software.

We will use this as a working definition for the purposes of this article with one very important modification: for our purposes we are referring to *instruction that is led by a facilitator in real-time using the Internet or intranet as the delivery medium.*

In my experience, simply telling people how synchronous training is defined is not enough. I have tried using definitions, case studies, "hands-off" product demonstrations—any means at my disposal. The people to whom I am speaking think they understand what I am saying, but time after time my experience proves out that until the other party has physically participated in a synchronous program they do not fully grasp the concept or the potential of this delivery method. Because of this, I strongly encourage readers who have not had the opportunity to learn synchronously to go to the web and sign up for some free online synchronous demonstrations right away. Start with programs offered by synchronous software providers (see "A Partial List Of Synchronous Software Vendors" at the end of this chapter). After you have had the experience of being a participant in this environment, you will be much better equipped to make decisions concerning implementation, design, and delivery of synchronous information, and the information in this chapter will be that much more meaningful for you.

This chapter focuses on two aspects of getting ready for synchronous learning. The first section deals with synchronous training implementation at your organization and includes information on developing a learning strategy, determining your organization's readiness for synchronous e-Learning, and finally some tips on selecting the right synchronous vendor for your organization. The second section deals with the effective creation and delivery of synchronous learning in your organization.

SYNCHRONOUS TRAINING IMPLEMENTATION IN YOUR ORGANIZATION

Designing a Synchronous Learning Strategy for Your Organization

Often the early synchronous initiatives at an organization are not viewed as successful—and it is very easy to fall into the trap of blaming these perceived failures on the learning technologies. While technical issues often create cumbersome and intrusive problems during learning events, frequently the difficulties were caused because the technology solution was implemented without adequate planning and assessment of desired outcomes. Like any other business initiative, organizations need to create an implementation strategy to ensure a successful initiative. Each organization must create their own e-learning team and create their own strategic process—but any learning strategy should be developed based on common themes.

The very first thing your team should do is to draft a statement that explains why you are creating an e-learning strategy. While this information may be known to the members of the e-learning team, there is a strong possibility you may need to provide documentation to support your decision later on. Be prepared for that eventuality.

After you have defined your business issues, it is critical that you conduct an environmental analysis to ensure that synchronous e-learning is a feasible addition to the mix of training deliverables in your organization.

To determine an organization's readiness you should complete the following action items:

1. **Examine the Climate Report.** If your organization does not have a climate that considers training to be critical to its success, it is likely that synchronous e-learning will be viewed as a "fad" and won't enjoy the success you are anticipating. Your training team may not receive the necessary resources and your participants may not be able to create a successful learning environment at their desks. To determine your learning climate, consider the following questions:

   ➤ Does senior management support employee development?

   ➤ What HR systems are already in place to support learning?

   ➤ What conditions in your organization create manager support for learning initiatives and motivate employees to learn? Knowing what these factors are will help you to sell the synchronous initiative to the organization.

   Based on your findings, you may determine that the current learning climate in your organization may not support a synchronous e-learning initiative.

2. **Assess Employee Readiness.** Even though synchronous training is a facilitator-led environment, employees need to be motivated to participate and learn at their desks. Are your learners ready for changes in the way they learn and receive information? To find out:

   ➤ If your organization is global, determine what you need to identify specific language and technology needs.

   ➤ Create learner profiles, including a "technological comfort" profile for each audience.

   ➤ Determine learner needs. Are they already getting the training they think they need? If so, what can you do to motivate them to learn in this environment?

3. **Assess Informational Technology Team Support.** I have had the unfortunate opportunity to see several synchronous initiatives fail because the IT department was not enlisted into the process early enough, if at all. The most extreme example I can recall has to do with an organization that spent tens of thousands of dollars on synchronous software licenses and never once consulted the IT department about security concerns, desktop configurations, and bandwidth availability. After the contract with the software vendor was completed, this organization found that they were not able to use the synchronous technology at all. It is essential that you get the IT group involved early and keep them involved throughout the process.

- Build a positive partnership between your training organization and your informational technologies group.

- Involve IT early in the technology selection process. If IT is not involved early you might make a selection that does not meet their requirements, and waste time and money along they way.

- Determine the security, desktop, and bandwidth concerns of your IT group. Often a training organization makes a synchronous software purchasing decision that does not meet IT requirements. Knowing this information up front can help you to avoid serious and expensive problems later on.

- Identify the software approval process.

While you are at it, dig a little deeper to find out about the technological capabilities already available to your training department. To be successful, you may need to invest in more than just software. Discover:

- What technologies are already in place to support your training environment?

- Are they working?

- Are they scalable? You may want to be able to have 500 participants online at the same time, but you might not have the bandwidth available to support those numbers.

- How can you take advantage of them?

- What do the learner's desktops look like? For example, is everyone standardized on PCs, or do you need to support Mac and Unix machines? What is the ratio of dial-up connections to high speed access? Do most of the learners have sound cards and headsets?

Development Implementation Plan

Now that you have determined that your organization is ready for synchronous e-learning, you should create an implementation plan that outlines your learning strategy and includes at least the following items:

- Definition of e-learning at your organization. It is important to have a standard definition so people have a clear understanding of what is being discussed. An example is " electronically delivered learning methods such as CD-ROM, web-based learning, online assessments, web-based reinforcement tools, and online coaching."

- Overall learning strategy

- Links of learning strategy to business strategy

- Roll out plan, including

  - What courses should be converted first? Early courses should not be courses that will have a negative organizational impact if they do not succeed. Select courses that provide useful information but allow the learners to adapt to the new way of learning.

  - Which audiences should be your test audiences? Select early adopters who won't get frustrated with technology problems.

  - Which instructors you will use and why?

  You want to use instructors who will not be frustrated with new technology and the issues that come from the resulting organizational changes.

  - Overall timelines

- Integration of learning technologies for individual courses. This means that you should identify where synchronous fits in your training mix. If you plan to blend with asynchronous tutorials, discussion boards, or other technologies you should record that information.

- Integration into existing technologies. If you have a learning management system (LMS) and/or a learning portal you probably want to integrate them with your synchronous technologies. Make a list of your internal requirements to ensure that you can include them in your request for proposal.

- Assessment plan. Identify the critical success factors that will determine if your synchronous e-learning is successful in your organization (number of people trained, ROI, number of new programs, etc.), and create a plan to measure these factors.

- Outsourcing recommendations. Do you want to take on this process internally, or do you want to use external resources to supplement your staff? Who is available and what is their experience level?

Selecting the Right Product for Your Organization

Now it is finally time to pick the synchronous product that is right for your organization. There are more than two dozen synchronous learning products on the market, and more coming out all the time. Each has its own special features and limitations. How do you choose the package that is right for your organization? The answer is to make sure you have done your homework before inviting vendors to the table.

First determine the feature set you would like to see in your product. Do this by **creating a matrix of synchronous features** (For assistance refer to the job aid, Appendix 17-A. With your team, make "must have," "nice to have," and "don't care" determinations. For example, if your focus is on software training, you may want the most high-tech application sharing that is available. Collaborative soft-skill programs with small group exercises may require robust breakout rooms. Identify what you might use each feature for, and create a short business case for your results. Knowing this up front will keep you getting lost in a bells-and-whis-tles pitch when attending software demonstrations.

Once you have determined your feature set, create a request for proposal (RFP) and send it to all of the synchronous software vendors. Make sure the RFP is very specific—and try to dig deeper than just features. There are other factors that should be influencing your buying decisions. Find out about customer service pro-vided by the synchronous vendor, look for real case studies by clients who have im-plemented the technology, and follow up with client references. Ask your IT rep-resentative to review the RFP and to incorporate questions that ensure the software finalists meet any technology requirements.

CREATING EFFECTIVE SYNCHRONOUS LEARNING INTERACTIONS

Now that you have ensured that your organization is prepared for this change and you have selected and implemented a synchronous platform, you are ready to teach. Right? Not quite. Your project plan needs to set aside time to prepare your train-ing teams and design interactions that are instructionally effective in the synchro-nous environment. Too often training organizations are given a mandate to have their first synchronous classes ready within a ridiculously short time after access to the synchronous platform is secured. In these cases, the tendency is to save exist-ing training materials as HTML without any thought to redesigning exercises or determining the appropriate blend of learning technologies.

In my opinion, training teams should strive to ensure that the e-learning ex-perience meets quality standards comparable to those set for the traditional class-room environment. Synchronous platforms are simply a delivery medium—noth-ing more. As any training professional will tell you, creating a successful program of any kind takes planning, design, and practice. As with any type of training initiative, instructional design must be applied to your synchronous content to determine the instructional mix, the learning objectives, and the instructional sequence.

Develop Competence in Training Development and Delivery Team

As a society we have been receiving education and training in a traditional class-room format since we were small children. We understand the advantages and dis-advantages of the environment, and recognize most of the tools available to tradi-tional instructors.

Avoid falling into the trap of assuming that the synchronous environment is simply a replication of the traditional classroom. It is not. It has its own tool set, its own set of ground rules, and requires that the trainers have a different communication style. Because of this our training teams need to be reskilled in synchronous content development and delivery techniques in order to be successful.

First, identify who in your organization will be impacted by the introduction of this new training technology. Trainers need to change the way they deliver content. Course developers need to design for this new medium. The Information Technology department may need to provide more regular support to the training department. Participants need to learn in a different way.

When a synchronous implementation fails it is very often blamed on a failure in technology. While sometimes technology is the root cause, too often the real culprit is organizational readiness. As with any new organizational initiative, the absence of appropriate training and preparation can cause the initiative to fail.

Early on in the implementation process you should determine how different groups in your organization need to be reskilled in order to support your new learning strategy. Then you should identify programs that will assist in developing these skills. Let us now considers some of the training needs and solutions for a few specific groups. (Remember—different organizations may have very specific needs.)

Trainers

The most obvious group affected by the implementation of synchronous training is trainers. Generally, synchronous software providers offer excellent "point and click" training concerning the technical operations of the software and its various features. Organizations should take full advantage of these programs to meet a goal of technical proficiency.

Too often, however, trainer preparation stops with software training. As most experienced synchronous trainers would tell you, mastery of the technology is not enough. A series of interventions around topics such as synchronous facilitation skills, multitasking, voice techniques, and disaster recovery (For example, what should you do if one participant has technical problems? What should you do if the server fails? Is it necessary to always have a "rain-date" for your programs?) should be offered.

It is also critical that "would-be" synchronous facilitators be participants first and should attend as many synchronous sessions as a participant as they can. Enroll in classes offered by your tool vendor, your colleagues, or by some other source. While participating in these programs note what the facilitator does that is effective and is not effective. How did you feel when nothing happened for 10 seconds or more? Did you feel your needs as a learner were being met? The purpose of participating in these programs is to have trainers truly understand the participant experience. Without this understanding the trainers will not be equipped to meet the needs of their audience. These sessions should be over and above the software training mentioned earlier. And, they needn't be offered on the same synchronous training platform as is being used by their organization.

Finally, there should be ample time built into the schedule to allow new synchronous trainers to develop a sense of conscious competency in this new skill.

Allowing for several practice sessions under realistic "battle-conditions" will help to ensure that early programs are early successes.

Designers/Developers

Instructional designers and content developers (I will refer to these individuals as "designers") are successful when they fully understand the training environment for which they are developing interactions. The traditional classroom setting has a known tool set—flip charts, white boards, projectors, desks, computers, and so on. Designers understand this environment and can design effectively because they have been participants and observers of traditional training interventions since they were small children. When asked to design for the synchronous classroom, designers often do not fully comprehend the differences between the traditional and synchronous classroom environments and wind up designing for the environment they understand.

Designers should attend the same training regimen as an organization's trainers. Complete software training and experiences as a synchronous participant are critical. I also advocate that trainers and designers team up for training in program design and delivery. If a designer understands how trainers will use the new tools it becomes easier to design programs.

While the differences are important, remember not to discard the effective elements of a traditional classroom. There seems to be an implied expectation that, since the classroom is now on the Internet, the technology will do the work for us. Instructional design, leader guides, participant guides, job aids, and reward systems are therefore often neglected. The result of this neglect is often that the quality of our synchronous programs fall far short of the expectations we set for more traditional events.

Producers

Your organization may decide that you want to use some sort of assistant instructor to enhance the quality of the training delivery. I call this person a "producer" based on a broadcast media analogy. In radio, for example, the job of the producer is often to make the "talent" look good. In the case of synchronous training, our talent is the trainer. Even with years of experience in this medium, I still feel the programs I deliver are much more effective, faster paced, and more engaging when I use a producer. Some of the functions of a producer may be to manage chat inactions, troubleshoot technical problems, write on the white board, and set up breakout rooms and application sharing exercises.

The type of training a producer receives would partially depend on how you define the role. Is the producer a "behind-the-scenes" role that runs the technology but never interacts with the participants? Is the producer a meeting facilitator? Is he or she a true assistant instructor that needs to be able to manage content as well as technology? (For those worried about trainer availability issues remember: If the producer does not need to manage content they needn't be full trainers.) No matter your definition, the producer needs to fully understand the functionality of the technology and disaster recovery procedures. If the producer is expected to write on the whiteboard, manage breakout sessions, or demonstrate shared applications they need to be trained as if they were full trainers. The leader guide should include explicit instructions as to what the producer needs to be doing at what time, and the trainer and producer should have a least one practice session to ensure that the each understands the role of the other.

Subject Matter Experts

One of the perceived advantages of the synchronous classroom is the ability to include subject matter experts in training sessions on a more regular basis. To reduce costs and get business critical data to the workforce more quickly, organizations are finding it expedient to reduce the dependency on the training organization (in other words, cut out the middle man) and give these experts the responsibility for educating the workforce. This and a variety of other factors (including the sheer amount of knowledge that needs to be transferred, short development cycles, small audience sizes, and minimal program shelf-life) often changes the traditional training model to a seminar lecture with an "Ask the Expert" component. Unfortunately, these experts often do not have the opportunity to learn the software, apply synchronous design techniques, or practice effective delivery techniques. If you are using subject matter experts to facilitate sessions (instead of trainers), I suggest that organizations use a producer to act as a meeting facilitator. An interview technique can be used as the primary delivery method. The producer can also provide assistance with content design and exercises as appropriate.

Participants

Synchronous software vendors often claim that their user interface is so easy to use that participants do not need more that a few minutes of training to master the software. I agree that the software is often intuitive—but I don't believe that this is a reason not to train our participants.

Learning the software is the easy part—the difficulty for our participants lies in understanding how to communicate and how to learn in this new environment. Organizations should create a prerequisite for synchronous class participation that teaches these skills so participants can succeed in the learning process.

A 75-minute learning orientation agenda might look like this[1]:

> ➤ **Warm-up.** This takes place 15 minutes prior to class start. As participants log on, you conduct a last-minute troubleshooting section to make sure everyone can use the audio features of your environment and that all software is properly installed. You can also teach whiteboard and chat tools using fun exercises. This time gives participants a chance to experiment in a low-risk environment. I find that, during their first 20 minutes in the synchronous classroom, participants aren't listening to the trainer anyway—they want to play. Give them this chance to do it.

➤ **Introductions.** Introduce the training team using photographs—and explain their qualifications to teach the course. Then, let the participants introduce themselves in a creative way—using the chat area, whiteboard, voice, or a combination.

➤ **Tools overview.** Train the participants how to use all of the communication tools in detail. Use accelerated learning techniques (games, word associations, varied instructional techniques) to make participants as comfortable as possible using the tools.

➤ **Ground Rules.** This is a new learning environment, so there are new ground rules to facilitate the process. Introduce and reinforce them now so that future classes will be better for everyone. Ground rules may include: come to class 10 minutes early so we can start on time; send a chat to the instructor if you need to leave class; remove distractions from your learning environment, be prepared to be called on by name even if you don't volunteer; and if you are using a telephone on audio never put your phone on hold ("Music On Hold" can be a disaster to the class.) You should create a set of ground rules that make sense for your learning culture.

➤ **The learning environment.** Give the participants some guidance on how to set up their learning environment to maximize learning and minimize disruptions. For example, participants should use a headset instead of speakers to minimize disruptions in the work environment. They should ignore people around them who are asking for attention, and remove any distractions from the work area. This is a good time to explain your organization's policy about being able to learn at your desk without interruption. For example, you may decide to send tent cards to all participants that say "Synchronous Learning in Progress. Do Not Disturb" and set a policy that insists that colleagues respect that sign. Participants should be encouraged to communicate the fact that they are in a class and inform colleagues of the scheduled end time.

➤ **Program details.** This is critical information; this is the time for you to explain your policy on prework, class participation, and the blend of your training programs. Take this opportunity to explain the e-learning initiative in your organization and how synchronous training fits in.

When Is Synchronous Delivery Appropriate?

Instead of making arbitrary decisions about moving to synchronous training ("75% *of all classroom offerings will be online by the end of the year*") you should take a more methodical approach. Start by cataloguing the current training curriculum and identifying programs that you want to add to your catalog. This is a great time to take a fresh look at what programs are being offered throughout your organization and to identify new programs. When creating this catalogue, remember to note the audience for each program. Having this information ready will help you to identify your synchronous content rollout schedule.

After you have a snapshot of your complete curriculum, you can begin to make the determination about what can be delivered synchronously.

The most obvious starting point to use a synchronous delivery method is when your audience is dispersed. Geography makes all the difference in the world. Often, worthwhile training initiatives are not even started because it is not economically feasible to bring people together. Synchronous training can help to eliminate this barrier and help your workforce access data they may never have had the opportunity to use before.

Another not-so-obvious reason to use synchronous technology is the ever-decreasing lack of classroom space. Organizations simply cannot afford to increase the "brick-and-mortar" real estate to support training events, and renting rooms from vendors can be extremely cost prohibitive. Increasingly, synchronous technologies are being used to support initiatives for audiences that are located in the same geographic locale.

You may also decide to implement a synchronous program because it makes more sense from an instructional perspective. Let's face it; it is very difficult for participants to retain six to eight hours of information when delivered in a traditional format. Synchronous technologies allow us to "chunk" instruction into smaller, more digestible units. Instructional modules can be scheduled in appropriate intervals to allow for practice and mastery of a skill before moving on to the next skill in the instructional sequence. We no longer need to fill up a day with instruction because we reserved valuable classroom space shipped everyone cross-country, and so forth.

What is The Right Blend?

When asked this question I inevitably respond with a qualified "To some extent, all topics can be taught synchronously." The real question to ask is: How do I appropriately blend synchronous events into a training curriculum? For example, I was recently part of a team that created a series of hands-on leadership courses in a blended format. There were a lot of skeptics because of the sensitive nature of such topics as creating collaborative performance reviews and giving and receiving constructive feedback. The questions facing the team were: *Can you teach soft skills online?* And: *Are synchronous practice sessions realistic?* The answer was a definite *Yes*—with the right blend.

Our final product included a variety of training technologies and processes. After looking at the instructional objectives, we determined that the content should be delivered in an interactive asynchronous format. The asynchronous modules presented content essential to the learning process and can be accessed at a learner's individual pace. We found that learners who didn't complete the asynchronous modules were less likely to be successful in the live event.

Skills practice sessions were to take place in an interactive synchronous format. The goal was to minimize lecture and to take as much advantage of the valuable "live" time as possible. The synchronous events were key to the learning design because they gave learners the opportunity to ask questions, interact with peers, and practice skills in a more realistic environment. Because the instructional design for the original classroom initiatives was based on small group interactions and practice, breakout rooms were a natural online tool.

Prior to any instruction, participants were required to log in for "Tech Checks" to ensure their computers had the appropriate hardware, software, and bandwidth capabilities. Then we required participants to attend a synchronous session we called "Learn How To Learn Online." Our team found that even though 10–15 minutes was enough time to learn how to use the technology, more time was needed to understand the blend and communications techniques required to be successful. Our technology instruction program consisted of introductions, a tools overview, ground rules, and tips for creating an effective learning environment. It also focused on the curriculum's blended qualities and explained policies for using the asynchronous module, such as attendance and participation.

For soft skills content this particular blend worked well. Other types of content would require different blends. For example:

> Textbooks and discussion boards might supplement *academic subjects* that are delivered over several months.

> Stand-alone synchronous events may comprise the entire blend for *product updates* and *marketing seminars.*

> *Technical training* and *computer skills training* will often require that traditional classroom experiences, especially lab environments, be blended with synchronous events. In this case you would not be eliminating classroom time, but reducing it.

Design Considerations

A common oversight when delivering synchronous programs is the inclusion of participant guides, leader guides, and other supplemental materials. There seems to be a subconscious assumption that since the delivery method is electronic we don't need to create any "paper" materials. The reality is that an interactive collaborative synchronous program may require more paper supplementation that its traditional counterpart.

For example, although participant guides are often absent in live training, a well-designed participant guide can be a critical success factor for synchronous programs. Take care to ensure your guides are not just copies of the same screens used online. This will take focus off the virtual classroom interface and direct it towards the participant guide. Participants will tend to read the paper slides instead of looking at the screen. Because observing the screen interactions (chat, whiteboarding, poll responses) is critical to maximizing learning, you want to ensure that the participants' eyes are always on the interface unless you direct them to be elsewhere. Instead, the participant guide should contain items like prework exercises, module instructions, self-study work, and other materials to supplement the live session.

Because of the new technical environment, detailed leader guides are more critical than ever. Besides the standard scripting, exercise set-up, and other instructions, the leader guide should contain technical instructions and specific deliverables for any assistant instructors.

CONCLUSION

As with any new trend, the possibilities and pitfalls of synchronous training technologies are not yet fully realized—and probably will not be for some time to come. Training professionals are creating their own best practices as they go along—best practices that may have a very short shelflife because it will not be long before we can improve on them. During this early stage of synchronous development, we need to rely on the things we do best to be successful: effective and thought-out implementation to create the right settings and learning environments, and delivering content that is well designed and in the right blend. Synchronous training seems to be here to stay: what is yet to be determined is it will be a welcome alternative to traditional formats because the quality of instruction meets or exceeds the classroom experience.

A PARTIAL LIST OF SYNCHRONOUS VENDORS

This short list represents synchronous solutions with which I have worked extensively. It is not meant to be an exhaustive resource, and no product recommendations are implied.

Centra—http://www.centra.com

Educata—http://www.educata.com

HorizonLive—http://www.horizonlive.com

InterWise—http://www.interwise.com

LearningSpaceLive—http://www.lotus.com

LearnLinc—http://www.Mentergy.com

PlaceWare—http://www.placeware.com

VClass—http://www.tutorsedge.com

WebEx—http://www.webex.com

Feature	Instructional Uses

Audio

One-way or two-way audio is available in most synchronous packages. Audio can be delivered via the Internet (VoIP) or by a phone bridge (audio-conferencing). When VoIP is used, sending audio is often initiated by pressing the <Crtl> key on your keyboard.

Some organizations opt not to utilize the VoIP. For various reasons, they find that audio-conferencing to be a better choice for their organizations.

The trainer's voice is perhaps the most important content delivery method available in a synchronous classroom. (This will be discussed more in the next chapter.)

Use the audio as you would in a traditional classroom—lectures, group discussions, and Q&A sessions are all effective in a synchronous classroom once the facilitation techniques have been mastered.

Text-based chat

Text-based chat allows the participants and trainer to communicate with one another through text messaging.

Private messaging allows participants to signal difficulties without disrupting a session.

Participants who are more reserved are more likely to interact when text chat options are available.

Questions can be "parked" to be answered later—either during or after the class session.

If you can save the text discussions, brainstorming sessions can be conducted and the results saved for later use.

A technical support person can monitor the chat to identify and fix technical problems without interrupting the class. A subject matter expert can monitor a classroom in order to answer content-related questions that may be out of the scope of the current lecture.

Independent or group exercise instructions can be pasted into a chat area for students to review during an exercise.

Considerations: Some software platforms offer group chat areas, while others have features that more closely resemble an Instant Messenger function (sometimes called "Notes"). These work very differently, and these differences need to be considered while designing exercises.

Feature	Instructional Uses

Breakout Rooms

This feature allows small groups to meet and share information during a larger synchronous session.

Breakout rooms are ideal for training sessions in which teams or groups can share specific content.

Students can be assigned to individual breakout rooms to complete a self-paced exercise or assessment.

Team competitions can be conducted.

You can work with groups or individuals on an as-needed basis.

Different groups can work with different content or on different exercises.

If there are varying levels of expertise in a class, a program can be divided and different trainers can moderate the breakout rooms.

Considerations: *Some applications limit the number of breakout rooms. Which features (whiteboard, application sharing) are available in the breakout rooms?*

Whiteboard

The synchronous equivalent of a traditional flipchart, whiteboards allow trainers and participants to post ideas.

Images can be placed on prepared whiteboards ahead of time or pasted on the fly.

Use the whiteboard for anything you would use a flipchart or marker board for in a traditional classroom setting. For example, you can capture expectations at the beginning of a class and revisit them at the end of a program.

Content changes and additions can be captured and used to revise the program.

You can capture participants' ideas flipchart-style.

Whiteboards can often be archived for reuse in asynchronous applications or emailed to class participants.

Content can be highlighted as it is discussed, which makes lectures more meaningful.

Icebreakers and games can also be created using the whiteboard.

Considerations: *Can you save whiteboards created during the event? Can graphics be pasted or imported to the whiteboard? How many people can write on the whiteboard at once?*

APPENDIX 17-A. *Continued*

Feature	Instructional Uses

Surveys/Polls
Polling your participants is a quick way to check the pulse of the class.

Use surveys and polls to determine whether the students understand the material and to keep them tuned-in to the lesson.

Use surveys to transition to a new topic.

Create icebreakers and introductory exercises by polling the audience.

Share results with the class to foster a sense of community.

Considerations: *What survey and/or polling tools are available with the platform? Can the results be shared with the class? Can questions be created on the fly?*

Pacing/Comprehension
This is a feature that allows participants to appraise the trainer on the pace and clarity of the content.

Asking students to provide feedback can be a good re-engagement technique if the audience is not participating.

Anonymous feedback allows participants to be honest without worrying about repercussions.

If you are not comfortable with receiving and responding to continual feedback, you might introduce this feature slowly.

Considerations: *Is the feedback anonymous/confidential?*

Testing/Evaluation
This feature allows the trainer to conduct pre- and post-session assessments and tests, the results of which can be automatically tabulated and saved.

Use this feature to assess your participants' comprehension and retention over the course of the session.

If these built-in solutions aren't robust enough, savvy users can create assessments in HTML and post them to participants over the application window.

Considerations: *How are the results reported?*

APPENDIX 17-A. *Continued*

Feature	Instructional Uses

Video

One-way or two-way video is offered by more sophisticated synchronous packages.

This is a very technology-intensive tool, which limits its use to participants using broadband connections. (An exception is the use of streaming media in one-way video configurations, which can be fed to participants with connections as slow as 56 Kbps.)

You can use the video to look directly into the camera for live Q&A sessions.

Using live video throughout a session can be very distracting; you should use it judiciously. If face-to-face interactions are critical, consider using a traditional classroom approach instead. Or, record video and distribute before the session using the Internet, videotape, or CD-ROM.

Considerations: What are the hardware and software requirements for live video?

Discussion Board

A discussion board is an asynchronous feature that allows participants to post messages and replies to messages by topic. Discussion boards are different from chat in that they are not real-time.

While a discussion board is an asynchronous feature, it is often bundled with synchronous packages.

If your software does not have a discussion board, you can incorporate a third-party product.

Use discussion boards to post class information, FAQs, pre- or post-session assignments, subject matter expert insights, or other information relevant to the synchronous session.

For multi-session classes, encourage participants to use the discussion boards for knowledge-sharing and community building. You'll need to stay involved to make sure this is successful.

Often, classes that include such asynchronous activities as discussion boards and short synchronous online sessions are more effective than using just one delivery method.

Application Sharing

This feature allows the trainer to share software applications (such as spreadsheets) with participants.

There are many varieties of this feature, ranging from "view only" on the participants' side to allowing participants to upload and use the applications from the synchronous tool server.

Use application sharing to demonstrate software features.

Small groups can collaborate by sharing common office software packages.

Individuals can walk-through software applications with which they are having difficulty.

Participants can use shared applications in breakout rooms. There, you can also assist individuals with assigned exercises.

Considerations: What types of applications can be shared? What are the bandwidth requirements for application sharing?

APPENDIX 17-A. *Continued*

Feature	**Instructional Uses**

Synchronized Web Browsing

This feature allows the trainer or participants to bring the class to an Internet site or corporate intranet.

Often, you can use this feature to run short, self-paced exercises as part of a synchronous session.

Instead of recreating content that already exists, you can use the Internet or corporate intranet as a content source.

Participants can share related content by leading the class to a website.

Independent exercises can be initiated for the entire group—including web-enabled, self-paced exercises created in authoring applications.

Last-minute content can be added to an existing program by placing it on the web.

Considerations: Can a participant bring the class to a website? Can bookmarks be created prior to class to speed navigation? Does this feature require a specific browser? Are hyperlinks available to individual participants?

Record/Playback

This feature allows individuals to record synchronous events and play them back later.

Often, parts of recordings can be edited into synchronous sessions.

This feature benefits individuals who miss sessions and allows for quick creation of asynchronous training content.

You can use the record/playback feature to practice and review the participants' and the facilitator's performances.

You can preview existing programs to review content.

Participants can use recordings to preview or review course materials.

Participants who miss one session of a multi-session program need not miss the content.

This is a relatively inexpensive way to create self-paced, videotaped classes.

This feature is a very efficient way to prep new trainers.

Considerations: Is client software required to view the recordings? Can recordings be viewed while not connected to the Internet?

Feature	Instructional Uses

Assistant Trainer

Feature that allows a second individual to assist the trainer with some of the facilitation tasks.

Assistant trainers do not need to be in the same location as the trainer, but they can still use an "instructor" version of the synchronous application to conduct various tasks—from dealing with technical support issues to helping with the content.

If your class requires a subject matter expert in the delivery, he or she can help in the assistant trainer role by answering questions and providing lecture assistance.

The assistant trainer role is perfect for a trainer-in-training. The assistant trainer can interact as a participant and assist you at the same time.

If you have a special guest trainer who doesn't know how to manage the synchronous technology, you can manage the technology while the assistant leads the discussion.

Considerations: What can a lead trainer do that an assistant trainer can't do (create breakout rooms, launch applications, etc.)?

Content Windows

Content windows are used to display content in HTML, PowerPoint(TM) or other web-ready media.

Remember that synchronous classrooms are a very visual medium. What you show in the content windows needs to be relevant and engaging.

Don't plan to read the content on your screen verbatim. If that's the nature of the content, consider an asynchronous or self-paced delivery instead.

Use multimedia when it makes sense—not just because you can. Remember that every time you add a new technology, you are also adding a potential technical obstacle.

Some software packages allow you to use pre-created content as whiteboard backgrounds. This can be a very effective engagement tool.

Considerations: Can content be added on the fly? How are plug-ins managed? What file formats can be used?

JOB AID: SYNCHRONOUS FEATURES AND FUNCTIONALITY DEFINED

Table 17-1 defines the major features of synchronous training packages. It also suggests some instructional uses for each feature that you might not have thought about. The names I have given each feature are intended to be generic—the features might be differently named in your software platform.

NOTES

1. The components of the learning orientation are reproduced from "The Synchronous Trainer's Survival Guide" (2002) with permission from the publisher, InSync Training Synergy, LLC.

RESOURCES

Readings

Avergun, Amy, and Del Gaizo, Edward. *Leveraging the Technologies of Learning to Improve Performance*. AchieveGlobal. Available at http://www.achieveglobal.com.

Hofmann, Jennifer (2001). *The Synchronous Trainer's Survival Guide*. InSync Training Synergy, LLC.

Palloff, Rena, and Pratt, Keith (2001). *Lessons from the Cyberspace Classroom*. New York: Jossey-Bass.

➤ABOUT THE AUTHOR

Jennifer Hofmann is training consultant who specializes in the design and delivery of synchronous learning. After eight years of managing technology-based training and development initiatives, Jennifer now owns and manages her own firm, InSync Training Synergy. Her team provides seminars and development services to individuals and organizations looking to implement a synchronous classroom.

Jennifer regularly contributes to the ASTD online publication Learning and Online Learning News, published weekly by VNU Business Media. She is a regular speaker on synchronous learning at national industry events and has taught the Certified Online Instructor Program at Walden University. Her most recent project was authoring—focused on preparing trainers for the synchronous environment. She is currently working on a companion piece to support content developers and designers in the synchronous environment.

CHAPTER 18

REPURPOSING MATERIALS FOR E-LEARNING

➤CAROLE RICHARDSON

INTRODUCTION

It is widely acknowledged that development of effective learning materials requires careful attention to traditional instructional design principles. When all design principles have been carefully followed resulting in the creation of an excellent instructional module developed for traditional face-to-face (f2f) instruction, how do you go about adapting that learning object for online delivery? And what about the teacher/trainer who has delivered that material in a traditional setting? Can that person be trained to be an effective online instructor? This chapter looks at these questions and proposes a blueprint for repurposing materials that will prove useful regardless of the instructional content.

Most instructional design "how-to" literature is geared toward an audience that is developing learning materials from scratch. However, increasingly teachers and facilitators are most interested in adapting existing instructional content for a technological delivery environment. Much has been written to assist those who plan to deliver their instruction in a televised, real-time environment. In this case, the similarities to a traditional f2f classroom are obvious. The differences in delivery type present more of a technological challenge for the teacher/trainer than a repurposing challenge for the instructional content. However, moving traditionally delivered content to an asynchronous, time-and-place independent, online learning environment requires an understanding of the technological challenges and how to effect the adaptation of the instructional content within these unique constraints.

To illustrate this process, I will describe in detail the steps I take to repurpose a course for online delivery. I will give you a blueprint for e-learning that you can adapt for use regardless of the specific content of your instructional activity.

REPURPOSING IS NOT THE SAME AS REDESIGNING

Over several semesters, I worked long and hard on building the perfect informatics course for my Masters in Public Administration students. I carefully developed my objectives with an eye focused on what the students would LIKE to know about the topic combined with what I am convinced they NEED to know. The particular course that I'm using for this illustration is expansive in its content. It is like many of those introductory or survey courses that immerse students in the subject matter to a relatively shallow level. The assumption is that students will enroll in future courses to acquire the depth in those specific subtopic areas that pique their interest. This is a very common scenario, whether in traditional educational institutions or employer-sponsored training programs. Survey, introductory, or overview courses are essential to provide a solid foundation upon which to build future learning. But they are the most difficult to design and develop.

This course is poised at the intersection of government and information technology. The objectives include both a review of basic computer applications (word processing, spreadsheet, and presentation) and an introduction to an array of e-government issues. After several semesters of teaching the subject, I felt I'd achieved a necessary balance that included enough flexibility to allow for both the dynamic nature of the discipline and the evolving computer skills of the students. This was no small challenge, but given the importance of the content, and the practically unquenchable thirst for knowledge the students brought to the class, it was a challenge I was proud to have met. Besides, the class was a lot of fun to teach. I was ready for the next challenge—taking the course online—but where to begin?

The instructional design work was done. If done well, instructional design is a laborious and deeply analytical process that requires questioning and probing the rationale behind every component of every instructional module. A well-designed course requires:

➤ an instructional analysis

➤ an instructional strategy

➤ an evaluation plan

Since the instructional design of the course was solid, I saw no reason to re-design the course to use another delivery method. All that was needed was a means of adapting the course to the e-learning environment. In other words, to create a seamless learning environment for students, you need to find a way to align your strategies for instruction and assessment with the technology used for delivery.

I began my repurposing project by creating a planning grid (see Figure 18-1). The purpose of this grid was to help me translate what I was doing in the f2f environment to the online delivery method. I had already defined objectives, the activities that supported them, and the assessments that measured their success. All that was needed to move to another delivery method was to adapt the activities and assessments. The objectives should not change. Sounds easy, right? Well, maybe. First, some planning is required.

PLANNING GRID

Step one of the repurposing project involves the drafting of a planning grid. The planning grid enables you to ensure that e-learning course activities meet course objectives by comparing them to activities you use in the f2f environment. If an activity does not result in learning that meets an objective, it should be eliminated. The grid demonstrates a methodical approach to making the transition from the old delivery method to the new. First, record what you do in the f2f environment. Once each objective and its related activities and assessments are listed, turn your attention to thinking through how you will accomplish the same goals through e-learning.

For example, the first objective states that "students will learn to name/explain theoretical concepts." For the traditional classroom, I have an array of activities associated with this objective. I deliver a lecture which reviews concepts related to public sector information technology management. I cover concepts like data sharing, information security, citizen privacy, universal access, and more. Students are required to read assigned text chapters prior to the class period when I lecture. Once the lecture is complete, the class views a videotaped simulation that demonstrates these concepts and how they are encountered in the "real" world.

Using the planning grid, I select some activities that will allow me to accomplish the same objective in e-learning mode. Instead of delivering my lecture orally, in front of a classroom, I type it and post the file to the class website. I use a WYSIWIG web editor (in this case, Microsoft Front Page), to create hyperlinks within my basic lecture to external websites that provide more extensive information about each concept. Students are still required to complete their reading prior to viewing my online lecture. However, for the online version of the course, instead of viewing a video, I describe a scenario, post it to the discussion board, and require

ONLINE

F2F

Objective	F2F		ONLINE	
	Activity	Assessment	Activity	Assessment
Students will learn to name/explain theoretical concepts	➤ Oral lecture ➤ Readings ➤ View videotape	➤ Multiple choice quizzes ➤ Exams ➤ Research paper ➤ Oral report	➤ Text-based lecture ➤ Readings ➤ Explore web sites ➤ Online discussion —individual postings	➤ Multiple choice quizzes ➤ Exam ➤ Research paper ➤ Discussion board content analysis
Students will learn to criticize arguments	➤ Oral lecture ➤ Readings ➤ Small group discussion	➤ Multiple choice quizzes ➤ Exam	➤ Text-based lecture ➤ Readings ➤ Online small group discussion ➤ Scheduled chat options	➤ Multiple choice quizzes ➤ Discussion board content analysis ➤ Analysis of chat archives
Students will learn to assess ethical implications of behavior	➤ Oral lecture ➤ Readings ➤ Small group discussion	➤ Multiple choice quizzes ➤ Exam	➤ Text-based lecture ➤ Readings ➤ Online small group discussion	➤ Research paper ➤ Exam ➤ Discussion board content analysis
Students will learn to construct reasoned arguments	➤ Oral lecture ➤ Readings ➤ Small group discussion	➤ Multiple choice quizzes ➤ Exam	➤ Text-based lecture ➤ Readings ➤ Online small group discussion	➤ Multiple choice quizzes ➤ Exam ➤ Discussion board content analysis
Students will learn to solve IT-related problems systematically	➤ Oral lecture ➤ Readings ➤ Small group discussion	➤ Multiple choice quizzes ➤ Exam	➤ Text-based lecture ➤ Readings ➤ Online small group discussion ➤ Scheduled chat options	➤ Research paper ➤ Discussion board content analysis ➤ Analysis of chat archives

FIGURE 18-1. **PLANNING GRID**

the students to post their reactions to the described case within a given period of time.

In the face-to-face classroom, student knowledge and understanding of these theoretical concepts is assessed using a variety of tools. I give a short multiple-choice quiz to ensure they can define basic terms. In addition, these concepts are fundamental to all subsequent instructional modules. Therefore, my assessment of student understanding of these foundational ideas is included in my grading of their research paper and the oral report based on that paper.

For the e-learning version, I still do quizzes and exams, but I do them online. I use quizzes for self-assessment and feedback to help students study for their on-line exam. The student requirement to do a research paper doesn't change, but they must send it to me as an e-mail attached file. I analyze student posts to the discussion board and grade the students based on the quality and quantity of their contributions to the asynchronous class discussion.

As you can see, the planning grid is a handy tool to help you systematically work through strategies for converting your course. It will inevitably be a work in progress and may be edited many times before you are comfortable with your choices.

TEAM APPROACH OR SOLO EFFORT

Once you've analyzed the individual learning modules of your course using the planning grid, it's time to decide how to proceed with the repurposing. Yes, you can repurpose a course independently, just as you can design and develop a new course independently. But given a choice, why would you want to? The fact is that e-learning is built on a technological infrastructure that requires specific **technological** expertise to successfully launch. No matter how wonderful and extensive your knowledge of a particular subject, the successful online instructional module relies upon a range of skills and abilities that are rarely combined in one individual.

Whether you decide to use a course management system (CMS), or to create a home-grown instructional website, at minimum, you'll want to work with someone who is skilled at HTML programming. The acronyms CMS and LMS (learning management system) are often used interchangeably. They refer to a piece of software which collects technological tools that support e-learning under one umbrella or gateway. Those tools usually include discussion boards, online quiz generators, chats, and web space for posting of a variety of documents. Generally speaking, if you have access to a CMS such as Blackboard or WebCT, it is more likely that your solo effort will not be so overwhelming as to discourage you from ever attempting the repurposing process again.

From the instructor/trainer perspective, a CMS is the most time- and cost-effective e-learning platform. Unfortunately, an institution or employer may not share that view and decide that the investment in hardware, software, and technical support for a CMS is too great an expense. If that proves to be the case, and you do not have access to such prepackaged instructional support software, you will most definitely enjoy the process, and have a more cohesive product, if you work with a team.

The team approach, where feasible, can result in instructional materials that are much more complete and effective than those produced through individual effort. I cannot stress enough the benefits of working with an array of professionals, each with expertise to contribute to the overall project. Having an extra set of eyes to edit your written material and perhaps even type your notes for you is truly a time-saver. By having all those professionals at your disposal, you may also have the opportunity to incorporate a variety of multimedia enhancements into your course. Today's computer graphic artists can do wonders with visual imagery and video clips, and many of them are talented at digital sound orchestration as well. Having an HTML programmer involved means that your content no longer has to rely on students having appropriate word processing software (or readers) on their computers in order to access the material you produce.

So, if you're fortunate enough to have team support, Table 18–1 is an example division of responsibilities for an e-learning repurposing project.

This ideal situation, however, cannot always be achieved. Still, the discrete components required to successfully repurpose and deliver e-learning content remain the same, whether one person does it all or the team approach is used. Likewise, the roles or skill-sets that are necessary to develop each component are constant. If you are fortunate enough to have all the skills represented in this table, then you should be able to successfully repurpose for e-learning on your own. However, if you feel that you lack any of the necessary skills, it is imperative that you find a way to include others in your project. In most cases, if the instructional goal includes a plan for large enrollments and/or long-term use, the institution/employer can justify the costs involved in the team approach. Regardless, whether solo effort or teamwork, this analysis of particular components and skills assumes that the original course is well-designed and that there is no need to revisit instructional design issues.

LESS IS MORE

Still, despite careful planning, the repurposed course was much bulkier than necessary. I learned after my first semester delivering it online that there was no need to substitute, item by item, each f2f assessment strategy with a corresponding e-

TABLE 18-1. **Division of Responsibilities**

Component	Required skill-set
Course outline	Instructor (content expert)
Planning grid	Instructor, typist, editor
Course map	Instructor, graphic artist, editor
Build web site	Programmer, instructor, graphic artist, editor
Course launch	Programmer, IT staff
Course site support	IT staff, teaching assistant
Student support	Teaching assistant, instructor

learning strategy. For example, the very fact that all synchronous and asynchronous communication was archived and available for careful review meant that the need for traditional writing assignments could be reduced.

The next time I taught the course, instead of requiring the usual three short papers during the semester, I adjusted the mandatory discussion board assignments to allow me enough written material to assess student learning. I required students to post a two- to three-paragraph response to an issue (described by me), and then post comments to two or three of their colleagues' responses. In this way I was able to meld two instructional strategies: student writing and class discussion. Students could demonstrate their grasp of key concepts while engaging in dialogue with their classmates.

As I moved through the Planning Grid (Figure 18-1), I found several opportunities to reduce the quantity of assignments by taking advantage of the unique qualities of the e-learning environment. This did not result in a reduction in workload, as you might expect. And it certainly didn't result in less "rigorous" instructional content for the students. I was able to reduce the number of assignments simply as a result of the seamless integration of writing into class interaction.

The e-learning environment is primarily a text-based world. As such, it relies heavily on text-based tools to support student/content, student/instructor, and student/student interaction. In fact, some students feel that e-learning unfairly favors those who write well. In many ways that is true. E-learning depends upon e-mail, discussion boards, and chats for communication. This communication can be both formal (related to course content) and informal (social in nature). Those formal communication opportunities should be viewed as additional input to the student assessment process. Since all interaction is text-based, there is often no need for the essays and small papers upon which many instructors rely to help us evaluate student understanding of key concepts. That understanding may well be more clearly revealed in an exchange between two students in one of the discussion board activities.

The point is, you should anticipate the ability to reduce the number of your formal assignments because the volume of text-based, written communication will be much higher than in a traditional learning environment. Therefore, despite the reduction in assignments, you will still have enough feedback to assess the extent to which student learning is taking place. In the future, as bandwidth continues to increase and end-user capabilities improve, use of full-motion, digitized video will become a more commonplace tool. This eventuality will limit reliance on the text-based modes of interaction that are essential components of e-learning today. Until that day, however, regard text-based communication as the primary tool for assessment of individual student learning.

RETOOLING YOUR SKILL SET

If you are like most of us who use e-learning, you may find that you often have no access to a team of skilled professionals to support your repurposing efforts. If this is the case, you need to review your skills to ensure all your repurposing plans are not derailed by inadequate technical knowledge. For example, let's say you're on your own and must repurpose your instructional material for delivery using a CMS. In this scenario, you'll need only a few fundamental technical skills. These include:

➤ Ability to use word processing software (the specific product depends upon what you are requiring your students to use—usually Microsoft Word)

➤ Basic knowledge of computer file and document management

Given this basic knowledge, you shouldn't find it too difficult to learn to manipulate the CMS. Blackboard is an especially easy product to learn, but others are not overwhelmingly difficult. Within that software environment, you'll need to master the techniques necessary to set up group areas, create discussion forums, launch chats, and upload the word processing files that you have created. In addition, the online grade book can be a nice feature since students like to monitor their progress. And if you have any interest in online quizzes, you'll want to learn how to use that feature as well. The important thing is to give yourself enough time to master the software before the course site is opened to students. Once your e-learning environment is available to students, you'll find that you have more than enough to do just managing the teaching/learning process without also having to learn how to create that quiz you have planned for tomorrow.

Repurposing is best when all course components are built prior to the delivery phase of the instruction. If you are one of the fortunate, and find yourself part of a team of individuals working on the repurposing project, you will still need to learn the software used as the delivery vehicle for the instructional module so that you can appropriately segment your instructional modules within that environment.

Essentially, your skill-set requirement is the same whether you're on your own, or you have a team of seasoned professionals behind you. You must know the software that you're using to develop your text and other files, you must know and use the delivery tool(s), and you must know how to organize and upload those files to the server from which the learning content will be delivered.

COURSE MAP

So far, you have used the planning grid to help you begin to conceptualize the transition of your instructional material from the face-to-face to the e-learning environment. You next determined whether you're going to be repurposing alone or with a team. Finally, you've reviewed the computer skills you'll need to complete the repurposing project. Now let's look at another tool that can help you systematically select those elements that will build a repurposed course. The course map (Figure 18-2) is a visual tool that you can print out and post on your wall. Or, depending on your skills, you can build a web page and post this at a site that you can access from anywhere.

The course map is simply a sequential blueprint of your repurposed activities. Well developed sequencing is a key component of successful repurposing. For ex-

FIGURE 18-2. **ELEMENTS OF A COURSE MAP**

ample, let's say you've repurposed a course that will be delivered online over an eight-week time period. You've taught it in the traditional classroom during a 15-week semester. Using icons to represent each module, each assignment, and each assessment activity, the course map enables you to develop an appropriate sequence of events.

The first step is to use word processing software and select clip-art icons to represent each of your course activities. Those icons can then be moved around as you decide the order in which you will deliver various components of your course content. I used the icons shown in Figure 18-2 to represent the items listed. Lay out the instruction based on what will be accomplished each week. Figure 18-3 displays an example course map.

Once you've created a map, you need to go back and synchronize it with your planning grid. In other words, you must ensure that all the activities you've described as essential on the grid are included on the map. Along the way, you will

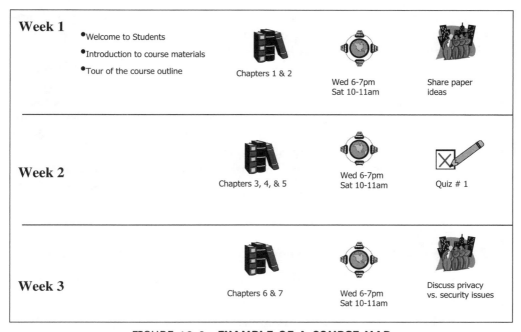

FIGURE 18-3. **EXAMPLE OF A COURSE MAP**

undoubtedly find that your map needs to be altered for one reason or another, but with this foundation, you'll find the adjustments to be relatively easy to do.

THE FOUNDATIONS OF COMMUNITY

Careful attention to community building is an essential component to consider when you are converting an f2f course to e-learning. The foundation of your learning community is built based on your planning grid and course map. The actual development of the community occurs during the delivery phase. While the construction is carefully guided by the instructor, it is built brick by brick by the students themselves. If the foundation is poorly constructed, the community will not survive.

Let's take a step back and address the issue of why community building is so important. One of the most attractive features of e-learning is its time-and-place independent nature. Learners can access their virtual classroom at any time of the day or night that is convenient for them. This means that after a busy day of being a dedicated employee, and an evening of being a committed parent, an e-learning student can still squeeze in some class time before going to sleep. The down side is that virtual classroom time is time spent in physical isolation from the instructor/trainer and other learners. For decades, researchers in the areas of correspondence study and independent learning have bemoaned the low completion rates of asynchronous delivery methods and proposed ways to minimize the isolation that leads to students feeling disengaged from the learning environment. E-learning shares the isolation risks of previous asynchronous delivery methods, especially the old correspondence model. The good news is that the modern technology that supports e-learning also provides a means of building bridges between learners to assist with creating a learning community.

Technology alone, however, does not make a learning community. Sure, the tools are there to bring learners together: e-mail, discussion boards, chats. But without your guiding hand, these tools will remain underused and some students may feel they are all alone. Of course, there are those individuals who prefer independent learning activity, work best in isolation, and have no particular interest in or need for that sense of community. Such people are rare. Most students are most successful in an e-learning environment that keeps them engaged with the instructional content, their fellow learners and their instructor/facilitator. Some techniques for building that sense of community include:

1. Build teams and assign group projects

2. Monitor chat and discussion board activity to ensure all are participating

3. Send personal e-mail to those who appear to be inactive and encourage them to join

4. Provide and encourage informal student-student interaction by creating a discussion forum and/or chat area that serves as a virtual student lounge

Clearly, some of these techniques can only be implemented during the delivery phase (numbers 2 and 3, for example). But to enable them during delivery requires building them during the repurposing process.

Once you build the use of collaborative tools (discussion boards, chats) into the structure of the course, monitor student involvement carefully and consistently, and provide encouragement to students who are in danger of "drifting" away, a growing, thriving community results. It is amazing to watch students begin to support one another, share their ideas enthusiastically, and even help those who are struggling with course content. Before long, you have a community of learners who are active participants in the instructional process. Every teacher's dream come true.

BUILDING THE REPURPOSED COURSE

With your course map in hand, the goal of achieving community in mind, and your skills dusted off, you are now ready to repurpose your course. To proceed from this point, all your files need to be in digital format. Create a folder structure on your hard drive and sort your files into the appropriate folders. I like to create a folder for each week labeled "week 1," "week 2," "week 3," and so on. Some e-learning instructors prefer to organize their folders based on specific content categories (i.e., "lectures," "assignments," "quizzes," etc.). Once your folder structure is in place, it is time to move your content into each of those folders. For example, my week 1 folder for the informatics course includes my syllabus in MS Word format, my PowerPoint lecture notes, and an HTML file that includes links to web resources.

Once everything is sorted, and you have all the files you need in conformance with your course map, you're ready to begin to upload them to the server from which your course will be delivered. To keep things organized easily, ensure that your folder structure on the web server parallels the one you've created on your hard drive.

Once your files are in place, build your discussion board forums, create your quizzes, and prepare your chat assignments. Next, develop an announcement or course guide that you can post prominently to inform students about their best strategy for navigating the e-learning course website. Although this is the last thing that you do, it is the first thing that students see when they enter your e-learning course. Spend as much time as you need making this document clear and complete.

An important note to keep in mind: students who struggle with the nonacademic components of e-learning too often fail. For example, I've known students who were so frustrated by a failure to get answers to their financial aid, registration, or tuition payment questions, that they dropped out of their e-learning course. As part of the repurposing process, it is important for you to provide direction to support options by inserting links to appropriate web pages (or at the very least listing phone numbers) within your e-learning course.

The last step is to arrange to find one or more people willing to serve as surrogate students. Ask them to take your e-learning course for a "test drive." They should login (if authentication is required), read your navigation guide or announcement, move about the course, and see if they understand what it is they are to do. Once you have incorporated their feedback into your final edits, your repurposed course is ready to launch.

EVALUATING THE END RESULT

As with any instructional project or course, evaluation is an essential tool to help you identify what worked and what didn't. You and your team will use this information to continually improve your efforts in future e-learning ventures. But e-learning evaluation is more than simple course assessment. You should regard your e-learning project as an interconnecting set of variables that together comprise a total teaching/learning system.

How do you evaluate this system? Well, certainly assessment of student learning is an essential ingredient. You conduct that assessment in conformance with your instructional design strategies following the detail laid out in your planning grid. But to provide sufficient feedback to refine and revise your repurposed course in the future, you need to look at the following as well:

➤ Technology—Did it impede the learning process? If so, how? And how often?

➤ Access—Were there impediments to student access to the e-learning material? Did they have major personal or work-related responsibilities that limited their time in the virtual classroom?

➤ Skills—Did students have essential prerequisite technical skills necessary to support their use of e-learning?

➤ Support services—Did students have sufficient support to enable their e-learning experience to be successful? Was there a telephone or online helpdesk available? Could they get information about how to navigate the CMS when needed?

Performing a comprehensive evaluation of the e-learning system is no small order. Most of us fail to cast our nets as widely as we'd like during the information-gathering process. A well-developed, end-of-course, web-based survey can be a very helpful tool. Together with your student assessment data, the survey results will help you determine where you may need to tweak things a bit, where you can eliminate certain tasks, and where others were so successful that you want to expand them. In addition, by asking students directly, you'll have the ammunition needed to request additional resources or to be able to pinpoint where existing resources should be reassigned.

CONCLUSION

Teaching in the e-learning environment is a lot of fun. It really is. Some of the frustrations of the face-to-face classroom disappear. No longer must you mourn for the student in the back who never speaks up in class. That student becomes actively engaged in dialogue in the online discussions. There is no reason to ever miss an online class; students visit their virtual classroom when it is convenient for them. No longer must you be irritated when students fail to come to class. No longer must you drag yourself to a classroom to teach when you have a cold; you can take your laptop to bed with you and work from there. But these alone are not sufficient reasons to repurpose your course for e-learning.

The truth is, e-learning is here to stay. Students enjoy the option of taking courses online. Employers enjoy the potential cost-savings of training their employees without attached travel and lodging costs. Teachers, trainers, and faculty all appreciate the reduction of emphasis on **being** somewhere physically which results in **time** that can be invested in an increased focus on learning. Repurposing learning materials is an essential first step that can be accomplished systematically, whether a solo or team effort. The real work begins once those students enter the virtual learning environment. Lay the foundation with a solidly repurposed instructional product, and the construction of your learning community will proceed smoothly. Enjoy!

TIPS AND HINTS

So, how do you repurpose your instructional materials for e-learning? Here is a summary of important things to remember:

➤ Repurposing is **not** the same as redesigning

➤ Take a team approach to development whenever feasible

➤ Use tools such as the planning grid and course map to help you plan your delivery

➤ If possible, combine activities and assessments that meet the same course objectives

➤ Carefully assess your skill-set and find ways to fill any gaps

➤ Build the foundation in which a learning community will thrive

➤ Evaluate the entire e-learning system and make appropriate adjustments

RESOURCES

Readings

Bates, A.W. (1995). *Technology, Open Learning, & Distance Education*. London and New York: Routledge.

Daniel, Sir John (September 7, 2001). Lessons from the Open University: Low-tech learning often works best. *Chronicle of Higher Education*, B24.

Dean, R., Biner, P., and Coenen, M. (1995, April). Distance education effectiveness: A systems approach to assessing the effectiveness of distance education. *Ed Journal*, J17–J20.

DeLeon, L. (2000). Comparing modes of delivery: Classroom and online (and other) learning. *Journal of Public Affairs Education*, *6*(1), 5–18.

Kemp, J., Morrison, G., and Ross, S. (1996). *Designing Effective Instruction*. Upper Saddle River, NJ: Prentice-Hall.

Moore, M. G. (1996). Tips for the manager setting up a distance education program. *The American journal of distance education*, *10*(1), 1–5.

Moore, M. G., and Kearsley, G. (1996). *Distance education: A systems view*. Belmont, CA: Wadsworth.

Reid, J. E. Jr. (1997, March). Preparing students for the task of online learning. *Syllabus*, 38–42.

Seels, B., and Glasgow, Z. (1998). *Making Instructional Design Decisions*. Columbus, OH: Merrill.

Venezky, R., and Osin, L. (1991). *The Intelligent Design of Computer-Assisted Instruction*. New York: Longman.

Watkins, B. L., and Wright, S. J. (1991). *The Foundations of American Distance Education: A Century of Collegiate Correspondence Study*. Dubuque, IA: Kendall/Hunt.

Workman, J. J., and Stenard, R. A. (1996). Student support services for distance learners. *Ed Journal*, *10*(7), 18–22.

➤ABOUT THE AUTHOR

Carole Richardson is an Assistant Professor in the Department of Public Administration at American University, where she teaches a range of courses with a particular emphasis in Government, the Digital Divide, Cyberdemocracy, and eLearning. Before going to American University, Dr. Richardson consulted in higher education technology and distance learning for a major computer company, managed Internet and web services for the Saginaw Chippewa Indian Tribe, and developed and directed the Distance Learning department at Central Michigan University.

Her doctorate in Public Administration is from Western Michigan University with an emphasis in Distance Education Administration.

Phone: 202-885-3796
e-mail: *caroler@american.edu*

YOUR E-LEARNING QUESTIONS ANSWERED BY THIS CHAPTER

➤ How do I motivate my employees to be responsive to e-learning?

➤ Is e-learning effective for all levels and types of learners, particularly those with low literacy levels?

➤ How do I retool my stand-up trainers to become e-proficient? What is available to help me?

➤ What is the right blend of e-learning and classroom instruction?

➤ Is e-learning effective for soft skills?

CHAPTER 19

USING TECHNOLOGIES IN A BLENDED LEARNING CURRICULUM

➤BRANDON HALL

Blended learning has been around forever. Ever since Socrates sent his young students out into the agora (market) to observe the behavior of Athens's citizens, instructors have been blending learning experiences with lectures and, in the last 500 years, with text. So it's arguable that there's nothing really new about blended learning in the same way it can be argued that the furnace in your basement isn't much different from the fires that early humans sat around.

If lectures and text and experiences are all part of blended learning, then we also must acknowledge that we've added a lot of new tools to this blend in the last five to ten years. Adding everything from e-mail to learning management systems to authoring tools to web editors to entire virtual classroom suites, the toolbox that instructors have traditionally depended upon got very heavy, very fast. It's no wonder trainers are feeling overwhelmed by the recent developments in e-learning. After all, we gave everyone plenty of time to get used to overhead projectors and flipcharts. We have been less patient recently, and less forgiving, when instructors don't pick up every technological tool that we sling at them.

Fortunately, blended e-learning is a reasonable voice above the din of technologies that clamor for the attention of those delivering learning. In the past, every time a new technology came along, there would be a collection of voices joined in a chorus of "this will be the end of classroom training" sing along. But the impending death of classroom training has always been greatly exaggerated. No one approach to training will replace classroom instruction, nor any other kind of learning, if we are going to be honest with ourselves.

The recognition that we need to take a blended approach to instruction shows that the industry is finally taking a mature, rational look at the tools we can now use. Classroom instruction will always be around because it's the best way to deliver certain kinds of skills. Likewise, text in books probably isn't going anywhere, either. Exercises and tests are useful ways to assess and build knowledge, and they always will be.

The trick is: we've got a ton of new ways to deliver tests, exercises, text, and even lectures. These new technologies—tools if you will—can all contribute to learning if we let them. So how many have we got? According to Paul Henry at Smartforce, his company has defined somewhere in the neighborhood of 40 instructional delivery methods now available to trainers. It's no longer a question of what you *can't* do instructionally using e-learning. "I think that question is becoming more and more academic as time goes by. There are so many interesting things being done in the online environment that, perhaps even two or three years ago, nobody thought possible. It's getting more and more difficult to say you can't do this," says Paul.

Most instructors are drifting or jumping whole-hog into some kind of blended e-learning, and they are immediately faced with the question of what to blend with what. Do we blend classroom with web-based training or with a discussion group or do we do it in a virtual classroom using live e-learning and blend that with something completely different?

An automatic response to matching instructional objectives to a plethora of delivery media is to set up a grid or matrix, to impose some kind of order on the apparent chaos. If you want something like that, you should really check out the article, "Leveraging the Technologies of Learning to Improve Performance," by Amy Avergun, Kathy Bunch, and Edward R. Del Gaizo. It's at Achieve Global's website *www.achieveglobal.com* and worth a look if you think a matrix would help you make some decisions about what to blend.

While this whole book is dedicated to examining the many e-learning tools currently available, it makes some sense to look at each in terms of its instructional effectiveness in a blended situation.

LMS

At first glance, it might not seem like a learning management system is a vital part of blended e-learning because it's not really a delivery medium. But like any good administrative function, an LMS is the glue that holds the rest of the blended learning environment together. And that's no easy task, says Paul Sparta, CEO of Plateau Systems. "In order for an LMS to get blended learning right . . . it has to bridge the logistics of classroom management seamlessly with the electronic delivery logistics," he says.

And that means, he says, you really must manage your training, not just let it happen. The LMS will help you do that, but it still means thinking seriously and continuously about certain learning issues. For example, says Sparta, scheduling class time and coordinating it with the web-based prework the learners need to accomplish is more complicated than it looks. One of the best things about an LMS is its ability to track and measure what's going on in the e-learning environment. When you mix in classroom experiences, capturing that data gets a lot tougher.

The mistake most blended learning beginners make, says Sparta, is breaking a course into a bunch of chunks—classroom, assessments, self-paced—without the connective tissue among them that tells the learner that they are all part of the same learning objective. That's why he tells clients that learning objects are all well and good, but it's important to remember that blended instruction units need context or it just turns into a huge repository of training elements with little rhyme or reason. People underestimate how tough it is to manage a blended approach, according to Sparta, but if they get it right, the LMS can be a vehicle that includes all the types of learning going on in an organization.

So how do you get it right? According to Sparta, the key is to keep your eye on your instructional objectives, not the technology or the tools. Don't fall into the trap of thinking every classroom needs to be shifted into a classroom/self-paced/discussion group hybrid. Once you align your delivery with the instructional objectives, he says, establish metadata for every element of the instruction. That's where an LMS can be very powerful and really act as management tool for your learning.

WEB-BASED TRAINING

The whole idea behind web-based training was that you would create a whole self-paced course, with all the media you might need to fulfill your learning objectives, and put it within reach of everyone with a browser program and Internet access. The idea of blending e-learning, however, challenges the notion that a self-paced course is all anyone will ever need.

In fact, blended learning may be just what the doctor ordered for self-paced, web-based training. The one drawback to WBT that has been written about recently is the dropout rate. It seems a lot of people will access the system, maybe go through three or four screens and then check out again. Electronic Performance

Support System proponents say that's to be expected because people are getting precisely what they need to perform and going back to the jobs. But in some cases you want learners to go through the entire self-paced course on the web.

By blending in some other elements, says Harvey Singh, former Chief Learning Technology Officer of Centra, you can add both accountability and motivation to increase completion rates. "To expect a learner to be motivated enough to go through each and every single screen, and go through all of that and complete it, is a very tough thing to ask for. But by adding a human element . . . it adds a whole dimension in terms of motivation for people to come together and learn and complete something," says Singh. His company makes live e-learning systems and blending a virtual classroom experience with self-paced e-learning has shown improved results in terms of completion. In one case, he says, a client had a forty-five percent completion rate for its web-based training. He suggested that blending in a virtual coaching approach, where learners could be coached and collaborate with each other through e-mail and discussion groups, might help. The organization tried that and completion rates jumped to ninety-five percent.

By requiring learners to show up for a class, whether a real class or a virtual class, Singh argues that it injects accountability. They know they will need to discuss what they learned, so they can't just click through the course or drop out completely. So even though it may be counterintuitive to add some classroom time (either synchronous or face to face) to your web-based training, it may pay off in ways you haven't imagined.

Of course, it's also important to remember what exactly web-based, self-paced instruction is good for. In most cases, what learners love about it is the ability to go at their own pace. Classroom instruction tends to proceed at a pace that leaves a lot of people behind and a lot of other people bored. Self-paced instruction can overcome a lot of that.

DISCUSSION GROUPS

Opening up a discussion so learners can share their own opinions, questions, and insights is a powerful tool in a blended learning approach. It's often overlooked because it's so easy, but in some cases it's overlooked because it gives a lot more control over the course to the learners. It's learner-centric and some instructors don't particularly like that.

A recent case study published by the University of Michigan's Business School describes a blended course taught by C.K. Prahalad. Part of the course was a discussion group where students could talk about the classroom discussion, the assignments and their own insights. One student wrote:

It is in your class that I feel liberated. The channels utilized to relay my thought is a safe harbor to voice my views. I do not have to do it under the scrutiny of others. I do not risk face-to-face opposition and I have time to conjure my thoughts. It is a beginning of confidence building and it makes me overcome my subconscious low self-confidence. It is great to know that my thoughts are worth a dime.

Another case in point comes from Smartforce's Henry. His company was working with Unilever in Britain and the company was talking about its annual get together. It seems the company had a meeting every year where it would fly the top twenty-five managers from all over the world to the headquarters. There these corporate leaders would go through two weeks of intense workshops and work on the direction of the company.

This seemed like a "must be done in the classroom" deal, says Paul, and in many respects it was. But the company decided to supplement the two weeks of workshops with a year round online mentoring. Often these managers would go back to their homes and lose much of what they learned as soon as the first crisis walked through their doors. By providing online mentoring, these leaders could not only get advice on things they learned from faculty and experts, they could also collaborate with each other. And that was key.

These leaders used the online collaborative mentoring environment, says Paul, to work together throughout the year. As the workshop approached, they worked on projects together before they met face-to-face, making their time together even more effective. This, says Paul, is "a great example of how you should never say you can or can't do this online anymore. It's also a great example of blended learning."

So one decision you may need to make if you're mixing discussion groups into the blend is: do you want to set up a discussion group or a learning community? In the case of Unilever, the leaders established a community. In the University of Michigan's case, the discussion groups, though asynchronous, were pretty limited. Students had roughly 48 hours on the discussion groups and then the board was shut down. John Setaro, Director of Research at THINQ Learning Solutions, agrees with the latter method in some cases. "Imposing that time limit," he says, "allows them or motivates them to get a lot of information during that period. Whereas I think one of the problems we see sometimes in e-learning are the drop-off rates. Imposing that time limit, I think, keeps them on task."

LIVE E-LEARNING

This combination of live instructors in an online environment is probably already a blended approach in its own right. It's a synchronous environment that tries to emulate the traditional classroom in every way except that everyone is sitting at a workstation in different locations instead of sitting together in a training room.

There's probably more than enough throughout this book about the complexities of getting instructors ready for live e-learning. Some of the problems and principles of live e-learning revolve around making the transition, as a traditional instructor, to the new environment. They have to learn to moderate a discussion when they can't see their students, work with a lot of media, and figure out which tool to use for different instructional objectives.

In that way, the traditional instructor is facing a lot of the same issues that organizations face with blended e-learning. Both organizations and trainers need to adapt to a new mix of media and reshuffle their ideas and expectations of the learning they deliver.

WHY DO BLENDED LEARNING?

There are only really two reasons to pursue a strategy of blended e-learning. Fortunately, these reasons aren't mutually exclusive, that is, you can have both. The obvious business reason to blend your training is to cut down on the time your employees spend in the classroom. If you've got a one-week course on database maintenance and you can trim that down to three days plus some other online learning exercises and readings, those employees will be back at their desks, being productive, sooner. That saves the company money and makes managers happy. Almost everyone understands that classroom learning is much more expensive in terms of lost opportunities than anything else—except ignorance.

The other reason to pursue a blended approach to learning is because it's a lot more effective. We already know the shelf life of learning when employees go off to a week-long series of workshops: in 72 hours about 75 percent of the learning will be forgotten, says Ara Ohanian, CEO of Vuepoint. "Blending becomes both a strategy for making instruction more effective and also a business decision for making it more productive," says Ara.

It's not difficult to imagine how blended learning can be more effective. A classroom session where everyone has already done the prework is much more likely to get to higher levels of learning because the instructor is working with an audience whose baseline of knowledge is much higher. In the past, you could assign a chapter of reading before the class occurred, but many students wouldn't bother reading it—figuring the instructor would go over it in class. Now, however, if you put the chapter or exercise or self-paced course online, the instructor can go into the LMS and see precisely how many trainees will be ready for the course. Then, if people aren't doing the prework, an e-mail can be sent out to remind them of the impending classroom course and warning them to be prepared.

It's often argued that classroom instruction tends to get bogged down because instructors need to teach the material to the least informed or lowest skilled people in the class. The promise of blended learning is to raise that bar, to get more learners more informed so that they are all on the same page and that page is further into the book at the beginning of the course.

One of the messiest issues in training is the issue of learning styles. It's generally recognized that different people learn differently: orally, visually, or using tactile or kinesthetic forms. Most instructors try to use a variety of styles in their classes, but for the most part learning is skewed heavily toward those who listen well. It's a snake pit, because learning styles are as complex as the individuals you end up training. At last count, Dr. Rita Dunn had categorized about fifty-four different learning styles.

Blended learning, however, comes closer to addressing the issues around different learning styles. The new package of tools we, as instructors, have acquired affords us opportunity to blend more elements into both classroom and self-paced exercises. Again, if we reach out to learners with a more diverse palette of learning options, they are more likely to show up to class with a higher level of knowledge and skills.

And let's not forget follow-up. One of the most often forgotten principles of adult learning theory is the three- to six-month follow-up after a class is held. This is to determine if the learners still remember what they learned or are using the skills they acquired. And in terms of retention, being able to send out exercises via e-mail in the weeks following the classroom experience is one of the best ways yet established to make sure the learning "takes." Singh says one of his clients showed a twenty percent increase in retention using a blended approach.

THE PROCESS

There's no magic formula or matrix that will answer all your questions about what to blend with what to optimize learning. About all you can do is follow the principles of instructional design (ISD) and use those methods to determine what you want to do. And that means asking yourself and your organization some general questions. Those answers should get you at least halfway through your journey.

To determine the most effective blended learning mix for your training project, you will need to gather information regarding the following:

➤ Audience

➤ Skills/Content

➤ Technical resources

➤ Personnel resources

➤ Budget/time constraints

The figures on the next few pages indicate the type of information you will need to gather.

Target Audience Description

It is critical to know as much as possible about your target audience when designing blended learning. In particular you will need to know their familiarity and comfort level with learning via computers (see Figure 19-1).

Skills/Content

The type of skills and content your learners need to master will greatly influence the delivery methods you select. Some skills such as supervisory and communications skills require interaction with an instructor, while others like technical skills and basic cognitive material are best learned in a self-paced environment. By matching the content carefully with the methods available you will ensure the effectiveness of your courseware (see Figure 19-2).

Primary audience:
Secondary audience:
Numbers to be trained:
Duration of training requirement:
Location of learners:
General skill, experience, and knowledge level:
Preferred learning methods:
Relevant skill mix:
Language/cultural issues:
Motivation to learn:
Comfort level/experience learning via computers:
Access to computer? Intranet? Internet? Satellite broadcast?
Access to labs?
Available to travel to classroom training?

FIGURE 19-1. **TARGET AUDIENCE DESCRIPTION**

Performance goals:
Learning objectives:
High level content outline:
Complexity, difficulty, and length of content:
Involves equipment:
Requires labs:
Requires role plays:
Requires teamwork:
Requires face to face interaction:
High value to organization/high consequence of error:
Changes frequently or is relatively stable:
Includes factual or procedural information:

FIGURE 19-2. **SKILLS/CONTENT**

Tips From the Trenches

Carefully map the course content to the most appropriate methods available to ensure the greatest learning effectiveness.

Technical Resources

Blended learning depends on the your organization's technical resources. Carefully cataloging what your organization does and does not have will narrow down the choices available to you and help you avoid making costly mistakes (see Figure 19-3).

Personnel Resources

Your choices will also be influenced by the personnel resources available for development, delivery, and technical support. If your training staff is not experienced with e-learning methods, you may want to provide some training and begin with the options that are easiest to design and roll out such as on-line discussion and chat groups. Another alternative is using third-party vendors for some aspects of your project (see Figure 19-4).

Do learners have Intranet/Internet access?
Do learners have sound cards in their computers?
Do learners have access to headsets or microphones and speakers?
The organization's slowest Internet connection speed is:
Can learner's computers play full multimedia CBT?
Do learners have access to Chat? Instant Messaging? Newsgroups?
Does the organization have access to satellite broadcasting or videoconferencing?
Has the organization purchased and deployed synchronous web broadcasting software like Placeware or Centra?
If distance labs are contemplated, do the learners have the appropriate hardware and software?
Does the organization have a Learning Management System? If so, what tools are compatible?

FIGURE 19-3. **TECHNICAL RESOURCES**

Expertise in traditional classroom instructional design:
Instructors with content knowledge available to travel:
Technical support for equipment and labs associated with classroom training:
Expertise in asynchronous and synchrounous on-line instructional design:
Expertise in asynchronous and synchrounous on-line production:
Instructors with content knowledge and on-line expertise:
Technical support for asynchronous and synchrounous on-line training:
Expertise in instructional design for satellite broadcasts:
Expertise in satellite broadcast production:
Technical support for satellite broadcasts:

FIGURE 19-4. **PERSONNEL RESOURCES**

Time/Budget Constraints

In the real world there are always budget and time constraints that must be considered in choosing your blended learning mix. If you only have a couple of weeks to develop and deliver content, you will probably not choose custom CBT or a satellite broadcast. On the other hand, if the project is high-profile and the content is stable, those may be appropriate methods. Always remember to consider maintenance costs and timeframes as part of the constraints you will need to manage (see Figure 19-5).

Tips From the Trenches
Always remember to consider maintenance costs and timeframes as part of the constraints you will need to manage.

Time available for training delivery:
Time available for training development:
Time available for course maintenance:
Budget available for for training delivery:
Budget available for training development:
Budget available for course maintenance:

FIGURE 19-5. **TIME/BUDGET CONSTRAINTS**

CONCLUSION

As we've stated before, just about any learning your organization delivers is going to be blended learning per se. But with the e-learning tools that have been developed in the last ten to fifteen years, you can reach learners in ways you never could before. A careful approach to blending can deliver better learning, with better retention, at a lower overall cost. It's been argued in the past that you can develop training that is faster, cheaper, and better, but you have to pick two of the three. With blended learning, that formula is going to be challenged on a lot of levels. Although some experts argue that a blended learning approach ends up being more work for instructors, others argue that it's a one-time charge, that is, once instructors get used to blending their new tools into the mix, it will be just as efficient as developing courses for the classroom alone. If blending encourages collaborative learning, as described in the Unilever example, the wise instructor will quickly figure out how to leverage the knowledge of students into future courses.

Maybe blending is more than just an approach. Jim Moshinskie, a professor at Baylor's Hankamer School of Business and a noted performance technology expert, likes to talk about it as an environment. "Blending doesn't have to be one event," he says, "blending could be the digital surround that you build."

Blended learning can have a significant effect on an entire organization. Dick Handshaw, president of Handshaw Inc. (the company that created LCMS product nogginware), helped Krispy Kreme develop a blended learning program for its managers. The chain of doughnut stores was going national and they needed a lot of people trained very fast. Handshaw evaluated their needs and struck upon a blend of videos, self-paced learning, lots of testing, and a week of classroom training. That week of classroom time was trimmed down from the 14-day training marathon the company was using previously. The training program was launched on the same day as the company's IPO because of one of the concerns of investors about the fast expansion of this franchise. It seems to have quelled investors' concerns, because it was a tremendously successful launch of the now public company.

Three months after the IPO, three senior executives approached Handshaw at a meeting to tell him about how important the blended training program had been for the company.

RESOURCES

Readings

Marsh, Julie (2001). *How to Design Effective Blended Learning*. Palo Alto, CA: Brandon Hall.

►ABOUT THE AUTHOR

Brandon Hall, Ph.D., is a leading independent expert in e-learning, helping organizations make the right decisions about technology through his writing, advising, and presenting. With more than 20 years as a training professional, Dr. Hall is the CEO of brandon-hall.com and the author of the groundbreaking Web-Based Training Cookbook. Since 1992 brandon-hall.com has been providing independent expert advice in the form of published reports and phone consultations on the tools of e-Learning: LMS, LCMS, authoring tools, content providers, and other tools that help organizations develop successful e-Learning solutions. Dr. Hall participates regularly as a featured speaker in conferences such as the ASTD and Online Learning. He earned his doctorate in educational psychology and has served on the faculty of San Francisco State University's Multimedia Studies Program.

CHAPTER 20

IMPLEMENTING E-LEARNING

➤**LORETTA DONOVAN**

LIGHTS, CAMERA, ACTION . . .

The script is written, the stage is set, the players take their places—
it's show time for your e-learning program! You are moving from
strategy and planning to development and the implementation
phase of your project. But unlike a theatrical production, the roles
and cues can't be memorized. To carry out e-learning in your
business, you must have a tactical plan and be ready to deal with
the variety of issues that pop up along the way. More than ever
before, you need focus to keep going as you implement—focus
on partnerships, access, value-added learning, and continuous
support.

Among other points we'll discuss in this chapter are:

➤ What tasks occur during the development of course content and media elements?

➤ How do you forecast development time and resource needs?

➤ Is delivery of e-learning just launching the course to the web?

FROM STRATEGY TO TACTICS

Introduction

Let's take a step back and look behind the scenes to what brought you to implementation. Knowing where you started, the points you hit in your e-learning episode, and how they lead into implementation puts the whole process in perspective. The overall approach you should have taken probably took you from a vision and strategic goals for your e-learning initiative, to the identification of the business, organizational learning, and technical requirements that would support those ideals, and on to macro level design decisions about the learning, technology, and security infrastructure. Now look ahead. You are ready to develop your program, create courses, and manage the delivery process. Continuous improvement is the final (and ongoing) phase of e-learning in your business. Figure 20-1 provides a graphical view of the process.

Defining Implementation

What do we mean when we refer to "implementation"? Betty Collis puts this pivotal phase in context when she says it's "moving a learning event from `special project' or `experimental' category, to some level of incorporation into the regular instructional routine of an instructor or institution" (1996). Implementation is making e-learning a regular part of your business's learning and development repertoire, not just a pilot project or one-time event. It requires skillful leadership and must be focused on results to overcome the inevitable stumbling blocks and unforeseen circumstances that are often encountered.

Implementation occurs after the preparation of a design document and storyboard to map the content flow, and identification of delivery mode—that is, through e-learning media. Depending on the scope of your e-learning initiative, implementation may be based on a programmatic model, such as a corporate university or certification; start with a few individual courses; involve blending face-to-face training; or be part of a knowledge management strategy; or a combination of these.

The key to implementation success is a dual focus: with a close-up lens, on the tactical processes of the entire e-learning initiative and, with a wide-angle lens, on the entire organizational and individual learning strategy that drives it. Keeping an eye on the tactical and the strategic continues throughout the various phases of implementation (described later). At each phase, there are decision points that are fateful for your program. While many of them are not irrevocable, the general idea

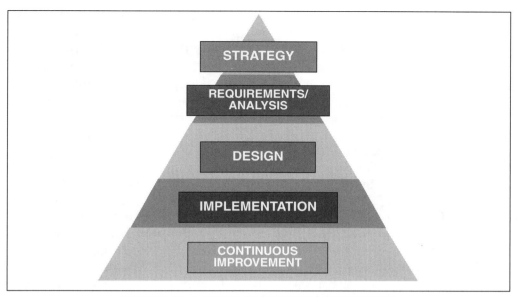

FIGURE 20-1. **YOUR E-LEARNING PRIORITIES**

is that you have examined your options upfront and decided which route you would take.

These options are related to three areas of decision-making that are essential to providing first-class e-learning within your business. Training professionals will be familiar with the first two areas, ones for which they may have set similar guidelines for face-to-face courses: instructional criteria and program planning. With some variations for new media technologies, selecting criteria for choosing the activities of training, and for laying-out and addressing the components of an integrated menu of courses are continued tasks. Now you will need to add decisions in a third area: learning data management—the storage and deployment of electronic content and media elements. What is their impact on your implementation? The instructional architecture, the technical architecture, and the security environment options will evolve from them. Together they are the infrastructure that will contain and support the programs and courses that you develop and deliver. When viewed in its totality, your e-learning priorities are essential elements representing the E-Learning Tactical Process Model (see Figure 20-2).

Why a process model for e-learning? Consider the cycle for course design, development and delivery that you are using for traditional training. The ADDIE model is one that is commonly used. It places training professionals in key personnel driving instructional processes. But when it comes to prescribed integration of the tasks of course design, development, and delivery with other organizational functions, things are outside of the trainers' control. Those touch points are out of sight. The assumption seems to be that they are inconsequential to the trainer's responsibilities. In an e-learning initiative, thinking along those lines can be devastating to your project's success. For that reason, you need a model that anticipates the indispensable resources and responsibilities from functions that must intersect with the work of training professionals. The model must convey the interactive nature of decisions and processes of all contributors for five critical priorities: Strategy, Requirements/Analysis, Design, Implementation, and Continuous Improvement.

Senior managers, including those who lead information technology and training, are important contributors as strategy decisions for e-learning position the company for the future, establish business goals, and take into account the operating structure, political environment, and traditions of the company. The requirements/analysis devised by training professionals determines quality standards for formulating plans and achieving goals for programs and learning. Management must be included in this process to ensure support and participation. In partnership information technology experts, specifications for creating, naming, and storing learning objects are drafted. This training/information technology collaboration continues during design, as hypermedia templates are set for consistency of the course interface; decisions are made about the authoring software, server, and network environment; and options for secure access to courses are selected. All of this precedes implementation.

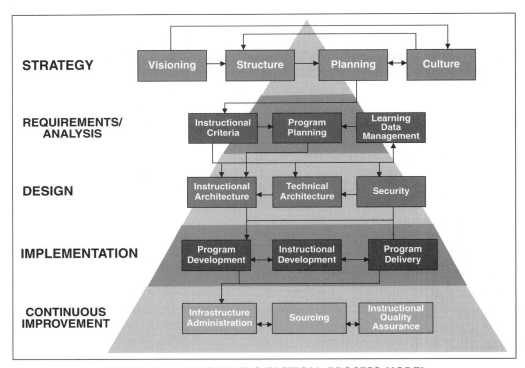

FIGURE 20-2. **E-LEARNING TACTICAL PROCESS MODEL**

Implementation: Priorities and Process

The tactics of implementation, as you have seen, are not about taking your old content and making it electronic. It's about aligning the activities of training development and delivery to a relevant model for new media learning within the larger context of organizational learning strategies and operations. The priorities for your business will be unique to your context, since they came from the plans from the previous phases in your e-learning initiative. The people who bought in to the ways e-learning ought to operate and look in your business, along with your employees, count on your follow-through on their decisions. Integrated operation is your ticket to an ongoing relationship with them and their continued interest and support.

In the implementation phase, there are three interrelated priorities underway: development of programs, development of courses, and delivery of both programs and courses. Program level and course level development of learning products affect one another as critical choices about resources for particular courses and their elements are made. Development at the course level, and delivery at the program and course levels, impact each other in relation to deadlines for deploying content and media elements. These relationships and the decisions they call for are shown in Figure 20-3.

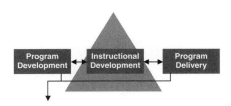

- How Are Elements of the Program Prioritized and Scheduled for Development? Are They on Track?
- How Is Project Management Used to Develop Courses & Media Elements?
- What Is the Launch Process?
- How Is Continuous Access Managed?
- What Synchronous/Asynchronous Practices Facilitate the Learning Experience?

FIGURE 20-3. **THE IMPLEMENTATION PRIORITY**

LEADING AND MANAGING DEVELOPMENT

Leadership Models

You will excel at development and delivery of e-learning if you act as a consistent and collaborative leader. It is up to you to bring partners into the process, to work through decisions with them, and to stand by agreements and deliverables. The organization and accountability of the people involved must be clear to everyone involved. Models for design and development teams vary from highly centralized and self-contained units with all the talent and technology in one place; to joint ventures in which a few departments work in tag team fashion for multiple projects, handing off deliverables to one another; to cross-functional teams assigned for the duration of an individual project. No matter which one you use, the lines of authority must be communicated publicly by a business sponsor or senior manager to avoid disputes about who's in charge, who's on the team, and who's in a supporting role.

Development Roles and Tasks

The implementation phase includes administrative, editorial, and technical roles. The first of these deals with overall management of the project, including scheduling and flow, allocation of resources, budgeting, and quality control. The second requires scripting skills for writing the screens based upon input from content experts. The third calls for programming skills related to the authoring tools, or the actual programming language, to generate code that communicates with servers and computers; technical skills for the preparation of audio and video files; and software and server administration skills to launch the course to the Web and maintain continuous access—that is the ability of end-users to receive learning anytime, anywhere as expected.

Administrative Aspects of Development

As leader of an e-learning project, your mission is to focus all efforts on the goals and deliverables. From your vantage point, you must see the big picture and use your peripheral vision for close-ups of your team's tasks. It's up to you to provide clear direction, to deploy resources, to juggle priorities, and to resolve dilemmas and conflicts. Your ability to communicate and motivate is essential. The administrative tools for e-learning will give you an edge on these responsibilities. Software like Microsoft Project or SureTrak by Primavera will help you to manage the project tasks and people. If you need a tool for budgeting, try Microsoft Excel. To graphically view the website architecture for the course, Visio is commonly used.

Editorial Tasks and Content Development

A key player on your team will gather and write digital content for courses. It is up to your content developer to negotiate with subject matter experts for primary sources, interpret the needs analysis for instructional priorities and objectives, and craft text-based learning objects that accurately and appropriately convey the knowledge and skills intended module by module. What are the deliverables of the team members who handle content? They are the content files containing scripted pages that will be handed off to the technical staff for the authoring process.

This seems like an easy role until you think of the influence and specialized writing skills necessary. Winning over SMEs takes interpersonal savvy. Without them e-learning projects may lack credibility or miss the nuances that only an expert can provide for scenarios and assessments. Copyediting their drafts will mean respecting the conventions of their field and the context of your business. A daunting task!

Finally, usability is a special issue with content on the Web. In other words, content must be written with an appreciation for readability on the screen, taking into account the reading level, culture, and context of the end users.

Features of Technical Development

The technical end of your project will take the most time and talent. At one time a team of highly skilled and specialized technicians were needed to create even a basic online course. They did everything from art direction, color, and graphic production; to editing content; to writing HTML; to recording and preparing audio and video files; to programming interaction and authoring the course. Even though the latest development products have made it easier to create your own course, it may be best to hire an experienced external developer to program your first project. Working side-by-side you will get to see how various issues and requirements are analyzed and solved.

Programming: What It's All About

Let's start with the raw materials. They are the design document, the storyboards, the content files, and the media assets.

The design document is similar to one that might be used for face-to-face training, but in addition it specifies the media and overall look of the e-learning course. Key elements of this document are: the course title, the concept or background for the course, a profile of the target audience, and course-level learning objectives. An annotated outline of the topics and subtopics is essential. The document also should indicate the types of programming required for navigation elements. See Figure 20-4 for an example of a design document.

The **storyboards** are a sequence of detailed snapshots of each screen of the course, including the text describing the action and screen-shots or rudimentary graphics showing the appearance. They are prepared during the design process, first by creating a flowchart that maps the structure of the instructional modules and then by drafting a miniature view of each screen in the sequence. Some developers prefer to use PowerPoint to show the text and graphics in a slide with navigation and action described in its notes. Many authoring tools, such as Authorware, have these functions built in.

Training Design Document

	Course Title	Manager	Project Background	ID
ID				

	After experiencing this:	This group of users:		Will achieve this result:	
Goal	☐ course ☐ content module ☐ topic or page ☐ lesson or activity ☐ media element			☐ do (apply) ☐ feel (emotion) ☐ believe (claim) ☐ explain (concept) ☐ create (synthesize)	

	Topic	Navigation Elements	Outcomes & Evaluation
Objectives	What must they do, learn, feel believe or understand?	In what circumstances? With what resources available?	To what degree must they succeed? Evaluation means? Evaluation criteria?

FIGURE 20-4. **TRAINING DESIGN DOCUMENT**

The **content files** that were scripted by the editorial members of the team were described above.

Graphics, still photos, audio, video, and animation are **media assets.** Adobe Photoshop and ImageReady, Paint Shop Pro and Macromedia Fireworks, and Flash are used for designing and developing images and animation. Files such as GIFs, JPEG, and bitmaps were once the domain of experienced art directors and designers. Selection of browser-safe colors once took some skills and placed limitations on graphic design. Since it's now easier to display graphics and colors with the most recent versions of Web browsers, such as Netscape and Internet Explorer, color selection is not as critical a step in designing graphics for e-learning. So you can create graphics for your web courses on your own. You may find that using a graphic designer will provide you with elements for visual media that you can use interchangeably across a number of courses. It is especially effective to use professional designers to create graphics templates that trainers can use to create graphics for specific e-learning courses. This means less development time for high-quality visual element.

Now, working with these raw materials, you can begin to create your course.

Authoring

Authoring is developing the interactivity of your e-learning course. While this work once required advanced programming skills, you may now choose an authoring tool that bypasses the high-end technology and makes you look like a pro. But when you shop, do not focus on simplicity of use when choosing an authoring program. It is more important to consider what you want to build with them.

A few examples may help. A linear course without feedback loops (that means users will just click from screen to screen and not make choices that receive responses) can be prepared in Microsoft's FrontPage by a relative novice. Also notable for their ease of use are Toolbook II Instructor, Toolbook II Assistant, Authorware Attain, Attain Objects for Dreamweaver, and DazzlerMax. But these tools aren't exactly the same. Some are better at producing a CD-ROM; others are better for programming courses for Internet/Intranet delivery. Spend some time browsing the Internet, lurking in distance learning listservs and talking to more experienced users to compare features and functions of popular applications.

Programming for testing and feedback is built into many of the authoring suites and learning management systems (LMS).

Functions such as discussion and chat call will require separate development software unless you are using an LMS. There are many options available.

On the cutting edge of development is open source software. As Patti Shank, a writer for *Online Learning* magazine with considerable experience in development, explains, "Not only is the software free of cost, but it also gives developers other forms of freedom. Since they have access to the source code, they're free to make copies [of the software], fix bugs, and add enhancements. . . ." Programmers and users of open-source are often found in academic institutions, like MIT with its Open Knowledge Initiative. But the possibilities for corporate e-learning developers, as well as consultants, are enticing so we are apt to see a lot of action on this front, as well as a fair amount of debate about its downsides.

A final word about authoring: when you select your tools keep three things in mind:

1. **The purpose of the e-learning projects.** Are you experimenting with a pilot, starting a scalable effort or launching an enterprise initiative? Is your primary product going to be a series of short tutorials that are developed with a quick turnaround, or are you looking forward to just a few projects that will have large time and effort invested in them?

2. **The compatibility of various systems and programming languages.** The technical infrastructure will only allow you to make e-learning available to users if the server from which you will launch the courses can communicate with other internal systems. Issues such as whether online forms are programmed in CGI script or as Active Server Pages will either stand in way of a successful launch or accelerate it.

3. **The viability of the vendor in the marketplace.** In the last few years, the number of technology firms that brought products to market swelled and then shrunk. Vendor capital, that was once available in unimaginable amounts, is now much harder to come by. And as businesses have become more conservative in purchasing technology, the market has contracted.

What this means is that you will have to do your homework regarding the stability of your suppliers. Online sources, such as Motley Fool and Yahoo Finance, provide basic background on publicly traded companies free of cost. The American Society for Training and Development (ASTD) has information available too.

Your investments will serve you well if they are made using those three criteria.

Forecasting and Managing Resources

For years trainers and instructional designers have wanted to know, "How long does it take?" That question referred to the development time for a traditional face-to-face course. With the shift to e-learning, we have to reply, "How long does *what* take?" Production time for courses that use new media technologies span a greater range than any traditional course.

To forecast production time and resources for e-learning, look at three components of the course: content, presentation, and interactivity. The **content complexity** (Figure 20-5) is related to the readiness of information that will be in the course pages. It may range from very low, in which all of the material for your course already exists and is formatted for the Web; to moderate, where the documents exist but need to be rewritten and reformatted; to high where complex content must be located or written, approved and formatted.

Presentation complexity (Figure 20-6) has to do with the desired sophistication of the graphics and media of the course. These vary from text that is unformatted, or formatted using WYSIWYG (what you see is what you get) editors, to complex programming of pages in HTML (hypertext markup language), XML (extensible markup language); a meta-language that is used to transmit formatted data, or VRML (virtual reality markup language) for graphical animation of three-dimensional images.

The **less complex** level of presentation also includes the use of slides or images prepared with simple software applications, like Microsoft PowerPoint or RealSlideshow from RealNetworks.

In the **mid-complexity range,** audio files or video files are involved. Products, such as Camtasia, are used to capture an activity from a computer screen and convert it for display within an online course. Digital video documentation may also require production to show everything from a lecture, to a demonstration of processes or skills, to a recreation of an event.

Increasing amounts of resources are needed to develop **high-end presentations** with Flash or Java applets, and two- or three-dimension animation.

The **complexity of interactivity** (Figure 20-7) at the learner, instructor, and system levels is the final component that predicts the investment needed for development. These range from the simple assets, like hyperlinks to other sites on the intranet or Internet, and one-to-one or one-to-many communication via e-mail, discussion or chat boards, or listservs; to assessment and feedback loops, and active agents; on to complex simulation responses and intelligent systems that are adaptive to the learner. At the high end of the spectrum, the production of avatars (graphical

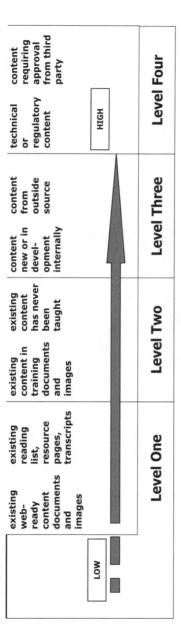

FIGURE 20-5. DEVELOPMENT COMPLEXITY: CONTENT COMPONENTS

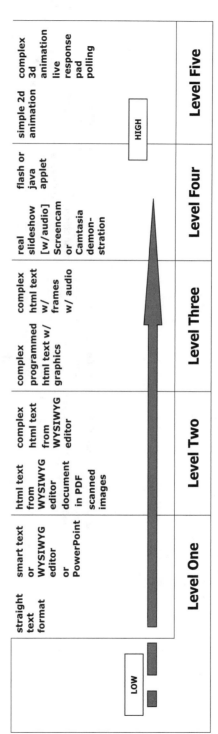

FIGURE 20-6. DEVELOPMENT COMPLEXITY: PRESENTATION COMPONENTS

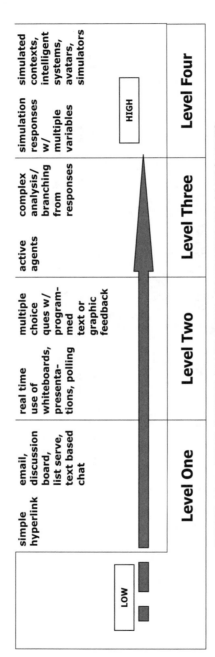

FIGURE 20-7. DEVELOPMENT COMPLEXITY: INTERACTIVITY COMPONENTS

representations of users, or fictional characters, that are three dimensional and animated) and simulators (an environment that mimics a real situation immersing the learner in it) are the most time consuming costly types of interactive e-learning.

Production Time

What sorts of time commitments are needed for production of media components? The guide at the end of this chapter will help you to guesstimate your development time in relation to the types of components and complexity you desire. When all is said and done, there are two additional issues that must be factored in as well: experience and authority.

Is this your first e-learning initiative? Is the hardware new? Are you using a new technology for authoring, or a version that has recently been released? If you said yes to any of these questions then, you should double the projected development time. Are the members of the team still growing their skills with the tools? Is the content new, out of the ordinary, or complex? If yes, add fifty percent more development time to your project. Is there more than one project on the drawing board? Are you planning to use an application service provider or launch from a hosted site? If so, increase development time by twenty-five percent.

Is the culture of your organization still hierarchical, requiring approval at several levels at multiple points in the project? Are there still some conflicting opinions about deliverables or budgets? If yes, give yourself fifty percent more development time. Do you require licensing, purchase or approval of presentation elements from outside vendors or third parties? Then development time should be increased twenty-five percent.

Once you have estimated your development time, share and reality test your calculations with your internal and external partners. They can judge the performance speed of individuals or teams, the difficulty of using particular technology, and likelihood of tasks being completed on time. A development time forecaster can be found in Appendix 20-A.

BRINGING IT ALL TOGETHER: DELIVERY

A Holistic View

In the end, the goal of implementation is preparing to deliver the right content, to the right people, at the right time, on the right technology, in the right context, and the right way. You might call this a **whole system/whole person perspective.** What does that mean? It's the way in which you position the project to the stakeholders and retain your focus on the business results as well as the end-users of e-learning. As a leader on the front line of e-learning for your business, you must champion this broader point of view of implementation to fend off some people's narrower and potentially harmful perspectives that the project is only about software or server administration.

The four performance nodes of the whole system/whole person perspective reinforce and delineate what you as an e-learning leader must do to stay on-course during implementation. Each node is a spot where you connect with others who have a stake in e-learning for your business and a philosophy that guides your expectations and performance. The nodes are:

- Partnership
- Value-added learning
- Access
- Continuous support

These nodes are next described in detail along with examples of ways in which they can be realized.

Partnership Node

Your key partnerships in leading as an e-learning champion in your business are senior leadership, management, and end-users. Senior leaders are your sponsors and advocates; managers are the leverage to move adoption of your program forward; end-users are your sounding board and word-of-mouth advertising. It is important that you build your relationships with these partners and communicate with them frequently and authentically. Before your program or course is ready for delivery, you must have provided information about what you will be expecting from each of these partners, what benefits they will receive from the e-learning initiatives, the progress and roll-out schedule of the projects, and any difficulties you are experiencing. Your candor and openness will pay off in the long run.

Communication

You must become an e-learning evangelist in your organization. Kim Kiser, managing editor of *Online Learning* magazine, explains how Chris Pirie converted the masses at Oracle. It's a story that points out how the e-learning manager must be an evangelist of sorts, to get the word out about what you will be doing and why.

> *As a member of the team that would move the $10 billion Internet software company into the e-learning age, it was Pirie's job to first convert Oracle's managers, course developers and 1,200 instructors into believers. . . .[He] took to the road, spreading the gospel according to e-learning. "I had a lot of convincing to do," he recalls, with a weary note in his voice. "We had to make this change happen. We kind of suspected we could do it, but we were as skeptical as everyone else. Business people, instructors, customers all had their doubts about e-learning."* (K. Kiser, 2001)

Motivation

The best e-learning program will go unnoticed unless you excite your audience. You know the reasons e-learning will make a difference for them. Before your launch, make sure they get it, too. Then watch the momentum grow, as Brooke Broadabent, e-learning consultant, sees it:

> *Bring issues alive. The difference between a good e-learning project manager and a great one is that a great one makes the issues alive for people, creates a sense of urgency, and helps people sing from the same song sheet.* (B. Broadabent, 2000)

Heads-up

Get the word out, especially at times when things are off-course. Your credibility will increase measurably when you are honest with your stakeholders. Whether there are scheduling issues, a glitch in the programming, vendor delays, or performance inconsistencies in testing your courses, don't keep them to yourself. Explain the issues and the steps you are taking to resolve them as simply as possible.

Value-added Learning Node

One of the most exciting uses of Web-based instruction is turning a course into a learning process that has impact. That means thinking beyond the bounds of the course—just like you probably do now for face-to-face training. Learning adds value when it transfers to the job. It's up to you to create pre- and postlearning tactics for learners to use solo, with their managers, or with peers who were participants in a course.

Advance Actions

Registration is the first step in taking an e-learning course. What's the next step? If you suggested, "taking the course," you're only partially right. Before the learner's first login, a message with the benefits of the course, some ideas for relating the content to the job, and tips for learning online will lay the groundwork for a higher quality experience.

Peer Groups

There's a lot of talk about the isolation of learners participating in e-learning. Whether there is collaboration in your courses or not, you can build a network for your learners to add value to their online course. Give those who successfully complete the same course a discussion board, listserv, or chat group. They can share ideas for using new skills and the challenges they have overcome.

Follow-up Sessions

Christine Duckworth in ASTD's Learning Circuits suggests using real time e-learning (chats or web casts) for "conducting follow-up sessions at prescheduled times without having all participants return to the training site. In addition, participants can refresh their skills with individual exercises or by reviewing discussion transcripts and using record and playback features."

Access Node

The ability of users to login to and participate in the course site using different types of internal and external connections to the server is what accessibility involves. The first challenge for learners will likely be browser versions and plug-ins. Bandwidth (the capacity of the network to deliver data) also strongly impacts access to e-learning. Large files on the server (especially multimedia files) and the number of users trying to access the server at the same time can all effect how easily users can access the course. For learners with physical or visual limitations, the layout of your course pages can aid or inhibit accessibility for them.

Plug-in Central

Download sites for plug-ins can be linked to a web page introduction to the program or course. These might include: audio and video players, for instance, Apple Computer's Quicktime, RealNetwork's RealPlayer or Microsoft's Windows Media Player; Acrobat Reader for PDF files; and Microsoft Flash or Shockwave for animations.

Options

Give your learners options. You can prepare course files in more than one format and offer an option of HTML or PDF files, for example. Or there can be a text-only version of your website available.

Friendly

Do you know if your course site is ready for learners who are visually impaired and use software readers to translate text to voice? By testing your site with Web Bobby, you will see firsthand the challenges that the course pages present.

Continuous Support Node

The people who access the courses on your server need all sorts of advice, explanation, problem verification, and quick fixes. The best assistance for them comes from staff who have a mix of technical, problem solving, and communications skills. They must be familiar with the courses and how they run; and they need access to the server. Whether you opt for sharing this responsibility internally or outsourcing it, be sure to quality control the help you offer to be sure it meets the needs of the users.

Support Structure

Consider establishing a variety of types of support for users. Does the learner need to get course information? How about a link to the training registrar on the portal or program website? What about learners wanting to connect to learners? A course roster with e-mailed linked names will help. Do learners or trainers have technical questions? E-mail or phone access to customer care is best. Extra help with content questions can be forwarded to an e-mail account for the trainer/facilitator. And feedback loops for completion of tests or courses can be built in to forward self-reports via drop box in the LMS to the learner.

Seamless Service

Anytime, anywhere learning needs 24/7 customer care. Whether or not you have the staff and facilities for round-the-clock coverage, there are many choices for connecting your end users to the help they need. Phone access via 800 numbers can lead to live support or monitored voice mailboxes. E-mail messages can be relayed to beepers or wireless devices. Online chat with a customer care specialist may be linked to your portal or course site. The goal should be a service that is available as it is needed and keeps the learning process going.

Service Tracking

Nothing is more frustrating to users than reporting a problem, receiving a commitment for service, and never reaching a point of resolution. Quality customer care includes systems for tracking incoming requests for service to their completion, and then checking back to insure that the solution and the process met expectations. From time to time you will also want to randomly evaluate the overall effectiveness of your e-learning program by using the data from your service records. It can provide clues to needs and issues related to people, courses, and technology.

IN CONCLUSION

In the final analysis, for implementation to be successful, an orientation towards comprehensive integration of business requirements, learning, and performance priorities with information technology, coupled with adaptation of the development and delivery processes, are essential to accelerating anytime, anywhere learning for your most important customer—the end user. For additional tips and hints, see Table 20-1.

TABLE 20-1. E-Learning Implementation: Tips and Hints

➤ **Implementation** involves development and delivery of an online program or course. It's the step after the preparation of a design document and storyboard, and identification of delivery mode. It signals that e-learning is a regular part of your business.

➤ **Successful implementation** aligns development and delivery to a relevant new media learning model and to organizational learning strategy and operations.

➤ **Requirements** need to be identified before courses and programs are designed and developed. These include instructional criteria, program planning, and learning data management.

(continued)

TABLE 20-1. *Continued*

➤ **The e-learning tactical process model** outlines the priorities in moving e-learning from strategy to delivery and continuous improvement.

➤ **Development must function** in the instructional architecture, the technical architecture, and the security environment.

➤ **Leadership** and team models for e-learning must be identified and communicated to clarify accountability and authority.

➤ **Administrative, editorial, and technical roles** are involved on the e-learning implementation team. If you don't have the necessary talent available, consultants or outsourcing may be in order.

➤ **Project management, budgeting, and visualization tools** are used to manage administration on the e-learning team.

➤ **Identification and attention** are important aspects of writing for the web. Be sure they are part of your editorial style.

➤ **The design document, storyboards, content files, and existing media** are the raw materials of development.

➤ **Templates** prepared by a professional have become a common practice, meaning less development time for the visual elements of e-learning.

➤ **Authoring tools** should be selected by the purpose they will fulfill, ease of use, compatibility with existing systems and programming languages, and the reliability of the vendor.

➤ **Complexity of content, presentation, and interactivity** impact production time and resources. Don't overlook the impact of experience and organizational culture on development.

➤ **A whole system / whole person perspective** on delivery will lead you to deliver the right content, to right person, at the right time, on the right technology, in the right context, and the right way.

➤ **Partnership, value-added learning, access, and continuous support** should be the hallmarks of your delivery of e-learning program.

Content development	+	Presentation development	+	Technical development	×	Experience	×	Culture	=	Total

Instructions: For each task your development team will perform, list the time in numbers of days. Add the totals for each type of development and multiply by the appropriate experience and culture factors to determine your forecast.

Experience Factor: 1.25: more than one project, using ASP or hosted site

1.5: still growing skills, new or difficult content
2: first e-learning initiative, new hardware, new authoring tool or version

Culture Factor: 1.25: licensing, purchase or approval of presentation
1.5: hierarchical approval, conflicting opinions

1 day

25 screens of text
15 screens of text + animation, audio or video
15 simple images
12 hyperlinks
8½-hr audio clips

5 days

30 simple animations
5 complex animations
5 simulation responses
2 15-min videos

10 days

20 complex branched questions
2 virtual reality models

20 days

40 complex images
1 complex simulation

APPENDIX 20-A. **E-LEARNING DEVELOPMENT TIME FORECASTER**

RESOURCES

Readings

Berge, Z. (2001). *Sustaining Distance Training*. San Francisco: Jossey-Bass.

Collis, B. (1996). *Tele-Learning in a Digital World*. London: Thompson Computer Press.

Gayeski, D. (1997). *Designing and Managing Computer Mediated Learning: an Interactive Toolkit*. Ithaca, NY: OmniCom Associates.

Lau, L. (2000). *Distance Learning Technologies: Issues, Trends and Opportunities*. Hershey, PA: Idea Group.

Rosenberg, M. (2001). *E-Learning: Strategies For Delivering Knowledge in the Digital Age*. New York: McGraw-Hill.

Websites

Boeing: *Who Keeps Moving the Cheese?: Lessons Learned from Multi-Format Conversions http://www.adlnet.org/library/library_details.cfm?Repo_Id=480*

Broadabent, B. Championing e-learning. *E-Learning Hub*. Available at *http://www.e-learninghub.com/championing.html#Managing an e-learning project*

Kiser, K. E-learning evangelism. *OnlineLearning* Magazine. January 2001.

Piotrowski, C. Are the reported barriers to Internet-based instruction warranted?: A synthesis of recent research. *Education*. Fall 2000.

Shank, P. "Something for nothing." *OnlineLearning* Magazine. January 2001.

Usability 101. Available at *www.beingoutdoors.com/mde615/testing.html*

➤ABOUT THE AUTHOR

Loretta L. Donovan is Senior Director, Organization and Employee Development for Girl Scouts of the USA. At Teachers College, Columbia University, she is an Adjunct Professor, teaching online courses in Staff Development and Training, and Leading and Sustaining Web-based Learning in the Adult Learning and Leadership Program.

Donovan was Director, Corporate Learning & Development for ClientSoft, Inc. managing employee development and product training. She previously was a Senior Consultant with SCT Corporation, with responsibility for distance learning clients.

She is an active member of the Academy for Human Resource Development, chairing its Technology Committee; the American Association of University Women, the American Society for Training and Development, and the Association for Computer Education and Technology.

CHAPTER 21

KEEPING E-LEARNING GOING: MOTIVATING AND RETAINING E-LEARNERS

➤**VICKY PHILLIPS**

"Telecommunications bandwidth is not a problem. Human bandwidth is."

Thomas Davenport,
E-Learning and the Attention Economy

Web-based courses are available 24/7/365; the mind of a working adult remains considerably less accessible. The information locked inside a course will not morph into practical knowledge without considerable human effort. E-learning often fails where education has historically stumbled: at the human level.

WHY DOES E-LEARNING FAIL?

Learning takes time. It takes mental effort. It takes motivation. It takes attention. During the average workday, with calls to return, clients to please, and budgets to meet, the anytime/anyplace promise of e-learning easily turns into a no time/nowhere reality. While most of the buzz to date has focused on e-learning technology—knowledge management systems and how they efficiently deliver large-scale educational events—the most formidable e-learning challenges of the future lie decidedly on the softer side. Whether or not e-learning "takes" is a question that the learners, not the technologists, will ultimately answer.

Failure in e-learning can occur at three interlocking levels:

➤ the learner level (poorly prepared learners, lack of motivation, no time);

➤ the product level (poor course design; inadequate technology infrastructure); or

➤ the organizational level (low managerial support, lack of reward structure).

The chart shown in Figure 21-1, The 3 Levels of E-Learning Failure, summarizes the success/failure matrix that impinges on all e-learning endeavors.

Notice that the product level has two possible evaluative pathways: content or conduit. Conduit refers to the technology itself—for example, a learning delivery system like Centra Symposium or HorizonLive. Content refers to the actual educational meat that makes up any instructional event, such as a single piece of courseware or series of predesigned learning modules from a vendor like Primelearning.com or SmartForce.com. The organizational level includes factors that constitute what might also be termed the external context. The external context refers to the macro environment where the e-learning takes place; this includes the greater organizational culture in regards to training and how it is valued and supported within the sponsoring corporation. In making assessments and e-learning evaluations we often refer to the learner level as "internal context." We use this term to signify that what happens inside the hearts and minds of learners. Internal context includes such things as learner motivation levels and poorly developed technical skills that are necessary for e-learning, such as knowing how to use a Web browser or download a lesson file.

CHALLENGES AT THE LEARNER LEVEL

> "In the training industry, if you build it—nobody cares."
> Tom Kelly, VP Internet Solutions Group,
> Cisco Systems

Learning is hard work. Even if we create the perfect piece of e-learning software (content) we still, as trainers, must go eye-to-eye with a generation of imperfect adult learners. We are not a nation of independent learners. Most of us learned how to learn within a coercive, expert-dependent educational system. Many of us were motivated to learn not to achieve rewards but to avoid punishments—such as F grades—or the embarrassment of being called on and found wanting in class. Remove the evaluative teacher and grade book from the electronic classroom and

Product Level (Content or Conduit)

Poor course design (chunks of theory and facts with very little real-life application/extension)

Poor e-classroom design (non-intuitive navigation, chat rooms that crash, ugly interfaces)

Ill-performing technology (poor audio, jerky video, interrupted data downloads, message boards that crash)

Poorly managed course social interactions (untrained or untried online moderators)

Slow instructor/mentor response times

Learner Level (Internal Context)

Lack of time

Low interest in subject matter

Low motivation for learning

Poor self-study skills

Poor time management skills

Disrupting life interruptions (divorce, shift change, parental duties)

Lack of necessary e-skills (downloading files, subscribing to e-mail lists)

Psychological resistance to losing face-to-face learning perks (social networking, travel, snacks)

Organizational Level (External Context)

Poor internal marketing of courses and events

Lack of clear reward structure

Failure to provide quality learning environment

Failure to provide quality learning equipment

Failure to provide managerial feedback and support of learning

Failure to provide time on-the-job to train

Corporate-wide lack of dedication to a learning culture

Blanket mandate of e-learning as the new-new thing; removal of all other methods

Failure to match Internet training to its most appropriate purposes

FIGURE 21-1. **THE THREE LEVELS OF E-LEARNING FAILURE**

many adult learners, not surprisingly, lapse into recess mode. You can make several interventions at the learner level to increase e-learning participation and completion rates.

Intervention: Select for Success

Two characteristics can aid success at the learner level. Learners who have historically been successful at learning independently, using CD-ROMS, printed books, videodiscs, or other correspondence methods, are the best first candidates for e-learning. These people have already learned how to learn independently, a crucial skill set for distance learning success regardless of the delivery conduit.

People who are comfortable trying out new things also are among the best early adopters within any organization. Surprisingly, these people are not always tech employees. Every team, whether in sales or customer service, includes people who are innovators. Identify these people and showcase them as peer e-learning leaders. Peer influence is almost always more persuasive in getting people to change their behavior than executive mandates.

One company we worked with identified three employees, each of them from different work teams—one from security, one from production, and one from sales—to serve as peer e-learning leaders. After receiving training in e-learning—the technology, what would be expected of them as learners, and the reward options—our peer leaders were off and running.

Three months later our client highlighted the three peer leaders in company e-mails, bulletin board displays, and their monthly newsletter, tagging them official "E-Learning Gurus." The three gave presentations at brown bag lunch gatherings and weekly department meetings, encouraging co-workers to come to them with their questions about e-learning. When the company launched their open e-learning program, available to all employees, a record number of curious trainees participated.

Generally, people are suspicious of new things. This includes e-learning. The best way to break down mistrust is to use real-life testimonials. In our client's case, they posted the photos and success stories of their e-learning leaders on the training Intranet splash page. Aspect Communications of San Jose employs a similar tactic. They pull favorable quotes from e-course evaluations written by employees and post them in banner ad style on the company intranet. They enlist the experiences of their own employees to internally promote the e-learning experience.

Intervention: Prepare Learners for E-Learning

Computers are like cars. Everyone drives a car, yet relatively few of us know how to perform common automotive maintenance tasks like changing a tire. Similarly, while everyone uses computers, surprisingly few of us are competent at the tasks commonly required to access an e-learning library. Can everyone in your company download a file? Highly unlikely.

If your e-learning program doesn't include a mini-course, handbook, or orientation program on how to e-learn, create such a resource ASAP. Create your orientation so it covers two major areas. Make sure your learners can perform the technological tasks required of them, such as signing onto and off e-mail list-servs for class discussions or downloading files. Go over your e-learning program with an eye toward idiot-proofing the technology access process. Never assume that your learners will know how to use any technology platform, whether that be an asynchronous message board system of a real-time audio wrap-around. Make every step explicit. In addition, include an e-mail or a phone number that links your learners to tech support in the most expedient way possible.

Make sure your learners are prepared psychologically for the e-learning experience. For example, if your program uses asynchronous communication, where learners can log on anytime, suggest to them that they establish and commit to a regular weekly learning schedule before they begin their studies. Most adult learners grew up and are comfortable with a weekly study schedule. Suggesting they establish one up front works well because it creates a familiar structure for progressing through what otherwise might be a completely unstructured course experience.

One client we worked with created a simple calendar program that popped up during course registration. The program explained to learners that while they could access their course anytime they would increase the impact of the educational experience if they committed to working on their course at least once a week, on the same day, at the same time. The pop-up calendar allowed learners to pencil in the day and time they would work on their course each week in half-hour blocks. Once the calendar was filled in, an automatic e-mail would arrive in the learner's e-mail box 24 hours in advance of the booked learning time to remind the learner it was time to log-on and crack the books.

Many large library course providers, such as PrimeLearning.com and SmartForce.com, have built-in e-mail agents that automatically send out messages to any learner who begins a course but then fails to return to work on that course for some preset length of time, such as 72 hours or a week. Such e-mail reminders are highly effective. They serve as an electronic tap on the shoulder, motivating learners to come back and complete their course of study.

Intervention: Lay-Out a Smorgasbord of Rewards

Learning is onerous work. When contemplating their commitment to e-learning, people naturally play station WIIFM: What's In It For Me. Make explicit the payoffs for each course taken. Don't try to get all your employees to accept one type of reward structure. People are diverse; they hold correspondingly diverse views of what they consider a reward to be. What motivates Adam to complete a course in C programming (a $10 gift certificate at Sportsman.com) may do nothing to motivate Eve to attend her customer service training online. (Eve craves managerial recognition. Kudos at the weekly staff meeting will go a long way toward keeping her nose to the educational grindstone.) Create a smorgasbord of rewards. Encourage employees to select what motivates them most from the menu.

Rewards
Material Rewards
Paper Certificates
> Tie courses together and issue company certificates upon completion of three or more courses in a sequence.

Gift Certificates
> Issue in small denominations from popular vendors like Eddie Bauer or Sears upon course completion.

Pay Raises
> Tie to the completion of educational and other performance milestones as part of an overall career plan.

Snacks
> When employees start e-courses send over a congratulatory box of doughnuts with a note saying these replace the doughnuts you would have gotten at the classroom seminar.

Psychic Rewards

Grant time on-the-job to learn.

Give employees Do Not Disturb signs to post when taking e-courses at work.

Grant time off for star learners who complete long training sequences.

Publicly mention employee educational achievements
> In team meetings,
> In the company newsletter,
> On the company training Intranet splash-page.

Hold competitions between work teams
> The team that completes more courses gets lunch on the company.

Intervention: Provide a Social Surround

E-learning practitioners are discovering that while self-contained, asynchronous e-learning is extremely cost-effective, participation rates often suffer from the absence of a social surround. The benefits of cost-effectiveness become less meaningful if employees refuse to use e-learning because of its lack of a social surround. For many, blended e-learning is becoming a wise compromise solution. Training events are being technology-enabled, helping to reduce travel and instructional costs, while social features, such as real-time group chat or live-peer audio conferencing, are being integrated to help make technology-enabled learning more psychologically and socially attractive.

New York University Online specializes in making and marketing courses for the corporate marketplace. NYU Online is also one of the few vendors that actively researches what flies and what flops in the corporate e-learning marketplace. Karen Frankola, E-Learning Solutions Manager at NYU Online, has found that the following human factors can significantly impact course completion rates in the corporate environment. Our collective client assessments echo and expand upon the research undertaken to date at NYU Online. Audit your program for these social factors.

1. Blend—Let learners do some of the course self-paced, but require live, synchronous sessions with peers and instructors at key points such as the beginning, middle and end of educational events.

2. Equip—Provide access to learning labs at work or fast-speed, home dial-in connections. Taking people away from their work desks to engage in e-learning will help them avoid disorienting interruptions like phone calls and office visitors.

3. Hold Accountable—Hold front line managers responsible for e-learning completion in their units. Publish the results in a comparative format for the whole company to review.

4. Observe and Measure—Maintain a central training tracking and reporting system where employees can see their progress as measured against their peers.

5. Intervene—Assign managers to send e-mails, make phone calls, or have face-to-face meetings with e-learners who fall behind in their coursework.

The American Society for Training & Development rates managerial and peer support as lead factors that set apart successful e-learning from less successful roll-outs. One of our clients, Management Vitality, assigns new e-learners to a buddy system. Students can choose to communicate with any classmate they like, but the buddy system ensures that everyone has a peer to turn to if they encounter uncertainty those first few crucial days of learning online.

In addition, Management Vitality (*www.managementvitality.com*), a Canadian e-learning vendor, offers a seven-week sequence of management training courses under the rubric of Teamwork Plus!. Management Vitality advises students in an eight-page downloadable "E-Learner's Handbook" that the most important thing to remember is to "involve your peers and your boss in your learning program."

Management Vitality's course is delivered in an asynchronous Web-based format to managers around the world. The "E-Learner's Handbook" is designed to help corporate learners prepare for the psychological challenges of online learning. The handbook also addresses issues such as how to get technical support. Notice that the letter on the next page also makes apparent for the learner and company management the take-away benefits or rewards of completing the TeamWork Plus! course sequence online. The handbook includes the following letter template to each person who enrolls in their seven-week online course TeamWork Plus! E-learners are directed to send copies of this templated letter to their bosses as well as their peers to help ensure that they obtain the peer and management support needed to complete online learning.

Management Vitality, Inc.
Template for Letter From New E-Learner to Boss and Peers
TeamWork Plus!

Dear ————————— :

From (date) until (date) I, along with several of our colleagues, will be participating in an online course called Teamwork Plus! The online course is offered by ManagementVitality.com, Inc. of Ottawa, Canada, and expounds upon the Adizes management principles.

They tell us that the course material, and learning how to navigate on the Web, are not nearly as difficult as the challenge of sticking to the course until the end. The self-discipline for me to do this will have continual competition from other on-the-job pressures. This is where you come in.

My goal is to take and complete this course in the allotted time in order to gain the immediate benefits of:

➤ Getting a certificate for successfully learning Adizes management techniques,

➤ Trying out and becoming experienced in this new phenomenon of online learning,

➤ Making online contact with managers from around the world.

You can help by getting involved with me.

(To the boss) My first suggestion is that we meet together before the course and discuss the objectives of the course that will benefit our organization, so that I can make sure that I am focused on them. Then let's meet weekly to ensure that you are aware of, and approve of, my weekly progress.

(To my peers) My second suggestion is that we meet together before the course so that I can share with you the nature of it and how I think it will impact our workplace. Then we can meet casually, each week if you like, for me to give you a summary of what has transpired so far, during the course.

(To my peers and the boss) My third suggestion is that you allow me "course time" which I will post at my desk, during which you will avoid contacting me over the approximately one hour per day, treating me for that hour as if I were out of the office. I'll post an "On Course" sign on my desk, as a reminder.

My fourth suggestion is that we have a post-course meeting so I can summarize its contents and its benefits to this organization as I see them.

Your cooperation in any of these ways will be a very big help to me.

Thank you very much,
The E-Learner

CHALLENGES AT THE PRODUCT LEVEL

Poorly designed e-courses will cause learners to click shut their browsers and their minds. L-Guide, a Washington State firm that reviews corporate e-learning, refers to the bulk of what's on the market for business skills training today as "the mediocre majority." Education demands attention, yet most corporate training has not been designed to compete for the attentive eye.

Many vendors that sell e-courses or create e-curriculum have operated for less than five years. Independent systems for rating the quality of e-learning courses are just emerging. To make matters more complex, a vendor that crafts great courses in one subject area may produce titles in another subject area that pale in comparison. Vast differences between information technology training and soft skills training have led to an uneven marketplace where pioneering companies that excelled at developing information intense courses, such as computer programming, may not possess the capability for developing socially complex courses on warm topics such as leadership. Follow these strategies to help mitigate failures at the product level.

Intervention: Consult Independent Evaluators

For all its size and convenience, the Internet remains a dimly-lit educational supermarket. The last time we counted, more than 126 vendors offered some type of e-training in project management. Don't shop in the dark. Independent authorities are striving to establish objective guidelines for both individual consumers and institutional buyers of e-learning. Check with the following sources to help identify the best training courses and e-learning degree programs.

L-Guide—www.lguide.com

Rates and ranks e-learning course titles from small and large vendors according to ease of use, appropriateness of subject matter, and other quality factors. Reviews are available by annual subscription. Sample reviews and report summaries are available free at the Web site.

American Society for Training and Development E-Learning Courseware Certification—www.astd.org/ecertification

For a fee, e-training publishers can submit their asynchronous Web-based courses to ASTD's certification program. The ASTD program reviews and rate courses along the dimensions of usability and instructional design. Courses in IT, desktop applications, and business skills are eligible.

GetEducated.com—www.geteducated.com

Issues free, online, in PDF book format, *Best Distance Learning Graduate Schools*, a series of targeted guides that profile the emerging "Internet Ivy" and "Consumer Best Buys" among accredited graduate schools that offer degrees or professional certificates through distance learning.

Intervention: Leverage Peer Networks Online

E-learning is a rapidly evolving industry. It may reasonably take a decade for standards and category leaders to emerge. In the meantime, tap peer-managed training grapevines on the Internet. Vendors rarely reveal the shortcomings of their wares. Trainers themselves are more likely to be forthcoming. More than one hundred specialized discussion lists dedicated to e-learning operate freely online. Below are two of the best online discussions lists to participate in for honest peer feedback online.

TRDEV

The Training & Development list-serv. To subscribe and participate in the open discussion, send an e-mail to trdev-subscribe@yahoogroups.com. *trdev-subscribe @yahoogroups.com*

E-Learning Leaders

The E-Learning Leaders list-serv. To subscribe and participate in the discussions, send an e-mail to elearningleaders-subscribe@yahoogroups.com

Intervention: Take a Team Test-Drive

The best way to determine the appropriateness of any e-learning library for your personnel is to assemble a test team from among your actual future e-learners. Assign the team to test-drive courses at random from potential vendor libraries. Use pull-out checklists like those provided in the do-it-yourself assessment kit from Lynette Gillis, *Quality Standards for Evaluating Multimedia and Online Courseware.* Gillis's standardized checklists will help ensure that team members compare e-courses along consistent data points.

Gillis' kit, which we've successfully used with corporate e-learning assessment teams of various sizes, provides pull-out lists that make it easy for geographically dispersed team members to rate courses across four sectors: usability, content quality, organizational appropriateness, and instructional design. (Gillis's off-the-shelf, e-learning quality assessment kit is incidentally central to the independent e-learning certification rubric under development by the American Society for Training and Development. The ASTD has partnered with Gillis to spearhead their own e-certification course rating program.)

Important: don't rely only on official demo courses to make your final decisions. Demo courses are often better developed than regular vendor libraries. Most vendors will open selected courses for a test-drive if you ask. Ask. Remember to test-drive titles that relate to subjects of the highest interest to your employees. A vendor who manufactures a good series on Java programming may not produce courseware of comparable quality in another subject area, such as project management.

CHALLENGES AT THE ORGANIZATIONAL LEVEL

Quality content is crucial. Robust flexible conduits are mandatory. Equipping learners to learn independently is equally essential. Yet creating a quality external context may prove the most crucial and difficult factor for building successful organization-wide e-learning campaigns that last. You can't buy context off the shelf. The context of e-learning is something that each organization must cultivate in congruence with their overall corporate culture. Before implementing e-learning, ask yourself if your company supports a learning culture. If e-learning is being adopted primarily to cut costs with little thought to the "softer side" of the success/failure matrix, it is likely to be met with immense psychological resistance.

For many employees, e-learning translates into psychological loss, not gain. Loss of a chance to network with colleagues. Loss of the annual training trip—read: working vacation—to Hawaii. For e-learning to succeed at an institutional level, corporations must create a culture that makes apparent and appealing the rewards of e-learning. Even a masterfully designed e-course will suffer from poor learner completion rates if the sponsoring company has failed to provide a motivational structure that adequately encourages employees to complete the training. Local management may build a grade-A, million-dollar, e-course library, yet completely neglect to engage in active internal marketing. Few employees might access the e-campus because few know it is there. In all these cases, context is king. If e-learning adoption occurs willy-nilly, it is likely to be used by employees in an equally haphazard manner.

Intervention: Adopt a Best Use Policy

One client recently called us with the introductory statement that a mandate had come down from headquarters to eliminate all face-to-face internal training, replacing it instead with e-learning. The goal: cut $1 million from the human resources budget in the current fiscal year. Headquarters had decided the best way to make this drastic reduction was to replace warm-body trainers with education online. E-learning can save money, but if it is implemented for this reason, and this reason alone, success, in terms of employee participation rates, is likely to remain elusive. Any company that eliminates all face-to-face training, replacing it instead with e-learning simply to cut costs, is not using e-learning at its best. E-learning is best used selectively in the following broad venues:

> **Repetitive uniform information transfer:** E-learning is great for any large scale, repetitive training that focuses on factual material: New employee orientations and new product roll-outs are excellent candidates for corporatewide conversion from face-to-face to Web-based delivery.

> **Just-in-time product update trainings:** Mobile sales forces must understand and present numerous products while in the field. Updates for products such as software can come as frequently as every three months. One of our clients, a drug company, uses e-learning to keep their globally dispersed sales force up-to-date on product approvals, drug recalls, and new studies that tout the effectiveness of their brand over the competitors.

➤ **Just-in-time training for mobile workers:** Field technicians have to diagnose and troubleshoot a variety of equipment and appliances while on the road. E-learning lets them access Web-based fact-files, product diagrams, and Q & A expert advice databases from mobile handheld devices.

Enlist e-learning for what it accomplishes best: cost savings, first and foremost. Blend e-learning with face-to-face events or real-time, synchronous features such as chat, electronic white boards, or phone conferencing the rest of the time to help shave time and travel expense. Adopting a blended, best-use policy will help ensure that your employees receive e-learning at its best.

HELPING LEARNERS COMPLETE E-LEARNING

Think Outside the Course—Leverage Less Formal Methods of Learning

Knowledge has a shorter shelf life today than a century ago. The packages we wrap it in should come in a corresponding array of new shapes and sizes. The historically familiar formal course represents only one kind of possible e-learning event. Moreover, the traditional course, with a textbook, a syllabus, and weekly assignments, probably ranks high among the adult learners' *least* favorite educational events.

In 1977 the Education Development Center of Massachusetts quantified the amount of career knowledge that the average adult learns not in formal courses but from co-workers: a shocking seventy percent. Don't limit your e-learning program to store-bought courses or knowledge databases. If you do, you'll be ignoring a great opportunity to leverage the informal knowledge networks that your employees spontaneously create and utilize every working day.

Diversify Your Approach To e-Training

Even large e-course library vendors such as Skillsoft and Smartforce offer knowledge outside the course. Skillsoft, for example, offers a library of just-in-time, online job aids. These aids allow employees to extract advice on common tasks like how to write a budget. Employees could take a course in managerial accounting, but a whole course would take a few weeks. If the truth be known, most employees looking for information on how to write a budget are looking because they need to include a budget with a report, both of which are due ASAP. A job aid is a great just-in-time tutor.

Peer Knowledge Communities

Daniel Tobin, author of *All Learning is Self-Directed*, writes little about e-courses in his excellent book. He sees the Internet and its connectivity as prized infrastructure for managing connections rather than content. "If you don't know a solution to your problem exists, for all practical purposes it doesn't exist. If you don't know that Joe in the next cubicle or Diana over in the company's Singapore office faced this same problem and solved it last week or last year, it is a new problem and a new solution," explains Tobin. The Internet Age solution is to build a company knowledge database. Make that database stop one for any team assigned to research pressing issues. Large companies such as Bechtel have implemented report databases in an effort to manage peer knowledge connections across divisions and geographically disperse locations. No team at Bechtel can begin a new project without consulting the database to see who/where/when a similar problem may have been encountered and solved by the collective brain trust of Bechtel. As Internet/Intranet search tools become more deeply embedded inside corporations the concept of managing knowledge connections is likely to ascend to prominence. Proctor & Gamble has built a knowledge portal that uses AskMe Enterprise software to manage the knowledge base of their 110,000 global employees. The AskMe technology allows employees to search for and connect with other P&G employees around the globe who are experts in thousands of areas.

Video On-Demand Training Libraries
Any educational broadcast or event can be archived in this day and age. Institutions can store and replay electronically archived presentations, speeches, team meetings, and report briefs at levels of granular specificity only dreamed of a decade ago. Cisco Systems provides employees with structured courses on hard and soft topics, but they also provide employees access to peer knowledge communities and video-on-demand libraries that use visual broadcasts to better illustrate new products and teach physical processes. Cisco broadcasts its live product road shows around the globe using an internal IP/TV network. Post-broadcast, Cisco creates a video-on-demand archive of the training. They also capture and archive the questions asked during the live broadcasts to create a Q & A text database that Cisco researchers and salespeople can access anytime to better understand client concerns.

BRINGING LEARNERS BACK

To escalate your rate of e-learning participation, you'll need to build a learning culture that actively encourages people to turn to e-learning to move their careers and the company forward.

Integrate E-Learning Into Career Plans

Make a course mandatory for pay raises or promotions and the number of people who take and complete that course will skyrocket. (Our studies show that making a course mandatory will likely double the number of attendees in any organization.) The bad thing about e-learning is that people can do it anytime, anywhere. People need more structure than this. If employees know that real consequences both positive and negative are attached to attending a course or not attending a course, they will attend to the course.

Orchestrate Internal Marketing

Kara Underwood, Senior Director of Education Services at Aspect Communications, realized that by implementing e-learning she was asking employees to change their behavior. She wanted employees to go to the Net rather than the seminar room (where many of them had been going for decades) to learn how to sell the company's products . "We treat all our training offerings, online or not, like they're product launches," reveals Underwood. E-learning can work. It can save time, and lower training costs, while simultaneously producing more knowledgeable employees—but only if companies take the time, like they do at Aspect, to "sell" employees on Web-based training and their new role as more independent learners.

In a survey of seven hundred learners at thirty companies, the American Society for Training & Development and the Masie Center discovered that e-courses with the greatest start rates (not completion rates) should include at least four out of five of the following features:

1. Use peer testimonials

2. Use formal means of internal promotion (targeted e-mail and print being popular)

3. Use direct managers/supervisors to inform learners about courses

4. Inform people more than once about courses

5. Locate and utilize internal champions (managers excited about and willing to promote e-learning)

To enhance your learner return rates implement the features listed above.

Focus on Competency, Not Completion

Low rates of course completion, sometimes as high as eighty percent, worry some in the field of technology-enabled teaching. Low course completion rates may signify several things. They may mean that your vendor offers a low-quality product, but they also may mean that your people came, learned what they needed to learn, and left. Adults are notoriously impatient. They take a pluck and play, practical approach to knowledge. Even in face-to-face seminars adult learners often prefer to skip the introductory material, focusing instead on the middle meat of an educational event. (Note: If we measured the number of people in any educational auditorium who remained physically present for a course while letting their minds drift elsewhere, we'd most likely have "mental" dropout rates as high as eighty percent for good old-fashioned lecture events.)

John Cone, Dell Computer's Vice President of Learning at Round Rock, Texas, recommends trainers deemphasize attrition rates. Dell sees drop out rates as high as thirty percent but drop in rates (for people not preregistered) just as high. Cone sees performance change as the critical metric to measure rather than course attrition. "We operate on the assumption that people drop in to get what they want and they drop out if they don't get it. All we care about is performance at the end."

Why bother to learn? People ask this question continually. Organizations can provide psychic and concrete rewards to help motivate people to begin and succeed at e-learning. One of the greatest motivators for corporations to adopt e-learning, as well as for people to return to it time and again, is to build your e-learning endeavor so that practical results are observable. The more immediate the results the better. If your marketing team knows that trainees who complete power marketing courses sell, on average, twenty percent more, their learning motivation levels will rise faster and remain stronger than if the top brass puts out an e-memo requiring everyone to take e-training with no visible performance metrics attached.

RESOURCES

Readings

American Society for Education & Training. *E-Learning: If We Build It Will They Come? E-Learning Motivators and Acceptance Levels.* ASTD/Masie Center, June 2001.

Caswell, Bill. "E-Learner's Handbook for Teamwork Plus." *Management Vitality,* July 2001.

Cisco Systems. "Case Study: Partner E-Learning Connections: Cisco Training, On Demand." September 9, 2001.

Cisco Systems. "Case Study: E-Learning via Cisco's IPTV Solutions." September 9, 2001.

Davenport, Thomas. "E-learning and the attention economy: Here, there, and everywhere." *Linezine.com,* Spring 2001, http://www.linezine.com/5.2/articles/tdeatae.htm.

Delahoussaye, Martin and Ron Zemke. "About learning online." *Training,* September 2001, pp. 49–59.

Delio, Michelle. Report: Online training "boring." *Wired News,* August 30, 2001, http://www.wired.com/news/print/0,1294,38504,00.html.

Frankola, Karen. (2000). Tips for increasing e-learner completion rates. *Workforce.com,* http://www.workforce.com/feature/00/07/29/0015576.html.

Frankola, Karen. Why online learners drop out. *www.Workforce.com.*

Gillis, Lynette (2000). *Quality Standards for Evaluating Multimedia and Online Training. Ontario Society for Training and Development.* Canada: McGraw-Hill Ryerson.

Lguide. *E-Learning Course Publishers: A Comparative Analysis and Industry Directory: March 2001,* Lguide, 2001.

Moore, Cathleen. "A case in point: Tapping knowledge: P&G deploys knowledge sharing software." *Infoworld,* October 15, 2001, p. 38.

Phillips, Vicky. "GetEducated.com's Best Distance Learning Graduate Schools: Business & Management Programs: 2002." GetEducated.com, 2001, http://www.geteducated.com.

Phillips, Vicky. "Motivating adult learners: The role of financial rewards." *Virtual University Gazette,* July 2001, GetEducated.com, http://www.geteducated.com/vugaz.htm.

Phillips, Vicky. "Visions: Death of the Course." *Virtual University Gazette*, November 2001, GetEducated.com, http://www.geteducated.com/vugaz.htm.

Online Learning Reviews. "Avoiding failure: How can you avoid failure in an e-learning initiative? John Cone's suggested steps." *Online Learning Reviews*, Thursday, June 21, 2001, *http://www.vnulearning.com/*.

Raths, David. "A tough audience: Getting employees revved up about e-learning can be difficult." *Online Learning Magazine*, June 2001.

Tobin, Daniel. (2000). *All Learning Is Self-Directed*. American Society for Training & Development.

►ABOUT THE AUTHOR

Vicky Phillips designed and directed America's first online counseling center for adult distance learners for the Electronic University Network on America Online in 1989. Today, as founding Director and CEO of GetEducated.com, LLC, Vicky researches and consults with corporations and colleges on the development of best of class e-learning curriculum and support systems.

She is the publisher of the free e-mail newsletter, The Virtual University Gazette, as well as lead researcher and publisher for the free online guide book series, GetEducated's Best Distance Learning Graduate Schools. You can reach her at vicky@geteducated.com or visit her online at *www.geteducated.com*.

CHAPTER 22

HOW DO I CHOOSE E-LEARNING SOFTWARE THAT WILL KEEP GOING AND GOING?

➤ALLAN BERGER

When considering the purchase of e-learning development tools, there are a number of things to consider beyond the package's basic features that will allow you to keep your e-learning on the mark and as trouble free as possible. This chapter will identify a number of those "technology type things" that you need to look for first, *before* you make a commitment to a set of e-learning tools.

HARDWARE REQUIREMENTS

One of the first "firsts" is to consult with your Information Technology people to determine what hardware they have in place in the organization. Vendors typically want to know what hardware you can support. This includes the manufacturer of the hardware and the amount of memory available to support the applications you want to run, what peripherals are common, data storage capacity, and network information.

By that same token you want to ask the vendor if there are specific hardware requirements to run their application. These requirements could include the amount of RAM memory, amount hard disk storage, graphics accelerators, sound cards, and so on.

Another thing you'll accomplish by going to your IT people early on is to develop a list of contacts, so that when the vendor asks a question you will either have the appropriate answers or will be able to direct the vendor to the appropriate internal contact at your organization. This isn't at all unusual so don't be surprised if you need to have your hardware people talk to the vendor on a number of occasions.

Additionally, you may learn that additional hardware may need to be purchased before the system can be installed. If this is the case, who will have to pay for the additional hardware? If it is your group, you will need to add the cost of the additional hardware (and installation) to the cost of acquiring the development package.

SOFTWARE REQUIREMENTS

Similar to hardware, each system has a set of software requirements. Questions you need to ask pertaining to software include but are not limited to:

➤ What version of the operating system is necessary?

➤ Are there any special software utilities needed?

➤ Does additional software need to be purchased in order to either develop or run the new applications? If so, what is the cost?

➤ Who will install necessary software?

➤ If there are plug-ins involved, how are they obtained and loaded?

Once again, these are questions to ask both your internal IT folks and the representative of the vendor.

INSTALLATION

The first thing you need to know is who will install the total software at your site? Many vendors offer to install the software on your machine as an option. There is frequently an optional charge for this service. If they do, you need to add that fee to the cost of the package. Conditionally you would like this to be the vendor. This is conditional because some IT departments don't like to have anyone else fooling around with "their" machines. Once again, you'll need to talk with them about this, probably with the vendor available to answer any questions and describe their capabilities and experience to your IT manager.

Even if your IT department is amenable, some vendors simply do not have the capacity (or manpower) to install your package, particularly if you are talking about user computers located all over the country or all over the world. Typically, these are small firms with limited manpower. Smaller firm's products and services are usually less expensive and somewhat less sophisticated than offerings from more well-established firms, but often they provide what you really need without too many expensive bells and whistles that you don't need or want to pay for. This become a balancing act between convenience and price.

If you assume the responsibility for software installation, you'll need to be sure that the vendor will properly train the number of company employees you will need to do it properly. Some vendors charge for this, and that adds more to your purchase price.

At the same time, you'll need to get a commitment from your IT department if you're going to use their resources. It doesn't need to be signed in blood, but. . . .

As a third option, you could turn to external help from competent IT professionals. The vendor should be able to tell you what the level of credentialsis required for these individuals.

If you are using a third-party firm to install the software, ask your vendor to recommend someone. Don't forget that one way or the other you will need to determine the cost of the installation and add that to the overall cost of acquiring the package.

If you decide that you (or your representative) will do the installation, determine clearly and up front what type of tech support the vendor will provide: documentation, training, a contact person or help line? What if the software causes a system crash or is simply incompatible with one or more programs already on the computer? What if it needs to be reloaded? Does the vendor charge for this assistance? Is there a specific amount of time they will spend assisting the installation? Are there specific hours when the vendor support is available? (i.e., if the installation will be on the east coast and the vendor is located on the west coast, there could be up to a three-hour time differential to be factored into the actual installation).

Regardless of who installs the package, you need to determine how long the installation will take. If the package is to be installed on an already existing system, you will need to find out if there are any restrictions on when the installation can take place (i.e., time of month, time of day, length of time you can have access to the system, etc.). If the installation is on new systems, when are the delivery dates of the systems? and how solid is it?

When you review your vendor's support options, also look to see if it would be helpful if new machines are purchased, or the software is revised due to bugs or enhancements.

It seems like a lot of "what ifs," but it will save you time, energy, and money if you get them answered now.

EASE OF USE

Next, you need to look at your users and compare them with the software.

What credentials or level of knowledge do the users need to use the package? (i.e., Do you need to know C++ or Word as two extremes?)

Is the package easy to learn? Is it intuitive? By this we mean, once you understand how the basic software operates, is it easy to learn to use new features because
they operate in a consistent way similar to the features you have already mastered?

Is online help available? It is easy to use?

TRAINING

Even the most user-friendly software usually requires some training. This training
may be for your designers who are creating your e-learning courses, for your users
who will be learning from them, or both. Here are some questions to ask your vendor concerning the type of training they provide.

> ➤ Is there any training provided by the vendor?

> ➤ Do you need to take a class?

> ➤ Is the class available on site at your location?

> ➤ Are public classes provided?

>> ➤ If so, where and when are the classes conducted?

>> ➤ How long is the class?

>> ➤ Is there a cost for the class?

> ➤ Are there self-instructional materials available to teach users or designers
how to run the software?

>> ➤ Are they technology based or print based?

>> ➤ Are they online?

> ➤ Can you learn the software on your own?

> ➤ Are internal tutorials provided?

> ➤ Is special equipment needed to use them?

> ➤ Do you need to learn the software before the system is installed?

> ➤ How much time does it take (on average) to complete the tutorials?

> ➤ What types of training materials are provided? (i.e., participant manuals,
job aids, on-line help)

> ➤ If follow-up training is needed how can that be provided? Is there a cost?

ONGOING SUPPORT

The most important question here is, "Is there a charge for on-going support?" or
perhaps simply, "How much is the charge for it?" Frequently, this takes the form
of an annual software maintenance contract that is prorated based on the number
of machines or sometimes the number of users.

It's also important to find out if the vendor offers remote diagnostic support. This capability enables the vendor to look into your system and determine if there is a problem without the need to send a technician to your site.

Ask who your contact will be to get answers to questions. Is there a cost for this service and when does it kick in? What is the typical turnaround time for receiving answers to questions?

Check out the help desk facility if they have one, and ask for references who can tell you about their help desk or ongoing support experiences.

How do you report general and specific problems with the software? Is there a particular way to document such problems? What is the typical turnaround time to resolve these problems? If the resolution involves installation of a software revision or correction, how is that accomplished? In other words, can it be online or do you have to wait for the next product enhancement release? If problem resolution requires an upgrade, who pays and how much?

UPGRADES AND ENHANCEMENTS

That brings up the whole topic of upgrades and enhancements. We all know from sad experience that there are upgrades and then there are upgrades. Some you need, and some you couldn't care less about, except that if you don't have them your software quickly becomes useless, and even worse, unsupported.

Is there a periodic schedule for upgrades? Some companies do an annual or semiannual release of software. These releases often correct problems identified in older versions of the software, so be sure you find out if there may be costs associated with the upgrade. Also ask about changes in hardware and software operating system requirements that may be in the works.

Some upgrades and product enhancements may be optional. They also may require newer versions of operating systems or upgrades to the hardware before they can be installed. These usually have a cost associated with them.

If you elect to install an upgrade, you need to ask all the questions discussed above before embarking upon the installation to insure that you are adequately prepared for the new package.

To sum it up, planning for the purchase of e-learning development and implementation software is very much like planning for the purchase of any company-wide software process. You need to look at all the variables to make sure it won't turn around and bite you when you least expect it. Appendix 22-A provides a question list that you can use to help you make the decision.

Hardware requirements

➤ What type(s) of hardware does your company support?

➤ What type(s) of hardware are compatible with the vendor's software

➤ Do we need to purchase additional hardware?

Software requirements

➤ What software utilities are supported by your company?

➤ What external software is needed to run the development tools?

➤ Do we need to purchase additional software components? If so what is the cost?

Installation

➤ Do we install the software ourselves?

➤ What type of vendor installation support is supplied?

➤ Is there a cost for installation support?

➤ Does the vendor do the installation?

➤ What type of vendor installation support is supplied?

➤ How long will the installation take?

➤ How far in advance do we have to schedule the installation?

➤ Is there a cost for installation support?

➤ Do I need to have my in-house IT department resources available to assist?

➤ What credentials or level of knowledge do my IT people need to assist with the installation?

Ease of use

➤ Is the software easy to learn?

➤ Is the software intuitive?

➤ Is there online help?

➤ Is the online help easy to use?

➤ What credentials do the users need?

➤ Do my employees need any prerequisite degrees or certifications?

➤ Do my employees need any prerequisite software knowledge?

APPENDIX 22-A. **A QUESTION LIST FOR CHOOSING E-LEARNING SOFTWARE**

Training

➤ Initial

    ➤ What types of training materials are provided?

    ➤ Are the training materials easy to use?

    ➤ Are multimedia training tools available?

    ➤ Are self-study training materials available?

    ➤ Is on-site training available?

    ➤ At what cost?

➤ Subsequent

    ➤ What type of reference material(s) are provided?

    ➤ Is on-site training available?

    ➤ At what cost?

Ongoing Software support

➤ How quickly can I expect answers to questions?

➤ What type of assistance do you provide to help define problems?

    ➤ Do you have toll free telephone support?

    ➤ Do you have online support?

    ➤ Do you have remote diagnostic support?

    ➤ Can you see remotely what is happening on my system?

➤ Is there a standardized way to report problems?

➤ What is the normal turnaround to resolve problems?

➤ What is the software support charge?

➤ Are there any extra fees?

Upgrades and Enhancements

➤ Is there a periodic schedule for upgrades?

➤ Is there a cost for upgrades?

➤ How are upgrades installed?

➤ Who installs the upgrade?

APPENDIX 22-A. *Continued*

➤ABOUT THE AUTHOR

Allan Berger is a Managing Director of Communispond Corporation, where he is responsible for managing client relationships with selected New York metropolitan area Fortune 500-based clients. Their primary products include communication skills and sales training, custom e-learning development, Knowledge Management Systems. He has also been a Managing Director of the PACE Divison, Sylvan Learning Systems, and the Executive Vice President, PACE Group of Greater New York.

He has spent many years in the information systems business in sales, marketing, product development, and sales support functions. His education includes a B.A. in Economics form Rutgers University, and an M.B.A. from Rutgers in Finance and Marketing.

CHAPTER 23

E-LEARNING AND PERFORMANCE

➤**THOMAS J. LABONTE**

INTRODUCTION

E-learning is a multibillion dollar industry that often combines the
allure of technology, the appeal of just-in-time training, and the
power of simulation. The benefits of e-learning are strongly advo-
cated by practitioners and vendors at conferences and in the literature of human performance improvement (HPI). What is sometimes lost in this movement to e-learning is the reality that it is one
of a number of performance support tools needed by line managers
and by you, as a HPI practitioner, to provide solutions to performance problems. Whether you are in the midst of adopting or expanding your initial investment in e-learning, there is no guarantee that improved performance will result if you are implementing
it as your primary solution to a performance problem.

This chapter takes the approach that e-learning is one learning action in an integrated set of learning and work-environment actions needed to improve performance and results. A new vision of e-learning and its relationship to improving performance is required to break free of the traditional approaches and single event training solutions of the past. This chapter will investigate e-learning and performance by focusing on two questions.

➤ Why does e-learning not equal performance?

➤ What is the role of e-learning in a complete performance solution?

WHY DOES E-LEARNING NOT EQUAL PERFORMANCE?

Many HPI practitioners have come to accept as fact that learning alone does not produce exemplary performance. Yet in the euphoria surrounding e-learning, these lessons often are forgotten in the workplace. Many profess to know and understand that learning does not equal performance and then confuse learning and performance in actual practice. The enthusiasm with the technical capabilities of e-learning may lead to talking and acting as if e-learning is the silver bullet, the miracle cure for organizational and individual performance problems. The frustration of a generation of line managers on the heavy investment in training with meager business results illustrates that most performance problems require a more comprehensive solution than training alone can deliver.

E-learning sometimes fails to deliver expected results due to the incorrect application of e-learning as a single-event solution to a multiple-cause performance problem. This misapplication of e-learning is sometimes driven by internal competition and ego rather than sound analysis and decision-making. The silos in organizations, the competition for resources, for internal client support and favored status, means that each silo, each department sells line managers on its learning and performance improvement tools and processes. The demands of running the business, the competing demands for resources and intellectual shelf-space, and the work-environment barriers often prevent the successful implementation of new learning.

E-learning must conform to the same rigor in design as any quality learning methodology. It may be a more sophisticated learning tool that other forms of learning, but its primary purpose, as with all learning in a business context, is the acquisition of skills and knowledge that are transferable in the workplace. The reality is that all too often e-learning programs are poorly designed. In the rush to get programs to learners, e-learning may not get the front-end assessment, the task analysis, audience analysis, and assessment of learner environment required for quality design and effective learning. The result is that often expensive yet ineffective courses become drills in page turning rather than performance-based learning. In the worst situations, the content of classroom programs are merged into e-learning without analysis or design appropriate for the differences and capabilities of each methodology. E-learning then becomes an exercise in reading content instead of a powerful learning tool for skills and knowledge that can generate results in the workplace.

WHAT IS THE ROLE OF E-LEARNING IN A COMPLETE PERFORMANCE SOLUTION?

E-learning is yet another performance improvement tool in the trainer's toolkit that to be effective cannot stand alone. Using e-learning as the sole performance solution places an unrealistic expectation on the capabilities of the technology to impact anything more than the skills and knowledge gaps of learners. This situation sometimes occurs when instructional needs are assessed but the workplace barriers to performance are not identified as part of that assessment. Your success as a HPI practitioner largely depends on learning and applying a performance improvement process for identifying root causes and the actions that generate business results. To maximize e-learning's potential return on investment, it must be designed and implemented using a performance improvement process. This process ensures that e-learning is designed and implemented in a systematic manner that blends into a complete performance solution. Learning and performance need to be viewed as mutually supporting components of this unified process. The phases of this process, outlined in Figure 23-1, provide an integrated approach to E-learning as one tool among many in delivering complete performance solutions.

Partnering

Partnering involves a long-term relationship between you, the HPI practitioner, and your internal client that is focused on improving performance and results. Often your client will contact you and request your help in designing and delivering e-learning to solve a performance problem. You have an opportunity in these situations to educate your clients that their performance problems have a number of causes and e-learning only addresses one set of causes, skills, and knowledge. It is important to help clients realize that investing in e-learning under these circumstances often lead to incomplete solutions, poor performance, and weak results.

Partnering
Assessment of Root Causes
Intervention Plan
Design Learning and Work-Environment Actions
Implementation and Measurement

FIGURE 23-1. **E-LEARNING PERFORMANCE IMPROVEMENT PROCESS**

Your objective in partnering is to understand the business, the issues, and the performance problems from your client's perspective. You help the client identify a performance problem for a potential intervention, quantify the gap between expected and current performance, and get agreement to assess the root causes of the problem. A complete performance solution is only possible based on root cause data identifying the few causes that, if addressed, will generate the most significant results. The client needs the data to make informed decisions on investments in learning and performance.

Assessment

The assessment phase involves you, the HPI practitioner, partnering with your internal client to gather data on the root causes, or the major barriers to performance, of a performance problem. The root causes or barriers to performance are found in the work environment and in skills and knowledge gaps. The work-environment barriers impede the ability of learners to apply what they have learned. Sustainable performance results cannot be realized from e-learning, or any learning for that matter, without designing and implementing actions to create a supportive work environment, preferably one that actually encourages the application of skill and knowledge on the job.

Once the data from the performance gap study are tabulated, you conduct a data-reporting meeting with your client to present the results. Clients tend to assume that a gap in learner skills and knowledge is the root cause of most performance problems and that training and only more training will automatically improve performance. This meeting gives you another opportunity to educate the client on root-cause analysis and the actions beyond training in the workplace, that are required for complete performance solutions. It is essential that the client understands and prioritizes the root causes for the next steps in designing appropriate actions.

An important and often overlooked component of e-learning assessment is the preliminary analysis of technical compatibility of the organization's operating environment with the e-learning system. This involves identifying high-level gaps in internal capability for potential learning actions that rely heavily on technology support. Appropriate action plans are developed to close technology support gaps.

Table 23-1 identifies the types of work environment and learning causes that you may find in the analysis of root cause data. This table presents a high-level overview and is not meant to be an exhaustive listing of potential categories of root causes.

The Intervention Plan

The actions identified by the client as a result of the assessment phase forms the core of an intervention plan. The beginning of the plan focuses on removing the work environment barriers that are responsible for approximately up to 80 percent of performance gaps. Focusing on the work environment before making plans to implement e-learning allows for a prudent investment of resources and the greatest positive effect on performance. E-learning is a costly investment. Implementing it before removing work environment barriers will often prevent a successful e-learning initiative.

You and your client share joint ownership of the intervention plan and for the ultimate success of the HPI intervention. The client prioritizes the work-environment and learning actions to be designed and implemented based on the potential individual and organizational intervention results. The plan lists the timeline, tasks, responsibilities, staff, competencies, budget, technology, and testing required for a successful intervention. The specific agreement with the client on HPI practitioner access to the workplace and to the client's employees and managers is a critical part of the intervention plan.

Design Learning and Work-Environment Actions

In presenting the data to your client, let the data speak for itself in identifying the specific actions needed for the performance improvement intervention. Table 23–2 identifies a list of actions that may result from the assessment data. No one action stands alone as a complete solution to the complex root causes to performance problems found in most organizations today. The actions should be designed to mutually support each other in providing a complete solution to the root causes identified in Table 23–1.

TABLE 23-1. **Categories of Root Causes of Performance Problems**

Work-Environment Causes	Learning Causes
Lack of or inadequate:	Lack of or poorly designed:
➤ Accountabilities and workload	➤ E-Learning solutions including: Computer based training, electronic performance support, web based and intranet learning
➤ Coaching, communication, team building	
➤ Competitiveness in the marketplace	➤ Knowledge management
➤ Goal setting	➤ Leadership development
➤ Policies and procedures	➤ Workplace development tools, job aids and templates
➤ Resources: tools, equipment, facilities	➤ Training programs and curricula
➤ Reward and recognition	
➤ Staffing and workload	
➤ Systems and technology support	
➤ Workflow	

TABLE 23-2. Actions Required for Complete Performance Solutions

Work-Environment Actions	Learning Improvement Actions
➤ Competency model to clarify job accountabilities and tasks	➤ E-Learning design, delivery method, and implementation
➤ Leadership accountability for coaching, communication, and teambuilding	➤ Knowledge management system for data retrieval and best practices
➤ Competitor and marketplace intelligence for identifying and implementing best practices	➤ Leadership development programs
	➤ Process, tools, job aids and templates for workplace support
➤ Performance management system for goal setting and evaluation	➤ Training programs and curricula
➤ Documentation assessment	
➤ Needs assessment to identify needed resources	
➤ Incentive and recognition plans	
➤ Staffing model and levels, employee selection and retention	
➤ Technology capabilities and support allocation plan	
➤ Process assessment of workflow	

HPI practitioners need to ensure that the appropriate human resources and information technology generalists and specialists serve on the intervention design team for the successful design and implementation of performance solutions. Human Resources staff must be partners in the design and implementation of work-environment actions that enhance learning and performance. All of the key actions listed in Table 23.2 require human resources expertise and support. Information technology specialists provide expertise on systems capability and usability for the workplace and learning actions identified in the intervention.

Work-environment actions that are often implemented in support of e-learning include:

> ➤ Creating a competency model to build employee selection profiles and to document performance expectations for a position. E-learning should, ultimately, provide for the application of specific skills and knowledge needed to help employees meet these performance expectations.

➤ Building a retention model to decrease employee turnover, increase employee stability, and improve employee skills, knowledge, and performance. Retaining learners is essential to the application of new skills and achievement of performance results.

➤ Designing a leadership model that helps the managers implement performance management, lead the team in achieving goals through quality service, and coaching. Leadership gaps, particularly in coaching, are often the most critical barriers to improving performance and achieving return on investment in E-learning.

➤ Developing a work-environment impact model with tools for improving workplace barriers that prevent employees from achieving expected performance. These barriers often include high employee turnover; incomplete or dated policies, procedures, and systems; lack of employee accountability for results; poorly designed and implemented staffing models; and ineffective reward and recognition systems.

The learning actions listed in Table 23–2 include a blend of facilitated, self-directed, and e-learning-based programs. These actions not only mutually support the work-environment actions but they are best implemented as an integrated set of learning actions. Often HPI practitioners and clients are surprised to realize that a generation of individuals raised on personal computers can be reluctant to embrace e-learning. Learners sometimes resist e-learning without live facilitation to orient them on the program content and software navigation. Job aids are useful in reinforcing critical skills and knowledge presented in e-learning programs.

Implementation

With the design of work environment and learning actions complete, the intervention plan is finalized. The e-learning portion of the plan is based on an integrated approach to workplace performance. E-learning is planned to be seamless with the business and integrates with the workflow and culture of the organization. This is accomplished by implementing e-learning to play to its strengths of on-the-job flexibility, just-in-time availability, and learner control.

It is important to identify and coordinate with the various departments in the organization that are involved with implementing the intervention. This is essential for the effective ongoing support of e-learning and the subsequent performance of the learner. Information technology is obviously a critical partner in supporting any knowledge management and e-learning actions. They ensure that the compatibility and system interface of the client's operating environment and e-learning application is fully documented. Any gaps are prioritized and appropriate steps identified in the technology section of the plan. There is nothing more devastating to the e-learner than not being able to access e-learning when motivated and scheduled to learn.

First-line and middle managers are also critical to the success of e-learning and performance improvement in providing learners the support and time needed to complete their e-learning programs. Managers need the support of HPI practitioners in helping them to own e-learning in the workplace. Managers must be willing and able to coach learners on the application of new skills and knowledge to improve performance. Without coaching there will be little to no measurable improvement in individual performance.

Managers often need a facilitated class on coaching techniques and the business unit's executive strong support to ensure frequent, effective coaching. Managers may also benefit from a performance guide on how to lead and support e-learning implementation. A guided walk-through of the implementation guide and e-learning program provide a level of knowledge and comfort that facilitates coaching and ownership of e-learning results. Managers may need your help in understanding the implementation plan and what performance gap root causes they are addressing. Then explain the role of managers and leaders in supporting learners in applying what they have learned to achieve those desired performance results. You may also assist the management team in building a communication strategy on e-learning implementation and the performance results achieved as part of the intervention.

Learners must observe in the words and actions of their leaders that the changes in the work-environment and the implementation of e-learning are part of the business strategy of the organization and not another passing event. There must be some compelling reason, need, or motivation for learners to change their work habits and learning routines for using new skills effectively. The application of e-learning is only as effective as the degree of learner motivation, leadership support and coaching, and supportive work-environment will facilitate.

Measure Success: The E-Learning Performance Scorecard

A complete intervention must include the measurement of results from the implementation of learning and work-environment actions. A performance scorecard of balanced qualitative and quantitative measures is used to evaluate the impact of the performance intervention to individual learning and performance and to business unit results. It's important to be thinking about the construct of the scorecard throughout the partnering phase and development of the intervention plan. It is critical that everyone involved in e-learning perceive the scorecard as credible and that it fits the organization's culture and metrics. Learners are given new accountabilities as part of the performance scorecard with stretch goals that require them to apply what they have learned. The HPI practitioner works with the client on the ongoing support required for the intervention to successfully achieve results.

Case Study

Michael, the HPI practitioner, completes a review of the organization's first and second quarter business results and notes that Sarah's business unit has several lagging indicators. In at least three key measures, her business unit is underperforming. Michael prepares a checklist of questions to clarify Sarah's current goals, her success to date in achieving those goals, and to discuss causes of her unit's performance problems. As Sarah's performance consultant, Michael calls her to request a meeting to discuss her business results. He hangs up the phone with Sarah after successfully setting an appointment for a client meeting. They agree that the purpose of this meeting is for Michael and Sarah to discuss her business needs and performance gaps.

The following week Michael starts the meeting with Sarah by reviewing his understanding of her business unit's performance during the first half of the year. Michael impresses Sarah with his knowledge of the performance data. Since the beginning of the fiscal year, the trends for quarters one and two have not improved. Customer satisfaction scores are down seven points, employee turnover is increasing at an annualized rate of thirty-six percent, and sales are off by eight percent. "I have spent well over a million dollars in the past year on e-learning and enhanced technology for my sales force. The training department manager told me that e-learning on product knowledge and service quality was a solid investment and that I would see a return in improved service quality and revenue growth. He also claimed that increasing the skills and knowledge of my sales force would lead to more satisfied employees and improved retention. It's obvious from these performance measures that e-learning has failed to deliver results. I need results and a return on my investment, now! Should I invest in more training, develop new courses, or put my people back through the existing e-learning programs? What do you recommend?"

Michael questions Sarah on the assessment and planning conducted to implement e-learning the previous year. Sarah vaguely remembers the trainers doing an instructional assessment on learning design. When questioned about root cause analysis of her performance gaps she draws a blank. Michael discusses the need for identifying barriers in the work environment as a requirement for improving performance. The assessment previously completed for e-learning, he explains, was probably conducted to develop a task analysis and learning objectives. "Unfortunately, the lack of assessment on the work environment may be one of the reasons why e-learning has not achieved expected results. There may be work environment barriers preventing learners from learning and applying new skills and knowledge." Michael convinces Sarah that before investing more resources on training to do a preliminary analysis on the root causes of her performance gaps and the work-environment barriers to e-learning in her business unit.

Weeks later Michael returns with a high-level assessment completed of root causes including learning and work-environment barriers to performance. "Remember several weeks ago we discussed that gaps in business results are often the result of multiple causes. We talked about how the work environment is often one of the critical barriers to performance. These barriers sometimes do not require a lot of resources to identify and change but they do represent up to eighty percent of the causes of why performance does not improve. Once we identify and deal with these barriers then we can see if an investment in additional training is needed to reach your business goals."

"With the support of your key managers I gathered data to identify some of these root causes in the work-environment." Michael reports the assessment data and uses it to help Sarah determine appropriate actions that will provide a complete solution. "There are six key causes of the business unit's performance problems, five are work-environment barriers and there is a skill and knowledge gap. The work-environment barriers include: insufficient staffing per the staffing model to provide quality sales and service, lack of time for learners to participate in training, high turnover of exemplary employees, poor to nonexistent coaching, and a lack of communication on goals, priorities, and successes. High turnover, insufficient staffing, and not helping employees create the time to take e-learning, appear to be the most critical barriers to performance. There was no coaching for those who did take the program so there was little if any application or reinforcement of new e-learning skills. The skills and knowledge gap is in call handling skills. Also, learners had problems accessing e-learning because of technical problems and difficulty navigating through the program once they gained access."

Michael advises Sarah that all of these causes need to be addressed to improve business results. He recommends that Sarah focus on gathering more data on all five work-environment barriers. "While working on these barriers, further analysis can be done to strengthen the e-learning performance objectives and review the design of the call-handling module. As the data is finalized, the intervention plan will be designed so that changes in e-learning are aligned with the work environment changes for the most efficient use of resources and best performance results."

Sarah and Michael agree to a more in-depth assessment of the root causes. A human performance improvement process is recommended that will involve a cross-functional team from human resources, training, organizational development, informational technology, and performance consulting to gather the data and prioritize the root causes, develop and implement actions that will remove barriers to performance. Sarah recognizes that what she needs is a complete performance solution. Her problems are complex, result from multiple causes, and require a holistic approach to changing the work-environment and employee skills. Sarah now recognizes that e-learning is not a quick fix to these types of business issues.

The next six months is intense as the team implements a series of work environment and learning actions in the workplace. By the sixth month all of the business metrics in decline have stabilized. With increased employee retention, the knowledge, skill, and performance base of learners dramatically improves. The work environment change is observable with managers coaching employees on e-learning participation and expectations, scheduling time for employees to take e-learning, and follow up coaching on applying these new skills. By the end of the fourth quarter the business metrics begin a positive trend that continues well into the new fiscal year.

Sarah and her management team begin to adopt a new vision and approach to improving performance. As a result of Michael's efforts and Sarah's leadership, the intervention has demonstrated the benefit of departments such as human resources, information technology, training, and performance consulting working together with the line to achieve results. E-learning, once thought of as the solution to performance problems, is now an important component of a more holistic approach to performance improvement. The relationship between learning and performance and a supportive work-environment lead to changes in the way the business unit integrates e-learning with work environment actions for individual and organizational success.

SUMMARY

E-learning and performance are presented in this chapter as part of a unified process for providing clients with complete performance solutions. As a HPI practitioner, you have an important responsibility to your internal clients in taking a consultative approach in partnering on their business and performance needs. This consultative approach may involve you initially working on an e-learning project at the client's request, or you may proactively help your client with a HPI intervention to address their performance problems. In either case, it is important for you to use a process that is based on gathering objective assessment data to identify performance gaps and causes, and determine the actions to remove barriers to performance. These actions often include the implementation of blended learning and work-environment actions delivered through performance consulting services. To successfully implement this process you will be constantly educating your client on the value of assessment to diagnose root causes and to develop actions that deliver complete performance solutions.

"What I Should Know About E-Learning and Performance is. . . .

➤ Learning does not equal performance. Performance is achieved through the application of learning in a supportive work environment with management champions providing leadership and coaching.

➤ Partner with the client to really understand his or her business needs and performance problems. You gain insight on learning and performance priorities that help you know how e-learning and performance can best be achieved.

➤ E-learning is a single event solution that supports skills and knowledge improvement. It is not a solution for complex performance problems that require multiple actions in the work environment to solve.

➤ Assessing root causes is essential for identifying the real causes of performance gaps and to determine the appropriateness of e-learning as one of the actions to improve performance.

➤ Be sure to include a high-level technical compatibility assessment early in the process as part of the e-learning section of the assessment plan.

➤ The outcome of a performance assessment is a listing of work-environment and learning improvement actions that forms the core of an intervention plan.

➤ Designing and implementing work-environment actions are critical to the success of a performance improvement intervention. E-learning fails to live up to performance expectations where work-environment change is not part of the intervention.

➤ Integrate e-learning into the existing business of the organization so that it is seamless to the workflow and accountabilities of learners.

➤ Coaching is a requirement of improved performance. New skills and knowledge gained from e-learning will not be consistently applied without strong leadership and effective coaching.

➤ Learners are held accountable by management for improving performance as a result of learning and applying new skills and knowledge gained from e-learning.

➤ Building a performance scorecard that integrates satisfaction, learning, process, and performance improvement measures is needed for alignment of learning and performance in the workplace.

➤ HPI practitioners need to develop a new vision of learning and performance with their key clients. This is a process of continuous education with clients built upon early wins, clear communication, and effective partnering.

RESOURCES

Readings

Cone, John W., and Robinson, Dana G. (August 2001). The power of e-performance. *T&D*, Vol 55, Number 8, pp. 32–41.

Horton, William (2001). *Evaluating E-Learning*. Alexandria, VA: ASTD Press.

LaBonte, Thomas J. (2001). *Building A New Performance Vision*, Alexandria, VA: ASTD Press.

Mantyla, Karen. (2001). *Blending E-Learning*. Alexandria, VA: ASTD Press.

➤ABOUT THE AUTHOR

Thomas J. LaBonte, Ed.D., is the Managing Director of Workplace Performance, LLC, specializing in improving performance through an integrated process to learning and workplace actions for breakthrough results. As the Director of Consulting Services at Ulysses Learning, Tom was responsible for implementing e-learning solutions and supporting client business results. He also held the positions of HR Executive with Centura Banks and SVP of Performance Improvement and Training at PNC Bank. Tom published *Building a New Performance Vision* in May 2001 through the ASTD Press. Tom is a frequent speaker on performance consulting, e-learning, and HR and HRD strategies. Tom served on the ASTD Board of Directors from 1998 to 2000 and currently serves as the Chair of the ASTD Global Nominating Committee. He can be reached at *tjlabonte@earthlink.net.*

CHAPTER 24

EVALUATING YOUR E-LEARNING IMPLEMENTATION

➤**WAYNE TURMEL**

OBJECTIVES

In this chapter you will learn:

➤ What some organizations have tried to measure in their e-learning initiatives

➤ What works and what doesn't

➤ How to assess your own readiness to evaluate your company's e-learning to levels I and II

> *Measure not the work until the day's out and the labor done,*
> *Then bring your gauges.*

> Elizabeth Barrett Browning *(1806–1861) Laura Leigh*

How do you measure the success or failure of an e-learning initiative? This is not a casual question given the time, money, and elbow grease involved in putting even the simplest learning on the web.

Because both the medium and the training world are ever-changing, it is hard to believe that anyone will ever be able to speak definitively about what can or should be measured. Still, there are two things that are becoming clear:

1. The challenges and successes of evaluating e-learning efforts are identical in many ways to those of more traditional types of training, and

2. That's not much comfort.

WHAT DO WE MEAN BY EVALUATION?

For our purposes, when we talk about evaluating learning, we are refer to the four levels devised by Donald Kirkpatrick. They are:

Level I—the effectiveness as perceived by the trainee

Level II—measured evaluation of learning

Level III—observed performance improvement

Level IV—business impact.

Most companies are familiar with Level I evaluation in relation to their instructor-led classroom training (ILT). They are the all too familiar "smile sheets" that are completed at the end of a program. Whether they are extensive or simple devices, they are designed to capture participants' immediate reactions to a program or event: Did the instructor do a good job? Was the material relevant to their job? Were the doughnuts fresh?

These have traditionally been done by paper and pencil at the end of the class although some organizations, such as IBM, now have learners fill them out on line so that their feedback can be automatically recorded in the company's learner management system, where data such as test scores and completion rates become part of their personnel file. Such integration is still rare in many organizations.

Level II feedback is truly measured evaluation of the learning. What did you learn and how do we know? An example of a simple Level II would be a quiz or skill test at the end of a program to determine whether they know the facts, or can complete a task to a given standard. More in-depth Level IIs include a precourse assessment so that you can then measure what they knew before the training and how much more they know leaving it.

Level III evaluation is measured by whether the behavior or skill is used back on the job. Simply put, are learners doing anything different than they did before the training, and is that new skill benefiting the organization that paid for it? This can only be measured back on the job, and over a period of time. The cost and time involved in doing this to a statistically valid degree of certainty means that it is seldom done, and even more rarely done correctly.

Finally, Level IV answers a deceptively simple question: was the training worth the time and money spent on it (Return on Investment)? In technical training, this direct line has been viewed as easier to prove—either they know how to use the new equipment or they don't—than in soft skills where there are any number of variables beyond skills and knowledge that impact behavior on the job.

These four levels of evaluation have been widely accepted in the world of instructor-led training and education for decades. Training professionals also know some of the pitfalls of attempting to implement them. How, then, does the task of measuring the impact of e-learning differ from instructor-led (if at all) and what are the challenges to measuring that impact effectively?

WHY MEASURE AT ALL?

According to a renowned psychometrician, Dr Robert Thompson, Ph.D., there are three main reasons to measure the success of training, particularly beyond Levels I and II:

For the Business—if you don't measure it, it won't be valued. If it's not valued it ultimately won't get supported or funded.

For the Educator—You want to know that the training works—that it does what you set out to do.

For the Learner—measuring success is vital to their psychological well being, the sense that "wow, I really am better at this now than I was." Such reinforcement greatly improves the odds of a learner overcoming objections to the skill being used back at the workplace.

According to Dr. Thompson, the reasons for evaluating training have not changed since the dawn of time. The difference, he feels, is that with e-learning the initial costs involved are so much higher that the spotlight of attention, brought by the large amount of money involved—and the attendant pressure—is on the implementer. Again, the demand to show return on investment is higher than in the more traditional training world where costs may consist primarily of instructor time and workbooks because it's such a large investment.

The corporate world seems to have adopted two strategies to measuring the success of training: treat it no differently than any other training event, or treat it as a completely separate beast with very specific needs and criteria for success.

Towers Perrin is one of the world's largest independent management and human resource consulting firms, with over 9,000 employees and 78 offices in 74 cities in 23 countries. As with most large, geographically diverse companies, they are in the process of moving much of their training function to the web. Julie Johnson, a key member of their Training and Development arm, says that they have decided to treat e-learning as just another part of their overall employee development strategy.

"There's an urgency to get the right training and evaluate learning opportunities, there's no urgency to rush to the web as such," she says. As a result, they have made the conscious decision to treat both web-based and instructor-led training as parts of a whole, and use the same criteria to measure them.

The Level I evaluations they use are essentially a variation of the questionnaire used for their instructor-led programs with a few questions, specifically about how easy it was to use the technology. This should indicate whether users were able to learn in that environment.

The company has no specific level II measurement, leaving that up to the program developer to use what's already in the courseware. Because well-designed training usually has some test or evaluation component built in, it saves them the time and effort designing it themselves. After all, psychometrics are not necessarily a core competency of people in HR. Since they are using third-party vendors, for the most part, they are relying on the evaluations built into the courseware and tracking them course by course. Sometimes different information is gathered, and sometimes similar information is gathered *by different means*, which can affect the analysis. At Towers Perrin each division has its own LMS, which means there is little coordination between divisions of the company at this point.

There is a different perspective over at Cisco, where the first online training was done in 1997. Tom Kelly, Vice President of Internet Learning, says they focused much of their early efforts on technical training and getting their folks access to information in a hurry. There, the primary concern was technological: could they find what they wanted when they wanted it.

"For the first year, they [the employees] were so grateful just to have the information available that they didn't care if it was any good," he says. The feeling around the company was, "Better fast and not completely right than completely right and too late." As a result, Cisco primarily focused its evaluation on the ease of use and navigation of its tools. Level II evaluation came months later.

Since the late 1990s they have conducted almost 200,000 tests for knowledge, mostly in the form of true/false quizzes. In October 2001 they piloted a Level II assessment based on role-play scenarios, and in January 2002 piloted assessments using online simulations. Results will be recorded in the LMS, and will become part of the participant's HR and Professional Development files.

Vendors of e-learning services have so far been more accommodating to those who fall into the former camp than the latter. Because so many of them sell to training departments, they have made the evaluation process look remarkably similar to the instructor-led world most of the buyers are used to. This makes sense, until you stop to think about what traditionally has happened with Level I evaluation at that level.

WHAT OFTEN HAPPENS WITH LEVEL I DATA

In organizations that don't have a strong history of objectively evaluating their training efforts, there are two things that generally happen when they conduct training of any sort, and one is as unproductive as the other. These folks tend to:

1. Not gather information—or at least information relevant to business goals.

2. Gather it, then don't act upon it.

In the first case, the person or team implementing an e-learning strategy needs to ask themselves two vital questions: what do we truly want to measure? (what would make the training a success?), and how will we gather *and report on* the results?

Deciding what you wish to measure is not an easy task. In the case of Cisco, Tom Kelly and his team centered their efforts on the ease of use for the web-based learning. Since most of the training was technical in nature, and relied on quick retrieval of small packets of information, this made the most sense to them. People needed facts in a hurry, could they get them? Once that was done, the quality of the training could then be examined more closely. Their evaluation process developed slowly, and in discreet steps.

Sabine Steinbrecher of Learning Library in Toronto, Canada, works with a lot of professional organizations who are using e-learning to offer professional development. Each of these organizations has its own standards and its own vision of what successful training looks like.

Some, like the Canadian Veterinarian Medicine Association, simply want to know that people are actively increasing their knowledge. Therefore, continuing education credits are granted simply for reading online white papers and articles. The fact that people read the latest treatise on canine hypothyroidism is sufficient to get a CE credit. Therefore, that's all they need to measure. What you thought of the paper is less important than that you read it.

This seems counterintuitive until you think about how continuing education is normally conducted in that environment. Doctors attend conferences (or claim they do on their taxes), listen to papers presented, and leave. No one measures their learning at those events, so why impose that standard on e-learning? Simply measure their attendance—did they register for the information online and complete the course—and give them their credits.

Other organizations demand more thorough evaluation. For these groups, CE credits are dependant on a pass/fail test of knowledge. These can be done on line and are recorded and the results passed on to the client organization. As a vendor, Learning Library is prepared to help their clients achieve the level of evaluation they need to achieve their goals.

A NEW WRINKLE, AS IF WE NEEDED ONE

When transferring the kind of learning that has traditionally been in the realm of training departments or instructor-led classes, companies traditionally measure two things: participant reaction to the learning (their feelings about the specific material presented) and the class experience (did they enjoy the program and/or the instructor).

Many e-learning implementers want to measure those two things as well, but there is a third factor that is a direct result of the e-learning environment.

When Frontline Group's Communispond division wanted to migrate its Write Up Front instructor-led program to a web-based version, it decided to measure both reaction to the program and ease of use. During the pilot, however, comments from participants indicated a third area of concern: e-learning itself.

Participants in the pilot program were asked about the program contents (learning objectives, were they better writers when they were done, etc.) and the EWUF program (ease of use, were the graphics attractive, was the testing sufficient) as a product. A number of comments were inconsistent with these questions, however. While liking the product itself, and agreeing they were better writers as a result (sounds like a success, right?) they still would be hesitant to recommend the product to others. In fact, some stated that they downright hated it! How could that be?

The truth is that participants liked the subject matter and thought the program was fine, but what they really didn't like was e-learning itself.

Those participating in the pilot were mostly from the training department or were senior employees very comfortable in the classroom environment and self-professed training junkies. They missed the instructor-led experience and that seriously colored their experience of the EWUF program. This was a different problem altogether.

This leads us to the second point—once information is gathered, what do you do with it? In a traditional scenario, numerical scores for the program would be gathered, averaged out, and a decision made on whether or not the program was any good. The number of negative comments probably would have doomed the program.

Had Frontline and its clients simply stuck with the two-tiered evaluation approach it would be easy to assume they had a dog on their hands. Instead, they analyzed the data from their evaluation and took action as a result. While there were some relatively expensive changes made to the courseware, most of the problem was solved by rewriting the letter that went to each course participant. It clearly explained how the course is designed to work, took more time to allay any concerns and gave them the name of a human being to contact in case of problems.

They now have a product that is popular with learners if the learners know what to expect before they sit down to take the course. This positioning can have a major impact on an organization's entire e-learning initiative, not just a single program.

Organizations that do a lot of instructor-led training tend to gather reams of data. Scores of paper and pencil evaluations are dutifully collected at the end of classes. They are quickly scanned to identify any problems that occurred in class.

These are generally little more than participant's gut reactions to the program and the facilitator. Sometimes the questions seem relevant yet really are subjective and say more about how the participants felt rather than what they know. A good example is a comment like "I found the program relevant to my workplace". Well, says Dr Thompson," that's really hard to say for sure until you go back and try to do it in the workplace." At this point the student is only "pretty sure" it's relevant.

At that point, for many organizations the process stops. The evaluations, or at least a summary of the numbers, are put in a file and stored away, never to be seen again. More sophisticated organizations actually track the numerical scores carefully, and generate numerous reports. Seldom do those changes result in a radical change in a program, although if the scores are below standard set by the organization there may be a change in training provider or a reexamination of the program.

When the end result is a pile of paper which is then put in a file cabinet and forgotten, evaluation is a process that gives the impression of due diligence but is often an activity that is done because it is expected. This is harder to justify—even to do—in an e-learning environment.

Think about what is involved in evaluating a program online. The evaluation must be translated into an electronic format. Programming time is not cheap. The results then are connected electronically to either a simple data collection database or a full-blown Learner Management System. These systems can do anything from report raw data to reporting seventeen ways from Sunday. Someone then needs to look at the data and make decisions about what those numbers mean.

After all this, of course comes the hard part—action is expected based upon those results. Do you kill a program, or just the messenger?

HERE'S THE GOOD NEWS—THAT WAS THE BAD NEWS

So evaluation is difficult and full of landmines—why do it if it's so difficult? Truthfully, measuring success is not that difficult if, in fact, you and your organization have clear ideas of what success looks like before you begin. That's before you begin to look at vendors, before you sell your soul to your IT people, and before you block off the six months of your life that will go into the implementation.

First you have to look at the drivers for the program. Why are you putting your learning and skill development online? This means ALL the reasons, and that can sometimes be a humbling experience.

Maybe your CEO saw an article on the airplane and mandated the move to the web as part of changing the culture of the company. In that case, the main metric to be evaluated is is it usable and accessible? Are people comfortable using those media? There is an assumption that if something is there, it will be used right away and used well. Some in the e-learning world refer to this as the "If you build it, they will come" syndrome. It's not true, and many well-intentioned initiatives have been derailed by this mindset.

Measuring learner's reactions to the courseware may be a secondary consideration. Success for that person will be measured by how many programs you have on line and how many people are using them.

This follows Tom Kelly's experience at Cisco—get it up and get them using it. In his words, "We'll determine if it's any good as we go." They tackled one metric at a time. First, is it useful and useable. If so, is the information accurate? Often it wasn't but it was good enough that people continued to use the system. Once they knew people were comfortable with using online learning, then the quality of individual programs was measured for accuracy, and finally the learning was measured.

Only now are they looking at Level II evaluation beyond the multiple choice quiz—and everyone from the CEO to the individual engineers must be somewhat happy with the results: they have 10,000 modules in over 50 topics available online, with more emerging almost daily.

Maybe the mandate has come down to you to get learning on-line as quickly as possible to save travel costs and time off the job. In that case one figure will be paramount—how much money was saved? This may not be the best evaluation of whether participants like the change, and in fact may have nothing to do with quality of instruction or ease of use—but it will be the kind of metric people can point to and ensure further funding and a mention in the annual report.

This may sound cynical, but remember that the definition of success depends upon the reason for implementing the project in the first place. If the goal is cost-savings, then that's the single most important item to be measured *at that moment*. It doesn't mean that other metrics can't be gathered and acted on at the same time or later.

That's the thought at Towers Perrin. Because Julie Johnson and her colleagues have decided to treat their e-learning as part of the general training and development activity, the same dynamics are at work as with their instructor-led training. Of particular importance are the application to the learner's workplace and the learner's perception of the content's relevance.

As a result, their e-learning evaluation form looks like a standard classroom Level I "smile sheet" with many identical questions with a few reflecting the technical aspects of the program (ease of use, navigation, and the like).

This is not necessarily a bad thing. The more familiar an online form looks to learners, the more comfortable they will be with it. Again, care has to be taken that the questions address all the concerns you might have about their interaction with the courseware.

Unlike Cisco's narrowly targeted assessment tools, these multiuse evaluations capture information in a large number of areas. That's good news on one hand—the goal is to be able to address multiple concerns at once. The bad news is that there's a lot of data captured—how much data will be analyzed and used? More importantly, has sufficient thought been given to prioritizing the results?

What do you do when there is conflicting data? For example, Frontline's EWUF program got very mixed results during their beta test. While scoring very high in usability and ease of navigation, it still was not rated very highly overall. The reason was the test group's overall discomfort with e-learning—these learners from the training department were people who dearly loved classroom training and all that went with it from interaction with instructors to the doughnuts in the morning. This meant that even though specific questions were answered positively, there was something negative which wasn't being captured and skewed the end results.

What a dilemma. If you simply acknowledge that there will be discomfort and just focus on the courseware itself, you've gathered a lot of information you have no intention of using and don't address participants' main concern. This can have a serious impact on future e-learning efforts.

If, on the other hand, you focus on the end number—the overall satisfaction number—you may throw out a perfectly useable writing course and never address the core issue: their discomfort with learning in a web environment. Ignoring that issue will have enormous ramifications as a company moves forward.

Fortunately, product developers at Frontline saw this and broke the evaluation into the three components (course content, ease of navigation, and comfort with the technology). They were then able to help clients measure the success of very different factors at once. This not only helps them separate the EWUF product itself from the other issues, but may help their clients address more global issues of techno phobia and discomfort with web-based learning as they move inexorably in that direction.

Knowing what you want to measure is one problem, and not an inconsiderable one. The next problem is knowing how to go about gathering it. Dr Thompson is one of a very small group of scientists—psychometricians—who specialize in the gathering and analysis of statistical information. Their job is to help design the methods of gathering proof of success at all levels of learning.

When Mark Twain made his famous crack about "lies, damned lies and statistics," he was pointing out what psychometricians know more than anyone else— the questions you ask and the methods used to gather that information can be used to skew the results in any direction. Sometimes that skewing is unintentional.

Sometimes It's Not

One leading off-the-shelf courseware designer has a program that asks a series of questions on a classic 1–5 Likert scale that would be familiar to anyone who's taken an instructor-led corporate program. It ends as so many such evaluations do by asking for written comments. The question reads, "What have you found to be the single most positive aspect of this e-learning program for you?"

Even though that question is legitimate, it forces the participant to say something nice about the vendor's product, even if they found the overall experience confusing, annoying, or not worth their time. These results are dutifully presented to the buyer who assumes everyone likes the program.

Asking something like, "Tell us one thing we could improve about this program" would get a totally different response. The problem, of course, is that someone might not like that answer, and why play with fire.

One reason Cisco has taken so long to build what many training professionals would consider basic evaluation systems is because they build every part of their system from scratch. While they work with a wide array of outside vendors, they buy very little infrastructure off the shelf. From the courseware and evaluation tools to a learner management system, everything is built to Cisco's order, designed to augment business goals Tom Kelly and his team have determined in advance.

Many organizations are trying to install large-scale e-learning projects with multiple courses and limited time to implement them. Since they buy much of their courseware from outside vendors, they use the assessment and course evaluation tools provided by those vendors.

The cost savings are obvious, and not every company has the luxury of so much time and management support. Many organizations are trying to implement large-scale implementations, with multiple courses and limited time to implement them. Because they buy much of their courseware from outside vendors, they use the assessment and course evaluation tools provided by that vendor.

Dr. Thompson and other psychometricians are leery of measurement tools designed by the same people whose courses are being measured. He urges companies to at least provide their own analysis of the numbers, and to carefully examine the questions asked.

Tom Kelly is somewhat less diplomatic. "Putting vendors in charge of evaluation is putting the fox in charge of the chicken coop," he says.

Other companies are more comfortable working with their vendors. Sabine Steinbrecher at Learning Library says her team is scrupulous about recommending what evaluation tools her clients should use. Because everything is built to order for their clients from scratch, and the clients provide all the raw courseware, "We always recommend the lowest level of evaluation that will allow the client to measure the results they want, the rest is useless information." Ultimately the final measurement decisions are made by the client before the program is built to their order.

Towers Perrin has taken the format provided by Net-G, one of their main vendors for soft-skills e-learning and tailored it to their purposes. This allows them some measure of control over the information gathered, but doesn't conflict with the learner management tools they've got to use these programs.

Most of the evaluation tools we've talked about so far capture Level I information. There is a second level of concern about what to do with Level II information, especially of the pass/fail variety. Taking a course online is one thing, but do companies simply want to measure whether someone took it, or whether they passed the course?

If they want to know if they passed the test, what will they do with that information? Does it go into their HR or personnel file? Will they lose their job if they fail? Will they have to take the program till they get it right? The answers to these questions will dictate whether test scores are worth gathering, and where the results are stored.

Certainly, Level II information is vital to the learner. It tells them whether their time was well spent, and may reinforce the behavior back on the job. For managers, it's important they feel like they "got their money's worth," that the course has given their employees the skill or knowledge to be better at their jobs. The organization may have expectations about competencies and knowledge that reflects their culture or affect succession planning and career development.

The beauty of modern computerized LMS systems is that the evaluation information can be captured and distributed in almost any manner imaginable. The questions that an implementer has to ask are: What information will be captured? Who will see it? and How will it be used?

Ultimately the criteria for using the information needs to fit the needs of the end users—the business, the managers and the learners.

➤ **The business** needs to know if the learner possesses the skills and knowledge they have deemed important to meeting organization goals. They will insist that whatever information is gathered is fully documented and will be passed on to all stakeholders.

➤ **The managers** wants proof that the skills have been passed on to the learner. Sometimes these skills are desired to assist in professional development, sometimes to meet goals the managers own goals, such as to assist them in discipline or other corrective actions. They will look for documented proof that the learner has achieved their goal.

➤ **The learners** wants to know that they have achieved what they set out to achieve—that the skills and knowledge are theirs, that they will be better at their job (or it will be easier) or that the item in their professional development plan has been "checked off" and their managers will be satisfied. Generally, they want the information documented only as far as it will further their personal goals.

LAYING THE GROUNDWORK FOR YOUR EVALUATION EFFORTS

We have already established that the hard work of evaluation is done before the first piece of data is collected. In order to lay this foundation, there are seven separate areas of inquiry you must be able to address to everyone's satisfaction. By slogging through this prework, you can identify potential pitfalls which might upset your plans and find areas where you can build support for future e-learning efforts.

More importantly, you'll be able to sort data into piles labeled "need to haves," "nice to haves" and "irrelevant." This way you'll know? Only measure?

1. What are the organization's business goals—both long-term and for this specific intervention?

2. Who are the stakeholders?

3. What information, if gathered, will indicate success or failure?

4. What will be the criteria for success?

5. How much time do you have to implement the initiative?

6. Are you building or buying?

7. What collection method will you use?

The Organization's Goals

Do you know why the organization has chosen to implement the training at this time? Is it money? time (which is money)? need to improve efficiency (ditto)?

Knowing the overall goals helps you frame the evaluation questions you ask and the type of information you gather. For example, if the company is concerned about travel cost and time away from the job, one piece of information you must gather is "how long did it take you to complete the course?" That figure can be easily captured and held against whatever your previous standard happens to be.

Let's take an example. You have been asked to reduce the training budget by 50 percent over two years. By having people take part in an e-learning program, there is no travel time or cost, and they are able to do their learning in small chunks at their desktop. What used to be a full day now takes about two hours total seat time over a couple of days with very little disruption of normal duties. Those are numbers you can take to your CFO and look like a hero. What do you think the discussion will be come budget time next year?

If, on the other hand, you gather reams of data on the quality of programs, show impressive learning and learner satisfaction but can't address the organization's goal, that will be an entirely different budget discussion come November.

Many of you will probably be worried that we are not evaluating the *learning*, concerned as we are with mere mammon. If you don't have the funding and buy-in of upper management it will be difficult to allocate resources to even offer the skill development in a meaningful manner. You may be forced to choose a solution based simply on price rather than overall value or strength of learning transfer.

Furthermore, it doesn't mean that the learning is divorced from organization goals. If better written communication is a core competency, and has been recognized as such from above, then by all means you'll want to measure whether people can write focused e-mails.

Notice that we qualified that statement. We said "focused" versus "better". One is measurable by an objective standard—is the subject clearly stated in the first line? The other may not be measurable at all, or is the result of several criteria which may be in competition with each other requiring a lot of data and analysis. This focusing on why the company wants to provide the training and what the *final business result or behavior will be* is the first step to determining what really needs to be measured, to what standard, and how you'll define success.

IDENTIFY STAKEHOLDERS AND THEIR NEEDS

While it sounds easy to say this is a surprisingly difficult thing to do. It demands not only identifying those with a stake in the success of an implementation, but determining what they really want to see happen. Careful analysis of this will tell you what you need to measure and, more importantly, the criteria for success. From there come all the implementation decisions you'll have to make.

Ignoring one of these factors can create major problems later. If you focus on the needs of the organization but ignore the needs of learners, you may wind up with a program that shows great cost savings, but learners would rather face an IRS audit than take the program. On the other hand, focusing solely on the learners but not showing that they truly possess the new skills and knowledge may make it tough for managers who are in control of their budgets to approve spending for training they can't justify.

It is helpful to drill down not only to each stakeholder's role, but be specific as to their name, function, and primary concern. Give some thought to both explicit (the statements appearing in company correspondence) and implicit (the things no one says out loud but "everyone knows"). An example of an explicit organizational goal is the reduction in overall costs associated with training. An implicit goal may be that the training department wants to appear competent and in control of the training.

Identifying and addressing both explicit and implicit goals at the onset may take a little extra time but can eliminate unpleasant surprises as you go forward with your implementation. Remember how the different players will view success:

The organization will be concerned with how the training aligns with their business goals. For example, If their number-one focus is cost control, are you planning to measure that?

The managers will be concerned with whether learners know or do (and you'd better be clear on whether they need to *know* something or be able to *do* something) something differently than they did before they took the training. Remember they have to justify every dollar they spend and good data will help them look at e-learning as an ally versus a cost item to be trimmed whenever possible.

Learners are where the rubber meets the road. They are doing the learning. What is vital to help them do that most effectively? At Cisco, it was initially the mere availability of information. At Towers Perrin, it's a series of issues, which must all work in conjunction.

Identify Criteria for Success

Measurement and evaluation is a pointless exercise in data collection unless you know what the numbers mean. An average score of 4.8 on a Likert scale looks very impressive, and will probably keep a program in your catalog for a long time, but what does it mean?

When is a program a success? The first criteria we've already addressed—do they need to KNOW something or DO something. In one case a multiple choice test may suffice, in another there may be a higher level of assessment required. What's the difference?

Well, if you are a nuclear power plant, and you are training people in preventing a reactor meltdown, do you want people to know which button to push, or do you want them to be able to push it? The two assessments require very different metrics.

Again, if you want them to know your company's return policy, is a simple pass/fail sufficient? Do they need to know it to 100 percent certainty (no returns without a receipt)? Is 70 percent sufficient (do nonfinancial managers know enough about how finance works to at least function in their job)? The managers in your department may have very definite ideas on this.

How Much Time Do You Have to Implement?

Cisco took five years from their first efforts in e-learning to their industry-leading program today. Tom Kelly's team has systematically built each piece of that program or had vendors build to their specifications. It has been a determined, rapid, but incremental development. Each step had discreet success criteria, which has been built on over time.

How much time do you have? Is your organizationrushing headlong to the web? Circumstances may dictate that you have to institute multiple measurement tools at the same time. Prioritizing those data is critical if you are not going to be overwhelmed. Planning to measure every conceivable facet of a course is of no use if they sit in piles on a desk or in a closet with no one to analyze them or act on what you find out—you may as well not have gathered the information at all.

Building or Buying?

Time and money are in short supply for almost every organization. Depending upon the business goals you are trying to address, and the level of in-house expertise you have, you have to decide whether to build the program yourself or buy from a third-party vendor.

The next question is, do you build your own evaluation tools or use those provided by the vendor? If a tool has been validated scientifically it may be perfectly functional. It will honestly and completely gather the information it has been programmed to gather whether it was created by you or your vendor. When looking at the vendor's evaluation, however, the important question is: Is that the information you and your organization need to determine success?

Towers Perrin has worked with their primary vendor to modify an existing evaluation form to capture information they deem relevant. Sometimes the information is the same, but the way the question is asked gets more precise data. Learning Library builds programs from scratch with evaluation criteria determined by the client and built in right from the beginning.

As long as the criteria for success has been determined, you can then hold any provider—internal or external—responsible for collecting the data you and your organization consider crucial.

Be aware, however, that because of the cost associated with programming and building effective e-learning, it may be harder to gather different data once your program is up and running, so planning beforehand is especially important.

What Collection Method are You Using?

Great. You've decided what you need to measure, and to what standard. You have built all the metrics into your evaluation process. Now people take the course. Where does that information go?

The final part of planning your evaluation and measurement is to determine how to gather the information and where do the results have to go. If you are a small training department, with sole responsibility for analyzing the results, a simple data base such as Access or its equivalent may be all the technology you need.

If, on the other hand, the results of assessments or course completions are part of someone's HR record, you will want to make sure that you have the mechanism for putting course records into the company's enterprise wide systems such as SAP or PeopleSoft.

Anyone who has ever tried to work with those systems knows that considerable work goes in to adding new data to those programs. The people who administer these systems are an important ally in your data gathering and dissemination efforts (did you include them as stakeholders?) and taking their needs into account before implementation will be critical to preventing information bottlenecks.

Also, please be aware that there are issues of security and privacy to be considered. Do you want everyone to know how the CEO did on a communication skills assessment?

Again, determining what information you need, then what to do with it once you have it, will ensure a systematic approach to your implementation.

Assessing Your Readiness

How ready are you to measure the success of your program? The checklist in Appendix 24-A will be of great help as you look at any e-learning initiative. It will identify the questions which must be answered if you are to both capture information and, more importantly, determine if the training you plan will accomplish your (and the organization's) goals.

FINALLY

You have done your homework. You've identified what needs to be measured, to what standard, and who will receive the information when it is gathered.

That was the easy part.

The hardest part is ahead: using the information wisely. Do you and your organization really plan to use this information to manage expenses and future plans, or is all this data gathering for naught?

Dr. Thompson makes no bones about the fact that most data die on the shelf. Internal politics, good intentions, and budgets all play their part to undercut the best of measurement efforts.

Ultimately, information is only useful if it is acted upon. Does this program achieve its goals? Is e-learning the best way for learners to gather this information? What can we do to help more people feel comfortable with this new learning style?

These questions underlie your measurement and evaluation efforts. The ultimate success or failure of your initiative lies in what happens AFTER you've gathered all the data and analyzed them.

Therefore, measurement and evaluation of your e-learning is not an end in itself, but is a part of a process which never ends. This is the true challenge for implementers of learning inside an organization, whether you're using state of the art technology or a live human being.

Good luck!

1) **Do you know the organization's business goals or reasons for instituting this project?**

   Stated Goals

   _____

   _____

   This planned training will support those goals by (be absolutely specific)

   _____

   _____

2) **Identify Stakeholders:**

Stakeholder's Name (if known)	Position (Organization, Manager, Participant)	Spoken Goals	Unspoken Goals

3) **What information is necessary to define success?**

   - **For the Organization:**

   _____

   _____

   - **For the Manager :**

   _____

   _____

   - **For the Learner:**

   _____

   _____

APPENDIX 24-A. **EVALUATION PRE-WORK WORKSHEET**

4) **What criteria will define success (specific and measurable)?**

■ **For the Organization:**

_____

_____

■ **For the Manager :**

_____

_____

■ **For the Learner:**

_____

_____

5) **How much time do you have to implement the initiative?**

_____

Can you evaluate isolated factors or will you measure multiple factors at once?

_____

6) **Are you building or buying?** _____

If Building:

■ **What IT and Learner Management System issues must be addressed prior to implementation?**

_____

_____

■ **Have you articulated all measurement criteria to the builder?**

_____

_____

■ **Have all stakeholders approved your plan?**

_____

_____

APEENDIX 24-A. *Continued*

If Buying:

- Is the vendor aware of your criteria for success?

  _____

  _____

- Do their standard tools capture and report that data in a form you can use?

  _____

  _____

- Can arrangements be made to tailor their evaluation tools to your needs?

  _____

  _____

- Is it possible to change metrics once the project has been completed?

  _____

  _____

7) What collection method will be used?

   _____

   _____

What level of assessment will be used?

_____

_____

Who will design the assessment?

_____

_____

Where does the information go?

_____

_____

Are the IT issues worked out in advance?

_____

_____

Who sees the final results? Are security issues addressed?

_____

_____

APPENDIX 24-A. *Continued*

REFERENCES

Readings

Beckshi, Peter, and Doty, Mike (2002). Instructional systems design: A little bit of ADDIEtude, please. *The ASTD Handbook of Training Design and Delivery*. New York: McGrawHill.

> ➤**ABOUT THE AUTHOR**
>
> **Wayne Turmel** is a freelance writer and full-time Manager of Products Development and Marketing for Communispond, based in Chicago, Illinois. He specializes in presentation skills, train the trainer, and other business communication issues.
>
> Wayne spent 15 years as a standup comic and broadcaster in Canada and the United States before moving into the real world. His years of experience training and developing curriculum for Fortune 1000 companies give him a unique vision of the training industry and the people in it. He is a sought-after speaker at ASTD and other industry gatherings. He can be reached at *wturmel@communispond.com* and at (630) 347-8369.

CHAPTER 25

LEVEL III EVALUATION OF E-LEARNING

➤JIM BURROW

FOCUS

The focus of this chapter is on the effective design and implementation of Level III evaluation. It is broadly focused in developing an
understanding of that specific type of evaluation. The chapter
specifically recognizes applications within e-learning as well as
unique qualities of e-learning that influence Level III evaluations.

Focus Questions

1. What is Level III evaluation and why is it important?

2. What problems and opportunities are presented when
   completing Level III evaluations of e-learning programs?

3. How can Level III evaluations be completed effectively and efficiently as a part of e-learning?

THE GROWING IMPORTANCE OF EVALUATION

More attention seems to be devoted to evaluation of education and training today than most other issues. However, at times it seems that attention is often directed more at discussing the topic rather than at making significant changes in the approach to evaluation or the use of evaluation results in many organizations.

The focus on evaluation is driven by the recognition in organizations of the level of resources allocated to education and training. Those resources include not only the direct cost of designing and delivering education and training, but the associated administrative costs; expenses of travel, housing, and meals, and the personnel costs for replacing employees involved in extended training and development activities.

Another factor encouraging attention to training and education effectiveness is the productivity issue facing organizations. Job output drops while employees are participating in training. Productivity is reduced as trainees build competence after training and as experienced employees and managers support the employee's development. If training is not effective, anticipated productivity gains may not be realized. Those costs and productivity issues are balanced against the costs to the business if training is not provided, if the organization relies on a strategy of trying to replace lower skilled employees with others who already have the needed skills so they do not require training, or if employees leave the organization due to a perceived lack of personal and professional development opportunities.

No matter what the organization's philosophy toward personnel and personnel development, the bottom line is that education and training must be effective in order to be a valued part of the organization. The organization needs information to determine the effectiveness of investments in learning and how to increase that effectiveness in the future. Evaluation of training, as well as other human resource development strategies, is a critical need in organizations today.

PLANNING MEANINGFUL EVALUATION

Evaluation begins with a clear identification of the purpose or results expected from the education program. By focusing on the purpose and results, evaluators are guided to the reasons why the training program has been developed and the changes and improvements in learner performance that should result. Evaluation planners should be aware of the knowledge, skills, and attitudes needed by the learners. Second, evaluation considers the design of training developed to achieve the identified results. A comprehensive evaluation plan matches the identified knowledge, skills, and attitudes (outcomes) to the sequence, activities, and resources that have been developed to achieve those outcomes (process). In that way, evaluation can be used to determine not only if the desired outcome was achieved but also if the related training strategy was effective.

THE STATUS OF EVALUATION IN ORGANIZATIONS.

Historically, most education and training models have incorporated an evaluation component as a part of the design process. There are many philosophies and approaches regarding when and how to evaluate, the type of evaluation data to be collected, and the use of the findings. Traditionally, the design of training directed at individual performance improvement has been guided by an ISD model (instructional systems development).

There are two primary goals of performance-based training. First, training must result in each trainee having the knowledge, skills, and attitudes necessary for effective performance. Second, each employee must be able to transfer the performance that was developed through training onto the job. The ISD model integrates evaluation extensively throughout the design and implementation process to ensure the effectiveness of the instructional process and to measure achievement of performance objectives.

Even in organizations that follow the ISD process, however, there appears to be a "practical" reality that evaluation does not receive the actual attention that is required to assure achievement of results. Arguments are lodged that "there is not enough time" for comprehensive evaluation, that "evaluation is not practical" within the ongoing operation of a business, or that "evaluation costs too much" when training and education budgets are already limited. So discussion continues on the need for and importance of evaluation while many organizations continue with limited or no evaluation or use traditional evaluations that do not provide the information needed for improving process and results.

KIRKPATRICK'S FOUR LEVELS

Traditional evaluation of training programs in organizations has been of two types—documentation of participation in training, and measures of participant reaction to the training programs. "Keeping the seats full" is obviously important to training personnel who want to be viewed as an important part of an organization's operations and can use the number of training programs offered and number of employees trained as a rationale for budget requests. Increasing the numbers of trainees in an organization, however, would seem to be counter to the assumed performance goal of organizations (i.e., to reduce the need for and costs of training while keeping performance levels high). In the same way, customer satisfaction (high ratings of training by participants) would appear to be a valid measure of training, but evidence is clear that trainees who have positive views of the training experience are not necessarily more productive when they return to the job. It could also be argued that trainees do not have the expertise to judge the effectiveness of complex training design decisions and that perceptions gathered at the end of a training program may be shaped by factors other than the effectiveness of the training program in improving job performance. At best, trainee perceptions of training is a very limited component of comprehensive evaluation.

Level III evaluation is derived from Kirkpatrick's (1959) well-known and seminal four-level approach for evaluating training. Kirkpatrick proposed that a comprehensive view of training effectiveness can only be gained through a multilevel focus on data collection (see Figure 25-1).

According to Kirkpatrick, each of the types of evaluation is necessary to obtain a complete picture of a training program and to make improvement in future training efforts. Other more recent training evaluation models have added an fifth and even a sixth level recommending measures of ROI (return on investment) and nonfinancial organizational benefits.

Arguments can (and have) been made as to whether the Kirkpatrick approach to evaluation is appropriate and provides adequate information to guide training professionals and organizational leaders in making decisions about human resource development strategies and investments. It is easily the most widely accepted approach to training evaluation in business today, however, and at a minimum provides a strong base for data gathering and improvement.

Differentiating the Levels

To review, Kirkpatrick's Level I calls for the traditional perception data. Participants in training are asked to provide their reactions to specific aspects of the training program design and outcomes. Level II measures learning. It determines what learning gains resulted directly from participation in the training. To accurately measure learning results, a premeasure of learners' relevant knowledge, skills, and attitudes is necessary as a baseline. Level III, the focus of this chapter, evaluates the improvement in learners' job performance following training. Are trainees able to transfer learning from training to the job? Again, to assess transfer in a meaning-

Level/Measure	Description
Level 1/ Reaction	Trainees' perception of training effectiveness
Level 2/ Learning	Trainees' achievement of training objectives (change in knowledge, skill and attitude)
Level 3/ Behavior	Trainees' change in performance in the job environment (transfer of training)
Level 4/ Results	Organizational change resulting from the trainees' participation in the training program.

FIGURE 25-1. **KIRKPATRICK'S FOUR LEVELS OF TRAINING EVALUATION**

ful way, both comparable prelearning and within-training measures of the important performance elements must be taken. Finally, Level IV determines if training had any affect on important organizational performance measures. If trainee performance has improved yet does not result in organizational improvement, the identification of training needs may have been incorrect leading to misdirected training investments.

The Importance of Level III Evaluation

It can be argued that Level III evaluation is the most meaningful and critical in judging the effectiveness of training. We recognized that Level I reactions provide useful insights into factors that contribute to learner motivation and satisfaction but do not directly measure training results. Level II, learning, is an essential measure. Did the training program achieve its objectives? Have trainees mastered the knowledge, skills, and attitudes at which the training was directed? If training does not result in learning, training has no value to an organization. However, there is ample evidence that learning from training is often quickly lost or not transferred to the job in a way that improves employee performance. There are a number of reasons for ineffectiveness of training transfer and ways to enhance transfer that are beyond the scope of this chapter.

The results of Level IV evaluations, improved organizational performance, are viewed by many as equal to or more important than Level III results. However, many variables in addition to the effectiveness of training and typically beyond the control of training personnel affect changes in organizational performance. Level III, the transfer of training results to the job, is therefore the most direct and meaningful measure of training effectiveness. If careful needs assessment is completed to focus training on important job performance elements of trainees, then training that leads to improved individual performance of those job components can be judged effective.

PROCESSES AND PARTICIPANTS

Whether applied to e-learning or to other types of organizational training and development programs, there is a specific set of evaluation procedures to use that involve specific participants. This section will give an overview of the design of Level III evaluations.

Purpose

The purpose of Level III evaluations is to gather data to make judgments about the effectiveness and efficiency of learning interventions (training) in improving individual and team performance. Level III Evaluations must be directed at the program outcomes (improved learner performance) and program process (the design elements used to achieve the outcomes) used to improve that performance.

Data

The data collected in Level III evaluations is of three types:

1. Direct evidence of learner performance in the work environment.

2. Evaluation of the work products of the learner that provide direct evidence of the learner's work.

3. Direct evidence of learner performance in simulated work tasks that recreate the work environment as closely as possible when either safety concerns or scheduling of actual job performance does not make on-the-job performance or the assessment of that performance realistic.

Design

The design of the evaluation procedures should make evaluation as unobtrusive as possible. The evaluation should be structured so that it will not interfere with job performance or create an unnatural performance environment. When possible, evaluation should be a part of the work procedure or a part of the normal work evaluation procedures used in the organization (assuming those evaluation procedures are well-designed).

Data Collection

Evaluation data should be collected by direct observation of the learner's work performance if possible. The observation can be completed by a trained observer using evaluation forms or through the use technology when appropriate such as video and audio recording equipment. Data can also be collected by careful analysis of the work produced by the learner in a way that identifies the effectiveness of the performance required to complete the work.

Timing

Level III evaluations should be completed after training when learners have returned to their work and after adequate time to practice and perfect the performance elements on which the training program focused. Multiple observations over a period of time should be completed to provide evidence of "typical" performance. To be able to make judgments about performance improvement, baseline data should be collected before the training begins and, if possible, at the end of training before the trainee returns to the job.

Evaluation Criteria

Judgments about performance should be based on specific, objective criteria that are drawn from the organization's performance expectations for the jobs of the learners. The same criteria should have been used to design the training and to complete evaluations within the training program. Criteria used for Level III evaluations should consider the job conditions under which the learner is performing. If job conditions are not "normal" at the time the evaluation is to occur, either the evaluation should be done at another time or the unique conditions should be noted as discrepancies and considered when making judgments about training effectiveness.

Evaluators

Level III evaluations typically should be completed by the people who are responsible for evaluation of the learner's job performance. That is normally a manager or supervisor, team leader, or in some cases, co-workers or even customers. Some organizations use trained evaluators who are often personnel from the training/ learning units. No matter who is identified as the evaluator, the person should be prepared for the observation and recording process and have an objective, understandable evaluation instrument.

Misperceptions and Misuses

Organizations may avoid implementing Level III evaluations, believing the evaluations are time-consuming, disruptive, and expensive. They also may try to short-cut the evaluation process by substituting perception evaluations for direct performance assessments. An employee or his/her supervisor may be asked a basic question: "Has job performance improved as a result of training?" A more precise question may be asked, "By what amount or in what ways has performance improved as a result of training?" In each case, if the person answering the question is not given specific performance elements and performance criteria to evaluate and is not directed to make specific observations of performance as the basis for the evaluation, the results are at best perceptions so do not meet the standards required of Level III evaluations. However, many evaluators and organizations are willing to substitute perception for direct evidence yet state they are completing Level III evaluations.

A related problem is the type of evaluation measures used to rate performance. Some rating instruments purported to gather Level III information use Likert-type rating scales (agree—disagree), comparative ratings (below average—above average), or numerical scales (1–5). Level III measures must be criterion-based (performance is measured against a standard) rather than comparative (measured against the performance of others). Without very carefully crafted definitions for the positions on a rating scale, the ratings will be both subjective and comparative.

A third problem with the way Level III evaluations are completed in some organizations is to make a very limited number of observations or complete evaluations at times or in conditions that are not typical of those in which the trainee normally performs. If we cannot be reasonably assured that the evaluation results reflect typical trainee performance over time, the results will have little value in either determining the effectiveness of training or in guiding improvements in the training program.

Finally, some Level III evaluations are completed using a standard or general form that is applied to many jobs and training programs. Level III evaluations are not the same as a performance appraisal. They are focused on the performance elements that were the basis for a specific training intervention, not the entire job of the trainee. A well-designed and job-specific performance appraisal instrument may have items that can be used for Level III evaluations. Organizations will benefit from using these documents for Level III evaluation only if there is a very close match between evaluations of training and the job performance elements that are assessed as a part of an employee's performance appraisal; however, the forms and processes cannot be easily or automatically interchanged. A legitimate Level III evaluation must:

- be designed specifically as a part of the education or training intervention for which it will be used,

- measure the specific job performance components that are the key elements of the intervention,

- gather direct evidence of learner performance,

- be implemented at a time when the learner has had a realistic opportunity to practice the performance elements on the job,

- represent the typical performance of the learner under normal job conditions,

- be based on the specific performance criteria that are used by the organization for that job, and

- have comparable pretraining and end-of-training performance data as a basis for comparison.

Matching Program Planning and Evaluation Design

Level III evaluation design begins with the learning objectives for the training intervention. Performance-based objectives have three parts—the performance, conditions of performance, and criteria or standards. Figure 25-2 describes the relationship between each part of a learning objective and the design of a related Level III evaluation.

E-LEARNING OPPORTUNITIES

Level III evaluations should be considered whenever e-learning is focused on improving learner performance within a specific organizational context. If the organizations that sponsor the learning, the educational professionals responsible for design and delivery, and/or the learners participating in the intervention are concerned about the capability of the intervention to affect performance, Level III evaluation strategies are essential. Level III evaluation is probably not appropriate

Parts Of A Performance-Based Objective	Level-Three Evaluation Design Considerations in e-Learning
Performance element—The specific knowledge, skill, or attitude that is the focus of this part of the training intervention	The evaluation procedure must identify the specific performance element(s) on which the evaluation will focus, provide the opportunity for the learner to demonstrate each element, and for the evaluator to observe the performance
Conditions—The restrictions (time, equipment, resources, environment) or resources (facilities, equipment, materials, personnel) available to the learner when they are completing the performance element on the job	The learner must perform within the identified restrictions and with access to the identified resources each timre the performance is being evaluated. If the conditions and resoources do not match those identified, the discrepancies must be specifically noted.
Criteria/Standard—The specific level of performance (time, accuracy, quantity, quality) or the standard (perfection, percentage correct or complete, minimum elements, sequence of performance) used by the learner's organization as evidence of mastery or achievement	The learner's performance must be judged against each of the identified criteria/standards by trained evaluators using reliable and valid procedures and evaluation instruments.

FIGURE 25-2. **THE RELATIONSHIP OF OBJECTIVES AND EVALUATION**

for learning that has a more general education rather than a performance focus, does not have a job or organization context, or for which educators are not accountable for the application of learning beyond the actual learning experience.

The availability of technology in the organizations designing and delivering e-learning or to the recipients may restrict the types of learning experiences that can be developed and provided. However, those limitations are rapidly being reduced by improvements in the capabilities of e-learning technologies and the affordability and availability of those technologies. In order to consider the use of Level III evaluations in e-learning, the technology (or a nontechnology alternative) must allow the learner to observe, practice, and demonstrate the key performance elements of the program. This would usually mean the capability of both instructors and learners to develop, send, and receive multimedia materials. Depending on the performance tasks, that can typically be accomplished with audio and video files transmitted either through network, e-mail, or Internet, or using more traditional exchanges such as personal mail and parcel delivery. The materials, especially those developed by the learner to demonstrate and document performance, do not have to be professionally prepared. They only need to be adequate for the evaluator to be able to recognize the important performance elements.

For the learner to master and demonstrate specific performance elements via e-learning, the developing, transmitting, and receiving media may need to be quite sophisticated. Each element of performance must be able to be easily and clearly studied and practiced. Factors (and changes) in the performance environment that can affect performance must be evident with specific procedures provided to the learner in order to perform within the environment. For example, in training the trainee may not typically experience the distractions that may occur in the real work environment that can often affect performance results. Those distractions should be a part of the environment when Level III evaluations are occurring. In the same way, the learner should demonstrate performance on the equipment configuration found at the person's workspace. Hopefully the training would have been done on the same equipment and configuration. Performance criteria that the learner needs to meet must be identified and observable. If each learner is not provided the opportunity to observe, understand, practice, receive feedback, and apply every key performance element as a part of the e-learning program, Level III evaluation of those elements is not appropriate. You should not evaluate what has not been legitimately developed to the level of acceptable performance within the program.

If there are technology limitations to conducting effective Level III evaluation virtually, it may be possible to involve personnel from the learner's location as the evaluator or to document performance results that can then be transmitted and used by the evaluators. Another evaluation option is for the evaluators to obtain sample products produced by the learner after training. Those products can be evaluated to determine the quality of the learner's performance. It is essential that e-learning programs incorporating Level III evaluations emphasize performance development and include opportunities for each learner to demonstrate performance after the program is completed. Without both components, Level III evaluation is not appropriate.

E-Learning Advantages

E-learning programs provide several advantages for implementing Level III evaluations. First, e-learning is not typically confined in time of delivery as is often the case with more traditional, classroom-based training. It is feasible to deliver part or all of an e-learning program at the workplace and even the specific workspace of the learner. By having access to learning within the work environment, resources needed for performance and evaluation should be readily available. There should be opportunities to observe performance being demonstrated by co-workers and to compare those observations with the standards presented in training. Learners can use the workplace to practice and improve performance prior to evaluation.

Using the same e-learning capabilities, experienced co-workers and managers can be prepared and used to complete some or all of the Level III evaluator activities at the time the learner is asked to demonstrate performance. Because of the availability of technology used to transmit and present the training, that technology can be used to prepare evaluators, to deliver evaluation instruments and instructions, and to transmit collected evaluation information back to the learning providers. Depending on the sophistication of the technology, complex simulations of the workplace can be produced and used to replicate performance conditions and to allow more controlled and safe Level III evaluations. Evaluators can use laptop computers, electronic writing tablets, and PDAs to facilitate data recording, summarizing, and transmittal.

In some jobs the leaner will be using computers that can administer training, monitor practice, and even provide preliminary and actual evaluation experiences. Software can be designed to unobtrusively collect evaluation data from the work completed by the learner and transmit it to evaluators for analysis. As an example, a person making repairs to an automobile engine after training can have performance data from the engine transmitted to the evaluator to determine if the performance met standards. A person completing customer reservations in a call center will have the amount of time to complete the task, and the resulting reservation information entered into a data base for review by the evaluator.

E-Learning Limitations

The primary disadvantage of completing Level III evaluations as a part of e-learning is the physical disconnect between the instructor and learners. Just as most instruction is delivered via technology, it is expected that evaluation will be implemented using that same technology. Without thoughtful planning and the consideration of alternative evaluation methods, it is easy to believe this disconnect restricts the capability for many commonly used types of evaluation, including work-based performance assessments. However, the accessibility of educators to the learners' work environments and the limitations on implementing evaluations of learner work performance is common to most education and training programs. Gaining access and designing strategies for observing performance and collecting data is essential for effective performance improvement whether in more traditional education programs or in e-learning.

One of the advantages of Level III evaluation that counters concerns often expressed about evaluation of e-learning is the integrity of the evaluation. It is often expressed that e-learning provides easier opportunities for learners to "cheat" by having others complete the evaluation or using restricted resources when taking the test. Because Level III evaluations require specific on-the-job performance by the individual, the identity of the person being evaluated is clear. They will be directly observed, video or audiotaped, or work submitted for evaluation must be prepared as a part of their regular work assignment so can be verified through normal organizational procedures.

Probably the greatest perceived limitation in completing Level III evaluations as a part of e-learning is the current stage of development of many e-learning programs. Those programs frequently emphasize knowledge development to the exclusion of performance improvement. However, the application of knowledge (especially higher-order cognitive skills) are a significant aspect of many jobs, and therefore evaluating that knowledge within the context and conditions of the job would be an appropriate Level III evaluation task (decision-making, problem-solving, completing intellectual tasks. If a learner has to make decisions based on specific information, the Level III evaluation would determine not only if the ultimate decision met specific criteria but if the "correct" knowledge (facts, procedures, information sources) were included in the decision.

A related concern is the independence (isolation) of many e-learning experiences. Even though increased attention is being focused on instructor-to-learner and learner-to-learner interaction and applications of group and even team learning within e-learning, there is concern that those "collaborative" skills such as consulting and team decision-making cannot be as effectively improved by e-learning. It appears, however, that this limitation is being rapidly overcome through both technology advances as well as the thoughtful development of methodologies that are appropriate for both the learning goal and the instructional media. As instruction in group processes is improved via e-learning, appropriate group process evaluations within the work environment can be planned and implemented as well.

THE EVALUATION INSTRUMENT

Level III evaluation instruments, whether used as a part of an e-learning program or in more traditional programs, need to include three components:

1. A description of the performance environment including restrictions that need to be imposed and resources that need to be available.

2. Clear instructions to the evaluator on how to conduct the evaluation so that there is minimal interference with performance, time limitations (if any) on the performance, and directions for documenting any discrepancies in the performance conditions that restricted or provided an advantage to the learner during the observed performance.

3. An easy-to-use data recording section that lists all important elements of the performance with specific, objective criteria/standards for each performance element. Most Level III evaluation instruments are designed using an observation checklist that includes each performance element, a sublist of performance criteria for each element, and a rating choice for each criterion. The ratings choice is typically organized in one of the following formats:

   ____ (check if observed)

   ____ below standard   ____ meets standard   ____ exceeds standard

A Level III evaluation sample form is shown in Figure 25-3. It is used to evaluate the effectiveness of an instructor facilitator after participating in a training program to develop specific instructional skills matched to effective training design characteristics. The Level III evaluation would be completed by a trained evaluator who is observing the instructor teaching an actual class. It could also be completed by viewing a videotape of the instructor's class or by viewing a live interactive teaching session via computer, or a two-way audio-video link. (Note that the same form could be used as an effective learning and review aid by the trainee as well as an evaluation tool to assess learning—Level II—as a part of the training program.)

ANALYZING LEVEL III RESULTS

Evaluations of education and training programs serve two purposes—to identify achievement of learning objectives, and to make judgments about the effectiveness and efficiency of learning strategies. While Level III evaluations occur after the completion of the intervention and in the job environment, the results are very important in achieving each of those purposes. If the goal of learning is a change in behavior, it cannot be judged successful without determining if any resulting change can be sustained and makes a difference in future performance. In addition, a high score on a test is of little value if the knowledge is not retained. One-time effective performance does little good if it cannot be routinely repeated. Level III evaluations provide evidence to judge whether learning has been mastered and sustained, is useable in the normal work environment of the learner, and if done carefully what learning strategies contributed (or did not contribute) to that mastery and maintenance of the performance.

In order to determine if training is effective, Level III evaluations must be matched against other data in order to determine if there is a change in learner performance (knowledge, skills, attitudes) as a result of training. That requires that comparable data be gathered from learners prior to beginning training so a pre/posttraining comparison can be made. Most evaluators recommend that a third evaluation be completed during or at the very end of training. This evaluation corresponds to Kirkpatrick's Level Two. Both the pre- and during-evaluations should focus on the same performance elements using the same criteria that will be used in the Level III assessment after the learner has returned to work. The evaluations should be completed in the job environment if possible or in conditions that are as close to job performance conditions as possible (laboratory, simulation).

After data have been collected, comparisons can be made on any documented learner change for each performance element. The analysis should focus on each of the criteria or standards for the performance element to see if the training was more effective in improving certain aspects of the performance but not others. Measures of change in performance elements can be matched to the types of learning strategies and resources used to develop that performance. With careful controls and analysis as well as multiple measures, it is possible to isolate strategies that are more and less effective in improving specific types of performance. It is impor-

Instructor/Facilitator Name _____

Session Title/Topic _____

Date of Observation _____

Instructions: Observe the instructor/facilitator at least two times with unique content and learners for each observation. Complete a separate form for each observation. Each observation should be for a minimum of 30 minutes. Obtain a copy of the instructional plan in advance of the observation.

Discrepancies: Use the session plan to identify the resources (facility, equipment, materials) that are required for effective instruction and note any that are not available to the instructor in this session.

          Discrepancies _____

Identify the learner qualifications required for participation in the training and note any differences in the participants for this session.

          Discrepancies _____

Evaluation: Observe for a specific demonstration of each skill listed. Base each rating on direct observation of the instructor/facilitator.

          Rate each skill using the following code: +   skill was used effectively in the session
                                           -   skill was used ineffectively in the session
                                       0   skill was not used in the session

Elements of Effective Training Programs	**Evaluation of Instructor/Facilitator Skills**
1. Measurable objectives directed at important results	__Instructor/facilitator presents one or more specific objectives for each critical KSA __Instructor clarifies the performance, conditions, and criteria with learners __Instructor/facilitator communicates the relationship between objectives and performance requirements in the job environment
2. Clearly related to previous experience and learning	__Early informal or formal learner assessment is completed to determine experience and training needs __Learners are asked to connect new learning to previous learning in discussion and other activities
3. Understandable and meaningful content	__Instructor/facilitator shows job relevance of content __Learners are regularly questioned and asked for feedback on content to insure understanding and relevance
4. Comfortable and motivating environment	__Instructor/facilitator begins the training program by establishing an inviting, involving atmosphere for all learners __Instructor/facilitator controls the physical environment (seating, temperature, lighting) as possible to maintain learner comfort __Environment, activities, and information demonstrate the job relevance of training
5. Instructional activities that support learning	__Instructional activities are sequenced to support learning __Instructional activities are matched to the type of learning (knowledge, skill, attitude)
6. Materials and resources that support activities	__Materials and resources are developed to focus learner attention and interest __Materials and resources clarify and support the content of the session and activities
7. Instructional equipment matched to resources	__Instructional equipment is included in the support of instruction __Use of equipment by instructor/facilitator and/or learners does not detract from learning
8. Adequate time to deliver content and implement activities	__A moderate amount of new information is included in the training program __The program includes an appropriate mix of knowledge, skill, and attitude development based on training objectives __Time is provided for each learner to practice, demonstrate learning, and receive feedback on key objectives
9. Meaningful interaction and involvement	__Learners are active rather than passive for the majority of instructional time __Learner experience is frequently incorporated into training __Activities encourage instructor/learner and learner/learner interactions
10. Realistic and relevant examples	__Learners are involved in realistic, job-related activities and instruction __Instruction and demonstrations incorporate job-specific examples and problems
11. Demonstrations and practice opportunities	__Training incorporates demonstrations of effective and ineffective performance __Demonstrations and practice opportunities are integrated into instruction for key objectives
12. Realistic practice environment	__Learners are given the opportunity to practice in realistic job conditions __Learners practice in a safe and supportive environment
13. Regular feedback and reinforcement	__Learners are given written or verbal cues for effective performance in advance of practice __Practice opportunities incorporates external feedback and correction
14. Evaluation using specific performance criteria	__Evaluation procedures and materials used match performance criteria from objectives __Learners are provided specific criteria in advance of performance
15. Planning for on-the-job applications	__Ending activities include goal setting and reentry planning __Trainees are given repeated and varied practice opportunities

FIGURE 25-3.

tant when completing preassessments and Level III evaluations to identify and document changes in work environment characteristics. It is apparent that changes in job performance can be affected by factors other than training. Changes in the environment should be considered whenever completing an analysis of training effectiveness.

Most e-learning programs are developed as an alternative to or as a replacement for more traditional program designs. Comparability of effectiveness and cost are normally a consideration as organizations integrate e-learning. Level III evaluations provide important information for that analysis. To be able to make reasoned judgments, the evaluation procedure and instruments should be as similar as possible for comparable programs focused on common objectives and job performance elements.

COMMUNICATING EVALUATION RESULTS

The results of Level III evaluations must be shared with those who have a stake and role in organizational performance improvement and in the design and delivery of learning programs if evaluation is to make a difference in the organization. Results must be communicated to each stakeholder in an understandable and meaningful way. Since e-learning is a relatively new undertaking for most organizations with the likelihood of strong feelings for and against its use and expansion, communicating evaluation results is especially important. Here, Level III evaluations (the affect of training on work performance) can be especially meaningful in directing the discussion about the value of e-learning.

It is obvious that those who are a part of the design and delivery of e-learning will want to be informed of any relevant information about the program and their role in the program. Instructional designers, instructors, administrators, and others can benefit from relevant results. Detailed attention should be given to the types of objectives and e-learning strategies that are most and least effective. Once again, when using Level III data, specific attention should be focused on the strengths and limitations of e-learning designs in performance improvement, transfer of skills to the job, and long-term retention of those skills.

Evaluation results are especially important to learners. Many will be concerned about their involvement in e-learning. Attitude and motivation are influenced by the knowledge they have about the training process and results. Feedback on performance prior to training can help set expectations going into the training program. Information on performance capabilities under job conditions during training prepares trainees for the transition back to the job. Feedback on the relationship between training and job performance after returning to work emphasizes the importance of training to the trainee and encourages sustained effective performance on the newly learned skills. Technologies used for e-learning delivery may increase the capability for more regular, varied, and in-depth assessments, as well as rapid, individualized feedback of informal and formal evaluation results to learners.

Supervisors benefit from learning-related performance information about their employees gathered before, during, and after training. Evaluation data can show supervisors the performance improvement that occurred during training and establish expectations for performance when the trainee returns to the job. Continuing information about evaluation that occurs on-the-job maintains focus on the value of training to improved performance as well as on work environment factors that affect evaluation results in addition to training. Level III evaluation data for e-learning programs can build support among supervisors for the newer delivery methods and encourage their future involvement in e-learning programs.

Finally, key decision-makers in the organization, both those who support e-learning and those who do not, must have regular access to evaluation data. Performance improvement data matched to learning programs will be viewed as much more meaningful than traditional evaluation data reporting numbers of training programs, enrollments, and learner perceptions of training. Level III evaluation information will result in improved decisions based on a clearer understanding of what works and does not work in e-learning. It will allow decision-makers to more objectively compare the effectiveness and efficiency of e-learning with other learning models, and will encourage them to consider its appropriate role in organizational planning and improvement.

RESOURCES

Readings

Combs, W., and Falletta, S. (2000). *The Targeted Evaluation Process: A Performance Consultant's Guide to Asking the Right Questions and Getting the Results You Trust.* Alexandria, VA: The American Society for Training and Development.

Phillips, J., ed. (1998). *In Action: Implementing Evaluation Systems and Processes.* Alexandria, VA: The American Society for Training and Development.

Russ-Eft, D., and Preskill, H. (2001). *Evaluating in Organizations: A Systematic Approach to Enhancing Learning, Performance, and Change.* Cambridge, MA: Perseus Publishing.

Schreiber, D., and Berge, Z. (1998). *Distance Training: How Innovative Organizations are Using Technology to Maximize Learning and Meet Business Objectives.* San Francisco: Jossey-Bass.

Additional Readings

Gaines, Robinson D., & Robinson, J. (1989). *Training for Impact.* San Francisco: Jossey-Bass.

Horton, W. (2001). *Evaluating E-Learning.* Alexandria, VA: the American Society for Training and Development.

Kirkpatrick, D. (1998). *Another Look at Evaluating Training Programs: Fifty Articles from Training and Development and Technical Training Magazines.* Alexandria, VA: The American Society for Training and Development.

Kirkpatrick, D. (1998). *Evaluating Training Programs*, second ed. San Francisco: Berrett-Koehler.

Multimedia Information in Mobile Environments Laboratory (MIME). Evaluation Matrix (A Planning Tool for Making Evaluation Decisions for Distance Learning Courses). Atlanta: Georgia Tech.

Philips, J. (1997). *Handbook of Training Evaluation and Measurement Methods* third ed. Houston: Gulf Professional Publishing Corp.

Schank, R. (2001). Designing World-Class E-Learning. New York: McGraw-Hill.

Todesco, A. (September, 1997). From Training Evaluation to Outcome Assessment: What Trends and Best Practices Tell Us. Learning Services Directorate, Public Service Commission of Canada.

Vella, J., Berardinelli, P., and Burrow, J. (1998). *How Do They Know They Know: Evaluating Adult Learning*. San Francisco: Jossey-Bass.

➤ABOUT THE AUTHOR

Jim Burrow is an Associate Professor and Coordinator of the graduate Training and Development Program at North Carolina State University. He has spent over twenty-five years in marketing and human resource development as a faculty member at the community college and university levels. He provides regular consulting to private and public sector organizations in the strategic integration and development of personnel and the design and evaluation of performance improvement strategies. Jim has provided leadership at NC State in developing distance education alternatives in professional education employing varied media (television, video, Internet). NC State now offers a fully distance-delivered masters degree in Training and Development. Jim Burrow can be reached at 919/515-6246, and at *James_Burrow@ncsu.edu*.

CHAPTER 26

E-LEARNING, THE NEAR FUTURE

➤ELLIOTT MASIE

WHERE IS E-LEARNING NOW?

The last five years have a been a whirlwind period for the learning, training, and development field. We have seen an amazing interest in the delivery of training, using the tools of the internet. We have seen the creation of a robust and risky marketplace, in part fueled by the internet mania and in part fueled by the need of organizations to rapidly deploy learning to the desktop. And, we have seen a changed set of expectations in both average learners and their managers, reflecting an acceptance (and demand) for alternatives to classroom instruction.

Yet, there is large and widespread misunderstanding about this "e" learning thing. This chapter will address the past, current, and future states of e-learning and advocate a different perspective about how this integrates with the needs of our businesses.

Let's Start With That Letter "E"

Let's look at the *e* in e-learning. It stands for many things, only one of which is electronic. We have been using electronics for the delivery of learning and training for some time now. Mainframe computers were delivering computer-based training forty years ago. We have seen the introduction of filmstrips, television, and the Internet into the classroom, and that process is continuing. So, the electronic aspect of learning is neither revolutionary nor all that exciting.

What makes the *e* intriguing derives from the experience dimension of our innovations. Organizations throughout the world are combining new technologies and methodologies to create new and quite different learning experiences for both individuals and institutions. CEO's and chief learning officers are talking about e-learning because it has the potential to change the fabric of learning through:

> **Global Delivery:** the capacity to provide workers or customers with the same learning experiences, regardless of physical location on the globe or whether or not they are working at a desk with computers.
>
> **Continuous Delivery:** the capacity to provide learners with an ongoing continuous set of learning, knowledge, and performance experiences, rather than a one-shot event of learning.
>
> **Rapid Learning Development:** the capacity to shorten the development time from concept to delivery.
>
> **Just Enough:** the ability to deliver exactly what is needed, by the learner, at that moment, rather than a set of content that is based on an average set of needs, or even worse, the needs of the slowest learners.

Each of these benefits reflects a fundamental desire to CHANGE the way that learners learn and how organizations develop and inject learning throughout the enterprise. In other words, the *e* is all about a change in our process of learning, not about a new delivery system. In fact, efforts that focus only on changing the delivery system are deeply overwhelming. For example, when web-based training first hit the scene, the loud (and often deserved) criticism was that it was only "digital page-turning". This form of e-learning proved not to be a new process. Rather, it was a step backward, merely substituting rich, interactive, in-person experiences with linear, reading from a screen delivery modes. What we learned from e-learning pioneers was that we had to change not only the delivery system, but also the assumptions, behaviors and models.

This has led us to richer simulation, live synchronous on-line events, blended learning, and in-depth case study models. So, let's take a look at what is being called e-learning today.

E-learning Models

Internet Computer-Based Training: Some of the more robust innovations in the e-learning field have occurred as vendors and implementers, CD-ROM-based, computer-based training modules to Internet or intranet delivery. In these formats, we see much the same learning assumptions as have been found in CBT for the past 30 years. Content is delivered to the learner, with opportunities for pretesting, checking for mastery, and practice, following a branched, behavioral model. Internet delivery has allowed this content to be more widely dispensed, sometimes with shorter development and deployment timeframes and with the promise of a more personalized instructional experience, leveraging information about the learner into a more appropriate set of modules or objects.

Linear and Data Base Content
A good amount of e-learning is being delivered without the behavioral reinforcement of CBT. Learners can access knowledge chunks or modules that are of shorter duration, linear in nature, and easy to digest. These content modules are often created from existing content or from knowledge management systems, allowing the worker to access just what she needs, when she needs it, in small chunks for learning, reminder or performance support.

Instructor Mediated e-Learning Content
Take one of the first two models and add access to an instructor. This is used extensively for longer duration and certification programs. The learner is given an instructional path and there is an instructor, subject matter expert, or facilitator on the scene, digitally. As your instructor, I might set the agenda, check your progress, evaluate your assignments, answer your questions, or host on-line chats. We are seeing vendors move towards this model as part of a pricing strategy that moves the value perception of the content significantly above just on-line, self-paced reading. It also addressed the challenge of keeping the learner's head in the game.

Simulations
Whenever I talk about e-learning to someone who is new to this field, their first assumption and hope is that they will see a robust, visually intensive, gamelike environment, similar to Microsoft Flight Simulator or SimCities. Why? The idea of learning delivered via technology seems to logically take us to a more intensive and engaging experience. The problem is money! These simulations are being successfully developed for areas where they are particularly appropriate such as flight training, manufacturing skills, and even some IT labs. But they cost significant amounts of money to develop and often have way too short of a shelf life or audience size to justify the expense; however, we are seeing more and more investment in the simulation model.

Case Study or Scenarios Models

These are often the "poor man's" simulations. Imagine a series of situations that are described to the learner, with pictures, words, audio, and even video. As the learner selects from a multiple set of choices, they see the consequences of their actions. This has been a very successful model in the business skills and "soft skills area." For example, a learner can build and test their selling skills by going through an in-depth set of case studies to see the consequences of choices made at each step in the selling cycle.

Live Collaborative Learning

This is one of the most explosive growth areas of e-learning. Simply, the learner is at a desktop, and the instructor and other students are at their desktops. At a designated time, the session starts. The instructor can "drive" the visuals and text on all of the learners screens. The audio can be delivered either through a parallel phone call or right over the Internet. Video can be added. The learners can be polled, taken on a web safari, broken into discussion groups, or access real time databases. This form of digital collaboration will grow into an assumptive form of learning, where we just assume that learners and instructors will be connected in this fashion.

Coaching

The role of the coach is to provide expertise, consultation, and compliance interventions, with or without a classroom curriculum. The power of the coach can be found in the short duration of the interactions and the influence on performance of the learner.

Blended Learning

Take any of the e-learning models above, mix them up, and perhaps add a short traditional in-person session, and you have blended learning. The yield is a multitechnique model, where learning is extended over time, and the best of each delivery system is used. Many traditional classroom offerings are being brought into the e-world, by adding a Digital Surround, before or after the event.

Learning and Content Management Systems

While these are not learning models, these systems play a significant role in the development and evolution of e-learning. Take the learner information, the content, the course logic, and you can imagine a robust way of assembling, delivering, and overseeing the learning process. The promise of these systems is delivering "just the right content" to learners as needed, and that we can use significant feedback to continually hone and improve the learning process.

Where E-learning is Being Applied

The fun part of e-learning is to watch where it is popping up. We are seeing e-learning used for:

- ➤ Worker development

- ➤ Career development

- ➤ New hire orientation

- ➤ Continuing education compliance

- ➤ Customer learning prior to the sale

- ➤ Customer learning post sale

- ➤ Supply chain learning

- ➤ Recreation and affiliation learning

- ➤ K–12 and higher education

THE TRAINER OF THE FUTURE

Some pundits have predicted that e-learning will lead to "trainer-less" learning. The idea of a wonderful portal, containing all the high-powered learning in the world, just a click away, would make the training process magical, without the head-counts and limitations of trainers.

However, there is a big flaw in that prediction. First of all, not all training will go to the internet. Even in the most e-learning-intensive organizations, there are still many, many classroom events. And, even in the best e-learning experiences, there are still important roles of people that might be called trainers, though we could change their title to facilitators or coaches, for example.

There are many situations where it is just flat-out cheaper to provide a trainer rather than author on-line content. For example, if there are only five people that need to learn a skill, it will always be less expensive and quicker to put them into a room with a subject matter expert who has at least minimal training skills, than to author the content. Likewise, when the learning needs to be immediate, or has a very, very short shelf life, a live trainer, either in person or over the Internet will still be essential.

Finally, there is a growing need for trainers for the delivery and mediation of virtual classroom, coaching, and teaching events. Every time an organization implements one of these digital collaboration technologies, there is a need for the development of a new skill set for the people that will teach and moderate in these formats.

Add to this list, the growing use of blended learning, which combines the best of on-line technology with human assets, and we are seeing the GROWTH rather than the shrinking of the need for training skills; however, the skills of the trainer in the Digital Age are going to be slightly different and in some cases, counterintuitive to classroom delivery techniques. Consider a few examples of what the Trainer of the Future will have in his or her skill set.

Compressed Delivery

The footprint of classes will shrink. Events that are delivered on-line are going to be shorter. We have significant evidence that the "learner-at-the-desk" will not be able to pay attention to consecutive hours of sessions. And, even the classroom duration will be shortened, by shifting some of the information transfer to an on-line mode, before or after the face-to-face session. Trainers will need to know how to say more with less time and fewer words. If something is available as a good resource site or there is a performance support tool, the delivery in the classroom will shorten. Trainers will need to be comfortable that the learner can learn something without hearing it from the mouth of the teacher. And, we will learn compression techniques to teach differently.

From Sage to Socratic Method

The best use of the actual classroom or on-line live session may not be the "sage on the stage" activity, where the learner is the receiver of audio content from the mouth of the trainer. The virtual classroom is the perfect environment for using case studies, Socratic teaching methods, group projects, simulations, and other learning processes which leverage the live environment. In order to do this on-line, the trainer will need to learn new techniques for facilitation in both the classroom and on-line environs.

Demand Loads

The e-trainer has to get ready for a huge increase in learner requests for support. In a classroom, the learners moderate their own requests and only a few students ask a few times for information or support. In an on-line or blended learning environment, each learner has the ability to access the trainer as much as they need. Trainers need the tools to manage this demand and to create ways to turn each request for information into a asynchronous resource for the rest of the learners.

Teaching with More Data

The trainer of the future has a unique opportunity to leverage significant data from the learning management systems to hone and personalize their interactions with each student. Trainers will know more about employee work history, learning experiences, and even style of learning. This is a gift to the trainer, assuming they know how to integrate and leverage this increased set of knowledge.

These are just a few of the skills of the Trainer of the Future. Of course, we will need to get more comfortable in front of cameras and microphones. We will need to learn how to work from anywhere and anytime. And, we will need to get our sense of success from clues that are more subtle than laughter or applause. The ultimate success will be in helping massive numbers of learners learn and perform better every day.

A FEW PREDICTIONS

This is the scariest aspect of thinking about the future of e-learning. How do you put on paper predictions for the future when our field is changing at the rate of twenty percent each quarter? Well, here is a simple attempt at predictions.

Growth of demand for e-learning from users will grow faster than our supply capability or innovation capacity. Learners will want and demand better and more interactive forms of e-learning, often getting frustrated by what is not yet available.

Digital Collaboration will integrate with organizational desktops and browsers. Just as every worker has a telephone, every worker will have the ability to add a virtual classroom or meeting space to any telephone call or on-line conversation.

Learning will be seen as less of an event basis and more of a subscription to a continuous, IV drip of content delivery and performance support. The learner will be part of an ongoing community of learning and practice.

Higher education institutions will become very involved and major players in the e-learning space. We will see degree programs start to include lifelong access to learning communities and feeds from these institutions.

Simulations will evolve to our expectation level. We will become used to "simming" a major decision, by trying it out before we do the actual sale, equipment assembly, or programming. Simulations will have multiplayer, ongoing, deeply visual capabilities.

Learning will become device agnostic. Old technologies like phones and voicemail will find new roles in e-learning, as well as mobile devices like handheld computers and cellular phones. In addition, we will see equipment developed that has Internet access for learning embedded within the hardware.

The "e" will disappear. The "e" is a temporary device to talk about the changes in learning we are all experimenting with. As learning becomes more integrated with technology, we don't really need to use the "e" anymore!

What is certain is that learning, whatever we call it, is in a very long relationship with technology. We will see steady increases in the use of technology for development, delivery, management, and marketing of learning. We will see new models of what a learning experience is like, when linked with the power of technology. We will see technology and learning integrated with daily business tasks and woven into our lives. And, I strongly believe, we will see classrooms, with instructors, for the duration of our species. All of these changes will take place in an environment of stress . . . stress to prove effectiveness, make profits, and deal with changing roles and careers for learning professionals. That kind of stress will fuel innovation. So, strap your seat belts on, the learning ride will be interesting and powerful.

➤ABOUT THE AUTHOR

Elliott Masie is the President of The MASIE Center, an international think tank dedicated to learning and technology.

CHAPTER 27

GLOBAL LEARNING, 2008

➤CLARK ALDRICH

It is hard to imagine the automobile industry in its early days, producing loud, noxious, unreliable vehicles trying to challenge the refined horse and buggy. It is hard also to picture a young pharmaceuticals industry, asking customers to ingest smelly powders and liquids to fix problems previously unfixable (or requiring invasive surgery), sometimes working, sometimes not. Yet both grew up to utterly change the world.

It is equally hard to imagine a mature e-learning industry. The issues that plague the industry are so basic:

➤ Does it really work?

➤ How should success be measured?

- When does it work? What is the relationship between traditional training and e-learning?

- How should vendors sell it? What should they sell? How should enterprises buy it?

- When will standards make implementation easier?

- Which vendors will be around next year? Next month? Thursday?

All of these issues are critical, but are being resolved. And as they are, e-learning will be as transformational and era-defining as automobiles were and pharmaceuticals are.

E-learning already has thousands of success stories. E-learning—the combination of tools, processes, and content—is already helping companies effectively achieve.

Greater Readiness, Responsiveness, and Alignment Throughout an Organization

It is one thing for senior management to come up with a new vision. It is quite another to have the enterprise understand it and apply it. Companies are rolling out four-to eight-hour learning programs around new strategic visions and directions, around new processes and tools, and are including not just employees, but also customers, suppliers, and vendors to create an immediate community around new terms, models, tools, and other ideas.

Faster Understanding, Selling, Use, and Servicing of New Offerings

One of the most common organizational transformations continues to be around the release of dramatically new products. Ford has to change when it releases a new type of vehicle. Bayer has to change when it begins to sell a new pill. Because when a product is first available, customers won't buy it, salespeople can't sell it, sales channels can't push it, and service and financing can't support it, until they "get it."

On its own, it takes the bulk of sales channels and customers five or six months to "get" a new offering. This is expensive for the launching company, because the most profitable time for a product is during the initial few months. It is also frustrating for the customers, because often newer products come out before they have understood and absorbed the last generation.

To compensate, high technology firms, leading manufacturers, and financial services organizations have had to use e-learning as a way of speeding up the "time to get-it." These companies are bell weathers, as more and more companies face increasing release schedules.

And More Loyal Employees, Vendors, and Customers

If companies do not engage new employees in the first 45 days, they probably will not be able to keep them, either mentally or physically. New employees need to feel that they are valued, and also that they have the necessary skills to complete what is asked of them. CD-ROM-based courses for high turnover positions have had measurable impacts in improved new-hire retention, especially in inherently high turnover industries like fast food, retailing, banking, or airport security.

New customers are even more demanding. To avoid buyers' remorse, companies have closer to 45 minutes to prove the value of the service or product. Palm, through an innovative website, was able to train people how to use their personal digital assistants (PDA) *before* a person even bought it, overcoming fears of complexity and increasing satisfaction at the moment of purchase. Charles Schwab continues to be a leader in training their customers, both in physical classrooms and their online site. Other companies are catching on.

E-learning is also building support at the individual level, as it is helping employees achieve:

Quick Ramp Ups for New Assignments or Jobs

Employees can get skills faster, and with lower disruption of their current situation qualifying them for jobs previously inaccessible. IT professional have proved the case, both gaining real skills and passing high-level certification exams. In doing so they have paved the way for dozens of other career types.

Greater Ability to Share Information and Be Recognized for Their Contributions

Most people are experts at something other than their official job, and in many cases what they are most interested in. For example, someone working at Kodak might, in her free time, research cultures, like Russia or Cajun Louisiana. This knowledge may become needed as Kodak expands in the region. Suddenly, that person is recognized as a resource and is freed up to spend more time becoming an expert in what she loves. Extended communities, driven today by both chat rooms and e-mails, have allowed this to happen much more comprehensively than the prewired world.

Less Repetitive Work, Including Working More Off the Work of Others

As we all know, the amount of redundant work in a company can be astounding. Network-based tools in experienced communities greatly facilitate the deployment of templates (such as new slide formats and new forms) and best practices (such as successful letters).

Learning On a More Flexible Basis

Instead of traveling to the training site, or never being trained at all, people can learn and participate through same-time different-location virtual classrooms. Even at midnight. Attire optional.

And Networks with People They Would Otherwise Have Never Met

Increasingly, synchronous sessions are organized by job type, not by location. For example, an organization rolling out a new piece of tracking software could organize a class for all of the warehouse managers, maybe one from Sydney, one from just outside Paris, one from Phoenix, and one from Atlanta. Not only is the information taught more relevant to learners, but networks of people have been brought together that end up sharing information and problems well after the class is over.

Because of the transformational nature of the benefits to both corporations and individuals, within fifteen years, enterprises worldwide will spend hundreds of billions in e-learning services. At least three of the Fortune one hundred will be e-learning vendors. The cost of organizational learning will be, on average, five percent of revenue (although that will vary by industry). Ten percent of an employee's time will be spent in formal learning, but much more tightly integrated into their broader work time.

The disparate corporate knowledge management groups will be joined into one organization. HR, knowledge management, and e-learning will all be much more aligned from a vision, organizational, process, and technology perspective.

CONTENT TYPES

Like mass media, and like the computer industry, global learning foremost requires content. Televisions without shows, computers without programs, fiber optics without data, and highways without cars couldn't sell for long, no matter how exciting is the technology. The failure of the expert systems market demonstrates what happens when enterprises are sold infrastructure without content. At the same time, as with the success of telephones and e-mail, there is a role for straight infrastructure tools as well.

The global learning market will use at least six different types of content, both internally and externally produced, each with their own benefits and costs. The first two, already in significant use today, are:

- ➤ extended books and
- ➤ extended lectures.

The other four, in early stages of being piloted and refined, are:

- ➤ extended community,

- ➤ extended expert access,

- ➤ role-playing/simulations, and

- ➤ embedded help.

Traditional Content Types

Extended Books

Today's asynchronous e-learning courses are extended books, workbooks delivered over the web. They have course outlines, modular structures, and often include multiple-choice tests. As time goes on, extended books will still be a major form of e-learning content, although they will not hold quite the same dominance that they have today.

Just as today, extended books will continue to be well edited, and often the result of multiauthor collaborations. The material is trustworthy, at least to the same standard as a hard copy magazine or book.

This type of content has flourished because the value is often much higher than a workbook for many reasons.

- ➤ Users and organizations can cheaply customize content.

- ➤ You can search the material electronically, instead of flipping pages or squinting at the index.

- ➤ The material is easily deployed using the web, instead of the mail.

- ➤ Because of this ease of delivery, the material can be updated seamlessly. When you go to a course on the web, unlike the textbook in your cubicle shelf, you expect the material to be up-to-date.

- ➤ These extended books have animations to improve comprehension, and hyperlinks to bounce around if some area especially catches your interest.

- ➤ The content may include testing and verification that the material was read and understood.

All of these features will become more powerful. More media sources, including traditional magazine and book publishers, will enter the e-learning extended books marketplace. They are learning that they will earn more money if they can chunk the content into categories that corporations care about, and put in an assessment test at the end and other tracking to make sure the material was read.

Extended books will get more and more extensive, and come to include simulations, branching storyboards, and screen shots. Portable, electronic books, wirelessly connected, will make this format easy to bring anywhere. Even heads-up displays integrated into eyewear with retina-activated information navigation will become standard issue for many repair jobs involving both hands, like aircraft or bridge repair.

Extended Lectures

Extended lectures (today called virtual classrooms or live e-learning) are based on the traditional lecture model, but stretch it in several ways.

First, they allow teachers and students to stay in different locations. Through using the right software, voices, slides, text, screen shots, icons of hands being raised, and sometimes video can be transmitted over the Internet. Because the sessions require no travel, instructors can have more frequent, hour-long classes as opposed to the two-day mind-busters. As important, participants can be organized by topic and interest, not geography.

Extended lectures can also change politics. Class sizes should be the same, about eight to twenty. But everyone can be pulled into the conversation. Quick polls can be taken of the entire group. People tend to be less self-conscious if they can't see their bosses. Questions can be asked both via text and voice, to just the instructor, to just one select classmate, or the entire group, and with your name or anonymously.

Finally, current virtual class applications can record sessions, much like someone can record a favorite TV show. While watching a previously recorded session precludes interaction, and therefore isn't nearly as interesting for the after-student (those people who miss the original lecture but watch it later), they still can be critically useful.

In the future, extended lectures will improve with

➤ Better quality of video and voice,

➤ faster slides and richer of interaction,

➤ easier set-up for first-time users,

➤ different on-ramps (including accessing sessions through palm tops),

➤ conversion of voice to text, language translation,

➤ increased number of users comfortable with the technology,

➤ easier editing of archived sessions, and

➤ more power for after-students, both to impact the polls and ask questions and get asynchronous responses.

Newer Content Types

Extended Community

Many of the elements that will make up extended communities exist in multiple, incompatible forms today. They include Internet chat rooms, some knowledge management implementations, even e-mail and telephone calls. In global learning, extended communities will be less ad hoc and significantly more productive. Their uses will grow from just information sharing, to coordination, to discussion, and then to collaboration. Fundamentally, extended communities will increase the size, geographical diversity, and levels of participation of any workgroup.

In many cases the material will also be divergent, not convergent. For example, fifteen people might discuss a common problem—how to improve employee morale. The goal might not be to come up with the one right answer. The goal is for all fifteen people to learn enough to improve their own approach to the problem. The group may brainstorm and develop fifty methods, and every participant takes away a subsection of twenty relevant to their situation.

Also, as more information is captured about a meeting or ongoing workgroup, that information becomes available to be analyzed. From a recorded meeting, we will be able to press a button to ask the program to sift through all of the dialogue to find out how stressed the group was, who the actual leader of the meeting was, who had ideas that were supported, who was shut out, and other aspects.

Finally, some members of your extended community will not be people at all. They will be automated, intelligent agents. As with other community members, they will search the web for areas of interest to bring back to you. The verification of the content will still be up to you.

Extended Expert Access

Mentorships flurried and then fizzled during the 1990s. But the underlying need of being able to talk to someone with answers is only increasing. From a practical perspective, today's call centers and IT help desk personnel are early pioneers here.

During the late 1990s, software vendors began putting together packages of technology for the purpose of identifying experts across an organization. These devices look through e-mails sent and chat room participation. They are being augmented by self-nominated and manager-populated skills management systems. Using other underlying global learning technologies, any employee will have an easier time gaining more immediate access to people with deep knowledge on a particular topic of interest.

"Experts" is not a definitive term. It does not apply only to those with certain degrees, or a certain number of years of experience. Useful experts could be in the category of semiconductor refrigeration or how to get past the secretary of the CEO of General Foods. In many cases, skill sets will not be identified *before* they are needed, but *as* they are needed.

The content produced through expert access represents only a single, pointed opinion. It will be intense. It will often be inspirational, as the experts are usually passionate about his or her area of expertise. These sessions will be two-way. A rehearsed speech, the crutch of many experts, would be a bad use of the time, although good prereading/watching. The expectation would be that shared work would be accomplished.

Role-Playing/Simulations

E-learning simulations, where people take on problem-solving roles in computer-created environments, are primitive today. But computer games and work in the military have vaulted ahead. Combining the best technology of both gaming and military simulations, future simulations will increasingly be a new and better way to learn.

- They will be about real, identifiable situations. Although some early simulation providers will use metaphorical settings, the scenarios must feel authentic and relevant to the employees' task at hand.

- They will be played in real time. The pressure of immediate decisions breaks through the attempts of most students to manipulate the course results. This is also critical as these tools are used for evaluations. As with life, time moves ahead, and doing nothing has to be an option.

- One of the best parts of the simulations will be replayability, taking on different approaches to the same problem. Just as pilots in flight simulators can try conservative and aggressive strategies, players using business simulations can to try out different personalities and approaches.

- Finally, the simulation will have a core engine with easily customizable scripts. When businesses spend large sums on simulations, they should expect to customize the experience to their unique culture, as least as much as people buying new cars can customize style and options.

Simulations will make up the bulk of most users' self-paced content. They will come closer to reality, teaching people at the emotional as well as intellectual level.

Personal computers will be the development platform of choice originally for simulations, but game consoles, such as Sony's PlayStation, will play a bigger part in the development and deployment over time due to their high power, low cost, and consistency across hundreds of thousands of units.

In global learning, students will be able to don 3-D headgear and stereo headphones for deep immersion, or even enter a room with the images projected around them. Perhaps the biggest irony will be for simulations to put you at the agora in Athens discussing with Socrates the serious issues of the day, using the highest technology to enable the oldest form of instruction.

Embedded Help

Embedded help gives users just enough help on how to use the program exactly when they need it. Ideally, the computer is psychic, at least as much as a golden retriever, and gives you the answer the moment the learners' brow furrows.

Today, part of embedded help is an online dictionary, where you can look up terms or questions to get answers wherever you are, instead of lugging fifteen pounds of manuals with you.

The other part of the system, like a shark sensing a wounded fish, figures out when a user seems lost, and tries to suggest a solution. While many of these systems are successfully in place today, especially around SAP and PeopleSoft implementations, most people connect the approach with the Office Assistant (also known as "that damn paperclip") in Office 2000. Microsoft's approach was ninety percent right, but because they used a less selective algorithm, ended up really annoying most people who used it.

Embedded help today can be triggered by steps or missteps while using a computer program. As more people carry around personal devices, this could change. For example, information could not only be just-in-time, but just-in-place. Imagine walking through a gallery, and seeing on your PDA a multimedia descriptive information and prices for every piece of art you stop at for more than three seconds. Or imagine a menu appearing as you approach a restaurant. Or parking rules as you approach a city.

CONTENT IN CONCERT

All of the content types can stand alone as meaningful learning experiences. But they are not stand-alone, and only the interplay between them will usher in global learning.

- ➤ Extended books will be annotated by colleagues, managers, or outside experts. Part of the process of reading a book will be selecting whose annotations you want to include.

- ➤ Content created from communities, lectures, and experts can all be broken up into knowledge chunks and then reassembled to form new books.

- ➤ Communities will build around simulated experiences, sharing techniques, and applications.

- ➤ Extended books will be intertwined with simulations to help people learn about big concepts.

- ➤ Some people will be identified through their sharp participation in chat rooms, and be elevated to the status of expert in their organization.

- ➤ People will build theories in communities, hone them through interactions as an expert, refine and synthesize the material in speeches, bring in other specialists for a book, and maybe be part of a simulation team.

Here are some deeper examples of how content interplay could happen.

Example 1: Just-In-Time Learning for Selling a New Product

Imagine a vendor that is rolling out a radical new product , perhaps a new type of enterprise software package. This is the first week it is available. A sales person is preparing to sell it to a large customer.

Community
The salesperson could both search a community database on recent contacts with that customer, or other salespeople who have tried selling the new service. Or the salesperson might ask current users in real-time for help and suggestions.

Expert Access

The same salesperson might find a specific expert for help. She might talk to the person who designed the product, or an outside consultant who codesigned the marketing. In either case, the session would be recorded for the use of others.

Extended Lectures

The salesperson may have already taken a lecture on selling the new product to large organizations. But she also might want a refresher course. She could take a live class, probably more generalized around selling the course to any organization. This class might have some real war stories from the product's first few days out in the field if the instructor was sharp, as well as all of the previously prepared launch material. Or she could review the recorded session she had participated in on selling to a large customer.

Extended Books

There may be early electronic documentation and trusted material, on the new service. But it would initially be flat, full of theoretical models and processes created from other rollouts. Over the next three or four weeks the documentation would be enriched dramatically.

Simulation

Because of the newness of the product, a specialized simulation probably wouldn't exist. Regardless, the salesperson could do a generic value based selling simulation, programmed for selling a new product to a traditional culture.

In a month or two, if the service is significant enough, an existing simulation might be tailored. For example, specific dialogue around features and barriers could be added to an interpersonal sim. Benefits and trade-offs could be added to a process sim. Early models could possibly be launched with the product, but only the feedback of real experience would make it truly useful.

Example 2: Global Curriculum

One of the killer applications of global learning will be the creation and deployment of a global curriculum. For example, this could be a week to a month-long program (depending on aptitude and focus), on the philosophy and protocols of business.

It will be privately developed and deployed, started around meeting the needs of high-potential employees. It will cover most areas of business, similar to an MBA, but with a higher emphasis on practical knowledge, including working with different cultures.

It will grow in use, spreading virally. Ultimately, the expectation will be that all professionals (or professional want-to-be's), all over the United States first, and then rest of the connected world, have taken the course. This body of work will become an intellectual standard, much like a technology standard. References from the program, such as to fictitious companies, characters, situations, or case studies, would be commonplace in both journals and personal conversations.

It will be canned, yet regionalized, and accompanied by a rich community. A single company will sell it, although competitors will offer some alternatives. It will also evolve sufficiently so that people will want to retake it every three to six years, depending on how fast-track the person is. Clearly the vendor offering the curriculum may drive the changes in order to have a higher retake level.

As with health care insurance, it will primarily be purchased by individuals and enterprises, but also bought in blocks by organizations such as the United Nations and philanthropic trusts.

Extended lectures, extended books, and simulations would provide most of the content in equal amounts. The extended community would also be well used, in part because the class metaphor, people going through the same material at the same time, would persist. In fact, the networks built around the courses will also be invaluable for professionals. People taking the global curriculum at the same time will have a special unifying bond, like recruits during boot camp.

The expert access would also be critical. Perhaps to finalize a degree or get an advanced one, a professional would have to serve as an expert for the next generation, even having to get good ratings themselves to move on.

Over time, the curriculum will expand to cover other areas, such as art, history, science, nutrition, medicine, and law. It will initially be criticized as being too American and Western Europe centric, but will evolve to tap the vast knowledge held by less developed nations. Having said that, politics will carefully shape many of these topics, and nations will outlaw segments.

VENDOR TYPES

E-Learning Vendors, 2000

To meet the needs of today's market, corporations and government organizations look at six different categories of e-learning vendors (Figure 27-1):

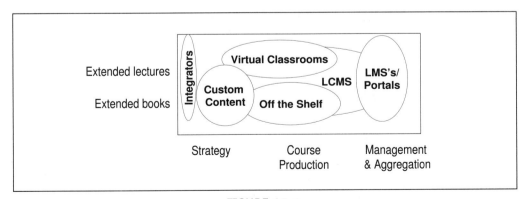

FIGURE 27-1.

- *Integrators*, skilled at applying the right e-learning solution to a given business problem, determining what to measure, and managing third-party software;

- *Off-the-shelf courseware providers* who supply business and IT skills courses, allowing companies to give up customization for lower price and/or higher production values;

- *Learning Management Systems (LMS)/Portals*, providing the infrastructure to make sure the right person gets the right course at the right time, record the event and the effect, and integrate different learning channels and vendors;

- *Custom Content*, to build custom courses;

- *Virtual Classrooms*, to provide an infrastructure for synchronous courses, as well as an authoring tool for capturing and integrating voices, slides, and gestures; and

- *Content Authoring Platforms /Learning Content Management Systems* (LCMS), which are the tools for enterprises to build their own content library.

The role of integrators in global learning will remain relatively unchanged, although most systems integrators will have to build up a significant capability to remain competitive here. Broadly, off-the-shelf content providers will have the same mission, but the quality and form of their offerings will change so dramatically that they will become unrecognizable compared with today's vendors. Simulations especially will become a mainstay of global learning.

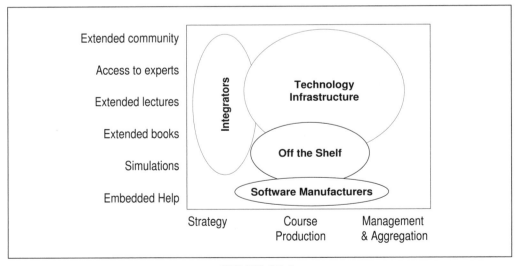

FIGURE 27-2.

Global Learning Vendors, 2015

The tectonic changes in learning vendors will be around the technology infrastructure, and not just around e-learning but the greater organization (Figure 27-2). Today, businesses use dozens of vendors to provide their technology infrastructure. These vendors come from a multitude of segments, software and hardware, including office document creation, knowledge management (KM), learning content management systems (LCMS), learning management systems (LMS), customer relationship management (CRM), enterprise resource planners (ERP), e-mail, internet browser, virtual classroom, telephones, palm top, lap top, and desktop computers, as well as wired and wireless network providers.

These services, if not the vendors themselves, will continue to come together, but in unpredictable, and sometimes irrelevant, ways.

Finally, custom content will be created in all three camps. Off-the-shelf vendors will customize their products. Technologists will create content based on their intimate knowledge of the tools. And integrators will have to do both.

Where the leading global learning vendors will cluster is far from certain (clusters are loosely defined as places where employees can change companies without changing their carpools). The United States is well positioned in this market, and will be a dominant position, tapping its strengths in software, military simulations, and mass media. Regions around the states that are already clusters are:

➤ Bay Area, California, including DigitalThink, Docent, and Saba;

➤ Route 128, Massachusetts, including Centra and WBT Systems;

➤ Hollywood, California, including Knowledge Universe;

➤ Phoenix, Arizona, including KnowledgeNet; and

➤ McLean, Virginia, including Thinq, Knowledge Planet, and countless military providers.

But other countries are already building capabilities and will produce vendors at least as competitive. Some regions that have taken early leads are

➤ Israel, with their expertise in communication and cognitive science, including Mentergy and InterWise,

➤ India, including Indira Gandhi National Open University and NIIT; and

➤ Ireland, with their strengths in courseware development.

China will become a reluctant mass user of e-learning, and will be a key component in the ongoing mix.

DISPLACED AND CHANGED JOBS

Global learning will change some existing jobs significantly. This is true of any new technology.

One of the big questions around e-learning has always been, will it replace instructors? The best analogy to the question is: has the pharmaceuticals industry replaced doctors?

Clearly some procedures that would have required surgical intervention twenty years ago can now be replaced both more cheaply and effectively with the right pills; therefore, the role of doctors is changed. They spend more time diagnosing, and they must know how to use drugs intelligently or they cannot perform their job. Yet, because the effectiveness of doctors increases through the use of pharmaceuticals, ultimately the number of doctors goes up, and the control they have goes up even faster.

Consider AIDS patients. There is no one pill today to allow a patient to continue living. It is accomplished only by doctors administering the right, ever-changing combinations of pharmaceuticals, drawn from multiple sources.

Still, the exact impact of global learning and existing training and development jobs will be different by professional segment.

Traditional Corporate Trainers

Many traditional corporate trainers will spend more time leading extended lectures sessions, as well as being experts on demand in certain areas. Others will be available for personal diagnostics of career paths and skill gaps. Still others will be consultants to the heads of businesses, developing and maintaining strategic learning objectives and programs.

Practical Higher Ed

Vocational/technical schools and community colleges will continue to be rapid adopters of global learning. They have fewer philosophical baggage, more short-term goals, and fewer egos at play.

K–12

The impact of global learning on government-run K–12 programs may both take longer but, when fully adopted, the impact will be greater than most other segments.

As content and processes get modularized, parents will finally have some real choices to make with the children about what to learn and how. This will increase parent involvement, perhaps to the chagrin of any remaining Luddites left in the schools in 2015. The reality will be education a la carte. Home schooling will continue to increase, and governments will be more accountable to paying for pieces of education, however delivered.

As self-paced technology draws students, teachers will be able to teach smaller classes. More classes will be made up of students from diverse locations. There will be a more pro-business direction to the work, for better or worse, as content that is developed for one market is ported over to the other. As in corporations and other enterprises, some people will be specialists in diagnosing skill gaps and prescribing regiments.

Traditional Higher Education

Many deans and professors of higher education have been pretending to get into e-learning, when in fact hoping for its disintegration. They have put forth a meager effort, failed, and then threw up their hands saying, "I guess this doesn't work." These universities will become increasingly marginalized as both corporations and more nimble enterprises teach more people more effectively, at lower cost, and in a lifelong learning capacity.

Other Impacted Jobs

In fact, most jobs will be affected. A turning point in sports came around cross-training. Football players, for example, learned that jogging and boxing made them much better players. All serious athletes cross-train now to avoid repetitive stress and burn-out. We will see more and more corporate cross-training.

Global learning will also change other ways that skills are managed within an enterprise. Some have said that there will be less job swapping as new skills can more easily be brought in-house without bringing in new people. Some other possible implications include the following:

Project Consultants

When enterprises traditionally do new things, they bring in consultants to bring in the needed skills, and then manage a skills transfer process to wean off the consultants over time. In the future change happens at a faster rate, the more cost-effective process will be to train more people sooner, and share best practices more aggressively, to reduce the need for external skills.

Computer Game Designers

As simulations get better and better, the pure computer game market will shrink for two different reasons. First, many of the adults who now play games will choose the more valuable global learning simulations instead. This will meet both self-improvement and entertainment needs.

Second, innovative developers who would have gone into designing computer games will go into global learning as well, both because it will be more profitable and more satisfying than building space people or dragons. The game industry will have to respond by breaking out of some intellectual ghettos it now occupies, and in some cases learn from the new genres being developed in the global learning world.

NEW JOBS

Global learning will also create jobs that do not exist today or that exist in different fields with different success criteria.

Artificial Intelligence/Artificial Life Designer

Simulations will require practical and sophisticated uses of artificial intelligence, artificial life, and fuzzy logic mathematics. This field will grow quickly as computing power increases and models are tested and refined.

Content Editor

Their mission increasingly will be to wade into the morass (read that mess) of knowledge management content, identify the valuable threads (using both their own savvy and also by the reactions of others), and weave these pieces into coherent, more linear modules, often interspersed with off-the-shelf content.

Let's say, for example, that GE's top Java programmer did a learning lunch on external web page requirements using live e-learning technology. Imagine she spoke for about forty minutes, with fifteen minutes of question and answer. The obligation of the content editor would be to tear apart the record of the presentation, edit out the best moments, clean up the sounds of people eating and rustling plates, and then intersperse these new knowledge chunks in the appropriate prepackaged GE courses. This brings in customization and good stories, and can even create heroes.

Experts On Tap

Content based around Expert Access will create a greater need for experts, both within and outside of an organization. Eventually, companies will even supplement internal experts with experts from other enterprises, time-swapping, or some other mutually beneficial arrangements.

Expert Locator

Some HR employees will have the authority to use a Google-style search engine to look through all of the nonprivate e-mails of every employee in the corporation. If, for example, a need for database recovery skills came up, they would have the ability to look for key words and passages in all e-mails to find employees talking about the issue, to identify the experts.

HR Expert Compensation

Compensation structures are changing as HR organizations use more tools to meet specific, rather than broad, employees needs. But as experts in an organization are identified, increasingly new compensation will be necessary to keep the experts motivated.

Imbedded Help Software Engineering

An emerging area of software development will involve designing help features that are actually helpful and not really annoying à la the MS paperclip.

Information Taxonomist

A critical job to optimizing any kind of knowledge repository is organizing the data into meaningful structures. The same information will have multiple structures. Any academic work in this area would also revolve around studying and suggesting different information metaphors.

Instruction Object Designer

Builders will construct "working" models of instructional objects, such as decks of cards or truck engines, that will have a role both in simulations as part of the furniture of the simulation space and will also have an instructional role in showing a student how something works, stripping layer after layer away to reveal an annotated structure.

Learning Integrators

Large consulting companies will need specialists in applying the various learning technologies to a given business problem. They also have to deal with the politics from the traditional training people.

Nonlinear Script Writing

Simulations require both dialogue and stories that are nonlinear. They have to evolve around the user. This emerging branch of both technical and creative writing requires the creation of plot and dialogue that allow pieces to be constructed on the fly.

Process Modelers

Mathematicians will emerge who can uncover and precisely convert relationships and systems to their fundamental mathematical and interdependent relationships.

Professional Moderators

Extended communities will involve chat rooms, and chat rooms require moderators. Their job will be to set the tone, elicit responses, and on occasion, if the community gets stuck, to find the outside expert to solve the problem. They will ensure organizational sharing occurs. They will also be critical in identifying participants with unusual knowledge and value to elevate to expert status.

Simulation Adapters

All of the large-system integrators will need staffs of people who will be able to customize generic simulations to both match a specific culture and also to meet identified business needs.

Simulation Graphic Artists

Simulations and other content types will require increasingly sophisticated 2-D and 3-D model building animation construction. Even though computer games will provide a bit of a template, graphics for the global learning marketplace will have to be much more subtle and realistic.

Skill Procurement

Either the HR department or the procurement groups will develop methodologies to make sure that the right external skills are on tap. They will negotiate rates with experts to make available. Third party guru-farms will also emerge to make this work easier.

Trainers Optimized for Extended Lectures

Leading a classroom is a hugely difficult task. Leading an extended lecture is as difficult, and also requires additional skills. The most important is how to continually draw in an audience you can't see.

Usage Anthropologist

Software companies will need scientifically trained observers of how users really use software to determine the best way to support them. Having the program be helpful with advice without annoying the user will be their holy grail.

CONCLUSION

The view presented here is incomplete, yet inevitable. The time frame is not. For global learning to be fully realized in seven years requires many factors. Consolidation and pruning has to happen among e-learning and tangential industries. Meanwhile enterprises have to become more sophisticated users of e-learning. Procurements have to be made intelligently. Choosing a content vendor based on low cost per course, high volume of courses, web deployment, and built-in tests at the end has resulted in vendors bulking up their libraries of boring content that doesn't have a chance of making a difference.

Ultimately, though, time frames aside, the future of e-learning is ensured because of the critical role it has to play. We are all just understanding that globalization and e-learning are inextricably linked. It is impossible for one to outpace the other for very long. In fact, the globalization of the 1990s created large numbers of "have-nots" that worked against globalization at the beginning of the new millennia.

On a more micro level, globalization without e-learning would be self-limiting because:

> ➤ too few technical skills would exist to maintain and build the infrastructure (as we saw with IT workers in the late 1990s),

- increased concentration of business skills accessed by the "haves," with increased numbers of "have-nots," would limit the human capital necessary to drive progress and generate new ideas, and

- too little ability to communicate meaningfully with people from different cultures, both within and outside of your enterprise, would create as significant a barrier to exchange as incompatible technical standards.

E-learning without globalization would be equally self-limiting because:

- the size of audience would not be sufficient to create next generation courses,

- people in under connected regions would be less interested in taking courses if the opportunity did not exist to practice and benefit from the new skills, and

- the technology infrastructure to deploy and run the content wouldn't exist.

Only by increasing both in concert will growth be sustainable. The opportunities to participate that are taken advantage of by a few can then be taken advantage of by nearly all. And when this happens, the world is in for quite a revolution.

➤ABOUT THE AUTHOR

Mr. Aldrich is an independent e-learning researcher who consults with implementing enterprises, vendors, and venture capitalists. Mr. Aldrich is also involved in several long-range projects. In one, Mr. Aldrich is researching how immersive simulations can be designed for the e-learning marketplace. He has spent over a year building a model of simulation-based learning, working with both subject matter experts from top universities and game manufacturers, which is available from SimuLearn.

Previously, Mr. Aldrich was the research director at Gartner responsible for launching and building their e-learning practice. Prior to joining Gartner, he worked for nearly eight years at Xerox. Mr. Aldrich earned a bachelor's degree in artificial intelligence and cognitive science from Brown University. He can be reached at *clark.aldrich@att.net*

GIF file format, 189
Gillis, Lynette, 346
Global learning, 431–436
    and education environment, 432–433
    and employment environment, 434–436
    global curriculum, 428–429
    and job displacement, 431–432
Graphic designer
    hiring tips, 147
    role of, 140
Graphics
    and caching, 185–186
    color, use of, 186–187
    compression versus optimization, 188–189
    cropping, benefits of, 185–186
    illustrations versus photos, 187
    and interactivity, 187
    low bandwidth design tips, 184–187
    photo file formats, 188
    software tools, 188–189
    visual size versus file size, 185
    and Webcasts, 199, 202–203, 205
Group work. *See* Synchronous e-learning
Guglielmino, Lucy M., 87, 89, 92, 98
Guglielmino, Paul J., 87, 88, 92, 98

H
Hall, Brandon, 305, 316
Handbook, for e-learners, 343
Handshaw, Dick, 315
Hardware, evaluation for system, 353–354
Hartley, Darin, 71, 86
Hartnett, John, 183, 190, 245, 253
Hawthorne Effect, 21
Help
    embedded help as content, 426–427
    learner access to, 94, 128
    software engineering of, 434
Hentschell, Patrick M., 229, 244
Higher education, global learning, impact of,
        432
Hofmann, Jennifer, 271, 285
Holistic approach, to delivery, 329–333
Home page section, 261
HorizonLive, 283, 338
Hosted learning management system (LMS),
        153
Hot spots, 9
Human performance improvement (HPI). *See*
        Performance improvement
Hyatt, Josh, 29
Hype, common reactions to, 27–29

I
IBM, learning management system (LMS)
        vendor, 153
Illustrations, versus photographs, 187
ImageReady, graphics program, 188–189,
        324
Implementation
    definition of, 318
    delivery stage, 329–330
    development stage, 322–329
    focus of, 318–320
    priorities in, 321
    process model, 319–320
    production stage, 329
    synchronous e-learning, 274–275
    tips/guidelines, 333–334
IMS Global Learning Consortium, Inc. (IMS),
        155
Indira Gandhi National Open University,
        431
Individual work. *See* Asynchronous e-learning
Industry trends, and e-learning, 74–75
Information taxonomist, 435
Information technology (IT) specialist
    and synchronous training design, 273
    technical certification requirements, 220
Information technology (IT) training,
        e-learning success, 31
Instant Messenger, 284
Institute of Electrical and Electronics
        Engineers, Inc. (IEEE), 156
Instructional designer
    hiring tips, 147
    role of, 139, 233, 278
Instructional Management System (IMS), 194
Instructional strategy
    in recommendations document, 53
Instructor object designer, role of, 435
InSync Training Synergy, 285
Integrators, role of, 430, 435
Interactivity
    authoring, 324–326
    complexity of, 326
    design for low-bandwidth, 187
Internet Learning, 376
Interoperability
    and closed systems, 157
    LMS feature, 153, 157, 160
Interview section, 261
InterWise, 283, 431
Interwise Millenium, 217
Israelite, Larry, 255, 269

George M. Piskurich Ph.D.

George Piskurich is an organizational learning and perfomance consultant based in Macon, Georgia. He provides consulting services and workshops in instructional design, management development, and performance improvement to clients throughout the country. He specializes in e-learning interventions, performance/training analysis, distance learning, the design and development of self-directed/individualized learning programs for all levels of the organization, telecommuting interventions, and knowledge centers.

His recent clients have included major multinational corporations for whom he developed Web-enabled problem solving and telecommuting interventions, as well as basic management programs; a small technology based organization for which he designed the company's training system; a state board of education where he managed and produced an interactive satellite distance-learning intervention; and a number of telecommunications, pharmaceutical, and banking clients for whom he has created e-learning programs and other self-instructional classes on various topics.

With more than twenty years' experience in every phase of learning technology, he has created classroom seminars, distance learning programs, and e-learning interventions. In his specialty of self-directed learning, he has created individualized programs on topics ranging from biological sciences to instructional and supervisory techniques, using print, slide, video, and computer-based formats.

George Piskurich has been a presenter and workshop leader at more than thirty conferences and symposia, including the International Self-directed Learning Symposium, the Best of America Conference, and the ISPI and ASTD international conferences. He is an active member of both ISPI and ASTD, in which he has held local and national leadership positions.

He has edited books on instructional technology, performance improvement, and e-learning; written books on self-directed learning, instructional design, and telecommuting; and authored many journal articles and book chapters on various topics. In 1986 he was ASTD's "Instructional Technologist of the Year" and won the "Best Use of Instructional Technology in Business" award in 1992 for his distributed SDL technical skills training design.

He can be reached at Gpiskurich@cs.com or through his Web site, GPiskurich.com.